PUERTO
THE RICAN
NATION
ON THE MOVE

JORGE DUANY

PUERTO RICAN NATION

THE

ON THE MOVE

IDENTITIES

ON THE ISLAND & IN THE UNITED STATES

The University of North Carolina Press
Chapel Hill and London

© 2002 The University of North Carolina Press
All rights reserved
Manufactured in the United States of America

Designed by Heidi Perov
Set in Electra
by Keystone Typesetting, Inc.

This book was published with the assistance of
the William Rand Kenan Junior Fund of the
University of North Carolina Press.

Library of Congress Cataloging-in-Publication Data

Duany, Jorge.
The Puerto Rican nation on the move: identities on
the island and in the United States / Jorge Duany.
p. cm.
Includes bibliographical references and index.

ISBN 0-8078-2704-5 (cloth: alk. paper)
ISBN 0-8078-5372-0 (pbk.: alk. paper)

1. Puerto Rico—Civilization—20th century. 2. Nationalism—
Puerto Rico—History—20th century. 3. Identity (Psychology)—
Puerto Rico. 4. Puerto Ricans—United States—Ethnic identity.
5. Ethnicity—Puerto Rico. I. Title.
F1975 .D83   2002
972.9505—dc21   2001057826

cloth   06 05 04 03 02   5 4 3 2 1
paper   06 05 04 03 02   5 4 3 2 1

To my brothers
and sisters,
Rafael, Lourdes,
Luis, Raúl, and
María Caridad,
with affection
and appreciation

In loving memory of
Herminia Guerra Rensoli

Contents

Acknowledgments *xiii*

INTRODUCTION. Rethinking Colonialism, Nationalism,
and Transnationalism: The Case of Puerto Rico *1*

1. The Construction of Cultural Identities in
Puerto Rico and the Diaspora *12*

2. The Rich Gate to Future Wealth:
Displaying Puerto Rico at World's Fairs *39*

3. Representing the Newly Colonized: Puerto Rico in the
Gaze of American Anthropologists, 1898–1915 *59*

4. Portraying the Other: Puerto Rican Images in
Two American Photographic Collections *87*

5. A Postcolonial Colony?: The Rise of Cultural
Nationalism in Puerto Rico during the 1950s *122*

6. Collecting the Nation: The Public Representation
of Puerto Rico's Cultural Identity *137*

7. Following Migrant Citizens: The Official Discourse on
Puerto Rican Migration to the United States *166*

8. The Nation in the Diaspora: The Reconstruction of
the Cultural Identity of Puerto Rican Migrants *185*

9. Mobile Livelihoods: Circular Migration,
Transnational Identities, and Cultural Borders between
Puerto Rico and the United States 208

10. Neither White nor Black: The Representation of
Racial Identity among Puerto Ricans on the Island
and in the U.S. Mainland 236

11. Making Indians out of Blacks: The Revitalization of
Taíno Identity in Contemporary Puerto Rico 261

CONCLUSION. Nation, Migration, Identity 281

Notes 287

Works Cited 297

Index 331

Figures and Tables

FIGURES

2.1 "The Philippines, Porto Rico and Cuba—Uncle Sam's burden. With apologies to Mr. Kipling" 52

2.2 Uncle Sam and his new babies 53

4.1 "Human poverty amidst nature's wealth— a beggar in Adjuntas" 98

4.2 "Porto Rican boys in their Sunday dress, near Aibonito" 99

4.3 "Rapid transit in Yauco" 100

4.4 "Be it ever so humble, there's no place like home—Cayey" 101

4.5 "Cock fight—a favorite holiday sport at Yauco" 102

4.6 "Dusky belles, Porto Rico" 104

4.7 "Amidst the charms of Porto Rico— delicious pineapples in the fields of Mayagüez" 105

4.8 "Military road" 110

4.9 "Street merchant, Viequez" 111

4.10 "Street scene. San Juan" 112

4.11 "The market. San Juan" 113

4.12 "The two first settlers, American occupation—Vogel, Day" 114

4.13 "Native soldiers drilling. Under American rule" 115

4.14 "Native girls. Upper class" 116

4.15 "Milk dealer. The support of two families" 117

4.16 "Weaving 'Panama' hats. Learning the stitch" 118

7.1 The Caborrojeños Ausentes at the Puerto Rican
Day Parade in New York City 173

8.1 The Puerto Rican and Hispanic League in
Brooklyn during the 1920s 189

8.2 The Unbeatable San Juan Baseball Club from
New York City's East Side, 1924 190

8.3 "Passengers disembarking from a steamship
in the port of San Juan" 192

8.4 The Puerto Rican Folk Festival in New York
City's Central Park 194

8.5 The Puerto Rican Day Parade in
New York City in the early 1960s 196

8.6 New York City's Versailles Restaurant menu, 1927 199

8.7 A Puerto Rican *bodega* in Newark, N.J. 200

8.8 Puerto Rican children in New York City dressed as *jíbaros* 205

9.1 "Spectators awaiting inbound passengers at the Isla Grande
airport in San Juan" 212

9.2 Luggage of a Puerto Rican migrant worker
in Wabash, Indiana 214

TABLES

4.1 The Underwood & Underwood and Helen Hamilton
Gardener Collections of Photographs on Puerto Rico 92

4.2 Basic Features of Persons Portrayed in the Underwood &
Underwood and Helen Hamilton Gardener Collections
of Photographs on Puerto Rico 96

6.1 The Vidal Collection at the Smithsonian: Basic
Identifying Information 152

7.1 Puerto Rican Voluntary Associations in the United States
Identified by Migration Division, 1953–1988 177

9.1 Characteristics of Sample, by Place of Origin 220

9.2 Number of Trips to the United States, by Place of Origin 224

9.3 Year of First Trip to the United States of All Movers
in Sample, by Place of Origin 225

9.4 Major Metropolitan Areas of Destination of Multiple Movers
on First and Last Trips to the United States 226

9.5 Major Metropolitan Areas of Destination of All Movers on
Last Trip to the United States, by Place of Origin 228

9.6 Sociodemographic Characteristics of Nonmovers,
One-Time Movers, and Multiple Movers 229

9.7 Employment Status and Occupation of Multiple Movers
during First and Last Trips to the United States 230

9.8 Social Networks of All Household Heads Who
Moved to the United States 231

9.9 English-Language Use among All Household Heads
Who Moved to the United States 232

10.1 Major Folk Racial Terms Used in Puerto Rico 238

10.2 Racial Categories Used in the Census of
Puerto Rico, 1899–2000 247

10.3 Racial Composition of the Puerto Rican Population,
as Reported in the Census, 1802–2000 248

10.4 Major Racial Categories Used in the Census of the
United States, 1900–2000 251

10.5 Mulatto and Black Populations of Puerto Rico, as
Reported in the Census, 1899–1920 252

10.6 Racial Composition of Puerto Ricans in the United
States, as Reported in the Census, 1940–1990 255

10.7 Racial Self-Identification of Puerto Ricans in the
United States in the Current Population Survey, 1992–1999 257

Acknowledgments

I completed the first draft of the manuscript for this book while enjoying a sabbatical leave from the University of Puerto Rico during the academic year 1999–2000. I appreciate the institutional support for writing this book, as well as the personal trust of my friends Raquel Dulzaides and Humberto Vidal, who served as witnesses to my contract with the university. During this period, I received a senior fellowship in Latino studies from the Smithsonian Institution in Washington, D.C. I thank Miguel Bretos and Marvette Pérez for hosting my research project at the Smithsonian. During the summer of 1999, I was also a visiting scholar at the Population Studies Center of the University of Pennsylvania, thanks to a generous invitation by Douglas S. Massey.

Much of the archival research for this book was conducted at the Smithsonian, especially the National Anthropological Archives of the National Museum of Natural History and the Archives Center of the National Museum of American History. I also conducted research at the American Philosophical Society in Philadelphia; the Centro de Estudios Puertorriqueños of Hunter College, City University of New York; the Luis Muñoz Marín Foundation in Trujillo Alto, Puerto Rico; and the Center for Historical Research of the University of Puerto Rico, Río Piedras. I appreciate the support of the staff at these institutions. Laura Larco offered expert advice and kind help in locating unpublished manuscripts and photographs at the Smithsonian. I received special attention from Pedro Juan Hernández during my research at the Centro de Estudios Puertorriqueños in August 1999 and later during the process of reproducing several photographs for inclusion in this book.

My colleagues César Ayala and Nancy Morris read the entire manuscript and made excellent suggestions for revision, most of which I have incorporated into this book. At the University of North Carolina Press, Elaine Maisner has been an enthusiastic and supportive editor. I also thank Nancy Raynor for her careful copyediting of the manuscript.

Several colleagues made perceptive comments and suggestions on earlier drafts of Chapter 1: Desmonique Bonet, Carol J. Greenhouse, Grace Dávila-López, Arlene Dávila, Michael Herzfeld, Gina Pérez, Moira Pérez, Juan Manuel Carrión, Frances Aparicio, and four anonymous reviewers for *American*

Ethnologist, where the chapter was originally published as an article. Manuel Valdés-Pizzini, Félix V. Matos-Rodríguez, Silvia Alvarez Curbelo, Luis Martínez-Fernández, Christopher Schmidt-Nowara, Pedro Cabán, Louise Lamphere, and Andrew Roth made thoughtful observations on earlier versions of Chapters 2 and 3.

Héctor Méndez Caratini, Fernando Coronil, Yolanda Martínez–San Miguel, Amílcar Antonio Barreto, and María Dolores Luque suggested changes to Chapter 4. Marvette Pérez, Miguel Bretos, Odette Díaz Schuler, Fath Davis Ruffins, Steve Velásquez, and Arlene Torres shared their insights on the Vidal Collection and exhibition. Lisa Maya Knauer made supportive comments on earlier versions of Chapter 6. Teodoro Vidal generously confirmed his personal information, provided access to primary documents, discussed his collecting practices with me, and commented on an earlier draft of the chapter. Thanks to Félix V. Matos-Rodríguez for his detailed criticisms and suggestions on Chapters 7 and 8.

I wrote the first version of Chapter 9 at the Population Studies Center of the University of Pennsylvania during June and July 1999. Douglas S. Massey and Jorge Durand invited me to collaborate with the Latin American Migration Project at the university. Mariano Sana and Nolan Malone helped to process and analyze the results summarized in this chapter. Ninna Nyberg Sørensen, Karen Fog Olwig, Douglas S. Massey, Juan Flores, Emilio Pantojas, and Raquel Z. Rivera provided useful comments and suggestions on earlier drafts. I would also like to acknowledge the efforts of the project's interviewers in Puerto Rico: Sonia Castro Cardona, Diana Johnson, Moira Pérez, and Rafael Zapata.

I thank Suzanne Oboler and Anani Dzidzienyo for their invitation to prepare the original version of Chapter 10. Lillian Torres Aguirre and Roberto R. Ramírez provided access to census data on race among Puerto Ricans on the Island and in the United States. Isar Godreau, Juan José Baldrich, Arlene Torres, Louis Herns Marcelin, Marvin Lewis, and María Zielina offered useful comments to strengthen my argument. I thank Arlene Dávila for her kind invitation to write the original version of Chapter 11. I also appreciate the comments and suggestions on earlier drafts by Luis Duany, Diana López, and Gabriel Haslip-Viera.

As always, I am pleased to recognize a great debt of gratitude to my family: to my wife, Diana, who has been a constant source of support, encouragement, and love for all these years; to my dear children, Patricia and Jorge Andrés, who give meaning and inspiration to my daily life; and to my late father, Rafael

Duany Navarro, whom I got to know much better during his last bouts of illness before his heart could not bear it any longer. They say that one's oldest friends tend to be one's siblings; in my case, that is true. This book is fondly dedicated to my brothers and sisters, Rafael, Lourdes, Luis, Raúl, and María Caridad, as a small token of our solidarity and affinity, despite all the differences that my mother used to analyze so well. I'm sure she would be proud of all of us.

As I correct the proofs for this book, I am saddened by the passing away of my mother-in-law, Herminia Guerra Rensoli. We will all miss her intelligence, good spirits, and love of music.

Finally, I am grateful to the Puerto Rican painter, Arnaldo Roche-Rabell, for allowing me to reproduce his work, *We Have to Dream in Blue*, on the book cover. I feel that this image visually encapsulates the personal and collective dilemmas—especially the racial ones—of living in a nation on the move.

THE PUERTO RICAN NATION ON THE MOVE

Introduction

Rethinking Colonialism, Nationalism, and Transnationalism

The Case of Puerto Rico

Puerto Rico has a peculiar status among the countries of Latin America and the Caribbean. As one of Spain's last two colonies in the New World (along with Cuba), Puerto Rico experienced the longest period of Hispanic influence in the region. On July 25, 1898, however, U.S. troops invaded the Island during the Spanish-Cuban-American War.[1] In 1901 the U.S. Supreme Court defined Puerto Rico as "foreign to the United States in a domestic sense" because it was neither a state of the union nor a sovereign republic (Burnett and Marshall 2001). In 1917 Congress granted U.S. citizenship to all persons born in Puerto Rico but did not incorporate the Island as a territory. Until now, Puerto Rico has remained a colonial dependency, even though it attained a limited form of self-government as a commonwealth in 1952.

As an overseas possession of the United States, the Island has been exposed to an intense penetration of American capital, commodities, laws, and customs unequaled in other Latin American countries. Yet today Puerto Ricans display a stronger cultural identity than do most Caribbean people, even those who enjoy political independence. At the beginning of the twenty-first century, Puerto Rico presents the apparent paradox of a stateless nation that has not assimilated into the American mainstream. After more than one hundred years of U.S. colonialism, the Island remains a Spanish-speaking Afro-Hispanic-Caribbean nation.[2] Today, the Island's electorate is almost evenly split between supporting commonwealth status and becoming the fifty-first state of the Union; only a small minority advocates independence.

Recent studies of Puerto Rican cultural politics have focused on the demise of political nationalism on the Island, the rise of cultural nationalism, and the enduring significance of migration between the Island and the U.S. mainland (Alvarez-Curbelo and Rodríguez Castro 1993; Dávila 1997; Kerkhof 2000; Negrón-Muntaner and Grosfoguel 1997). Although few scholars have posited an explicit connection among these phenomena, they are intimately linked. For instance, most Puerto Ricans value their U.S. citizenship and the freedom of movement that it offers, especially unrestricted access to the continental United States. But as Puerto Ricans move back and forth between the two countries, territorially grounded definitions of national identity become less relevant, while transnational identities acquire greater prominence. Constant movement is an increasingly common practice among Puerto Ricans on the Island and in the mainland. Under such fluid conditions, what is the meaning of Puerto Rican identity? Where is it located? How is it articulated and represented? Who imagines it and from what standpoint? How can a people define themselves as a nation without striving for a sovereign state? These are some of the basic questions addressed in this book. Reconsidering the Puerto Rican situation can add much to contemporary scholarly discussions on colonialism, nationalism, and transnationalism.

MOVING BACK AND FORTH

The Spanish folk term for the back-and-forth movement of people between Puerto Rico and the United States is *el vaivén* (literally meaning "fluctuation"). This culturally dense word refers to the constant comings and goings in which large numbers of Puerto Ricans are involved (C. Rodríguez 1994b). It implies that some people do not stay put in one place for a long period of time but move incessantly, like the wind or the waves of the sea, in response to shifting tides. Furthermore, it suggests that those who are here today may be gone tomorrow, and vice versa. More ominously, *vaivén* also connotes unsteadiness, inconstancy, and oscillation. In any case, contemporary Puerto Rican migration is best visualized as a transient and pendulous flow, rather than as a permanent, irrevocable, one-way relocation of people. *La nación en vaivén*, "the nation on the move," might serve as an apt metaphor for the fluid and hybrid identities of

Puerto Ricans on the Island and in the mainland. I have therefore chosen that image as the title of this book, to suggest that none of the traditional criteria for nationhood—a shared territory, language, economy, citizenship, or sovereignty—are fixed and immutable in Puerto Rico and its diaspora but are subject to constant fluctuation and intense debate, even though the sense of peoplehood has proven remarkably resilient throughout.

In the past few years, the metaphor of Puerto Rico as a nation on the move has taken new meanings. On May 4, 2000, the U.S. Navy carried out Operation Access to the East, in which it removed more than two hundred peaceful demonstrators from its training grounds in Vieques, a small island off the eastern coast of Puerto Rico. Those practicing civil disobedience included a wide spectrum of political and religious leaders, university students, and community activists. The protests had been sparked by the accidental death of security guard David Sanes Rodríguez during a military exercise in Vieques on April 19, 1999. Soon thereafter, Puerto Ricans of all ideological persuasions called for an end to live bombings, the navy's exit, and the return of military lands to the civilian residents of Vieques. As a result of this prolonged struggle, the Puerto Rican nation was symbolically extended beyond the main island to Vieques—*la isla nena*, or "the baby island," as it is affectionately known—as well as to Culebra and other smaller territories of the Puerto Rican archipelago. It is now more appropriate than ever to speak about the *islands* of Puerto Rico.

A noteworthy development has been the active participation of leaders of the Puerto Rican diaspora in the grassroots movement to end the U.S. Navy presence in Vieques. Two of the three Puerto Rican delegates to the U.S. House of Representatives, Luis Gutiérrez and Nydia Velázquez, were detained in Vieques during Operation Access to the East. The third, José Serrano, was arrested inside the White House grounds demanding peace for Vieques. Many other Puerto Rican leaders from New York have publicly expressed their support for the peace movement on the Island. Thus, Puerto Rican national identity has moved abroad in two main directions—both across a short distance to Vieques and across the "big pond" of the Atlantic Ocean to the U.S. mainland. For the moment, the public discourse on the Puerto Rican nation has broadened beyond territorial boundaries and across political differences.

Despite the strong ties of solidarity displayed by Puerto Ricans on and off the Island, the U.S. government has insisted on continuing military exercises in Vieques until May 1, 2003. Although motivated by a host of political and strategic factors, this insistence reveals the colonial nature of U.S.–Puerto Rican relations. Without effective representation in Congress, islanders have been forced to accept a presidential directive (timidly negotiated by former governor Pedro Rosselló), which does not please most opponents of the navy's continued presence in Vieques. This directive called for the resumption of military training activities, although with inert bombs, as well as for a plebiscite to tap the views of the people of Vieques. (On July 29, 2001, 68.2 percent of those polled in a Vieques referendum supported the navy's immediate exit.) Throughout the controversy, high-ranking members of Congress have raised the question of Puerto Rican loyalty to U.S. citizenship and commitment to American security needs. On April 29, 2000, President Clinton's key adviser on Puerto Rican affairs, Jeffrey Farrow, reiterated the official position that Puerto Rico is not a nation but a territory of the United States (see García Passalacqua 2000). As such, the Island is supposed to follow the defensive strategies established by the White House for the entire American nation.

Contrary to such opinions, I argue that Puerto Rico is indeed a nation, but a nation on the move. In so doing, I redefine the nation not as a well-bounded sovereign state but as a translocal community based on a collective consciousness of a shared history, language, and culture. Furthermore, Puerto Rico may well be considered a "postcolonial colony" in the sense of a people with a strong national identity but little desire for a nation-state, living in a territory that legally "belongs to but is not part of the United States." The prevailing juridical definition of the Island as neither a state of the Union nor a sovereign republic has created an ambiguous, problematic, and contested political status for more than a hundred years. Paradoxically, it has also strengthened the sense of peoplehood among Puerto Ricans.

One does not have to espouse an essentialist or primordialist viewpoint to acknowledge that the vast majority of Puerto Ricans—on and off the Island— imagine themselves as part of a broader community that meets all the standard criteria of nationality, such as territory, language, or culture, except sovereignty. The public outcry over Vieques suggests that the "baby island" has been popularly redefined as part of the Puerto Rican, not the American, nation. At the same time, the massive displacements of people between the Island and the mainland over the last half century complicate any simple equations among territory, language, and culture. In particular, the mobile livelihood of many Puerto Ricans challenges static approaches to national identity. Nonetheless, recent essays on the construction and representation of Puerto Ricanness concur on its sheer strength, intensity, and wide appeal (Dávila 1997; Guerra 1998;

Morris 1997; Rivera 1996). Unfortunately, most of this work has centered on the Island and neglected how identities are transformed and reconstructed in the diaspora.

THE RECURRENT THEMES OF THIS BOOK

Two key questions guide my analysis. First, how can most Puerto Ricans imagine themselves as a nation, even though few of them support the constitution of a separate nation-state? I address this issue by making a careful distinction between political nationalism—based on the doctrine that every people should have its own sovereign government—and cultural nationalism—based on the assertion of the moral and spiritual autonomy of each people. While the former is a minority position in contemporary Puerto Rico, the latter is the dominant ideology of the Commonwealth government, the intellectual elite, and numerous cultural institutions on the Island as well as in the diaspora. Most Puerto Ricans now insist that they are a distinct nation—as validated in their participation in such international displays of nationhood as Olympic sports and beauty pageants—but at the same time they want to retain their U.S. citizenship, thus pulling apart the coupling that the very term "nation-state" implies.

Second, what has been the cultural impact of the massive migration of Puerto Ricans to the mainland over the past five decades? I argue that diasporic communities are an integral part of the Puerto Rican nation because they continue to be linked to the Island by an intense circular movement of people, identities, and practices, as well as capital, technology, and commodities. Hence, the Puerto Rican nation is no longer restricted to the Island but instead is constituted by two distinct yet closely intertwined fragments: that of Puerto Rico itself and that of the diasporic communities settled in the continental United States. The multiple implications of this profound territorial dispersion are explored throughout the book.

In what follows, I approach the construction and representation of Puerto Rican identity as a hybrid, translocal, and postcolonial sense of peoplehood. Here I appropriate the suggestive notion of "hybrid cultures" developed by Néstor García Canclini (1990) to analyze the interpenetration of local, regional, national, and transnational forms of culture, as well as folk, rural, urban, popular, and mass culture. Furthermore, the interpretation of Puerto Rican culture on the Island and in the mainland calls for a transnational approach (Basch, Schiller, and Blanc 1994; Schiller, Basch, and Blanc-Szanton 1992) that moves beyond territorial boundaries to characterize the continuing socio-cultural links between the diaspora and its communities of origin. The book also draws insights from contemporary writing on the public representation of collective identities, especially the idea that all identities are constituted through particular discursive practices (see Hall 1997). By insisting on the performative aspects of people's sense of who they are, I do not claim that discourses take precedence over material experiences but that the former always mediate the latter through culturally patterned forms of imagination. Finally, I engage critically with a central strand of postcolonial criticism that takes the analysis of colonial discourses as its point of departure. Above all, the material presented in this book challenges homogeneous portrayals of racial and ethnic others, which cannot account for the specific historical and cultural junctures in which such portrayals emerge.

The Puerto Rican Nation on the Move deals with several interrelated topics, such as the politics of representation, the construction of colonial and anticolonial discourses, and the myriad intersections between race, ethnicity, class, and nationalism. In examining these issues, I dwell on certain historical moments and cultural practices shared by the Puerto Rican people, both on the Island and in the United States. First I assess the impact of the American occupation of the Island after the Spanish-Cuban-American War on the construction and representation of Puerto Rican identity. Then I emphasize recent social changes on the Island, such as industrialization, urbanization, and migration. I am particularly interested in the cultural effects of the massive displacement of Puerto Ricans to the United States since the 1940s. The 1950s can be considered a bridging decade between the colonial and nationalist discourses that dominated the first and second halves of the twentieth century, respectively. I also focus on emergent trends in the first years of the twenty-first century, such as an ever increasing ethnic diversity on the Island owing to foreign immigration and the persistence of migration between the Island and the mainland.

The present work draws on neglected primary sources for the ethnographic and historical analysis of Puerto Rican culture, such as its public display through material objects and photographs. Methodologically, the book weaves together findings from ethnographic fieldwork, archival research, surveys, censuses, personal documents, interviews, newspaper articles, and literary texts. Because of the shifting nature of my object of study, I myself had to move back and forth between Washington, D.C., Philadelphia, New York, and San Juan. I scrutinized the texts, images, and other cultural artifacts produced by several social actors, including American anthropologists and photographers, Puerto Rican writers and artists, as well as various institutional sites, such as the Smithsonian Institution, the New York Academy of Sciences, the U.S. Bureau of the Census, the Institute of Puerto Rican Culture, the Commonwealth's Migration Division, and Puerto Rican community organizations in the United States. I analyzed various genres of representation, ranging from ethnographic essays and census statistics to museum exhibits and world's fairs.

Throughout this book, I trace the development of certain emblematic figures of the Puerto Rican people (such as the *jíbaro*, or "independent subsistence farmer") during the twentieth century, to interpret the historical process of nation formation and consolidation on the Island and in the diaspora. As a consequence of massive and sustained migration to the United States, popular images of Puerto Rican identity have been thoroughly deterritorialized and transnationalized over the past few decades. For instance, the jíbaro's *pava*, or "straw hat," is constantly displayed as a visual icon of Puerto Ricanness in the United States. The pava reappears in the most unlikely places, such as folk festivals in Central Park, public schools in Brooklyn, and Smithsonian Institution exhibits. Another example is the construction of *casitas*, small wooden houses reminiscent of the Island's rural dwellings, in the abandoned lots of the South Bronx and the Lower East Side of Manhattan (Aponte-Parés 1996). The diaspora has mobilized standard concepts of the nation, culture, language, and territory on the Island and elsewhere. Population displacements across and within the boundaries of the imagined community have resulted in the weakening of political nationalism and the broadening of cultural identities in Puerto Rico, as well as in other countries of the world (Basch, Schiller, and Blanc 1994). While Puerto Ricans lack a separate citizenship, they have a clear sense of national identity. Any definition of the Island's political status must take into account the growing strength of cultural nationalism, as much as the increasing dispersal of people through the diaspora.

IMAGINING THE PUERTO RICAN NATION

Nations are not natural and eternal essences but contingent, slippery, and fuzzy constructs, always in a process of redefinition (Chatterjee 1993, 1995; García Canclini 1990; Hall 1994). At the same time, national boundaries have practical implications for people's daily lives as well as long-term political repercussions, especially in colonial settings. National identities are not completely artificial or abstracted from everyday experience; on the contrary, they are historically grounded in social relations, cultural practices, and shared conceptions of what constitutes a people, a country, and a community. While some aspects of national identity can be fruitfully considered "invented traditions" (Hobsbawm 1983) or "imagined communities" (Anderson 1991), the process of inventing or imagining the boundaries of the nation has much symbolic and material significance. Even though nations are collective imaginaries, they have concrete consequences for one's sense of self and relations with others. The debate between constructionist and essentialist views of the nation remains sterile unless it is recognized that all forms of identity are imagined, invented, and represented—but not necessarily arbitrary, immaterial, and irrelevant.

Anderson's suggestively titled *Imagined Communities* has been the point of departure for much of the rethinking about nations.[3] Anderson (1991: 5–7) defines nations as political communities imagined by their members as limited and sovereign territories sharing a horizontal comradeship. Modern nations emerged as cultural artifacts toward the end of the eighteenth century in western Europe, particularly through new forms of literary representation, such as the novel, the newspaper article, biography, and autobiography. Nationalism is also expressed in state institutions of power via censuses, maps, and museums, all of which help to define and classify the nation as a separate entity. For Anderson, nations are not necessarily fabrications but rather cultural creations rooted in social and historical processes—that is, ideological constructs with personal and collective significance.

Unfortunately, some analysts (such as Elie Kedourie, Ernest Gellner, and Eric Hobsbawm) confound the meaning of the word "imagined" with "imaginary" in the sense of "fictitious" or "false," thereby suggesting that nations do not exist apart from the ideological machinations of nationalist elites or popular movements engaged in struggles for self-determination. However, the practical impact of national identities on people's everyday lives should not be neglected. As Etienne Balibar argues, nothing is more real than what someone imagines. All human communities are imaginary insofar as they are "based on the projection of individual existence into the weft of a collective narrative, on the recognition of a common name and on traditions lived as the trace of an immemorial past" (Balibar and Wallerstein 1991: 93). For Balibar, a nation constitutes a "fictive ethnicity" because it is "represented in the past or in the future *as if* [it] formed a natural community, possessing of itself an identity of origins, culture and interests which transcends individuals and social conditions" (96). The key question then becomes how representations of national identity are constructed, institutionalized, and communicated.

In their most extreme versions, such as those advanced by Kedourie or Gellner, critical views of the nation are as off the mark as essentialist approaches. Kedourie (1993) has correctly faulted the political doctrine of nationalism for assuming that nations are natural divisions of humankind and that the nation-state is the only legitimate form of government in the contemporary world. But he dismisses all too quickly the potency and endurance of national identities and their roots in earlier forms of human association, such as kinship, religion, and ethnicity. For Gellner (1983), nationalism arose in social formations undergoing modernization, as in much of western Europe during the nineteenth century. In his view, the loss of cultural homogeneity produced by industrialization leads to nationalism as a way of creating new bonds of solidarity and exclusion. Gellner's often-quoted dictum that "it is nationalism which engenders nations, and not the other way around" (55) resonates strongly with Hobsbawm's equally counterintuitive notion (1990: 10) that "nations do not make states and nationalism but the other way around." The major problem with this thesis is that it cannot account for nations without states, such as Scotland, Catalonia, Quebec, or Puerto Rico.

A more reasonable, if less controversial, attempt to define nations has been made by Anthony D. Smith in *The Ethnic Origins of Nations* (1986) and in more recent works (Smith 1991, 1995, 1998). Smith argues that ethnicity has historically provided the main model for the construction of national identities, particularly with regard to myths, memories, symbols, and values. His study documents the continuity between ethnic communities and modern nations as bases for popular mobilization throughout the world. Nationalist ideologies incorporate elements of enduring ethnic identities to legitimize the creation of a nation-state. In this sense, nations are not entirely invented traditions or imagined communities but historically grounded in earlier modes of association, such as kinship and religion. As Smith (1986: 211) points out, "Nations are not fixed and immutable entities 'out there'. . . ; but neither are they completely malleable and fluid processes and attitudes, at the mercy of every outside force."

In his 1991 volume, Smith (vii) has argued that "we cannot understand nations and nationalism simply as an ideology or form of politics but must treat them as cultural phenomena as well." National identities are cultural practices involving specific kinds of icons, myths, and rituals. The symbolic repertoire of the nation is based on a limited set of images that must be interpreted according to local canons of knowledge. The foundational myth of an ancestral home-land, along with the preservation of an original language and the embodiment of these ideas in public ceremonies, is amenable to ethnographic description and analysis. Furthermore, nationalism often develops the ritual idioms of kinship, religion, and ethnicity as metaphors for the bounded solidarity among the citizens of a country. Thus, it becomes possible to reject essentialist and primordialist approaches to the nation without neglecting the lived experiences of ordinary people, whose subjectivities and material relations are shaped by that particular form of collective identity. Smith's call for the careful study of "the various 'myths' and 'memories,' 'symbols,' and 'values,' which so often define and differentiate nations" (1986: xix) outlines a useful research agenda.

This book contributes to the growing literature on the construction and representation of national identities in four basic ways. To begin, it locates precisely the multiple social actors who define and articulate the nation. In the case of Puerto Rico, several groups can be readily identified, such as colonial administrators, American scholars, nationalist intellectuals, Commonwealth officials, and leaders of migrant organizations, each with their own special interests, social positions, and ideological perspectives. Second, the book poses the question of when these discourses arise and how they gain broad institu-tional support. For instance, the historical context for the emergence of colo-nial, national, and transnational representations of Puerto Rico can be dated to the early part, the middle decades, and the last half of the twentieth century, respectively. Third is the issue of from where the nation is imagined: on the Island, from the United States, or from a diasporic standpoint? Among other factors, one's place of residence makes a huge difference in the construction and representation of the nation. Last, I analyze how identities are portrayed and communicated—through literary texts, visual images, government reports, ethnographic collections, museum exhibits, and so on.

This project has broader implications for the understanding of national imaginaries beyond the case of Puerto Rico, specifically, the idea that all identi-ties are constructed and represented from particular locations in time and place, according to the subjects' positions, and with practical repercussions for people's everyday life. Revisiting the case of Puerto Rico can shed new light on current debates about the local and the global, the national and the transna-tional, the colonial and the postcolonial, as contested sites for the construction and representation of cultural identities in the contemporary world. Thousands of Puerto Ricans have developed mobile livelihood practices that encompass several places in the mainland as well as on the Island. Those who live abroad, speak English, and participate in U.S. politics must be included in public and academic discussions on the future of Puerto Rico. They are part and parcel of a nation on the move.

The Construction of Cultural Identities in Puerto Rico and the Diaspora

More than one hundred years ago, the French scholar Ernest Renan (1990 [1882]) posed the question, "What is a nation?"[1] Renan answered that it was a "spiritual principle" based on shared memories, the cult of a glorious past, as well as the ability to forget certain shameful events, and above all a "daily plebiscite": the collective affirmation of a national "will" by the citizens of a country (1990 [1882]: 19). But how is this spiritual principle translated into practice? How does the cult of the past relate to the present and project into the future? How exactly is the national will expressed in everyday life? Who defines the nation, and for what purpose? Who is included and excluded in the nationalist discourse? How does one map the territorial and symbolic boundaries of the nation?

The search for the essence of the nation has continued unabated throughout the twentieth century, especially among colonized peoples such as Puerto Ricans. In such situations, questions of cultural identity are far from academic but instead touch on people's struggles for survival, lived experiences, and rights to political representation. Intellectual and public debates on the Island suggest that it may be too premature to announce the end of nationalism or to romanticize transnationalism in an increasingly global world. Nationalist ideas and practices continue to circulate worldwide and organize much of people's daily lives.

As I argued in the introduction, the case of Puerto Rico is distinctive because of its persistent colonial condition. Although Puerto Ricans have been U.S. citizens since 1917, the legal definition of their identity does not correspond to their self-perception as "Puerto Ricans first, Americans second." The juridical status of Puerto Rican citizenship (as opposed to U.S. citizenship) has been debated in both the United States and the Island's legislative and juridical branches. One dispute was sparked by the pro-independence leader Juan Mari Bras's well-publicized resignation of his U.S. citizenship in 1995. Yet most Puerto Ricans see no contradiction between asserting their Puerto Rican nationality at the same time as they defend their U.S. citizenship (Morris 1995, 1997). On December 13, 1998, Puerto Rico held a plebiscite on its political status, and more than half of the voters supported neither annexation to nor independence from the United States but voted instead for "none of the above," including the current commonwealth formula, the Estado Libre Asociado.

A second distinctive element of the Puerto Rican case is the sheer magnitude of the diaspora. Few other countries in recent memory have exported such a large share of their population abroad—more than half a million out of a total of roughly 2 million people between 1945 and 1965. The exodus resumed massive proportions in the 1980s and 1990s. Between 1991 and 1998, nearly 250,000 Island residents moved to the U.S. mainland (Junta de Planificación 1998). In 2000 the census found 3.4 million persons of Puerto Rican origin residing in the mainland, compared with more than 3.8 million persons on the Island (Guzmán 2001). At the same time, thousands of returning Puerto Ricans, Dominicans, Cubans, and other foreigners entered the Island. In 1990 more than 321,000 residents of Puerto Rico, roughly 9 percent of the total population, had been born in the U.S. mainland and in foreign countries—most of whom were persons of Puerto Rican parentage, but many were born in the Dominican Republic and Cuba (U.S. Bureau of the Census 1993b). Demographically and geographically, Puerto Rico is a nation on the move, as well as a nation without a state.

At this juncture, Island intellectuals are sharply divided between those who believe that Puerto Ricans should fight for independence to preserve their cultural identity and those who believe that this struggle necessarily invokes a homogenizing, essentialist, and totalitarian fiction called "the nation." Roughly speaking, local nationalists of various strands tend to assume the former position, while some postmodernists have espoused the latter. Hence, the battle between the two intellectual camps has multiple implications for ideological discourses, political strategies, and tactical alliances. For a nationalist sympathizer such as Juan Manuel Carrión (1996), the defense of the Spanish language and other icons of the Hispanic heritage has the practical advantage of uniting the Puerto Rican people against a common foe: U.S. imperialism. For a skeptical postmodernist such as Carlos Pabón (1995b), the Hispanophilia of the native elite is a discursive practice that glosses over the internal diversity of the collective imaginary. For the former camp, the rise of cultural nationalism is an integral part of the anticolonial struggle in Puerto Rico; for the latter, it is merely a "light" form of nationalism or neonationalism, devoid of its subversive and progressive connotations.[2] The two camps have probably overstated their opposition in the heat of the discussion, and neither has systematically considered the diaspora in their reflections on the Puerto Rican nation.

Much of the current controversy among scholars on Puerto Rico centers on their standpoints vis-à-vis the question of national identity and sovereignty. The influence of poststructuralist theories in the social sciences and the humanities, as they have developed in Western Europe and the United States, has led many scholars to question the very existence of a national character, essence, or substance that can be fixed, defined, and preserved unequivocally (see J. Duany 1996, 1998a).[3] Still others have argued that the deconstruction of the nationalist discourse need not imply surrendering all practical commitments to progressive social movements such as the quest for independence (Coss 1996). More recently, some Puerto Rican scholars living on the Island and the mainland have asserted that a radical democratic agenda can be accomplished only under complete annexation to the United States (Duchesne et al. 1997). To a large extent the politics of decolonization (whether through statehood, independence, or increased autonomy) is contingent on competing discourses of identity.

In this chapter I analyze recent intellectual debates on the Puerto Rican nation and its persistent colonial relation with the United States. First I trace the development of a nationalist discourse on the Island, primarily among creative writers, artists, and scholars during the twentieth century, and then I identify several problems with this discourse, especially the exclusion of ethnic and racial others from its definition of the nation. I also examine the recent challenges to nationalist projects in Puerto Rico from the growing ethnic diversity of the Island's population, especially Dominican and Cuban immigrants. Next, I argue that public and academic discourses on Puerto Rican identity must encompass the diaspora in the United States. It is especially urgent to think about the nation in nonterritorial terms because of the increasing numbers of people who now live outside their country of origin.

In what follows I engage in a critical dialogue with Benedict Anderson's seminal book *Imagined Communities* (1991). Although I agree with Anderson that nations "are cultural artefacts of a certain kind" (4), I do not believe that they are necessarily imagined as sovereign or as limited to a particular territory.[4] Moreover, the idea of the community as a "deep, horizontal comradeship" (7) should not obscure the internal cleavages within all nations or that identities are constructed in different ways, from various social positions. Anderson's original formulation of nationalism tends to take for granted that communities are imagined from a fixed location, within a firmly bounded space. Although Anderson (1992) has more recently paid more attention to "long-distance nationalism," further work is needed to spell out the theoretical and political impact of population movements on nationalist thought and practice. I intend this chapter as a reflection on this wider topic, with a focus on contemporary Puerto Rico and its diaspora.

CULTURAL POLITICS IN A STATELESS NATION

Public and academic debates about whether Puerto Rico has its own national identity have always been fraught with strong political repercussions because of the Island's colonial relations, first with Spain and now with the United States. For decades the main conceptual and political paradox in the construction of cultural identities in Puerto Rico has been the growing popularity of cultural nationalism, together with the weakness of the independence movement. Culturally speaking, Puerto Rico meets most of the objective and subjective characteristics of conventional views of the nation—among them a shared language, territory, and history—except for sovereignty. The Island also possesses many of the symbolic attributes of a nation, such as a national system of universities, museums, and other cultural institutions; a national tradition in literature and the visual arts; and even a national representation in international sports and beauty contests. Most important, the vast majority of Puerto Ricans imagine themselves as distinct from Americans as well as from other Latin American and Caribbean peoples (Morris 1997).

Yet the Island remains a colonial possession, and most of the electorate does not currently support an independent republic in Puerto Rico. Rather, it has reiterated an overwhelming preference for U.S. citizenship and permanent union with the United States.[5] A key issue is the freedom to travel to the United States under any political status option. Under the Commonwealth, Puerto

Ricans have unrestricted entry into the U.S. mainland. In a striking gesture, the Puerto Rican Independence Party president Rubén Berríos has recently argued that the U.S. Congress should grant Puerto Ricans the right to enter the United States freely, even if the Island became independent. Berríos acknowledged the importance of U.S. citizenship for most Puerto Ricans, especially as a practical way of facilitating the movement between the Island and the mainland (Magdalys Rodríguez 1997). Questions of citizenship, migration, and identity in Puerto Rico acquire a sense of urgency seldom found in well-established nation-states that do not have to justify their existence or fight for their survival. Consequently, the affirmation of a separate cultural identity is closely linked with the unfinished project for self-determination, which is typical of colonial liberation movements throughout the world (Chatterjee 1995).

Since the mid–twentieth century, the pro-independence movement has been unable to retain a mass following in Puerto Rico. As Carrión (1980, 1996) has argued, the struggle for independence has not represented the bulk of the native ruling and working classes. Instead, independence has been primarily the political project of a radicalized sector of the petty bourgeoisie—including small merchants, manufacturers, independent artisans, liberal professionals, and government employees. For instance, the leadership of the Nationalist Party during the 1930s was primarily composed of lawyers, journalists, physicians, dentists, pharmacists, and small business owners (Ferrao 1990). Most local entrepreneurs have not embraced a nationalist discourse because they identify their class interests with continued association with the United States (González Díaz 1991). Moreover, the massive extension of public welfare benefits through transfer payments from the federal government has strengthened popular support for annexation. Without the allegiance of either the native bourgeoisie or the proletariat, resistance to colonialism has largely been displaced from party politics to the contested terrain of culture. As a result, local intellectuals—especially college professors, scholars, and writers—have played a role in the construction of a nationalist discourse disproportionate to their numbers. Here as elsewhere, the local intelligentsia has helped to define and consolidate a national culture against what it perceives as a foreign invasion. In John Hutchinson's terms (1994), native intellectuals have sought to regenerate the moral fabric of the nation as an organizing principle in the daily lives of the people.

Since 1898, national identity in Puerto Rico has developed under—and often in outright opposition to—U.S. hegemony. During the first third of the twentieth century, the local movement to obtain sovereignty garnered growing support, and several political parties included independence as part of their ideological platforms. But after World War II, the autonomist and annexationist movements became the dominant forces in Puerto Rican politics. Recent studies have focused on the fall of political nationalism and the rise of cultural nationalism on the Island since the 1940s (see, for example, Alvarez-Curbelo and Rodríguez Castro 1993; Carrión 1999; Carrión, Gracia Ruiz, and Rodríguez Fraticelli 1993; Gelpí 1993). In Puerto Rico, cultural nationalism became increasingly disengaged from political nationalism and identified with populism after World War II (Díaz Quiñones 1993). As I develop in Chapter 5, the charismatic leader Luis Muñoz Marín, the Island's governor from 1949 to 1964, was a key figure in that ideological transition.[6] During this period, Muñoz Marín came into direct confrontation with the president of the Nationalist Party, Pedro Albizu Campos, who advocated independence for the Island.[7] Muñoz Marín adopted an autonomist position that sought to reconcile the Island's political and economic incorporation to the United States with the preservation of Puerto Rican identity or, as he preferred to call it, "personality."

Muñoz Marín, then, was one of the chief architects of cultural nationalism in postwar Puerto Rico. I would argue that this is not a lesser or minor form of political nationalism, as the pejorative labels "neonationalism" and "*lite* nationalism" imply. Cultural nationalism represents a serious (though perhaps limited) attempt to assert Puerto Rico's distinctive collective identity, within the context of continued political and economic dependence on the United States. Like Arlene Dávila (1997: 3), I approach cultural nationalism "not as an apolitical development but as part of a shift in the terrain of political action to the realm of culture and cultural politics, where the idiom of culture constitutes a dominant discourse to advance, debate, and legitimize conflicting claims." Unlike Dávila, I argue that this turn to culture has a strong potential to subvert ideologically the colonial regime in Puerto Rico. In Chapter 5 I assess the repercussions of cultural nationalism for the anticolonial struggle on the Island.

Today, cultural nationalism transcends political party loyalties on both the left and the right. It is now the official rhetoric of the three political parties on the Island—pro-independence, pro-commonwealth, and even pro-statehood. In the 1998 plebiscite campaign, the pro-statehood party prominently displayed the traditional symbols of the Puerto Rican nation, such as the flag, the Spanish language, and Olympic representation. The other two parties also employed a nationalistic language of collective self-respect to advance their respective causes. Thus, Puerto Rico exemplifies better than other places the significance of cultural nationalism in that it is still a colony, rather than a nation-state, and yet most people on the Island (as well as on the mainland) continue to identify themselves as Puerto Ricans as their primary collective affiliation. I would argue that the construction of cultural identities in contemporary Puerto Rico involves a profound ideological rift between citizenship and nationality, as well as the constant transgression of the boundaries of territory, language, and ethnicity established by standard views of the nation.

On the Island, Puerto Ricans from different political parties share a strong consensus with regard to their primary collective affiliations, a clear dichotomy between "us" and "them"—that is, between Puerto Ricans and Americans (Morris 1995, 1997; Rivera 1996). Cultural nationalism has become one of the leading discourses of identity in contemporary Puerto Rico, even though it is articulated across various social positions, including class, gender, race and color, age, and ideology. In the 1940s Julian Steward and his colleagues (1956) also found substantial regional differences, but these have diminished since the advent of industrialization, migration, and urbanization. Moreover, the dominant representations of Puerto Ricanness are no longer confined to an intellectual elite, the petty bourgeoisie, or the pro-independence movement. Rather, popular icons of national identity (such as the omnipresent flag or salsa music) have filtered down, sprung from the bottom up, or recirculated through the Island's class structure. Such symbolic expressions of Puerto Rican culture have penetrated the colonial state apparatus, local political parties, the mass media, and grassroots organizations (Dávila 1997).

INTELLECTUAL DISCOURSES OF IDENTITY

Nationalist thought has permeated academic discussion on Puerto Rican culture at least since the 1930s. Ideologically, nationalism has been characterized by the defense of local values and customs against the U.S. occupation of the Island in 1898—or, to cite the revealing title of a book on the topic, "the North American cultural aggression in Puerto Rico" (Méndez 1980). According to another well-known scholar, "the essential dilemma" of twentieth-century Puerto Rico was "cultural assimilation vs. national consciousness" (Maldonado-Denis 1972). Nationalists have insistently denounced "Yankee imperialism" on the Island and have claimed the right to the self-determination of the Puerto Rican people, including the preservation of their national identity. During the first half of the twentieth century, most Puerto Rican nationalists embraced the Spanish vernacular as the dominant symbol of their culture, as well as other elements of the Hispanic heritage such as Catholicism. Contrary to nineteenth-century Latin America (Anderson 1991: 47–48), language is a crucial element in Puerto Rican nationalism, partly as a reaction to the ill-fated attempt by the U.S. colonial government to impose English as the official language of public instruction on the Island until 1948. Today, critics often equate Puerto Rican nationalism with Hispanophilia—the cult of all things Spanish—or at least with a special preference for the Hispanic basis of Creole identity (Pabón 1995b), usually at the expense of the African sources. The recent revitalization of Taíno culture has also served to root national identity in mythical pre-Columbian times (see Chapter 11).

Nationalism faces three recurrent problems in the analysis of contemporary Puerto Rican society. First, it has historically set up an artificial binary opposition between American and Puerto Rican culture—one English-speaking, the other Spanish-speaking; one Protestant, the other Catholic; one Anglo-Saxon in origin, the other Hispanic; one modern, the other traditional; and so on. But such a rough dichotomy no longer exists in Puerto Rico, if it ever did anywhere. For instance, many Puerto Ricans born and raised in the United States now use English as their dominant language; many Puerto Ricans on and off the Island have converted to Protestantism; and many Puerto Ricans have mixed ancestry, not just a Spanish background. Several of the traditional symbols of the Puerto Rican nation were invented during the late nineteenth century, such as the national flag and anthem, and some are even more modern, such as salsa music. In 1998 the controversial privatization of the Puerto Rican Telephone Company led to its popular reinterpretation as part of the national patrimony. In 2000 all three political parties reached a consensus that the U.S. Navy should stop its military exercises in Vieques, which is now portrayed as an integral part of the national territory.

Second, nationalists have tended to idealize the preindustrial rural past under Spanish rule and to demonize U.S. industrial capitalism in the twentieth century. Like other colonial intellectuals, Puerto Rican nationalists have depicted their native land as the source of all moral values and the imperial power as the root of all evil (see Chatterjee 1995). As a result, they have erected the noble highland peasant (the *jíbaro*), supposedly of European origin, as a romantic icon of a pure Puerto Ricanness (Guerra 1998). By the end of the eighteenth century, the Creole elite sought to identify with the local peasantry, while maintaining the basic contours of the colonial relationship with Spain (Scarano 1996). Although the elite's discourse included "white" subsistence farmers within the boundaries of Puerto Rican identity, it excluded African slaves, free people of color, and recent immigrants from its definition of the nation. As other scholars have noted, the founding myth of *la gran familia puertorriqueña* (the Great Puerto Rican Family), with Creole landowners as benevolent father figures and subsistence farmers as their grateful peons, obscures important conflicts and tensions within nineteenth-century coffee and sugar plantations (Quintero Rivera et al. 1979; Torres 1998).

Finally, nationalist thinking and practice have tended to embrace an essentialist and homogenizing image of collective identity that silences the multiple voices of the nation, based on class, race, ethnicity, gender, sexual orientation, and other differences. A troublesome area has been the neglect and mistreatment of diasporic experiences, both on and off the Island. In the 1950s, Puerto Rican writers began to reflect on the resettlement of hundreds of thousands of their compatriots in New York City and other places along the eastern seaboard of the United States. But most of these authors did not write from the migrants' own standpoint and failed to capture the complex and dynamic texture of their bilingual and bicultural communities (Flores 1997). Similarly, in the 1970s, writers began to approach the immigration of Cubans and Dominicans into Puerto Rico from a biased perspective, usually focusing on the threats posed by the "alien invasion" rather than the strengthening of cultural diversity (Martínez–San Miguel 1997a). In sum, most nationalists have not fully acknowledged the implications of spatial dispersion and cultural fragmentation, perhaps because, following political doctrines prevailing since the nineteenth century, they have typically defined national sovereignty and identity within strictly territorial boundaries.

In the following sections, I draw primarily on creative writers who articulate the official discourse on the Puerto Rican nation. I do not wish to privilege literary texts over other kinds of discourses, such as political speeches or academic essays, which I analyze in other chapters. Rather, I focus on literary texts here simply because they clearly raise the questions of cultural identity that have dominated the Island throughout the twentieth century. The conceptions of canonized writers—predominantly male, white, and middle or upper class— have been subject to intense contestation from the start, especially by women, blacks, the working class, and migrants. Thus, elite views of the nation are not the only or even the ruling ideas in society; they may be contradicted, revised, or discarded by other groups and classes. Nonetheless, the cultural production of intellectual elites has shaped hegemonic, popular, and even subaltern approaches to the nation. In Puerto Rico and elsewhere, creative writers often set the broad parameters for the public debate on cultural identities.[8]

The constitution of a nationalist canon in the Island's literature has been well documented (Flores 1993; García-Calderón 1998; Gelpí 1993). This canon was established and consolidated by the so-called Generation of 1930, a notable group of intellectuals, writers, and artists that included Antonio Pedreira, Tomás Blanco, and Vicente Géigel Polanco. The Generation of 1930 helped to define the contemporary discourse on the Puerto Rican nation, based on five ideological premises. First, this discourse considers the Spanish language the cornerstone of Puerto Ricanness, as opposed to English, which it typically views as a corrupting influence on the vernacular. Second, the Island's territory is the geographic entity that contains the nation; beyond the Island's borders, Puerto Ricanness is threatened with contamination and dissolution. Third, the sense of a common origin, based on place of birth and residence, defines Puerto Ricans. Fourth, the shared history of a Spanish heritage, indigenous roots, and African influences offers a strong resistance to U.S. assimilation. Fifth, local culture—especially folklore—provides an invaluable source of popular images and artifacts that are counterposed to icons of U.S. culture, avoiding unwanted mixtures.

The classic text in the development of a nationalist discourse on the Island is Pedreira's *Insularismo*, or Insularism (1992 [1934]). Significantly, Pedreira is an ideological heir to the moderate autonomist tradition of the nineteenth-century Creole elite, rather than radical separatism from Spain. In this book the author asks the key questions, "What are we, or how are we Puerto Ricans, globally considered?" (1992 [1934]: 21).[9] He answers the questions in three main ways: (1) culturally, Puerto Rico is a Hispanic colony; (2) racially, it is an extremely mixed and confused population; and (3) geographically, it is an island marginalized from world history. According to Pedreira, the Puerto Rican character was primarily determined by territorial isolation, hence the title emphasizing insularity. The Island's geographic situation conditioned Puerto Ricans to feel small, dependent, and passive. In the end, the islanders' collective personality was dominated by an intense inferiority complex that forced them to rely on more powerful, continental countries such as Spain and the United States. Pedreira's philosophical pessimism permeates his entire argument, from the so-called degeneration of the races in a tropical environment to the practical difficulties of leading the Puerto Rican people to an independent state.

Despite its shortcomings, *Insularismo* remains one of the basic sources of contemporary thinking and writing on the Island's culture. As such it is part of the dominant narrative of the Puerto Rican nation and required reading on public school curricula. Pedreira's image of geographic isolation was inscribed as a master metaphor for national character. His dramatic description of Puerto Rico as a "ship without direction" (*nave al garete*) has been restated by several authors of various ideological persuasions, most prominently the noted playwright René Marqués in his infamous essay "El puertorriqueño dócil" (The docile Puerto Rican [1977]). Pedreira's text illustrates how Hispanophilia and Negrophobia, as well as elitism and androcentrism, converged in the thought of the intellectual elite on the Island during the first half of the twentieth century. The author's biological determinism—especially as it shaped his negative view of racial mixture—was tempered only by his equally strong geographic reductionism. His rhetorical strategies, including the use of metaphors such as the ship, the house, the family, the child, and disease, have become standard features of the Island's cultural nationalism (Gelpí 1993). For all these reasons, Pedreira is a foundational figure in the contemporary discourse on Puerto Ricanness.

The current intellectual discussion on national identity in Puerto Rico is still framed largely in Pedreira's terms. Now as then, scholars, writers, and artists often feel threatened by the Americanization of Puerto Rican culture through the school curriculum, the mass media, and the massive Protestant "penetration" of popular religiosity (Silva Gotay 1997). In response to that perceived threat, local intellectuals have tended to reassert the Hispanic roots of Puerto Rican culture and to cultivate Creole topics such as the jíbaro, the landscape, and folk customs. Much of the Island's literary activity during the first half of the twentieth century—when the traditional icons of national identity were first defined—was characterized by a romantic return to the mountains, as the leading nationalist Juan Antonio Corretjer titled his 1929 book of poems (Corretjer 1977). As the traditional home of the jíbaro, the highlands have long been hailed to be the heart of Puerto Ricanness. Similarly, until the 1950s the Island's plastic arts were primarily concerned with the creation of a national iconography based on local types, customs, and landscapes (Hermandad de Artistas Gráficos 1998). As writers and artists elaborated the dominant representations of Puerto Ricanness, they tended to gloss over the Island's internal diversity.

After World War II, cultural anthropologists appropriated the nationalist discourse in Puerto Rico and promoted it from various academic and government institutions, such as the University of Puerto Rico and the Institute of Puerto Rican Culture (see Alegría 1996b; Fernández Méndez 1980; Seda Bonilla 1980). At the time, most influential intellectuals shared the view that Puerto Rico had a strong national culture, even though it lacked a sovereign state. From their standpoint, the Island's cultural identity revolved primarily around the Spanish language, Catholic religion, and other Hispanic values and practices, such as respect and dignity (Lauria 1964). In the mid-1960s, a controversy arose over the publication of Sidney Mintz's essay on national culture in Puerto Rico for the U.S.-P.R. Status Commission (Mintz 1966). From a cultural ecological perspective, Mintz raised doubts about the existence of a homogeneous national character on the Island and posited instead a series of distinct regional subcultures. Local reception of Mintz's work continues to be tainted with political suspicion.

In the 1970s, Marxist critics underlined class distinctions in the formation and consolidation of national culture in Puerto Rico (Quintero Rivera et al. 1979; Ramírez 1976). From this standpoint, the bourgeoisie and the proletariat developed different, often opposing, views of cultural identity. Since the 1990s, as I have already noted, postmodernist writers have charged that the nationalist discourse tends to obscure the multiple fissures and fragments within Puerto Rican society, including class, race, gender, and sexual orientation (Negrón-Muntaner and Grosfoguel 1997; Pabón 1995b). For many of these writers, nationalism can be as exclusionary and oppressive as colonialism. Hence, a key intellectual and political issue within contemporary Puerto Rico is the characterization of national identity as homogeneous or hybrid.

One of the recurring themes in the debate on Puerto Rican identity has been the binary opposition between Hispanic and U.S. culture. But the mass exodus from the Island to the U.S. mainland, especially between 1945 and 1965, challenged such clear-cut dichotomies. In the 1960s, Puerto Rican scholars began to approach the diaspora with trepidation. The work of anthropologist Eduardo Seda Bonilla (1980) is typical of a nationalist stance toward Puerto Rican migrants in the United States. In a series of influential essays published during the 1970s, Seda Bonilla posed the "problem" of the assimilation of Puerto Ricans into American society and concluded that second-generation immigrants had practically lost their cultural roots. Seda Bonilla was especially concerned with the erosion of the Spanish language among the so-called Nuyoricans, second-generation immigrants born in the United States, as well as the negative impact of American racism on Puerto Rican culture. From his perspective, migration to the mainland threatened the survival of the Puerto Rican people and announced a "requiem for its culture" (see also Maldonado-Denis 1984). The diaspora was therefore represented as an obstacle to the consolidation of a national consciousness and the growth of the independence movement on the Island.

EXCLUDING THE OTHER

The nationalist discourse in Puerto Rico has traditionally omitted racial and ethnic minorities and other subaltern groups from its nation-building project, whether they were inside or outside the Island's frontiers (see Martínez–San Miguel 1997a). These exclusions run through political speeches, literary texts, historical chronicles, journalistic articles, paintings, films, and other cultural representations that constitute the textual corpus of nationalist thought (Negrón-Muntaner and Grosfoguel 1997). The need to establish clear-cut territorial, linguistic, and cultural borders vis-à-vis the United States has ideologically framed the pro-independence movement in Puerto Rico. Hence, Puerto Rican nationalism throughout the twentieth century has been characterized by Hispanophilia, anti-Americanism, racism, androcentrism, homophobia, and more recently xenophobia—as well as a more positive attempt to define and uphold local values and customs. I have already noted how the legendary figure of the jíbaro—the white male peasant from the inner highlands—was put forth as the essence of Puerto Rican nationhood, neglecting other sectors of the Island's population, such as urban dwellers, wageworkers, blacks and mulattoes, women, gays, and lesbians. Nowhere was this "man of the land" more commonly reified than in twentieth-century Puerto Rican literature, especially in the poetic and narrative genres. Since its inception, Puerto Rican nationalism has been very masculine in orientation, as feminist scholars have shown (see Martínez–San Miguel 1997b; Roy-Fequiere 1997). More recently, nationalists have found it difficult to incorporate in their discourse the growing immigrant population within the Island's borders as well as the massive diaspora that overflows them.

The paternalist image of the Great Puerto Rican Family presupposes the harmonious integration among the three main roots of the Island's population:

Amerindian, European, and African. This traditional conception considers Africans the third root of Puerto Rican identity not only in chronological terms but also ranked according to their avowed contribution to the Island's contemporary culture. Thus, many scholars have claimed that the descendants of African slaves, as well as the remaining Taíno Indians, were quickly amalgamated into Creole culture, primarily of Hispanic origin, which tended to erase ethnic and racial differences (Alegría 1996b; Fernández Méndez 1980). The myth of racial integration insists on the physical and cultural homogenization of the Puerto Rican population, based on an ideology of *mestizaje* (racial mixture). The absence of racial prejudice in Puerto Rico was supposedly achieved through the acceptance of interracial marriages and the progressive whitening of the local population, as social distinctions based on skin color became secondary to class inequality (see Chapter 10). In the view of nationalist intellectuals such as Tomás Blanco, *la gran familia puertorriqueña* overcame the invidious racial divisions prevalent in the United States (Díaz Quiñones 1985).

Nonetheless, stereotypes persistently stigmatize the black population of Puerto Rico and practically exclude it from the nationalist canon. In elite as well as in popular forms of culture, Afro–Puerto Ricans continue to be represented as marginal and subaltern outsiders, as less Puerto Rican than white people. A catalogue of racial slurs against dark-skinned people runs through folk humor, proverbs, aesthetic concepts, school texts, museum displays, media representations, literary texts, and political speeches (Zenón Cruz 1975). In an infamous 1988 speech, former governor Rafael Hernández Colón held that the African contribution to Puerto Rican culture was merely "a rhetorical ascription" (cited by Pabón 1995b: 23). Still, the dominant narrative portrays the Island as a racial paradise, where white, brown, and black people mix and mingle freely. In the 1990s, Puerto Rican intellectuals began to revisit "the conspiracy of silence" that has enveloped the racial question on the Island and in the diaspora (see, for instance, *Centro* 1996; Torres 1998).

As Puerto Rico has become more diverse ethnically over the past four decades, the nationalist discourse has also attempted to exclude other minority groups, especially Cuban and Dominican immigrants, from the official definition of the nation. This exclusion of Cuban and Dominican immigrants is ironic, given that much of the pro-independence movement in Puerto Rico since the end of the nineteenth century has embraced the ideal of an Antillean confederation. However, this discursive practice is primarily oriented toward establishing ideological links between the three countries of origin (Cuba,

Puerto Rico, and the Dominican Republic), rather than among their diasporas in Puerto Rico and the United States. At the same time, intermarriage among members of the three migrant groups is common today in the United States.

The public image of Cubans in Puerto Rico is highly ambivalent: although most Puerto Ricans grant that Cubans are hardworking and independent, they continue to characterize Cubans as a whole as dishonest and selfish. Moreover, Cuban contributions to Puerto Rican culture and politics are not well known or appreciated (J. Duany 1999). Cuban immigrants have not been completely assimilated into Puerto Rican society insofar as negative stereotypes about them continue to shape their relations with the host population. By and large, Cubans are still perceived as marginal and unwanted outsiders.

Since the early 1960s, nationalist intellectuals have tended to reject Cuban immigrants in Puerto Rico primarily for ideological reasons. Marqués's previously cited essay (1977) portrays them as "aggressive and without scruples in their struggle for their own survival" (209), as well as "unconditional supporters of the United States . . . cynically colonialist . . . fierce enemies of Puerto Rico's national sovereignty and dignity" (208). Cubans have also been shunned because of their popular association with the white elite of San Juan, the so-called *blanquitos* and *riquitos* (literally, "white" and "wealthy" people) (Cobas and Duany 1997). Contemporary writers have tended to represent Cuban immigrants as foreign to the national imaginary of Puerto Ricans, regardless of their cultural and linguistic affinities. A paradigmatic case is Ana Lydia Vega's short story "Trabajando pal inglés" (Working for the Englishman) (1981b), a literary inventory of standard clichés about Cuban immigrants (for an excellent analysis, see Martínez–San Miguel 1997a).

"Trabajando pal inglés" takes the form of a letter written by Marta, a Cuban woman in Puerto Rico, to her niece in the United States. Marta's letter revolves around her daughter's romantic involvement with a Puerto Rican man, despite her parents' objections. In the end, the ungrateful daughter elopes with her left-leaning social scientist boyfriend to—of all places—Cuba. From an anthropological viewpoint, the most significant element of this story is the skillful re-creation of the narrator's attitudes, prejudices, and values. Marta emerges as the archetypal Cuban in exile: from a privileged class background in her home country, alienated from the local culture, biased against Puerto Ricans (especially against blacks), and politically reactionary. Vega's close attention to Cuban mannerisms and regionalisms makes Marta appear sympathetic, if ridiculous. Overall, the story articulates many of the dominant discursive practices that construct Cubans in Puerto Rico as racial, cultural, linguistic, and ideological others.

Contemporary Dominican immigration has generated much more hostility in Puerto Rico than has Cuban immigration. The causes of the growing anti-Dominican discourse include the immigrants' legal condition (many are undocumented), socioeconomic composition (most are lower class), gender (the majority are women), and, above all, racial appearance (most are black or mulatto). The figure of the Dominican—especially the undocumented immigrant—appears as the Other par excellence: a strange, dangerous, and incomprehensible character who occupies a marginal and clandestine status. The Dominican way of speaking Spanish, for example, has become the focus of numerous jokes told by Puerto Ricans. Television and radio programs, as well as journalistic and literary texts, constantly recycle the public perception of Dominican immigrants as illegitimate and undesirable aliens. Most Puerto Ricans consider that foreign immigration to the Island, especially from the Dominican Republic, is out of control and that the government should restrict the number and kind of immigrants to the Island. As one survey respondent claimed, "Corruption and crime have increased because of the foreigners" (J. Duany 1999).

The dominant representations of Dominicans in Puerto Rico emphasize their peasant origins, poor background, low educational levels, and limited intellectual capacity. The Puerto Rican stereotype of Dominicans as dumb, ignorant, dirty, disorderly, and violent recalls that of Haitians in the Dominican Republic or, for that matter, Puerto Ricans in the United States (see Duany, Hernández Angueira, and Rey 1995). The contemporary racialization of Dominican immigrants in Puerto Rico associates them closely with black Puerto Ricans, who remain on the fringes of the nationalist imaginary. It also serves to denationalize and alienate Puerto Rican blacks. Racial exclusion, as currently applied to the Dominican community of San Juan, is one of the most problematic elements of the national project on the Island. Hence, the popular conflation of the term *negro* (black) with *dominicano* (Dominican) is a sign of increasing concern to those interested in promoting cultural diversity in Puerto Rico. It represents the growing ethnicization of racial stigmas on the Island, as well as the continuing perception that being black is foreign to national identity.

As the anti-Dominican discourse has grown in popularity over the past two decades, literary texts on the Island have begun to articulate (and criticize) that trend. A recent example is Magali García Ramis's (1995) brief short story "Retrato del dominicano que pasó por puertorriqueño y pudo emigrar a mejor vida a Estados Unidos" (Portrait of the Dominican who passed for Puerto Rican and was able to emigrate to a better life in the United States). The story humorously narrates the attempt by a light-skinned undocumented Dominican, Asdrúbal, to bypass U.S. immigration authorities in San Juan in order to board an airplane to New York City. His Puerto Rican friends teach him how to walk, dress, look, cut his hair, and talk like a Puerto Rican. The protagonist even has to change his exotic name to a more Puerto Rican–sounding name like Willie or "Ilving." He finally manages to cross the inspection point at the airport and enter the U.S. mainland. In so doing, he crosses over not only the geopolitical frontier between Puerto Rico and the United States but also the cultural border between Puerto Rico and the Dominican Republic.

CULTURAL IDENTITY AND THE DIASPORA

Alongside the enduring "colonial dilemma" (Meléndez and Meléndez 1993) and increasing ethnic heterogeneity, a major challenge to contemporary thinking on national identity on the Island is the Puerto Rican diaspora to the United States.[10] A key issue is that migrants do not meet most of the traditional criteria of nationalist discourse on who is a Puerto Rican. Today, almost half of all persons of Puerto Rican origin do not reside in their "national" territory, the Island, but in the U.S. mainland. Many Puerto Ricans—especially those born and raised in the United States—do not use the "national" language, Spanish, as their primary means of communication. Nor do most participate actively and directly in the political and economic affairs of their nation of origin. It is even doubtful that most U.S.-based Puerto Ricans share with islanders a common sense of history or a "psychological makeup," to cite Stalin's classic definition of the nation (Stalin 1994).

Scholars cannot even agree on a common terminology to refer to Puerto Ricans in the United States. The papers for the 1996 Puerto Rican Studies Association Conference in San Juan suggested the following alternatives: Neo-Rican, Nuyorican, Niuyorrican, *nuyorriqueño*, mainland Puerto Rican, U.S.-born Puerto Rican, Boricua, Diaspo-Rican, and even Tato Laviera's curious neologism *AmeRícan*—but never that hyphenated mixture, Puerto Rican–American. Several studies have found that Island-born Puerto Ricans perceive Nuyoricans as a different group, and Nuyoricans also tend to view themselves distinctly from both Island-born Puerto Ricans and Americans (Lorenzo-Hernández 1999; Morris 1995; Rodríguez-Cortés 1990). As popularly used in Puerto Rico, "Nuyorican" refers to all Puerto Ricans born or raised in the United States. The term is often used pejoratively to imply that Nuyoricans are somehow less Puerto Rican than those who live on the Island. Still, most Puerto Ricans in the United States maintain strong cultural, psychological, economic, and political ties to the Island (Alicea 1997; Falcón 1993). As Arjun Appadurai has argued in another context, the diaspora has developed into a *"transnation, which retains a special ideological link to a putative place of origin but is otherwise a thoroughly diasporic collectivity"* (1996: 172; emphasis in the original).

The nationalist discourse on the Island has traditionally shunned the diaspora in its definition of the nation, primarily for linguistic reasons (Barradas 1998; Díaz Quiñones 1993). The main issue has been the gradual substitution of the Spanish vernacular by the English language, especially among second- and third-generation Puerto Ricans in the United States (see Zentella 1997). Until recently, most scholars based in Puerto Rico located the emigrants outside the territorial and symbolic boundaries of their own identity. Island intellectuals usually considered Nuyoricans to have an identity crisis or to have assimilated into U.S. culture; in either case they treated them as Other, just as they treated the gringos or the Cubans and Dominicans who later moved to Puerto Rico (see Fernández Méndez 1959; Maldonado-Denis 1984; Seda Bonilla 1972). As Marvette Pérez (1996: 192) puts it, "Almost all of the Puerto Rican nationalist discourse implicitly excludes Nuyoricans because of their physical and metaphorical proximity to the United States. In these discourses, Nuyoricans are discursively constructed as dangerous, hybrid, and contaminated beings, and in danger of, upon returning to Puerto Rico, contaminating Puerto Ricans." Even today many local scholars and creative writers deride Puerto Ricans in the diaspora because they cannot speak Spanish well or conduct themselves in a proper Puerto Rican fashion. The resistance to incorporation of migrants into a broader view of the divided nation has taken various forms, particularly in the sphere of cultural politics and specifically language policies.

The issue of cultural identity in the diaspora has been hotly contested by Puerto Rican writers on the Island. As noted before, cultural nationalism—and especially linguistic nationalism—has constituted the dominant canon in Puerto Rican literature throughout the twentieth century (Gelpí 1993). In part, this assertion of language as the essence of national identity stems from the intellectuals' resistance to the imposition of English as the Island's official language. From their standpoint, to be touted as Puerto Rican, a literary work must have been written originally in Spanish.[11] Hence, the literature of the

Puerto Rican diaspora, mostly written in English or in "Spanglish," lies outside the national canon (C. Hernández 1997). No Puerto Rican writer currently living in the United States and writing in English is now included in the Island's official curriculum at the elementary and high school levels. Very few are taught in elective courses at local universities. Neither Spanish nor English departments have made these authors required reading, largely because of their hybrid, bilingual writings.

Vega's well-known short story "Pollito Chicken" (1981a) is emblematic of the traditional local stance toward Puerto Rican migration. The story narrates the return of a second-generation Puerto Rican woman, "Suzie Bermiúdez [sic]," to the Island. The text satirically explores the psychological impact of code-switching between Spanish and English on the protagonist, creating a kind of cultural schizophrenia, a neither-nor identity. On her first night at the Conquistador Hotel in Fajardo, Suzie picks up a bartender. Her Island-born lover concludes, "That woman in room 306, you don't know if she's a gringa or a Puerto Rican, brother. She asks for room service in legal English, but when I make love to her, she screams her life out in Boricua" (A. Vega 1981a: 79). What she exclaims, rather implausibly, is, "¡Viva Puelto Rico Libre!" ("Long Live a Free Puerto Rico!"). Despite the author's humorous intentions, the ideological implications of her narration are serious and debatable.

Vega's story has been a constant source of friction between Puerto Rican and Nuyorican writers. A Puerto Rican author born and raised in New York, Nicholasa Mohr (1987: 90) has complained that "the use of what the author [Vega] considered to be a cross between Spanish and English, which is referred to as Spanglish, was incorrect and ludicrous. No one here speaks that way. The storyline was quite silly and the story rather far-fetched and stupid, much like a cartoon. This writer had very little knowledge of who we are, and I suspect holds quite a bit of disdain and contempt for our community. This author is not the only one with this attitude. Unfortunately, it is quite common among the Island's intellectuals."

Mohr goes on to argue that the separation between Island and mainland-based writers transcends the use of the Spanish or English language. In her view, Puerto Rican and Nuyorican literatures have distinctive themes, narrative strategies, and audiences. Mohr herself has "found their work [that of Island-based writers] to be too obsessed with class and race, thus narrowing their subject matter into regional and provincial material. Their commonly used baroque style of writing in Spanish seems to act as filler rather than substance" (1987: 90). I would add that Puerto Rican literature on the Island has been primarily concerned with the assertion of a national identity, whereas Nuyorican literature is better understood as part of an ethnic minority canon, especially as developed by African American and Chicano writers in the United States (C. Hernández 1997). While both literatures provide significant insights into the Puerto Rican experience, they do so from different standpoints.

Although the acute tension between Vega's and Mohr's positions may be atypical, it reflects the passionate tone of current polemics on Puerto Rican and Nuyorican literature. Related debates have centered on the possible participation of stateside Puerto Ricans in a plebiscite on the Island's political status (see Falcón 1993; Marvette Pérez 1996). Most Island residents do not imagine Puerto Ricans living abroad as part of their community, while Nuyoricans continue to claim inclusion in a broader view of the nation, both in literary and political terms. In this highly contested context, the noted Puerto Rican writer Rosario Ferré (1997: 9) made a startling revelation for an Island-born intellectual: "Not too long ago I was convinced that language and culture were like Cuba and Puerto Rico, two wings of the same bird. This has long been an axiom of intellectuals on the island, who have been deeply concerned about losing our identity as a people. Now I am not so sure the axiom holds true. After seeing how the Puerto Rican population on the mainland has tragically lost Spanish while firmly holding onto its culture, I feel it must be reevaluated. Language is an important part of a culture, but exclusivity is not fundamental to that culture's survival."

This statement by a former pro-independence supporter (who now advocates statehood for the Island)[12] suggests the growing realization among creative writers and literary critics—such as Arcadio Díaz Quiñones (1993), Juan Flores (1993, 1997), Carmen Dolores Hernández (1997), and Efraín Barradas (1998)—that the dialogue between Island and mainland Puerto Ricans need not take place in Spanish alone but will most probably occur in English as well—and in Spanglish, that interlingual form of communication so typical of second-generation Latinos in the United States. Slowly but surely, Puerto Rican academics on the Island and the mainland have begun an important rapprochement based on mutual respect and tolerance. It remains unclear whether the bilingual character of the diaspora will undermine what until now has been considered a nonnegotiable aspect of the Puerto Rican nation: the Spanish language. At the very least it will require broadening the boundaries of cultural identity to include the more than 3 million people of Puerto Rican descent living abroad.

The Nuyorican experience has already produced ample evidence that migration does not always lead to assimilation into the dominant U.S. culture. On the contrary, Puerto Rican migrants often believe that they can preserve their culture of origin in the United States (Cortés and Vega 1996). As Flores (1993) has suggested, Puerto Ricans live on either side of a divided border that they transgress and remap continually in their everyday language, popular music, visual arts, and creative literature. It is this straddling of two linguistic and geopolitical frontiers that most precisely defines cultural identity in the diaspora. The interlingual poetry of Tato Laviera, the autobiographical essays of Judith Ortiz Cofer, the graphic collages of Juan Sánchez, the documentaries of Frances Negrón-Muntaner, and the music of Willie Colón all attest to the bilingual and bicultural texture of Puerto Rican communities in the United States.

Both in the mainland and on the Island, Puerto Ricans are creatively blending cultural icons and symbolic repertoires of various origins. The polar opposition between Spanish and English has given way to various degrees of bilingualism and the much misunderstood practice of code-switching (the combination of English and Spanish within the same linguistic structure) in Puerto Rican communities throughout the United States and back on the Island. The rhythms of salsa, merengue, rock, reggae, and rap have fused imperceptibly in popular music tastes. The spiritual battle between Santa Claus and the Three Wise Men has been resolved in favor of a peaceful coexistence between the two icons, at least in commercial terms. Protestantism can no longer be portrayed as an alien importation from U.S. imperialism or as entirely antagonistic to popular culture. American fast-food chains have adapted to local preferences by incorporating traditional staples such as *arroz con habichuelas* (rice and beans) and *tostones* (fried plantains) in their menus. Lest these trends seem trivial, readers should note the significance of dietary habits for most Puerto Ricans as a key symbol of their culture (Morris 1995). I next discuss how the bidirectional flow of people further unsettles the antinomy between the Island and the U.S. mainland.

EL VAIVÉN: MOVING BACK AND FORTH

In recent years the increase in circular migration between Puerto Rico and the United States has reinforced hybrid identities in both places. "Circular migration" can be defined operationally as two or more extended round-trips between the Island and the mainland (see Chapter 9). This bilateral movement of people creates a porous border zone between Puerto Rican and Nuyorican communities, which migrants continually cross and transgress, sometimes several times a year. Estimates of the volume of circular migration between the Island and the U.S. mainland range widely (see Ellis, Conway, and Bailey 1996; Hernández Cruz 1985; Meléndez 1993a; Ortiz 1994; C. Rodríguez 1994b). Regardless of the precise numbers, more and more Puerto Ricans are remapping the borders of their identity by moving frequently between their nation of origin and the diaspora throughout their life.

The best known literary image for circular migration between the Island and the mainland is Luis Rafael Sánchez's "La guagua aérea," or "The Flying Bus" (1987). Sánchez's short story takes place aboard the "flying bus that ferries every night between the airports of San Juan and New York" (1987: 17)—that is, the cheap late-night flight that Puerto Ricans affectionately call El Quiquiriquí (from the Spanish word for cock's crow). The narrator's ironic but sympathetic voice registers the myriad gestures and poses that distinguish "between them, the gringos, and us, the Puerto Ricans" (1987: 18). While the gringos stay calm in the middle of turbulence, the Puerto Ricans make a lot of noise, tell each other the stories of their lives, and laugh loudly and contagiously. For the Puerto Rican passengers of the flying bus, traveling to or from New York is like jumping across a pond (*brincar el charco*). As one character quips, *"I live with one leg in New York and the other in Puerto Rico"* (1987: 21; emphasis in the original). Sánchez's depiction (1987: 24) of the existential dilemmas posed by shuttling between the two nations is worth quoting at length: "Puerto Ricans who want to be there but must remain here; Puerto Ricans who want to be there but cannot remain there; Puerto Ricans who live there and dream about being here; Puerto Ricans with their lives hanging from the hooks of the question marks *aquí? allá?* [here? there?], Hamletian disjunctives that ooze their lifeblood through both adverbs. Puerto Ricans installed in permanent errancy between 'being there' and 'being here' and who, because of it, deflate all the adventurous formality until it becomes a mere 'ride in a bus' . . . however aerial, so it may lift them filled with assurances over the blue pond . . . the *blue pond*, the Puerto Rican metaphor for the Atlantic Ocean."

Sánchez's powerful allegory for circular migration helps to redefine the geographic terms (here/there, Island/mainland, us/them) in which Puerto Rican identity has usually been couched. Even the binary opposition between Puerto Rican and American, so pervasive in cultural nationalism, becomes problematic as the characters move between and betwixt two cultures. More-over, the image of a flying bus helps to revise the standard notion of migration as a permanent change of residence with an irrevocable shift in identity. As the literary critic Hugo Rodríguez Vecchini (1994: 53) has pointed out, contempo-rary Puerto Rican "migration" exceeds the conventional connotations of the term, including moving, visiting, traveling, commuting, and going back and forth from the Island to the mainland. Thus, Sánchez's text suggests a radical decentering of the nationalist discourse on cultural identity, insofar as it pro-poses that being Puerto Rican is no longer a matter of living here or there, in Puerto Rico or in the United States. It is rather a question of how a person defines herself subjectively, like the passenger in the flying bus who claims she comes from the town of "New York, Puerto Rico."

Although Sánchez has explored well the literary dimensions of circular migration between Puerto Rico and the United States, several issues require further research and reflection from a social scientific perspective.[13] First, how does the Puerto Rican diaspora compare with other transnational movements, both currently and historically? As noted before, most Puerto Ricans in the United States reject the hyphenated label Puerto Rican–Americans, in contrast to groups such as African Americans, Italian Americans, or Cuban Americans. Perhaps, as Frances Aparicio has suggested (letter to the author, February 1, 1997), it is because Puerto Ricans, as U.S. citizens, find the term redundant to their self-identification. Or perhaps, as Desmonique Bonet puts it (letter to the author, January 30, 1997), it is a sign of a deeper resistance to cultural assimila-tion. In any event, Puerto Ricans in the United States continue to represent Americans as cultural and racial others (Urciuoli 1996). Moreover, the so-ciocultural effects of circular migration should be assessed at both ends of the transnational circuit—in Puerto Rico as well as on the U.S. mainland. Trans-national ideas and practices have reshaped the cultural landscapes of both countries—for example, the maintenance of strong kinship networks between Chicago and San Lorenzo (Alicea 1997) or the reconstruction of rural housing types, casitas, in the Puerto Rican barrios of New York and Boston (Aponte-Parés 1996). More fieldwork is needed to document which cultural practices travel between the Island and the mainland and how they move.

Finally, the back-and-forth movement has redrawn the contours of Puerto Rican identity in many sites of cultural production, including literature, popu-lar music, the visual arts, and theater (see Dávila-López 1996 on Nuyorican theater). The emergence of salsa music as a product of the incessant traffic of performers, instruments, genres, and styles between Puerto Rico and New York City—the so-called *cuchifrito* (fried food) circuit—is only one example (Aparicio 1996, 1998; Glasser 1995; Leymarie 1994). Another has been the rise of a transnational artistic community linking New York and San Juan through a network of museums, galleries, and other cultural institutions. Even Island scholars are beginning to participate in a transnational system of intellectual exchange with their colleagues on the mainland, though they were traditionally reluctant to do so for political and linguistic reasons.

CONCLUSION

During the twentieth century, Puerto Rican intellectuals developed a nationalist discourse based on the celebration of a unique cultural identity, the moral regeneration of the people, and the rejection of outside influences, particularly from the United States (see Hutchinson 1994 for a general description of cultural nationalism).[14] As a result of their control over powerful cultural institutions such as the university, the intellectuals' discourse has become the official version of Puerto Ricanness, widely accepted across various social classes and political ideologies on the Island. In Anthony Smith's terms (1991), Puerto Ricans now share an extensive repertoire of collective myths, memories, icons, and rituals that distinguish their nation from other countries—such as the founding figure of the jíbaro, the romantic view of the Taíno Indians, the enduring myth of racial democracy, the iconography of the flag and anthem, the consecration of the Spanish language, and the cult of la gran familia puertorriqueña. Cultural nationalism has achieved a popular consensus over what constitutes Puerto Rican identity, even if that consensus has been contested from the start. Still, the idea of a national culture has become embedded in the everyday life of a colonial people, the majority of whom do not subscribe to the doctrine of political nationalism.

Today, nearly half the population of Puerto Rican origin reside in the United States, but islanders have not traditionally considered them part of the Puerto Rican nation. And yet most of the emigrants and their descendants continue to define themselves as Puerto Rican rather than American. At the same time, the growing ethnic diversity of the local population—especially as a result of the massive influx of Dominicans and Cubans—tests the limits of canonized views of the Puerto Rican nation as a homogeneous and bounded entity, as an island unto itself. In sum, rethinking the diaspora entails approaching the nation as a dispersed and fragmented subject that flows across various spaces, classes, and other social locations. Circular migration, in particular, forces one to move away from the easy dichotomy between here and there, between the Island and the mainland, between identity and alterity. The Puerto Rican nation is better defined as the crossroads of these borders.

Like other diasporas, Puerto Rican migration to the United States (and back to the Island) has deterritorialized and transnationalized identities (see Basch, Schiller, and Blanc 1994; R. Rouse 1991, 1995; Schiller, Basch, and Blanc-Szanton 1992). The spatial boundaries between the two places have been blurred by increasingly cheap and rapid means of transportation and communication, especially the airplane, the telephone, the videotape, the fax machine, and e-mail. Over the past few decades, the worldwide movement of capital, people, commodities, technologies, images, and identities has grown greatly in speed, scale, and volume (Appadurai 1996), particularly between the continental United States and Puerto Rico. Economically and politically, the sending and receiving societies are so closely intertwined that the conventional distinction between sending and receiving is itself questionable. Linguistically and culturally, the borders between the Island and the mainland are increasingly difficult to map. Thus, the Puerto Rican diaspora raises many problems regarding the conceptual equation between state, nation, people, territory, citizenship, culture, language, and identity. Each of the terms in that series is now under critical interrogation.

The cultural dilemmas posed by the diaspora may well signal the future of the Puerto Rican people as an increasingly transnational community. On the one hand, Puerto Rican migrants and their descendants have not completely assimilated into American culture, if the measure of assimilation is discarding Spanish and replacing it with the English language, becoming a hyphenated ethnic minority, or abandoning their emotional attachment to the Island. This lack of assimilation is caused at least partly by popular resistance to Americanization and the public discourse in which this resistance is grounded. On the other hand, the process of transculturation—or, better still, hybridization—has advanced swiftly, especially in the second and third generations of the so-called Nuyoricans. Still, diasporic communities in New York and other places in the United States construct their identities primarily as Puerto Rican and imagine themselves as part of the Puerto Rican nation. As Ana Celia Zentella (1997) has argued, Nuyoricans have redefined Puerto Rican identity away from an exclusive reliance on the Spanish language in order to incorporate monolingual English speakers with family ties to the Island. Circular migration between the Island and the mainland is only the most dramatic example of continuing attachments to "dual home bases" (Alicea 1990). The broader implications of this reluctance to incorporate into U.S. mainstream culture merit further study. For now, it is clear that transnational migration has not undermined—and has perhaps even strengthened—popular claims to national identity on the Island.

In short, Puerto Rico is a nation on the move. Its cultural identity is not legally defined by citizenship, because all Puerto Ricans are U.S. citizens by birth. Its geographic frontiers span two clearly bounded territories—the Island and the mainland—for there are no formal barriers to travel or trade between both places. Spanish is no longer an exclusive identity marker because many Puerto Ricans now speak English as their first language and are bilingual to some degree. Yet contemporary Puerto Rican culture flourishes along the porous borders of political, geographic, and linguistic categories long taken as the essence of national identity. If anything is clear at this juncture, it is that such categories can no longer capture the permeable and elastic boundaries of the Puerto Rican nation. The spatial practices and subjective affiliations of Puerto Ricans in Puerto Rico and the United States are now characterized by massive physical and cultural displacements.

Reflecting on the Puerto Rican experience, on the Island and in the diaspora, can advance current thinking on national and transnational identities. First, it suggests that cultural rather than strictly geopolitical definitions of identity play a key role in forging the collective will that Renan (1990 [1882]) identified as the core of the nation. Second, as Anderson (1991) suggested, intellectuals are still using literature to articulate and disseminate foundational views of the nation, based on territorial and linguistic criteria, which tend to exclude diasporas as part of the homeland. Third, contrary to Anderson's argument, nations are not always imagined as inherently limited and sovereign communities; the symbolic borders of the nation do not correspond neatly with state frontiers, and the subjective sense of a separate nationality can thrive without the formal recognition of citizenship. Fourth, the construction and representation of cultural identities have far-reaching practical implications in colonial and postcolonial societies—among them, the symbolic struggle to assert a separate nation, even within a nonsovereign state. Fifth, contemporary diasporas undermine the traditional anchoring of identities in a single territory, government, citizenship, and language. Finally, transnationalism should not be equated with crossing state borders but should include migration to and from stateless nations as well. At this point in the history of the global economy, the nation-state is increasingly unable to contain the ideological and cultural contours of people on the move. The future of the Puerto Rican people, like that of other transnational communities, depends largely on incorporating migrants and other subaltern groups within a broader discourse on identity.

TWO

The Rich Gate to Future Wealth

Displaying Puerto Rico at World's Fairs

In the last chapter I argued that Puerto Ricans developed a well-defined sense of national identity during the second half of the twentieth century. Throughout the first half of the century, however, American colonial discourse systematically denied Puerto Rico's right to self-determination, precisely on the grounds that it was not a nation and therefore unsuitable for independence. According to the dominant imperial narrative, the Island was destined to remain a territory of the United States. Through various means, including world's fairs, museum exhibits, photographs, and postcards, U.S. government officials and private entrepreneurs tended to portray Puerto Ricans as a dependent people in need of tutelage. In particular, world's fairs played a key role in the public representation of Puerto Rico and other colonial acquisitions, which reached millions of Americans and other peoples.

In this chapter I focus on how U.S. public authorities represented Puerto Ricans to popular audiences during the first decade of the twentieth century, a key moment in the development of a colonial discourse on Puerto Rico. Specifically, I examine how the Smithsonian Institution displayed Puerto Rico at two world's fairs (the 1901 Pan-American Exposition in Buffalo and the 1904 Louisiana Purchase Exposition in St. Louis), as part of its exhibits of the "outlying possessions" of the United States, including the Philippines, Hawaii, Alaska, and Samoa. United States government displays at both world's fairs rendered

Puerto Ricans as whiter, more civilized, and easier to incorporate into American culture than Filipinos. Popular images of Puerto Ricans and Filipinos became increasingly distinct and often opposed to each other, partly as a result of their dissimilar portrayal at world's fairs. Colonial discourse became more sophisticated (though no less stereotypical) as a consequence of the encounter between American colonizers and the various colonized subjects after the War of 1898.

Since the mid–nineteenth century, displaying living human groups has been a popular feature of international expositions. In 1851 the Crystal Palace Great Exhibition in London introduced the concept of "native villages," representing indigenous peoples and customs in their "natural" surroundings. The 1889 Paris Universal Exposition expanded the practice, and the 1893 World's Columbian Exposition in Chicago turned it into a mass spectacle. Seventeen villages were built at the Chicago Midway to illustrate the customs, sports, ceremonies, and festivals of Africans, Native Americans, Javanese, Samoans, and other "savage tribes" (Carr and Kurney 1993; Greehalgh 1988; Maxwell 1999). After Chicago, most U.S. government exhibits in world's fairs featured live displays of "primitive" groups, especially Native Americans and Filipinos. Fairs in the United States acquired a distinctively imperial flavor during the first decade of the twentieth century, beginning with Buffalo in 1901 and culminating in St. Louis in 1904. Until the 1930s, the federal government routinely organized huge displays of material artifacts and cultural practices from its outlying territories, particularly the Philippines, Hawaii, Alaska, Samoa, Puerto Rico, and the U.S. Virgin Islands (see Greehalgh 1988; Hinsley 1991; Rydell 1993).

According to Robert Rydell (1998), half the world's fairs between 1851 and 1940 were colonial expositions. During this period, the fairs celebrated the colonial appropriation of primitive others through ritual displays of archaeological and ethnological objects collected in the conquered lands. This celebration was part of the exhibitionary complex in western Europe and the United States at the height of the imperial era. As Burton Benedict (1983) notes, all the major imperial powers displayed the inhabitants of their colonial possessions as living spectacles in world's fairs. Native villages became a popular way to dramatize the racial and cultural differences between savagery and civilization from an evolutionary perspective. Moreover, such exhibits legitimized British, French, Dutch, Belgian, Portuguese, German, and American colonialism on the basis of the presumed racial and cultural superiority of whites over other peoples

(Baker 1998; Greehalgh 1988; Hinsley 1981, 1991; Lidchi 1997; Rydell 1994, 1998; Rydell, Findling, and Pelle 2000).

Scholars have analyzed the origins and development of world's fairs as imperial representations of non-Western peoples. Many authors have interpreted the ethnological display of Native Americans, Filipinos, and other "primitives" as "living proof" of racial and cultural hierarchies prevalent during the colonial era (Breitbart 1997; Rydell 1998). Some have argued that native villages popularized the racial discourse of social Darwinism, which correlated the relative position of human groups with their skin color and geographic origin (Baker 1998; Maxwell 1999; Rydell, Findling, and Pelle 2000). Anthropologists working for prestigious museums and universities played a prominent role in the design and implementation of these villages, giving them an air of scientific respectability and divulging the ideas of their new discipline. Frederick W. Putnam, Franz Boas, and Otis T. Mason were active at the World's Columbian Exposition as well as William J. McGee at the Louisiana Purchase Exposition (Hinsley 1981; Rydell 1994; Stocking 1985). Moreover, colonial exhibits at world's fairs were part of ongoing public debates about European and American imperialism. Previous research has shown that international expositions tended to justify the acquisition of non-European territories on moral as well as economic grounds (Benedict 1983; Greehalgh 1988). In the United States, the main ideological rationales for imperialism were the notions of Manifest Destiny and the Roosevelt Corollary to the Monroe Doctrine, which asserted the supremacy of the Anglo-Saxon race and culture in the Americas. Such ideas were extended to the newly acquired territories of the Caribbean and the Pacific after 1898.

Absent from most scholarly accounts of world's fairs is a detailed analysis of how the U.S. government represented Puerto Rico at such public occasions. Much of the related research has centered on Filipino villages, especially in St. Louis, as the largest anthropological exhibit ever assembled for a world's fair (Breitbart 1997), one of the most lavish ever devoted to a single territory (Greehalgh 1988), the most costly colonial project undertaken by the U.S. government (Kramer 1999), and the most popular midway attraction at the fair (Zwick 2000). Clearly, the representation of the Philippines on such occasions epitomized an imperialistic image that underscored the islands' savagery and buttressed the American mission to civilize them. However, restricting the analysis of U.S. colonial discourse to Filipino displays at international expositions runs the risk of oversimplifying and homogenizing American images of the Other. As Lanny Thompson (1998) argues, Americans developed distinctive views of each of the main components of their "imperial archipelago"—Cubans, Puerto Ricans, Hawaiians, and Filipinos.

MILITARY ANNEXATION AND SCIENTIFIC INTEREST: PUERTO RICO AS AN ETHNOGRAPHIC CURIOSITY

During the Spanish-Cuban-American War, Puerto Rico became the object of growing public and academic attention in the United States. In 1898 the War Department issued a pamphlet called "Military Notes on Puerto Rico," and the State Department published a bulletin on Cuba, Puerto Rico, Hawaii, and the Philippines. In 1899–1900 the *National Geographic Magazine* published nine articles on Puerto Rico, or Porto Rico as it soon became known. In 1899 the Smithsonian Institution reprinted Otis T. Mason's catalogue of Puerto Rican antiquities from the Latimer and Guesde collections, specializing in pre-Columbian archaeology (O. Mason 1877, 1899).[1] According to the archaeologist Jesse Walter Fewkes (1970 [1907]: 90), this decision "stimulated an ever-increasing interest in the subject that was heightened by the annexation of the island to the United States."

The U.S. National Museum organized several expeditions to Cuba and Puerto Rico during and after the Spanish-Cuban-American War. As the museum's 1899 annual report stated, "On the breaking of the war with Spain it was recognized that an important epoch in our national history had been initiated, and measures were taken to secure for the Museum such relics and mementos of the campaign as would be of interest to the people" (U.S. National Museum 1901). In 1899–1900 the geologist Robert T. Hill visited the Island to "obtain photographs and other data of ethnological character" for the Bureau of American Ethnology (Powell 1903). Hill (1899c) wrote one of the first extensive surveys of the Island for the *National Geographic Magazine*, as well as technical reports on the forest conditions and mineral resources of Puerto Rico for the U.S. Geological Survey (Hill 1899a, 1899b). He later published a book on the geography of Cuba, Puerto Rico, and other Caribbean islands (Hill 1903).

The Smithsonian sent Paul Beckwith to Cuba and Puerto Rico in 1901 to gather archaeological objects that were never delivered to the museum. However, a few of his photographs of Puerto Rican landscapes are stored at the National Anthropological Archives of the National Museum of Natural History. His pictures show mountains, plants, roads, and bridges, but few people.

These images offer a striking visual example of Western conceptions of the Other as absence or emptiness (Spurr 1993). In Chapter 4 I return to the question of how American photographers idealized Puerto Rico's tropical nature in the first two decades of the twentieth century.

Other scientific expeditions were geared toward collecting specimens of tropical plants and animals as well as information on the pre-Columbian inhabitants of the new colonies. Between 1899 and 1901, Leonhard Stejneger and Charles Richmond gathered birds, mammals, toads, reptiles, and batrachians in Puerto Rico. About 900 of these specimens were collected for the Pan-American Exposition in Buffalo (Stejneger 1904). O. F. Cook also researched plant resources for the Department of Agriculture's exhibit. A selection of 630 specimens from Fewkes's collection of Caribbean archaeology was displayed in St. Louis (Fewkes 1970 [1907]; Holmes 1907). From the beginning, American scholars were more concerned with the Island's natural resources and indigenous past than with its living population.

The Bureau of American Ethnology officially initiated fieldwork in the Caribbean in 1900, with the visit of the director, John Wesley Powell, and William H. Holmes, his successor, to Cuba and Jamaica (Holmes 1907). Fewkes was first commissioned on a reconnaissance trip to Puerto Rico in April–May 1902 to collect "data and specimens of this West Indian island which had lately come into the possession of the United States" (Fewkes 1970 [1907]: 17). Otis T. Mason himself had lamented that "while the museum is rich in objects from Porto Rico we know nothing of its archaeology" (O. Mason to True, October 1, 1898). Fewkes's excursions more than doubled the number of archaeological objects from the Island at the U.S. National Museum. Altogether, he purchased or excavated more than twelve hundred artifacts in Puerto Rico and the Dominican Republic (Fewkes 1970 [1907]). The director of the Bureau of American Ethnology, Holmes (1907: xiii), proudly proclaimed: "Not only is this collection the largest which has been brought to the Smithsonian from Porto Rico and Santo Domingo at any one time, but it is also one of the most significant on account of its wealth in typical forms previously unrepresented at the museum."

Fewkes's numerous voyages to Puerto Rico and other Caribbean and Latin American countries (including Cuba, Haiti, the Dominican Republic, Trinidad, and Mexico) were part of larger Smithsonian efforts to expand fieldwork in the natural and social sciences outside the continental United States (Holmes 1907). As early as October 1898, Otis T. Mason (1838–1908), the first curator of ethnology at the U.S. National Museum, had urged the exploration of Puerto

Rico as "a magnificent field of research," especially in pre-Columbian archaeology. "Porto Rico must have been the sacred island of the ancient inhabitants
of the Caribbean sea," Mason wrote poetically to the executive director of the
U.S. National Museum, Frederick W. True. "I do hope provision will be made
by which we shall be the first on the field" (Mason to True, October 1, 1898). In
Chapter 3 I analyze in detail Fewkes's ethnographic diaries on Puerto Rico, but
now I turn to examine how the Smithsonian portrayed Puerto Rico at the
Buffalo and St. Louis fairs.

"WHAT SORT OF COUNTRY? WHAT SORT OF PEOPLE?": PUERTO RICO AT TWO WORLD'S FAIRS

In 1899 the Government Board of the Pan-American Exposition in Buffalo
began to organize a display of objects from Cuba, Puerto Rico, Alaska, Hawaii,
and the Philippines. The Smithsonian created a Special Committee on Exhibits from Outlying Possessions in response to a request from the exposition
management to show "not only the products, resources and possibilities of these
possessions, but also and particularly the ethnological features available" (Rice
to the Board of Management, October 9, 1899). One of the main proposals
discussed by committee members was the re-creation of native villages from
each territory, including Puerto Rico. Because the Special Committee (1899)
felt that "the Philippine Islands will afford the most valuable collecting field," it
focused its efforts on that territory. Nonetheless, the minutes of the committee's
meetings reveal how its members imagined Puerto Rican culture, compared
with the other territories.

On November 27, 1899, the director general of the Pan-American Exposition, William I. Buchanan, a former U.S. diplomat in Argentina, first formulated his proposal for a U.S. colonial exhibit at Buffalo: "Throughout the
United States there exists an intense interest and a great desire to learn and
to read exactly what sort of countries, what sort of peoples, what sort of native customs, arts and industries, and what sort of products and resources, the
United States now has to deal with in the islands of Hawaii, Cuba, Porto Rico,
and Guam, and the Philippine Islands. The Exposition seems the best and the
proper medium to present such an exhibit to the people of the United States"
(Cox 1899). A week later, Buchanan wrote to J. H. Brigham, the president of the
Government Board, to insist on the benefits of the colonial exhibit:

Even now the greatest importance should attach to a proper representation of what they (the Phil.) and other Islands possess; and, to a correct first impression being formed here with regard to the problems we have to solve, and, as to what we have gained by the acquisition of these new possessions.

. . . The inhabitants of the different Islands we shall speak of, not having a Government of their own, and being under the direct control of our general Government, can not do so by and of themselves. It would seem logical, therefore, and in every way proper, that our general Government should through your Board undertake to do for these people what they cannot do so for themselves.

This is the first and therefore the best opportunity we have had, or will have, to justify, by means of the most available object lessons we can produce, the acquisition of new territory. (Buchanan to Brigham, December 5, 1899)

Buchanan's plan was clearly framed in the paternalistic mentality of American expansionism popular at the time: it combined educational, political, and commercial interests in a single project—"the acquisition of new territory." From this perspective, the U.S. government had the moral right and duty to represent those who "can not do so by and of themselves" through ethnographic collections, exhibits, expeditions, surveys, reports, and other "object lessons" (see Said 1994).

A memorandum by the government board thus outlined the proposed U.S. colonial exhibit for the Pan-American Exposition: "The [exposition] Management desired the Government Board to transport from the Islands and Alaska to Buffalo, and there absolutely reproduce typical scenery of each, and to erect on the Exposition grounds houses actually used in the respective countries; landscape to be represented largely by artificial means. Some houses to be occupied for living purposes by natives; others for exhibits of products and resources. The plan to include the bringing of 100, more or less, natives, housing and maintaining them during the Exposition period. The principal tribes of each island and Alaska to be represented; including a few entire families" (Special Committee 1901). The plan, then, was based on standard exhibition practices at world's fairs (Baker 1998; Benedict 1983; Greehalgh 1988; Rydell 1994). The main idea was to display the indigenous peoples of America's newly acquired possessions—the memorandum calls them "tribes"—as realistically as possible, in their "natural" habitat. Such a display would educate and entertain the general public, profit the exposition organizers, and legitimize the incursions of the federal government into distant lands.

The project was not entirely executed for several reasons. Foremost were legal ones: the congressional act approved on March 3, 1899, providing moneys for the Pan-American Exposition, did not earmark funds for the proposed villages. According to a memorandum of action from the Special Committee (1899), "The Board was advised that the solicitor of the Treasury had rendered an adverse opinion upon the legality of spending any portion of the Government appropriation for bringing into the country for exhibition at the Exposition, natives from outlying possessions, and maintaining them at Buffalo." One attorney strongly warned that " 'villages' are out of the question as far as the US [government] is concerned, they must be concessions" (Wheeler to Cox, August 17, 1899).

Moreover, the committee decided to focus on the Philippines for economic and practical reasons. When the chair asked if the exhibits should equally represent all the outlying possessions, "the opinion seemed to prevail in the Committee that the allotment was inadequate for that purpose." The committee recommended that the government board not make an exhibit for Cuba, because the War Department would organize its own display from that island (Special Committee 1900). A U.S. National Museum report on the Pan-American Exposition stated that efforts to form general exhibits from Cuba and Puerto Rico were abandoned because the governors of those islands were already planning to organize several displays (True, Holmes, and Merrick 1903). Finally, the Special Committee on Exhibits from Outlying Possessions judged that the Philippines constituted "the most valuable collecting field," apparently because it considered that territory to be more exotic, primitive, and alien to Americans than the other colonies.

Hence, legal, financial, and ideological reasons led U.S. government officials to emphasize the Philippines as the most important overseas possession, from an anthropological standpoint. At Buffalo, small Filipino, Hawaiian, and Cuban villages (but not a Puerto Rican one) were built through private concessions (Greehalgh 1988). In addition, the Pan-American midway included Eskimo, African, Japanese, and Native American villages. However, the popularity of the Filipino village was so enormous that Smithsonian anthropologists went on to organize a grand Philippine exposition at the 1904 St. Louis fair. United States government displays of Puerto Rico were never as large and prominent as those of the Philippines.

At Buffalo, American colonial exhibitions of Puerto Rico concentrated on its agricultural products and natural resources, rather than on "native customs, arts, and industries," as Buchanan had proposed. The U.S. Government Building displayed tropical products from the Philippines, Cuba, Puerto Rico, and Hawaii. The Department of the Interior also showcased photographs of Puerto Rican public schools. The U.S. Post Office building exhibited a large collection of old stamps and machinery from Cuba, Puerto Rico, and Hawaii. In addition, a Porto Rican Expedition Society Day was held in the New York State Building (Anonymous 1901).

The architecture of the Pan-American Exposition was a liberal treatment of the Spanish Renaissance style as a compliment to the Latin American countries represented at the fair. A supposedly typical Puerto Rican "rancho" contained most of the exhibits from the Island. This building stood next to those of other Latin American republics such as Mexico, Ecuador, and Honduras at the entrance to the fairgrounds. The location symbolically associated Puerto Rico with other Spanish American countries, rather than with American possessions in the Pacific or with other U.S. states.

In addition, a Puerto Rican exhibit occupied about twelve hundred square feet in the U.S. Agriculture Building. Here, the colonial government built an elaborate Moorish-style, castlelike structure, complete with arabesque arches and medieval coats-of-arms (Anonymous 1901; Warshaw Collection 1901).[2] This Spanish revival style became a standard architectural practice in Puerto Rican exhibits at local and international fairs. In 1882 an Arab pavilion imitating the Alhambra palace in Granada had been erected in the center of the plaza for the fair at the Puerto Rican city of Ponce (Abad 1885). In 1939 the designers of the Puerto Rican display at the New York's world's fair created "an atmosphere typical of old Spain, a cloistered esplanade with balconies surrounding a Spanish Patio," as well as a diorama of El Morro Castle and Casa Blanca Fortress, the two most significant Spanish colonial buildings in Old San Juan (Warshaw Collection 1939).[3] Such popular representations insisted on the Spanish heritage of Puerto Rico, as opposed to the non-Western culture of the Philippines and other insular possessions in the Pacific.

United States colonial exhibits of Puerto Rico at world's fairs resembled those organized by the Island's elite for local consumption during the nineteenth century. This continuity suggests that the quasi-hegemonic ideas of the Island's upper class influenced the interpretations of Smithsonian anthropologists, who were familiar with the work of local intellectuals (see Chapter 3). As

Libia González (1998b) shows, the Creole elite was imbued with liberal ideas of progress and modernity popularized at the Paris and Chicago fairs. This group of well-educated professionals enthusiastically embraced the idea of the fair as a place to promote their country's civilization and industry. In a catalogue prepared for the World's Columbian Exposition, members of this elite invited American capitalists to invest in Puerto Rican agriculture, especially in the sugar industry, in order to modernize it (González 1998b). After the Spanish-Cuban-American War, U.S. colonial exhibits of Puerto Rico were partly the product of collaboration between American anthropologists and local elites. Many Puerto Rican merchants and agriculturalists were listed as exhibitors in the fairs' catalogues.

Prominent Puerto Ricans participated actively in expositions and fairs during the second half of the nineteenth century, when the Spanish Crown encouraged such activities to foster the Island's economic and cultural development. Local expositions focused on tropical agricultural products, such as sugar, coffee, tobacco, cacao, and cotton, as well as cattle growing and mining. However, they also featured the Island's accomplishments in the fine arts, such as paintings by José Campeche and Francisco Oller, and orchestra music, such as the *danzas* composed by Juan Morel Campos. The 1882 Ponce Fair included an exhibition of archaeological and historical objects, notably those collected by Agustín Stahl for his projected Museum of Natural History (see Abad 1885; Anonymous 1871; Viña 1854). The first official exposition, celebrated in 1854 in the capital city of San Juan, was subsidized by Spanish colonial authorities, while the Ponce fair was organized primarily by influential citizens with the support of the municipal government. The latter fair was an elaborate urban spectacle, complete with a civic procession, religious ceremonies, fireworks, dances, horse racing, and literary and scientific gatherings (Provincia de Puerto Rico 1882).

The Puerto Rican exhibition at Buffalo dwelled on the Island's economic assets and opportunities and downplayed its cultural traditions and artistic achievements. A catalogue produced for the fair, titled *Puerto Rico and Its Resources* (Anonymous 1901), highlights the Island's location, climate, soil, sanitation, population, and "industrial possibilities," especially in coffee, sugar, and tobacco. It also provides a partial list of agricultural and other products exhibited at the exposition, including coffee, sugar, rum, tobacco, cigars, bananas, coconuts, rice, beans, cotton, textile fibers, woods, and medicinal plants. In a few scant references to the Island's inhabitants, the author recognizes that "islanders are essentially a home-loving people, and remarkably attached to their native land" (20). The physical and cultural characteristics of Puerto Ricans did not attract as much American attention as did those of Filipinos.

The catalogue does not contain any visual images of Puerto Rico or an extended discussion of its historical background, supposedly because it was "gathered in a very short time without preparation of any kind" (20). Thus, the catalogue "can only serve as a partial demonstration of the varied resources of that country, which needs the fertilizing influence of American capital to develop its wealth and richness." Claiming that "Puerto Rico is really the 'rich gate' to future wealth" (23),[4] the text unabashedly endorses U.S. economic and political hegemony on the Island: "Puerto Rico has plenty of laborers. The Island needs men with capital, energy and enterprise to develop its latent industries and to reclaim its sugar, tobacco, coffee and fruit estates; to build factories and railroads, and make the country hum with the busy round of commerce" (20). This kind of writing illustrates the concept of the capitalist vanguard, characterized by an economistic and efficiency-driven rhetoric, which Mary Louise Pratt has identified in many colonial discourses (cited by Matos-Rodríguez 1999).

In St. Louis the Puerto Rican exhibition elaborated the theme of agricultural wealth and added another—the progress of American education on the Island. Both Puerto Rico and Hawaii were included in the U.S. government representation, but not Cuba, which as a newly independent nation had its own pavilion (Buel 1904). The U.S. Department of Agriculture showcased agricultural colleges and experimental stations in Hawaii, Alaska, and Puerto Rico, especially in the field of tobacco growing in the latter case (Warshaw Collection 1904). Puerto Rico's colonial government contributed $30,000 to the fair's budget (out of $7.7 million from the U.S. government). The Puerto Rican section, located in the Agricultural Building, displayed the Island's leading agricultural and manufacturing products, especially coffee, tropical fruits, dye woods, rubber, and needlework. Another exhibition housed in the Education Building celebrated the proliferation of English-language public schools since the American occupation of the Island. The author of the fair's general catalogue writes, "Porto Rico, one of our most recent acquisitions, while still in the reformative state, nevertheless participated with no small sense of pride in the Educational Exposition." He adds, prophetically, "Spanish will probably remain the prevailing tongue in the country and remote districts for several years to come" (Buel 1904: 3093).

Meanwhile, the Philippine exhibition in St. Louis was the largest anthropological display of living peoples, including four separate villages for the Igorot, Negrito, Bisayan, and Moro tribes. Nearly twelve hundred Filipinos were showcased in a forty-seven-acre reservation built on the fairgrounds at a cost of more than $1 million. The exposition included 20 exhibition palaces, 100 native huts and lodges, and 70,000 material objects. Supervised by the government anthropologist Albert E. Jenks, the villages featured live demonstrations of tribal archery, spear warfare, weaving, dancing, game playing, and ritual dog eating. Americans were fascinated with the seminude, dog-eating, head-hunting people from the remote mountainous regions. In St. Louis the most popular event was the weekly killing of dogs by the Igorots, who were widely taken to represent the most savage tribe of the Philippines (Baker 1998; Kennedy 1998; Kramer 1999; Maxwell 1999; McCoy 2000; Warshaw Collection 1904). According to the exposition's official catalogue, the main purpose of this display was to show "what the US has done for the strange people whom we are now trying to assimilate" (Buel 1904: 1532). A contemporary account noted that America's mission in the Philippines was to "civilize the natives," specifically to teach them the art of self-government (Foreman 1906: 9–10).

As far as can be determined, no comparable exhibition was organized for Puerto Rico in international expositions. The extensive Zim and Warshaw collections of world's fairs at the National Museum of American History do not contain any records of ethnographic villages of Puerto Ricans. Nothing of the scale and scope of the Philippine encampments or Native American villages was ever built to represent Puerto Rican culture to the American public.

UNCLE SAM'S BURDEN:
PUERTO RICANS, FILIPINOS, AND OTHER COLONIAL SUBJECTS

The only known attempt to re-create a Puerto Rican village for public display was a private initiative. In March 1900, Myndert Starin, son of John H. Starin, the millionaire owner of Glenn Island in New York, traveled to Puerto Rico to collect materials for exhibit at the summer resort. He was accompanied by his assistant, J. McCornick, who also represented the Smithsonian Institution. As a local newspaper article noted, "Last season the chief attraction at Glenn Island was a Phillipine village and this venture was such a success that Mr. Starin decided a Puerto Rico village would prove even more interesting" (*San Juan*

News 1900: 1). The planned exhibition would consist of twenty-five to thirty men, women, and children living in "typical Puerto Rican shacks," covered by palm trees and surrounding a plantation structure. During the daytime, the natives would sort coffee and weave straw hats, and during the evening they would play and dance to Puerto Rican music. Whether this project was actually carried out is unknown, but it was typical of ethnographic villages at colonial exhibits, such as the one contemplated by the Smithsonian for the Pan-American Exposition (Special Committee 1900). As Anne Maxwell (1999: 27) writes, such villages displayed "colonized peoples in physical settings that implicitly justified colonization by suggesting that indigenous peoples had low levels of moral development and technological competence."

Aside from this episode, efforts to display Puerto Rico to the American public between 1898 and 1940 focused primarily on the Island's natural resources and tropical agriculture and secondarily on its material artifacts.[5] The federal government in general, and the Smithsonian in particular, paid little ethnographic attention to the contemporary people of Puerto Rico, compared with other outlying possessions, especially the Philippines, but also Hawaii, Samoa, and Alaska. Why were the Philippines considered a "more valuable collecting field" than either Puerto Rico or Cuba? Was it because Filipinos were classified as more "primitive" and therefore more appealing to American anthropology? Why was Puerto Rican culture silenced at world's fairs, other than some references to its quaint Hispanic heritage? Was this discursive practice part of the strategy to Americanize the Island? What role did the active resistance to colonial rule in the Philippines and its relative weakness in Puerto Rico play in dominant images of the two territories?

Although not enough information is currently available to answer such questions fully, late-nineteenth- and early-twentieth-century cartoons and photographs suggest that popular representations of Puerto Rico and other U.S. colonies were initially undifferentiated (see also Chapter 4). An 1899 stereocard published by the Keystone View Company, based in Meadville, Pennsylvania, has the following caption: "The Philippines, Porto Rico and Cuba—Uncle Sam's burden. With apologies to Mr. Kipling" (see figure 2.1). The photograph shows a faceless white man carrying three half-naked black boys on his back, wrapped around with an American flag. The man wears a military hat, boots, and bullet belt and carries a bag labeled "U.S." A banana tree and a wooden veranda serve as backdrops. This image encapsulates many of the rhetorical strategies of colonial discourse, such as the identification of the colonized as

FIGURE 2.1. "The Philippines, Porto Rico and Cuba—Uncle Sam's burden. With apologies to Mr. Kipling." 1899 stereograph by B. L. Singley. Courtesy of the Olmos Collections, Centro de Estudios Puertorriqueños, Hunter College, CUNY.

"children of nature" (see Spurr 1993). It also reveals that for many Americans who produced and consumed such visual images, the newly acquired territories were all inhabited by childlike, dark-skinned, poor, and primitive peoples.

At the same time, some popular representations drew finer distinctions among Puerto Ricans, Cubans, Filipinos, and Hawaiians (see Thompson 1995). A cartoon published in the popular magazine *Puck* on August 3, 1898, shows Uncle Sam and an unidentified white woman in front of a building labeled "U.S. Foundling Asylum" (see figure 2.2). On the left side of the image, four light-skinned and well-dressed children dance in a circle inside the premises. The children are identified as Texas, New Mexico, Alaska, and California. In

FIGURE 2.2. Uncle Sam and his new babies. 1898 *Puck* cartoon.
Courtesy of *Boricua* magazine.

front of the building, on the right side, two hands hold a basket with four crying, dark-skinned, and naked babies. The lower arms have written on them "Manifest Destiny." The four babies are labeled Puerto Rico, Cuba, the Philippines, and Hawaii. Those representing Puerto Rico and Cuba are lighter-skinned than the ones representing Hawaii and the Philippines, and the former wear straw hats while the latter have flowers and long hair. But the main contrast in the visual composition is between the happy light-skinned children (including an Alaskan native) inside the asylum and the unhappy dark-skinned babies outside. The racial and cultural overtones of this comparison are remarkable.

Over time, practical experience and growing ethnographic knowledge led to more nuanced views of America's overseas possessions. Colonial administrators as well as anthropologists elaborated the physical and cultural diversity among the territories. As Americans came to know better "what sort of countries, what sort of peoples" they had conquered in the Caribbean and the Pacific, they began to treat them differently. Although the original colonial project was very

similar, it became increasingly differentiated as a result of political and economic considerations, such as the lowering of customs duties for raw sugar
exports from Puerto Rico but not from the Philippines. Census reports showing
that the Island's population was predominantly white bolstered legislation con-
ferring U.S. citizenship to Puerto Ricans, but not to Filipinos. In Puerto Rico a
more centralized colonial regime emerged than in the Philippines, where local
elites were used to keep the peace and raise revenues (Cabán 1999; Cabranes
1979; Go 2000). By the second decade of the twentieth century, American
colonialism had developed distinctive practices in the two territories.

Part of the difference in colonial administration was based on racial and
ethnic stereotypes. Soon after the Spanish-Cuban-American War ended, popular texts and photographic albums often referred to the "primitive natives,"
"aboriginal savages," "heathen races," "unattractive Mongolian types," and
"picturesque villages" of the Philippines (see White 1898; Willets, Hamm, and
McIntosh n.d.). One American traveler characterized the "domesticated natives" of the Philippines as indolent, ignorant, shifty, erratic, superstitious, cred-
ulous, unoriginal, inefficient, and disorganized. In his opinion, "The reasoning
of a native and a European differs so largely that the mental impulse of the two
races is ever clashing" (Foreman 1906: 167).[6] United States colonial officials
often photographed Filipinos in timid, awkward, and half-naked poses that
suggested their inferiority to Westerners (McCoy 2000). As a result of their racial
and cultural exoticism, the Philippines became a primary object of the American ethnographic gaze.

In contrast, American images of Puerto Rico were more benevolent. As
mentioned before, the Island was mainly appreciated for its natural resources
and agricultural products. According to Frederick Ober (1899: 4), Puerto Rico
was "a potentially lucrative investment individually" as well as a strategic naval
station for the United States. A contemporary photographic album depicted the
Island as beautiful, prosperous, curious, pretty, comfortable, and attractive
(Willets, Hamm, and McIntosh n.d.). A Presbyterian minister who spent ten
years in Puerto Rico extolled the natives' courtesy, aesthetic sense, idealism,
intellectual capacity, sympathy, generosity, and emotion (James n.d.). An early
Keystone View Company stereocard of a public school in Caguas portrayed the
Island's inhabitants as gentle, docile, intelligent, moral, and good workers.
Whereas Filipinos were classified as racially and culturally alien, Puerto Ri-
cans—particularly women—were usually described in more favorable terms.

Hill, the geologist (1903: 167), lavishly praised upper-class Puerto Rican women: "The ladies are handsome and refined, and as strictly secluded as in other Spanish countries. Their goodness of heart and unaffected frankness with their friends are charming. Those of gentle birth and breeding are sweet and flower-like, with the bright alertness of a Latin woman transplanted to American soil and climate. Their glances are swift and meaning, and their great black eyes full of expression." In this archetypal description, the white but swarthy Latin woman becomes an object of desire by the American colonizer. Yet few contemporary portraits of native Filipino women highlight their beauty, charm, or intelligence (see Foreman 1906; White 1898). While most Americans considered Filipinos either half-primitive or semibarbaric, they judged Puerto Ricans to be more receptive to civilization and progress. To what extent these images of otherness and difference shaped U.S. colonial policies is the subject of scholarly dispute (see G. García 1997–98; Rivera Ramos 2001; Thompson 1995).

In any case, various representations of American colonial discourse were encoded at world's fairs as well as in legal forums. Congressional debates in the United States clearly differentiated Filipinos and Puerto Ricans on racial, cultural, geographic, and political grounds. Whereas Congress promised the former eventual independence in 1916, it conferred U.S. citizenship on the latter in 1917. José Cabranes (1979) documents that American legislators handled Filipino and Puerto Rican affairs very differently during the first two decades of the twentieth century. Whereas many took it for granted that Puerto Rico would remain a U.S. possession indefinitely, they perceived the Philippines as unsuitable for annexation. A key factor in this contrasting perception was that most Puerto Ricans had welcomed the American occupation, whereas Filipinos continued to struggle for independence. While Puerto Rico still inhabits a juridical limbo as an unincorporated territory of the United States, the Philippines finally obtained sovereignty in 1947.

The distinct treatment of Puerto Ricans and Filipinos was intensely racialized. American observers were well aware of the decimation of Puerto Rico's indigenous population during the early Spanish colonial period. As an early traveler noted, "So in Puerto Rico: not a man is to be found there to-day who is a pure-blooded aborigine" (Skinner 1900: 50). Less charitably, a photographic album claimed that the Island's "farming class is about on a par with the poor darkies down South, and varies much even in race and color, ranging from the Spanish white trash to full-blooded Ethiopians" (Willets, Hamm, and McIntosh n.d.: no page number). However, U.S. government reports insisted that the Puerto Rican population was predominantly of European, not African, origin. Hence, they typically depicted the Island as "the whitest of the Antilles," inhabited by a large majority of people of Spanish background, many of whom had immigrated to the Island during the nineteenth century (see Chapter 10).

In contrast, congressmen often portrayed Filipinos as "the yellow men of the Orient," who threatened to perturb the presumed racial purity and cultural homogeneity of the United States (quoted by Cabán 1999: 88). According to a member of the U.S. House of Representatives, "The inhabitants [of the Philippines] are of wholly different races of people from ours—Asiatics, Malays, negroes and mixed blood" (quoted by Nieto-Phillips 1999: 59). Among other results, such racial and ethnic images distracted anthropological attention away from Puerto Rico and toward the Philippines as a privileged field of "savages." Conversely, Americans valued the Caribbean island mainly as a new site of opportunities in agriculture, industry, and commerce—as well as a strategic military outpost for their budding overseas empire. Because Puerto Ricans were considered to be mainly of Mediterranean Caucasian "blood," they were also supposed to be more similar (and yet inferior) to white Anglo-Saxons than the "Asiatic" Filipinos.

CONCLUSION

The Smithsonian was the first American scientific institution to engage in the public representation of Puerto Rico and other territories acquired after the Spanish-Cuban-American War. The Special Committee on Exhibits from Outlying Possessions seriously considered displaying Puerto Ricans in native villages, similar to those created for Native Americans and Filipinos. Although such Puerto Rican villages were never built at world's fairs, they were clearly modeled after the dominant colonial representations of non-Western groups (see Benedict 1983; Rydell 1994). U.S. government exhibits of the Island actually focused on its archaeological and agricultural resources, rather than on native beliefs and customs. Puerto Rico was therefore represented as a valuable collecting field for pre-Columbian artifacts and tropical specimens, but not for contemporary ethnographic purposes, as was the Philippines.

Anthropological displays of Puerto Ricans and Filipinos at the Buffalo and St. Louis fairs worked to sort out the countries and peoples recently conquered by the United States. On the one hand, Puerto Rico was considered an invaluable asset because of its compact size, geographic proximity, strategic location, agricultural potential, and predominantly white population (Nieto-Phillips 1999). Hence, American exhibits of its Caribbean colony emphasized its natural resources, promising market, Spanish heritage, and European background. On the other hand, the Philippines were considered more problematic because of their geographic fragmentation, distance from the U.S. mainland, cultural and linguistic diversity, and predominantly "Mongolian" types. Hence, American displays of its Pacific colony emphasized its "savage tribes," primitive culture, racial inferiority, orientalism, and sheer strangeness. These dual images of Puerto Ricans and Filipinos placed them at different points on the scale of human evolution—Puerto Ricans at an intermediate rung of barbarism, Filipinos (especially Igorots) at the lowest stage of savagery. The elaborate ethnographic attention given to the Philippines (and the scarcity of such attention to Puerto Rico) was inversely related to their status in congressional debates on whether they should be awarded U.S. citizenship and fully incorporated as territories (Cabranes 1979; Nieto-Phillips 1999; Rivera Ramos 2001). In the end, Puerto Ricans but not Filipinos became U.S. citizens, and Puerto Rico remains an overseas possession of the United States, while the Philippines is an independent nation.

Historical analyses of world's fairs have rightly stressed that they served primarily as instruments of symbolic domination over colonial peoples from the mid–nineteenth to the early twentieth century. But they have paid insufficient attention to the multiple and diverse representations of the Other contained within such fairs. Although both the Pan-American Exposition and the Louisiana Purchase Exposition celebrated the rise of the United States as an imperial power (Rydell 1993; Rydell, Findling, and Pelle 2000), they elaborated distinct views of the new overseas possessions. In particular, standard binary oppositions—such as West and East, European and non-European, civilized and savage, white and black—between Americans and Puerto Ricans could not prosper as well as those between Americans and Filipinos. Thus, U.S. government displays sharply distinguished the two territories and helped to imagine their inhabitants in contrasting ways.

At the same time, American authorities judged both Puerto Ricans and Filipinos to be unfit for independence. Both possessions were subordinated as military and commercial outposts of the U.S. empire. Both peoples were portrayed as racially and culturally inferior to white Americans of Anglo-Saxon origin. Both were considered uncivilized and racially mixed populations that could not fully develop their intellectual abilities in a tropical environment.

These racial perceptions had long-term historical consequences for U.S. colonial policies in Puerto Rico, which I explore in subsequent chapters. In the next chapter, I examine how two American anthropologists helped to constitute colonial subjects in Puerto Rico as people of an alien race, language, and culture during the first two decades after the War of 1898.

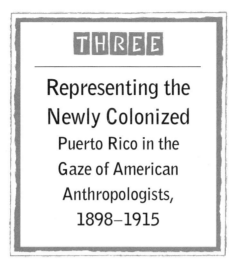

THREE

Representing the Newly Colonized
Puerto Rico in the
Gaze of American
Anthropologists,
1898–1915

In his seminal essay "Representing the Colonized: Anthropology's Interlocutors," Edward Said characterizes anthropology as a discipline founded on "an ethnographic encounter between a sovereign European observer and a non-European native occupying, so to speak, a lower status and a distant place" (Said 2000 [1989]: 300). Historically, anthropology defined itself as the comparative study of "primitive" societies, especially the indigenous peoples of North America, Africa, Asia, and the Pacific. The classic ethnographic project during the first half of the twentieth century consisted of rescuing traditional beliefs and practices in danger of extinction as a result of the expansion of Western imperialism and capitalism. In the United States, Franz Boas championed the dominant approach to "salvage ethnology," first to Native Americans, then to African Americans, and eventually to other colonized peoples outside the mainland, including Puerto Ricans (see Baker 1998; Hinsley 1981; Stocking 1992). Following Boas's call, many ethnographers saw their mission as documenting, preserving, and speaking for rapidly fading non-Western cultures.

Over the last few decades, anthropology has undergone a profound crisis of representation. The swift decolonization of the so-called Third World after World War II and recent changes in the global economy have altered the links between Western and non-Western countries. The formal end of colonialism in most places reshaped the connections between anthropologists and their traditional objects of study, which closely paralleled the unequal power relationship between "civilized" and "primitive" peoples or, to put it more politely, developed and developing economies (see Asad 1973; Said 1978, 1994; Thomas 1994; Williams and Chrisman 1994). Moreover, the new international division of labor has entailed the deindustrialization of the core countries of the capitalist world system, such as the United States, Great Britain, France, and Germany, and the industrialization of peripheral and semiperipheral countries such as Singapore, Korea, Brazil, and Mexico. Massive migration from former colonies in Asia, Africa, Latin America, and the Caribbean to their North American and Western European metropolises has further blurred the traditional geopolitical borders on which much of the anthropological imagination had rested (Basch, Schiller, and Blanc 1994; Gupta and Ferguson 1997; Olwig and Hastrup 1997). Within academic circles, the rise in the number of "native" anthropologists in many postcolonial countries has contributed to questioning the conventional distinction between ethnographic observers and their subjects (see Fahim 1982). Finally, the reflexive turn in anthropology has scrutinized the discursive practices on which ethnographic authority was established (Clifford 1997; Clifford and Marcus 1986). In this context, the question of whether ethnographic texts can speak for the colonized has arisen with great urgency.

The issue acquires poignancy in the case of Puerto Rico. American anthropologists were one of the first professional groups to travel to the Island after the U.S. invasion of 1898. Together with soldiers, officers, missionaries, administrators, entrepreneurs, journalists, and photographers,[1] anthropologists were keenly interested in the new colony. Since the nineteenth century, a small number of U.S. seamen, agriculturalists, merchants, and government employees had moved to Puerto Rico. After the Spanish-Cuban-American War, the American presence on the Island expanded greatly in all walks of life—from government, the economy, and education to religion, sports, science, and the arts—and developed into a colonial elite (Bender 1998). According to a contemporary travel writer, the U.S. military occupation facilitated the "advancement of American ideas and [the] promulgation of American methods" in Puerto Rico (Ober 1899: 231). "It is in this island," the American treasurer of Puerto Rico declared, "that the United States has made its first essay in the government of a dependency partaking of the essential character of a colony" (Willoughby 1905: 81). The colonial project included exporting the political, legal, economic, and cultural institutions from the metropolitan power to the newly acquired Caribbean possession (Rivera Ramos 2001). Even the Island's name was officially changed to Porto Rico to make it easier to pronounce in English.[2]

Between 1898 and 1945, American scholars displaced an incipient native tradition of academic research on the Island's archaeology and folklore (see J. Duany 1987 for more details on this process). Prominent anthropologists such as Franz Boas, Jesse Walter Fewkes, William H. McGee, and Otis T. Mason saw the acquisition of Puerto Rico as an ideal opportunity to expand the research agenda of American social science beyond the mainland (see Baatz 1996; Hinsley 1981; Rydell 1994). Together with the Island's colonial government, the Smithsonian Institution as well as the New York Academy of Sciences funded fieldwork, sponsored collecting expeditions, and organized displays of Puerto Rican artifacts in world's fairs and museums. Many of these activities were divulged in leading professional journals in the United States. Thus, anthropologists played a key role in representing the manners and mores of the Puerto Rican people to a large American audience. In this enterprise, as Christopher Schmidt-Nowara (letter to the author, October 26, 2000) has noted, "US social scientists positioned themselves as inheritors of the Spanish colonial tradition. Though they criticized Spain as a backward and decadent colonial power, they nonetheless identified more readily with Spanish imperial authors than with the peoples of the new colonial possessions."

Postcolonial scholars have documented the common rhetorical strategies of British, French, and American colonialism (see Gandhi 1998; Loomba 1998; Moore-Gilbert 1997; Said 1978; Spurr 1993). Many writers have noted that colonial discourse tends to rely on binary oppositions between colonizer and colonized, such as civilized/savage, mature/immature, developed/underdeveloped, and masculine/feminine. Until the mid–twentieth century, anthropological research on non-Western peoples usually depicted them as backward, primitive, exotic, and radically different from Westerners. Much of this research also supported the notion that blacks and whites were distinct and ultimately irreconcilable races (see Baker 1998). During the high period of Western imperialism (1860–1920), ethnographers helped to codify the dominant stereotypes of conquered peoples as racially and culturally inferior to peoples of European origin. Although such a general characterization serves to underline the continuities in colonial discourse, it glosses over the varied activities of anthropologists and other scholars in specific colonial settings at particular moments (Stocking 1991; Thomas 1994). More broadly, it fails to account for the historical and cultural differences in imperial renderings of the Other.

In this chapter I address a recurrent problem in postcolonial theory—the representation of the colonizer and the colonized as homogeneous subjects. First I review the unpublished diaries and notebooks of the American archaeologist Jesse Walter Fewkes, who articulated many archetypal images of the natives while collecting pre-Columbian pieces for the Smithsonian between 1902 and 1904. Then I analyze John Alden Mason's letters from the field (1914–15) as an instance of the ethnographic imperative to rescue the Island's Hispanic folklore before the onslaught of Americanization. Comparing the published and unpublished writings of these two anthropologists will shed light on the differences and similarities in the complex images that Americans formed of their newly acquired colonial possessions.

REVISITING COLONIALISM AND ANTHROPOLOGY

Fewkes and Mason developed distinct forms of representing the "natives": Fewkes depicted Puerto Ricans primarily as the contemporary descendants of Taíno Indians, whereas Mason basically envisioned them as transplanted Spanish peasants. Despite their theoretical, methodological, and even political differences, the two authors articulated a similar colonial and racial discourse. In both cases, they distanced themselves from the African origins of Puerto Rican culture and attempted to "whiten" the Island's population (see Chapter 10), while recognizing widespread racial mixture. Hence, both highlighted the racial and cultural differences between the Puerto Rican population and the white Anglo-Saxon population of the United States. These two anthropologists, each in his own way, attempted to domesticate Puerto Ricans by including them in an American narrative of material prosperity, commercial expansion, and moral progress (see Spurr 1993). According to this narrative, Puerto Ricans may have occupied a distant and lowly place, yet they could be pliable colonial subjects.

Mason's writings illustrate a more problematic relationship between anthropology and imperialism than do Fewkes's. Contrary to Fewkes, Mason did not espouse an imperialistic rhetoric or an evolutionary perspective; he identified closely with his subjects of study. Just as expansionism sparked a public debate over the incorporation of racially and culturally distinct peoples in the United States (Burnett and Marshall 2001; Cabranes 1979; Rivera Ramos 2001), it generated multiple reactions among anthropologists. During the first decades of the twentieth century, one of the main cleavages within the profession pitted the evolutionism of well-established Smithsonian anthropologists (such as John Wesley Powell, William McGee, Otis T. Mason, and Fewkes himself) against the historical particularism espoused by the emergent group of Franz Boas (1858–1942) and his disciples at Columbia University. Part of the difference between Fewkes and Mason is due to Boas's strong influence on Mason's research agenda. Rather than speculate on the origins and development of pre-Columbian peoples, as Fewkes did, Mason concentrated on collecting and documenting oral texts and cultural artifacts.

Moreover, the two anthropologists traveled to Puerto Rico at two different junctures. Fewkes went to the Island only four years after the conclusion of the Spanish-Cuban-American War (in 1902) and produced an unsympathetic account of contemporary Puerto Rico, partly as a result of his lack of knowledge of the vernacular language and local customs. Mason arrived in Puerto Rico well after the consolidation of U.S. colonial rule (in 1914), spoke Spanish, lived on the Island for about ten months, and rendered its inhabitants in a much more positive light.[3] Perhaps their different theoretical orientations were tuned to distinct moments in the colonial appropriation and administration of the Island. Prior research has suggested that evolutionism provided the intellectual and moral justification for the expansive phase of Western imperialism, while other schools of thought (such as Boas's historical particularism) were more congruent with established colonial regimes, which required practical kinds of data in order to rule more efficiently (Stocking 1991). Last, Mason's ideological inclinations were those of a liberal reformer, in contrast to Fewkes's conservative stance.[4] As will be shown presently, their political affiliations permeated their writings on Puerto Rico. Even their physical types differed markedly, with the young Mason posing in informal clothes, in the field, with a monkey hanging from his side, while the mature Fewkes appeared as a bearded and respectable man in formal attire. Nonetheless, Mason and Fewkes shared a common ideology as American anthropologists.

Boas's esteem of Mason's work diminished greatly during World War I as a result of Mason's participation in "a secret mission for the U.S. government" (Boas 1917). A German immigrant, Boas defended German cultural traditions and military policies and criticized American intervention in the war. As a pacifist, Boas opposed the war from the beginning as an imperialistic conflict. In 1919 he published a letter in *The Nation* accusing four anthropologists of serving as American spies in Mexico under pretense of working under Boas's patronage. Although Boas did not name these individuals in the letter, he referred to Mason, Samuel Lothrop, Sylvanus Morley, and Herbert Spinden (Price 2000). Mason had told Manuel Gamio, a Mexican colleague of Boas, that he would conduct archaeological research for the Field Museum in Chicago. Mason defended his position in a letter to Boas (February 18, 1920) as follows: "The United States Government desired and requested no more than accurate information concerning the activities of their enemies known to be partial to them." Boas eventually considered Mason "a very harmless young man whom I think did not understand clearly what he was doing and who is perhaps the only one in the whole group whom I would excuse" (Boas 1921). Nevertheless, the correspondence between Boas and Mason was greatly strained after this episode.

In 1920 the American Anthropological Association censored Boas and removed him from office as a result of his public criticism of U.S. government activities during World War I. A coalition of anthropologists affiliated with the Smithsonian and Harvard University temporarily imposed its nationalistic and conservative agenda on the profession. This group, organized around the Anthropological Society of Washington, feared that Boas's accusation of espionage would taint the reputation of all American anthropologists working outside the United States (see Lesser 1985: 23–26; Stocking 1992: 102–5). In turn, Boas (1919) strongly condemned scholars who "prostituted science by using it as a cover for their activities as spies." Boasian anthropology would increasingly define itself as antiracist, antifascist, and sometimes anti-imperialist.

This key moment in the history of anthropology suggests that the relationship between anthropologists and U.S. political interests was complex and equivocal, including significant internal conflict and contestation. As noted above, Mason did not define himself explicitly as an anti-imperialist and participated in undercover intelligence-gathering activities in Mexico. Yet his work in Puerto Rico suggests that he could also "soften" the colonial discourse and be seduced by the oral popular traditions of the Island. Compared with the blatant racism, imperialism, and evolutionism of scholars such as Fewkes, Mason portrayed Puerto Ricans much more favorably. For one thing, Mason spent more time in one field site (Utuado) and was able to communicate better (in Spanish) with his informants than Fewkes. For another, following his mentor Boas, Mason assumed a culturally relativistic posture toward his subjects of study rather than advocating the moral superiority of the Anglo-Saxon race and culture.

Nevertheless, Mason's sympathetic gaze was as much a product of colonialism as Fewkes's more critical outlook (see Spurr 1993). Both derived their ethnographic authority from a privileged and distant position that allowed them to survey Puerto Rico's history and culture, as well as to roam the Island. Both worked closely with representatives of the U.S. colonial regime. Both were attracted to the more exotic, bizarre, and quaint aspects of the new possession. Both were concerned with tracing the ethnic and racial origins of the Island's population. Finally, both constructed Puerto Ricans as less savage than other groups (such as Filipinos or the peoples of the African diaspora) but more primitive than (white) Americans. As I argued in Chapter 2, such images rendered Puerto Ricans less wild but more tamable subjects for U.S. imperialism.

THE "SACRED ISLAND OF THE ANCIENT INHABITANTS OF THE CARIBBEAN SEA": SEARCHING FOR THE INDIGENOUS PAST OF PUERTO RICO

Jesse Walter Fewkes (1850–1930) was probably the first American anthropologist to visit Puerto Rico for an extended period. Born in Newton, Massachusetts, Fewkes was originally trained in zoology at Harvard University. After spending several years at Harvard's Peabody Museum of Archaeology and Ethnology, Fewkes worked at the Bureau of American Ethnology from 1895 to 1928, serving as bureau chief between 1918 and 1928. Fewkes was also president of the American Anthropological Association between 1912 and 1913. He carried out fieldwork in the U.S. Southwest, especially among the Hopi Indians; Mexico; and the Caribbean. Fewkes was one of several Smithsonian scholars to shift his research focus from Native Americans to the newly acquired possessions in the Caribbean and the Pacific (see Hinsley 1981). Unlike other researchers who specialized in the Philippines, Fewkes devoted his full attention to Puerto Rico, "the sacred island of the ancient inhabitants of the Caribbean sea," in Otis T. Mason's phrase (O. Mason to True, October 1, 1898).

Between 1901 and 1904, Fewkes completed seven archaeological and ethnographic field notebooks and diaries on Puerto Rico, including many drawings, photographs, and maps. These documents are now located at the National Anthropological Archives (NAA) of the National Museum of Natural History in Washington, D.C. Fewkes's unpublished materials shed light on emerging American images of Puerto Ricans during the first few years after the U.S. occupation of the Island. Because these manuscripts were not meant for publication, they candidly record his first impressions of the Island's geography, culture, population, and difficult socioeconomic conditions. They also display many of the textual practices associated with U.S. colonial discourse.

In 1907 Fewkes published his monograph *The Aborigines of Porto Rico and*

Neighboring Islands as part of the annual report of the Bureau of American Ethnology. The text quickly became the classic of American archaeology on the Island. Here Fewkes combined historical, ethnological, and archaeological methods to reconstruct the cultural practices, beliefs, and artifacts of the Taínos, a term he used in a generic sense to refer to "the original sedentary people of the West Indies," as opposed to the Caribs, who were supposedly recent immigrants from South America (Fewkes 1970 [1907]: 25). The author believed that the Taínos were a "primitive race," inferior to indigenous groups such as the Mayas of Mesoamerica, because of their low level of technological and urban development, but superior to the native peoples of North and South America (Fewkes 1970 [1907]: 219). He also thought that the aboriginal population of Puerto Rico was in a prehistoric stage of cultural evolution because it lacked written documents other than pictographs "of the rudest kind." However, Fewkes (1902c: 496) argued that "the ancient Porto Ricans were not troglodific" and, like Otis T. Mason (1899: 395), suggested that "they were not savages, but were in the 'middle status' of barbarism." Note the parallels between Fewkes's characterization of the indigenous population of Puerto Rico and other authors' descriptions of its twentieth-century inhabitants. Such evolutionary schemes, based on the theories of Lewis Henry Morgan and others, dominated the writings of Fewkes and his contemporaries.

Fewkes's main research strategy was to describe and classify a vast number of archaeological objects found in twenty different sites throughout the Island. Especially notable were the stone implements carved by the Taínos, which were excavated from the land or located in isolated caves and indigenous ceremonial centers. In particular, Fewkes identified the Caguana site in Utuado and another in Jayuya as ancient burial places as well as several caves in Ciales, Adjuntas, and other remote regions of the Island as the best preserved (Fewkes 1902c, 1903). He concluded that indigenous crafts were distinct from those of other cultural areas in North and South America. On the one hand, he postulated the South American origin of the Taíno population and its diffusion throughout the Caribbean basin during the pre-Columbian era. On the other hand, he explained the indigenous culture of Puerto Rico as a response to the Island's climatic, topographic, and physiographic conditions. Like many other anthropologists at the beginning of the twentieth century, Fewkes (1970 [1907]: 21) believed that "the culture of a people is largely determined by its environment."[5]

In 1901 Fewkes began to study the secondary sources and private collections of Taíno artifacts, especially the Latimer Collection at the Smithsonian and the Stahl Collection at the American Museum of Natural History in New York. He was familiar with the writings of the leading Spanish-language authors on the pre-Columbian population of Puerto Rico, including Salvador Brau, Alejandro Tapia y Rivera, Cayetano Coll y Toste, and Manuel Fernández Juncos. Fewkes quickly noted that, according to Brau, "there are Indian mounds near Utuado" and that "the purest Indians lived near San German [sic] where the type is still present" (Fewkes 1901). He would later travel to those two towns in search of archaeological artifacts.

On April 26, 1902, Fewkes sailed from New York and arrived in San Juan seven days later. His first impressions upon disembarking included the following:

Temperature delightful—weather moist and sticky.

Bayamon [sic] is situated in the hills beyond, which are very beautiful.

Palms over balconies as in Spain.

Sometimes see naked children; many children have only a single garment. All colors from white to black but almost all have negroid features—Rather unintelligent faces.

There are many characteristic Porto Rican homes in Bayamon [sic]. They are built on tiles ordinarily thatched with palms; small single room.

Furniture simple gourds with [illegible] figures which are probably survivals of ancient patterns. (Fewkes 1902a)

In a few broad strokes, Fewkes characterized Puerto Rico's tropical climate, hilly terrain, Spanish atmosphere, poverty, racial mixture, simple housing patterns, and indigenous heritage. His published work elaborated more systematically on these elements of the Island's physical and cultural landscape (Fewkes 1902c, 1970 [1907]).

Upon arriving in Puerto Rico, Fewkes behaved like a typical colonial emissary. He first contacted a certain Captain Scott, "a secret service agent of U.S. in the [Spanish-Cuban-American] war [who] published a map of the [Morro] fort in N.Y. Herald before bombardment."[6] He then met with the American governor of Puerto Rico, William Hunt, and "found him very affable and interested in my work." Fewkes also called on William Henry Latimer, the nephew of the American millionaire who had donated his archaeological collection to the Smithsonian, but Latimer was of little help. He later spoke with "Mr [Federico Vall y] Spinosa,"[7] a local Protestant minister who "thinks the region about Yunque is the most primitive in the island" and that "the Indian types predominate in this region." Fewkes stayed at the Bay View Hotel in Old San Juan, owned by Mrs. Skinner, and traveled to Corozal with a Captain Wilson (Fewkes 1902a, 1903). Because he spoke "poor Spanish," he could not communicate well with ordinary Puerto Ricans and relied on American officials and Puerto Rican intermediaries for translation and transportation. At one point he called Puerto Ricans "Spiketties," apparently referring to their Spanish accent when speaking English (Fewkes 1902b). As an American correspondent in San Juan wrote around the same time as Fewkes was on the Island, "We know very little about these people or about their language, since we have little or no relation with Puerto Ricans, or 'spiketies' as we all call them" (cited in Gettleman 1971: 309).

As a specialist in Native American archaeology, Fewkes relentlessly sought the Island's Indian legacy in Utuado, San Germán, Luquillo, Río Grande, Manatí, Yauco, and Ponce. His monograph on the Island's archaeology mentions that "marked Indian features were casually observed everywhere, especially in the isolated mountainous regions" (Fewkes 1970 [1907]: 24). He believed that the Taíno heritage could still be detected "in the bodily form and mental characteristics of the existing natives; their peculiar customs, characteristic words, music, and legends" (Fewkes 1970 [1907]: 20). His search for the pre-Columbian roots of the Puerto Rican people first took him to El Yunque on the northeast coast, following Spinosa's suggestion, and then to La Indiera on the southwest end of the inner highlands, following Brau's intuition. He also thought that the people of Utuado and Comerío preserved Indian customs and physical traits. In his first published account of his trip, Fewkes (1902c: 491) claimed that "in the inaccessible region of Porto Rico called Loquillo [sic] we must look for the purest Indian blood among the present mountaineers of the Island." In the end, Fewkes (1970 [1907]: 24) held, "It is probable that the entire mountainous interior of Porto Rico, from the eastern to the western end, was the last refuge of the aboriginal population."

The contemporary evidence for Fewkes's indigenous interests was mostly anecdotal. With regard to El Yunque, Fewkes (1902a) commented: "It appears that the natives in the mountains still preserve legends about the high peak Yunque which may be ancient traditions. The [American] officers and soldiers are said to have collected a good many antiquities which the native Porto

Ricans brought in and sold at small prices." He also wrote: "Many almost pure types of Indians live there. They are very conservative and have many of their old arts and customs." As to La Indiera, Fewkes followed Brau's lead that "probably this [is] one of the last places when the Indians (puer) lived." However, he could not locate the place exactly, noting variously that it was "near San German," "near Yauco," "south of Lares," and "east of Las Marías." The place is actually located in the *municipio* of Maricao.

In his romantic search for the primitive, Fewkes found Indian traits throughout the Island. In his mind the "characteristic Porto Rican homes" in Bayamón and Pueblo Viejo were Carib survivals (Fewkes 1902a). He also thought that the "primitive habitations" of Luquillo, Loíza, and Barceloneta did not differ much from those of the Island's prehistoric inhabitants, even though they were currently occupied by "poorer negroes" (Fewkes 1902c: 491). Elsewhere he observed that "Porto Ricans do not like to enter caves, evidently because once used for religious purposes" by the Indians. In Río Piedras, Fewkes (1902a) visited the "old governor's palace" and church in the middle of the plaza, which he thought looked "much the same as was probably the cacique's home in old times." In Río Grande he "saw many signs of Indian types" (Fewkes 1903). On his last trip to Ponce, Fewkes (1904) found more Indian survivals. "Evidently there are many others [*sic*] things in the barrio called Indios, where there was formerly an Indian settlement."

To the American anthropologist, many current cultural practices showed remnants of Puerto Rico's indigenous past. The art of making canoes and hammocks was supposedly an ancient Carib custom. Carrying bundles with a bamboo stick was "evidently the survival of the old Indian," as was the peons' "easy gait or kind of dog trot." An old mill was similar "to those no doubt formerly used by the Indians." In Manatí, poor people "use tin cans as Indians in our southeast" (Fewkes 1903). He even attributed a possible Carib origin to the Island's national anthem, "La Borinqueña," as well as other musical genres popular in the countryside (Fewkes 1902c). Fewkes hastily concluded that much of Puerto Rico's racial composition, material culture, and folklore could be traced to the Taíno or Carib Indians.

Aside from his previous fieldwork in the Southwest, his readings on Puerto Rican archaeology, and his studies of museum collections, Fewkes was ill acquainted with Puerto Rican geography, history, language, and culture. His first published paper on "prehistoric Porto Rico" (Fewkes 1902c) contains numerous incorrect renderings of the Island's place names, such as "Loquillo," "Utuardo,"

"Cabo Roja," "Yubucoa," and "Curabo," and names of indigenous chiefs, such as "Aguenaba" and "Guaronix." More problematic were Fewkes's paternalistic views of Puerto Ricans and their contemporary culture. Here are several entries from his diary written during his first trip to the Island:

> Everything is very crude about their life; few know how to read and write and are astonished to find that one could read what was written. There are said to be many idols in this region [of El Yunque].

> In the morning a row of beggars sat on the sidewalk in front of our hotel (Mrs. Skinner, Bay View) and a man came out and gave each a cent. Today beggars allowed through town, and in many stores boxes of food laid out for them. Many beggars were seen on the street.

> There are streets in both Luquillo and Rio [sic] Grande which reminded one of an African or Phillipine town: Nothing but small homes with palm coverings; no nails employed in the manufacture of these houses.

> They say that the mothers bath the eyes of their infants in their own urine as soon as born.

> It is no uncommon thing to see a man half naked sitting in his house or stretched out in a hammock. Children often naked. (Fewkes 1902a)

On his second trip to Puerto Rico, Fewkes (1903) further noted:

> The country people [in Utuado] have no seats in their bohíos [huts]; all are seated in the floor. They have no table or furniture. A dirt floor a hammock or cot bed seems to constitute their only furniture. They apparently cook in one [or] two earthen or iron dishes.

> Sorcery is found among the negros [sic] of Porto Rico and appears in several different forms—e.g., the witch collar.

> The jagua homes on the outskirts of the town [of Manatí] are very primitive, people poor.

> They (the "gibaros") tell me that life at Loisa [sic] is very primitive and that it would be a good place for "stones."

Fewkes depicted the inhabitants of the new U.S. colony as primitive, illiterate, idolatrous, destitute, superstitious, and dark skinned. In documenting the miserable living conditions of Puerto Ricans, his portrait was marked by a strong racial prejudice against the natives, most of whom he considered to be Africans, "negros," or "Negroid" in physical appearance. Fewkes (1970 [1907]: 20) clearly noted that "the present population [of Puerto Rico] is composed of several amalgamated races." He described Puerto Ricans in terms that resonated strongly with those conventionally assigned to other nonwhite peoples, such as Filipinos (see Foreman 1906). Such racialized images served to buttress American rule over Puerto Rico. As Homi K. Bhabha (1994: 70) puts it, "The objective of colonial discourse is to construe the colonized as a population of degenerate types on the basis of racial origin, in order to justify conquest and to establish systems of administration and instruction."

In his notebooks and diaries, Fewkes described some of the contemporary cultural practices of Puerto Ricans, which he often found intriguing from his Protestant Anglo-Saxon perspective. During his visit to the town of Río Piedras, he observed the traditional Hispanic paseo: "In the evening went to the plaza to witness a custom of the Porto Ricans, which is common when the band plays Sundays and Wednesdays. The plaza is a place for [illegible] the inhabitants promenating [sic] to the music. The peons on one side of the gaslight posts; the higher classes on the other between the two lines of rockers (?) (price 10 cts.). This continues from 8–10 pm. The promenade closes with a rendering on the Star Spangled banner." On a trip to Ponce, Fewkes was fascinated with the Catholic rituals surrounding Holy Week: "Visited the Church this morning to hear Mass. The services were elaborate and instead of bells a rattle was used, when the congregation knelt down. This rattle which is also used elsewhere in Catholic countries symbolizes the thunder which [illegible] the veil of the temple. The altar very elaborately lighted and there was a procession with mistral (?) circuit in the Church. This procession formed of a priest with a veiled cross and candle bearer with candles and after them a priest with the host under a canopy: After these a procession of men and women with candles—the host deposited in a coffin above altar" (Fewkes 1902a).

The author was most impressed with the religious ceremonies held on Good Friday: "Found the altar covered with a black veil. There was an elaborate Mass and procession about the Church in the morning about 9. The figure of Christ on a cross with figures of the thiefs [sic] one on each side stood on the altar and before them the box in which the body was later carried about the town. This latter was filled with flowers . . . then there were sermons on the last words spoken by Christ on the cross. At about 3:30 the body was formally lowered from the cross in the presence of a great crowd filling to Church to overflowing and extending into the plaza. About 5:30 PM there was a procession through the streets of Ponce" (Fewkes 1902a).

Several elements stand out in these ethnographic descriptions. First, Fewkes relies primarily on a visual mode of representation, partly because he does not master the vernacular language (see Clifford 1997). Second, the author is notably absent from his own narrative, which tends to adopt a third-person, distanced, and realistic standpoint. Third, the text dwells on the cultural differences between Puerto Ricans and Americans, such as their patterns of social stratification or religious beliefs and customs. Fourth, the American presence on the Island is taken for granted (note the casual reference to the "Star-Spangled Banner" in the first cited passage), as the precondition for Fewkes's own fieldwork. (On another occasion, Fewkes noted in passing that the 1902 San Juan Carnival had two queens, one Puerto Rican and one American.) Finally, the text reveals a sense of discovery and wonder, of charting unexplored terrain, of encountering a new culture that needs to be recorded and interpreted by adventuring American scholars. Elsewhere Fewkes (1902c: 512) wrote enthusiastically that "a vast amount of new material awaits the advent of the archaeologist and ethnologist in these [Caribbean] islands." He concluded with a telling geographic metaphor: "The unknown anthropological material opened to us by territorial growth is vast."

In both his published and unpublished manuscripts, Fewkes combines professional curiosity with a missionary zeal and an unabashed expansionary spirit. These elements are clearly enunciated in the following fragment: "Late historical events have brought into our horizon new fields for conquest and opened new vistas for anthropological study. In the last years the political boundaries of the United States have been so enlarged that we have come to be regarded as a 'world power,' and with this growth new colonies beyond the seas now form parts of our domain . . . and we have been brought closer than ever before to problems concerning other races of man besides the North American Indian . . . these new problems will occupy our attention with ever increasing interest in years to come as Anthropology advances to its destined place among sister sciences" (Fewkes 1902c: 487).

This passage contains several unnamed references to the Spanish-Cuban-American War and its aftermath ("late historical events," "the political boundaries of the United States have been so enlarged," "new colonies beyond the seas now form parts of our domain"). Moreover, Fewkes uses the collective pronoun "we" as well as the possessive term "our" five times in four sentences, by which he means both Americans and anthropologists. The two processes—U.S. territorial expansion and the advancement of archaeological and ethnographic knowledge—are inextricably linked in the writer's mind. Like other contemporary American authors, Fewkes frequently employs images of possession, acquisition, annexation, and expansion throughout his essays.[8] His writing illustrates the strategy of appropriation that David Spurr (1993) has identified as common in the rhetoric of empire. Last, Fewkes proposes that the "new problems" raised by the overseas colonies should displace American anthropology's traditional object of study, Native Americans. The future of the science lay in the study of the indigenous cultures of the Caribbean and Pacific islands.

Although Fewkes engaged mostly in collecting archaeological objects for museum exhibition, he was aware of the broader implications of his fieldwork. Fewkes (1902c: 488) argued that "among all the acquisitions which came to the United States by the treaty of Paris, Porto Rico is pre-eminent from an anthropological point of view." Among other reasons, he mentioned Puerto Rico's size, location, insular environment, and favorable conditions for cultural development during pre-Columbian times. Studying Puerto Rican prehistory would help to elucidate larger questions about cultural origins and development in the Americas. Pursuing his main intellectual project was facilitated by U.S. colonization of the Island, which guaranteed the material and ideological conditions for anthropological research. After 1898, Fewkes's professional career was entirely reoriented from the study of American Indians toward West Indian archaeology as a result of the transformation of the United States into an imperial power.

In summary, Fewkes's archaeological expeditions confirmed the wealth of "Porto Rican antiquities" already noted by Otis T. Mason (1877, 1899). Responding to Mason's call to be "the first on the field," Fewkes quickly gathered one of the largest collections of pre-Columbian objects in the world for the U.S. National Museum. Fewkes's excursions, supported by the Bureau of American Ethnology, revealed the potential of anthropological research on the Island, not just in archaeology but also in ethnography. As Fewkes argued, it was necessary to use ethnological methods to discover Indian survivals. Moreover, Puerto Rico could serve as an overseas station for U.S. fieldworkers concerned with "other races of man besides the North American Indian." The Island could provide historical and cultural material to develop anthropology into a full-fledged professional enterprise. As Fewkes (1902c: 487) saw it, the territorial expansion of the United States could only improve the status of the discipline among its "sister sciences."

PEASANTS IN THE HILLS: RESCUING THE
HISPANIC SOURCES OF PUERTO RICAN FOLKLORE

In contrast to Fewkes, John Alden Mason (1885–1967) began his fieldwork in Mexico and Puerto Rico and developed his career elsewhere. Born in Phila-delphia, Mason studied anthropology with Edward Sapir at the University of Pennsylvania and earned his Ph.D. degree in anthropology at the University of California at Berkeley with Alfred Kroeber. Both his mentors had been students of Franz Boas at Columbia University. After graduating from Berkeley, Mason spent two years (1912–14) at the International School of American Archaeology and Ethnology in Mexico under Boas's tutelage. He was later appointed curator at the Field Museum of Natural History in Chicago and the American Mu-seum of Natural History in New York. In 1926 he became a professor of anthro-pology and curator of the University of Pennsylvania Museum, from which he retired in 1955. He served as vice president of the American Anthropological Association in 1944 and as editor of the *American Anthropologist* between 1945 and 1948.

Mason's research in Puerto Rico was part of a much larger study of the Island's natural history. In 1913 the New York Academy of Sciences approved a five-year plan to conduct a "scientific survey of Porto Rico and the Virgin Islands," focusing on tropical biology and geology, with a significant compo-nent devoted to anthropological fieldwork under Boas's direction (see Baatz 1996). The academy originally requested $25,000 from the colonial government in Puerto Rico for the first five years of research and was twice granted $5,000. The academy itself appropriated only $500 annually for the survey between 1913 and 1918 (Anonymous 1913; Britton 1919–22). The results were published in nineteen volumes of the *Annals of the New York Academy of Sciences*, extending well into the 1940s. The project was initially coordinated by Nathaniel Lord Britton, a botany professor at Columbia University who founded and directed the New York Botanical Garden and who became a prominent advocate for the study and conservation of the Island's natural resources.

Boas's research agenda in Puerto Rico included the Island's "ancient aborigi-nal inhabitants," as well as the effects of "race mixture" and "the tropical environment" on "the development of the modern population." This agenda was divided into "three distinct lines of anthropological work": "1 an investigation of the physical characteristics of the Porto Ricans; 2 an inquiry into their folklore; 3 researches on the antiquities of the island" (Boas to Britton, August 5, 1915). The first line of research was directly related to Boas's larger project on environmental influences on human types, for which he became well known. Whereas Boas conducted the fieldwork in physical anthropology, Mason completed most of the research in folklore and archaeology. Boas boasted that Mason's collection of Puerto Rican folklore "should have an influence similar to that of the European fairy tales collected a century ago which have been a source of pleasure and instruction for millions." Boas also praised Mason's archaeological excavations in the Capá site near the town of Utuado as "the most important site so far investigated in any of the Antillean islands" (Boas to Britton, August 5, 1915). Here I focus on Mason's fieldwork in folklore.

During his first visit to Puerto Rico between December 1914 and May 1915, Mason made one of the most extensive compilations of Spanish American folklore of its time. Altogether, he published more than 800 riddles; 600 *coplas* (quatrains); almost 400 *décimas* (ten-line poems), *aguinaldos* (Christmas carols), *canciones de cuna* (nursery rhymes), and other songs; more than 130 folktales; and about 30 traditional ballads. He also recorded 174 audio cylinders of funeral music, rumbas, games, tangos, and other songs in the course of his fieldwork (Lastra 1999). Mason's collection of folktales was the most abundant in Spanish America, while his compilation of riddles was only second in importance to those of Argentina. The bulk of the collection was published in Spanish in ten parts in the *Journal of American Folk-Lore* between 1916 and 1929, first edited by Boas and later by his disciple Ruth Benedict, and in the *Revue Hispanique* by Aurelio M. Espinosa (1918). Espinosa (1880–1958), a New Mexican scholar of Spanish descent who specialized in Hispanic folklore, oversaw the publication of the entire series but gave Mason most of the credit.

Mason's materials suggested that Puerto Rico's folklore was chiefly of Spanish origin.[9] As Espinosa wrote Boas (March 17, 1920), "The African elements are easily discernible in some [tales], but not important. The European element predominates." The most popular narratives on the Island were picaresque tales such as the stories about Juan Bobo, a local version of the Hispanic trickster Juan Tonto or Pedro de Urdemales (Mason 1921, 1924; for more recent interpretations of their significance, see Guerra 1998; Lastra 1999). Similarly, canciones de cuna were practically identical in Puerto Rico and other Spanish

American countries. Puerto Rican décimas and aguinaldos followed Spanish traditions of the sixteenth and seventeenth centuries, "showing the great vitality and vigor of that class of poetical compositions among the people" (Espinosa in Mason 1918: 289–90). Only on one occasion did Espinosa acknowledge the possible African influence on local folklore: the popularity of aguinaldos may be "partly due to the large number of people of Negro blood" on the Island (Espinosa in Mason 1918: 293). For Mason and Espinosa, the traditional culture of the Puerto Rican peasantry was fundamentally a Spanish transplant. Because Puerto Rico had been in continuous contact with the "mother country"—more so than any other Latin American nation except Cuba—Spanish folklore was conserved more "purely" on the Island than in other parts of the New World, such as New Mexico, Argentina, or Chile.

While in Puerto Rico, Mason completed twenty notebooks of folklore, which he phonetically transcribed from his informants in Utuado and Loíza. (Much of this material is now deposited in the Archives of the University of Pennsylvania Museum of Anthropology and Archaeology in Philadelphia.) Mason also collected twenty-five notebooks of poetry and riddles in Loíza, Coamo, and San Germán, as well as numerous copybooks written by school-children from fifteen districts of the Island, mostly from the western half of the interior, especially Utuado, Adjuntas, and Lares. Mason's original purpose was to study the Island's Spanish dialect and to compare it with that of Mexico and Spain, but eventually he changed his mind because "my knowledge of Spanish was never great enough to do a good job of this, and it was later well done by [Tomás] Navarro Tomas [*sic*], so I'll never do that" (Mason to Espinosa, November 23, 1956).

The extensive correspondence between Mason and Boas during 1914–15, preserved at the American Philosophical Society in Philadelphia, reveals constant frictions, negotiations, and clarifications with regard to the scope and intent of Mason's project. Initially, Mason dwelled on the linguistic aspects of his fieldwork, marveling at the "peculiar dialect" of Puerto Ricans. He noted, for example, the common aspiration of the final *s*, the trilled voiceless *rr*, the elimination of the intervocalic *d*, and the substitution of *l* for *r*. At the same time, Mason (December 28, 1914) frankly wrote Boas, "I have absolutely no idea how large a body of phonetic text you wish me to take or what you are going to do with it when I get it." In the end, Boas (1915c) instructed Mason, "You have, however, a very definite problem; namely, that of the relation of the folk-lore of Porto Rico and of Spanish America, as we know it from the various sources."

Following a typically Boasian agenda, Mason shifted his attention from "the philological question" to documenting folklore itself. Other scholars would later focus on the dialectology of Puerto Rico (see Alvarez Nazario 1992).

Armed with some prior knowledge of Spanish and research experience in Mexico, Mason arrived in Puerto Rico in December 1914 and proceeded to a twelve-day reconnaissance trip to Utuado. He saw E. M. Bainter, the Island's commissioner of public education, "immediately after arriving in town," to secure official support for his project. He also called on "the best scientist I have yet met and consequently the least pretentious. Needless to say he is of German blood, Mr [Robert L.] Junghanns"[10] (Mason to Boas, December 14, 1914). He later moved from Utuado to San Juan, where he stayed at the Hotel Nava and the Axtmayer Apartments in Santurce, working on his notebooks. "I have also received a Guest's card," Mason wrote Boas, "entitling me to the privileges of the American Club just across for a month, so I take my meals there and it is better and cheaper than at the hotel." There he saw the auditor of Puerto Rico so often that Mason feared he might belittle Mason's work, which depended financially on the colonial government (Mason to Boas, January 19, 1915).

"My trip [to Utuado] was a very successful one," Mason wrote Boas, "as far as folklore and philology are concerned, but fruitless as regards archaeology and anthropometry." From the beginning, Mason reported that Puerto Rican folklore "was practically identical with that of México and absolutely different from that of Jamaica and the Bahamas." Following Fewkes's footsteps and Boas's instructions, Mason attempted to identify the "Indian area" but became "more and more convinced that there is none." Instead of traveling around the Island, as Fewkes had done, Mason concentrated in Utuado—"probably the most interesting region on the island from an archaeological point of view"—and perhaps another place on the "eastern end near Luquillo," such as Loíza (Mason to Boas, December 8, 1914).

As Mason later explained, "Many persons have told me, Dr. [Henry Edward] Crampton included, that the most interesting town on the island from the point of view of folk-lore is Old Loiza [sic] on the northeast coast" (Mason to Boas, January 19, 1915). Mason was drawn to that town, "where there is a rather homogeneous and isolated negro population and said to be practices of voodooism" (Mason to Boas, January 30, 1915). He finally "ran down to Old Loiza" accompanied by a Major Dutcher. Like Fewkes before him, Mason had chosen Utuado as the center of "the mountain Gibaro who is prevailingly white" and saw Loíza as the center of "the negro of the shore" (Mason to Boas, February 2,

1915; see also Mason 1960: 9). Thus, Mason's work reinforced dual representations of Puerto Rican culture as epitomized by the interior town of Utuado and the coastal town of Loíza. The racialized image of the Island as a counterpoint between the white jíbaro of the inner highlands and the black former slave from the lowlands persists to this day.[11] Like other scholars before and after him, Mason privileged the Island's Hispanic heritage and downplayed the indigenous and African sources of its folklore (see Cadilla de Martínez 1938; Garrido 1952; Ramírez de Arellano 1926; Tió Nazario 1979 [1921]).[12]

Methodologically, Mason's research was uneven. He suspected that many folktales written by schoolchildren in several municipios had been corrected at their teachers' request. He also recorded dozens of popular songs on phonograph but could not ascertain if "all of them were indigenous" (Mason to Boas, January 5, 1915). Mason transcribed much of the material on the spot from interviews with adult informants in Utuado and Loíza. As he later recollected, "I personally wrote while on the island twenty copybooks of miscellaneous folklore in hasty phonetic text for the purpose of making a study of the island dialect" (Mason to Espinosa, January 22, 1956). "I was writing as fast as I could as the informant gave the tale, poetry, or adivinanza [riddle]" (Mason to Alegría, October 23, 1957). His choice of informants was also haphazard. When he traveled to Loíza, Mason interviewed Melitón Congo, an elderly man born in Africa who claimed to have been brought on the last slave ship to Puerto Rico. Mason's informant gave him "a vocabulary of several hundred words, unmistakably African. Unfortunately, he knows no African stories or songs which would be of interest in tracing negro influence here" (Mason to Boas, February 16, 1915). Mason did not pursue this line of inquiry, because he was primarily interested in the verbal expressions of highland peasants. Furthermore, his main ethnographic objective was documenting the folklore of Spanish rather than African origin.

From the start Mason was concerned with authenticating the materials he collected: "All of the stories are told by illiterate persons who have learned from others. Most of them are learned at 'velorios,' 'wakes' held over the dead. . . . I think there is small doubt that they have been handed down from mouth to mouth for a very long time" (Mason to Boas, December 8, 1914). At the same time, Mason paid little attention to folk poetry because "these, decimas, bombas, versos, refranes, are innumerable, are being composed continually and have a short life" (Mason to Boas, January 22, 1915). Thus, he defined a corpus of narrative texts that met the standard criteria of folklore at the time—anonymous, traditional, oral, popular, and rural. Mason also sought to capture the everyday language in which these stories were told. He preferred informants "who do not try to improve on their natural speech when dictating to me" (Mason to Boas, December 8, 1914) and wrote Boas from Utuado, "My principal regret here is that I have not yet been able to secure any informants [*sic*] who talks *muy bruto* [very rough]" (Mason to Boas, January 5, 1915).

Mason's editor, Espinosa, took many liberties when he prepared the collection for publication. Mason was initially unhappy with Espinosa's intervention (Mason to Boas, March 2, 1915, March 15, 1917). Mason wrote Boas that "I was never informed at all regarding your dealings with Espinosa and all that I have learned has been from him. I had an idea that he would read all the material carefully, correct it and give it to the typist for publication, but he claims, and of course justly, that he is too busy to do this, so is merely classifying and leaving it to the typist to correct errors, punctuate and paragraph and interpolate any missing words" (Mason to Boas, August 26, 1916). In turn, Espinosa repeatedly complained about Mason's sloppy research (Espinosa to Boas, May 10, 1917, March 17, 1920). "There are all sorts of words," Espinosa wrote, "which Dr Mason has put down which he thinks he heard, but which I am sure were not recited" (Espinosa to Boas, June 8, 1918).

After transcribing the phonetic texts into "good Spanish," Espinosa corrected their spelling "to conform with the Spanish orthography" and eliminated some pieces "because of offence to good taste, defective condition, or on account of evident literary sources" (Espinosa in Mason 1916: 424). Mason himself wrote Boas (February 22, 1917), "I wonder which the ones he censored because of 'offence to good taste' can be, for some of those included are pretty raw."[13] Nor did Mason like Espinosa's "strictly alphabetical arrangement" of the material and his lack of editorial care. In turn, Espinosa felt "a distinct disappointment" with Mason's collection because he felt that "the tales are too short, unfinished or incomplete; fragmentary." Espinosa discarded much of the material for publication "because it is mere repetition or copied" (Espinosa to Boas, March 17, 1920).

Espinosa classified Mason's collection according to genre or title, with brief introductory notes on the parallels between Puerto Rican folklore and that of Spain and Spanish America. Other contemporary compilations of the Island's folklore followed a similar format (Ramírez de Arellano 1926; Tió Nazario 1979 [1921]). In a typical Boasian stance, Mason as well as Espinosa believed that the material spoke largely for itself. As Mason wrote Boas, he would publish his results "merely as *data*, as a collection of the folk-lore of Porto Rico, without going deeply into the question of the origin, the different elements, etc." (Mason to Boas, January 22, 1915). Consequently, his material was presented as a meticulous compilation of oral literature, with little analysis or theoretical discussion. Nor did Espinosa have the time or inclination to interpret the contents of Mason's collection. Appraisals of the broader implications of the "data" would have to wait several decades (Guerra 1998; Lastra 1999).

Nonetheless, Mason's letters to Boas from the field are replete with personal observations and interpretations of the nature and significance of Puerto Rican folklore. At first he believed that "it is exclusively Spanish in origin," "the same as found in México, NM, etc." (Mason to Boas, December 8, 1914), although he later granted additional influences in Loíza. "If an African element is to be found anywhere on the island," Mason wrote Boas, "it will be there" (Mason to Boas, February 2, 1915). But, after spending two days in "Old Loiza," Mason felt "a little disappointed": "There is no dearth of material here and it can be gotten very easily but it seems to be practically the same as elsewhere, almost entirely of Spanish origin. . . . About the only local characteristic seems to be a considerable number of witch tales. But the great majority of stories, adivinansas [*sic*], *etc.*, are the same as those found all over the island and in Mexico and elsewhere in America. The dialect spoken here is of course practically the same as in Utuado" (Mason to Boas, February 9, 1915). Upon further inspection Mason found that "the dialect spoken on the coast seems to be considerably better Castilian than that used by the Gibaros in the mountain" (Mason to Boas, March 2, 1915). However, his observations led him to posit that Puerto Rican language and culture were relatively homogeneous throughout the Island, despite some regional, racial, and class distinctions. As he noted, "Even the most cultured classes use more or less of the characteristics of the island dialect in their ordinary speech" (Mason to Boas, December 8, 1914).

Apart from the possible African influence in Loíza, which he did not explore in depth, Mason could not identify many aboriginal elements in the folklore or racial composition of Puerto Rico. One of his key informants "Mr Junghanns agrees with most of my other authorities that the 'Indian area' is a myth, all cases being due to atavism" (Mason to Boas, December 13, 1914). At Boas's insistence Mason traveled west to Maricao and San Germán, "looking for Indian blood and archaeological sites," but concluded that "I am inclined to doubt their existence in either place" (Mason to Boas, April 6, 1915). Unlike Fewkes, Mason could not find much evidence of indigenous traits—either cultural or physical—in the contemporary Puerto Rican population. After reading both Fewkes and Coll y Toste, Mason noted that the Indian cacique Guarionex "had his stronghold about ten miles west of Utuado" (Mason to Boas, April 14, 1918). But he failed to see "any unusual amount of Indian blood in that region" (Mason to Boas, April 6, 1915). Instead, he emphasized the prevalent mixture between Spanish and African types in Puerto Rico.

When Boas requested samples of hair colors and textures for his own research on the Island, Mason conceded: "Individuals are found of practically every type of hair color and form and of eye color, though of course, in greatly varying proportions. On the coast nearly all the individuals are negroid. . . . The Gibaros in the hills present greater variations as the negro blood is less, the white blood predominating with traces of Indian blood" (Mason to Boas, March 19, 1915). Once in the field, Boas himself echoed Mason's assessment: "It can hardly be assumed that there is a great deal of Indian blood in the towns" of Utuado, where he measured the stature and dental arches of 350 schoolchildren, and San Juan, where he reviewed the medical records of numerous soldiers of "the Porto Rican regiment" under Major General Basil N. Suthar at the Insular Constabulary (Boas to Britton, January 5, 1915, August 5, 1915). In his published article on Puerto Rico, Boas (1916) doubted that Indian types had persisted on the Island to any great extent, although he acknowledged the popular belief that the Indiera area of Maricao had a larger proportion of residents of Amerindian origin. Boas and Mason were both "greatly puzzled at the many diverse physical types met here" (Mason to Boas, April 6, 1915). As Mason wrote Boas (March 13, 1915), "It strikes me that a place where there is such a varying mixture of blood as here and consequently so little race feeling, and therefore practically equal opportunities given to either race, would be an ideal place to make a thoroughgoing scientific investigation of the racial intelligence of the negro and white." Other American scholars would take this issue as a point of departure for their research in the 1940s (see Chapter 10).

Mason's work on Puerto Rican folklore practically ended with Boas's six-week trip to the Island between May and July 1915 (Boas to Mason, May 21, 1915; New York Academy of Sciences 1915).[14] After Boas concluded his research in physical anthropology, Mason briefly traveled to the United States but returned to Utuado from August to December 1915. During this period Mason worked with the archaeologist Robert T. Aitken excavating a large burial cave and several ball courts in the barrio of Caguana in Utuado (Aitken 1917, 1918; Haeberlin 1917; Mason 1941). Boas (1916) published a brief report on his fieldwork in Puerto Rico, which supported his contention that human types were highly unstable in different environments (Boas to Britton, June 13, 1915; see also Spier 1918, 1919). But he soon lost his connection with the Porto Rico Committee that sponsored his research. "I am rather disgusted with the whole thing," Boas (1940) later wrote Mason, "because the Academy practically took the matter out of my hands in 1916."

Although Boas's professional correspondence does not shed much light on the academy's withdrawal of support for anthropological fieldwork on the Island, the decision was apparently based on economic considerations. At the end of 1915 Boas submitted a financial report to the New York Academy of Sciences in connection with anthropological research in Puerto Rico. His expenses, including transportation, research assistance, and photographic work, totaled $1,601.08—more than the entire $1,500 per year at the disposal of the Porto Rico Committee (Britton n.d.; New York Academy of Sciences n.d.). In 1917 the colonial government in Puerto Rico did not approve the requested $5,000 for the scientific survey (Britton 1917). Local authorities were reluctant to fund the expensive, presumably unscientific, and impractical work of Boas and his collaborators in folklore and ethnology. Mason's research was deemed irrelevant to the study of the Puerto Rican economy and its natural resources (Baatz 1996). The academy would not grant more money for anthropological studies of the Island until Froilich Rainey's archaeological expedition in 1934 (Rainey 1940).

Mason's fieldwork in Puerto Rico was part of the first sustained attempt to export "imperial science" beyond the boundaries of the U.S. mainland (Baatz 1996). It was also part of Boas's emerging vision of an applied anthropology centered on the problems of administering an American colony in the Caribbean, such as "the hygiene of childhood," "the actual management of schools," and the development of "reading matter for rural schools" (Boas to Britton, August 5, 1915). A decade later Boas (1925) lamented that fieldwork in physical anthropology had been abandoned in Puerto Rico, "particularly relating to the important question of the influence of tropical climate upon growth and development." Research of this type would not resume until the 1940s.

For anthropology, the most enduring legacy of the *Scientific Survey of Porto Rico and the Virgin Islands* was launching J. Alden Mason's long and distinguished career. Mason returned to the United States in 1915 and later moved on to other field sites on the mainland and in numerous Latin American countries such as Panama, Guatemala, Colombia, Peru, and Costa Rica. He developed a solid reputation as an expert in the archaeology of South America and Mexico. He did not go back to the Island until October 1956 (Mason to Alegría, July 31, 1956), when the Institute of Puerto Rican Culture invited him to promote the government's purchase and preservation of the Capá site as a historic monument, as Boas had urged four decades before (Boas to Britton, December 17, 1915). The site now boasts a public recreational park known as the Centro Ceremonial Indígena de Caguana (see Chapter 11).

Mason completed the first systematic compilation of Puerto Rican folklore as well as the most significant archaeological excavation on the Island for its time. His research agenda stemmed from Boas's attempt to move anthropology away from evolutionary and racial theories and toward relativistic and particularistic fieldwork. Mason's work in folklore was the only effort of its kind supported by the New York Academy of Sciences through its massive *Scientific Survey of Porto Rico and the Virgin Islands*. It was also part of an academic effort to salvage the last vestiges of Hispanic folklore in the New World. Painstakingly recording his informants' words and music, Mason deeply sympathized with ordinary men and women, the peasants in the hills. His collection of folktales, riddles, songs, and other forms of verbal art enshrined the mountain jíbaro as the archetype of the folk. It thereby contributed to construct Puerto Ricans as a predominantly white population with strong ties to European traditions. At the same time, Mason's research depicted the Island's inhabitants as much closer to the Mediterranean than to the Anglo-Saxon race and culture.

CONCLUSION

Between 1898 and 1915, American anthropology in Puerto Rico was framed by the unequal encounter between outside observers and dependent natives. This encounter was itself predicated on a colonial power structure that made the Island accessible, feasible, and safe for field research (Asad 1973). American anthropologists such as Fewkes and Mason often relied on colonial authorities—including the presidentially appointed governor, the commissioner of education, school superintendents, military officers, and even a former secret service agent—as well as such metropolitan institutions as the Smithsonian and the New York Academy of Sciences to carry out fieldwork in the Island. Neither Fewkes nor Mason collaborated extensively with Puerto Rican scholars, although they were familiar with the work of local intellectuals such as Brau's and

Coll y Toste's writings. Both Fewkes and Mason sought to produce ethnographic and archaeological knowledge that might be useful to the U.S. colonial
government, on such practical issues as public health, education, agriculture,
immigration, and historic preservation. They also constituted the Other as a
legitimate field of study through constant references to the need to advance
scientific knowledge beyond the mainland, especially in the newly acquired
overseas possessions in the Caribbean and the Pacific.

In varying degrees, the two American anthropologists articulated a colonial
discourse on Puerto Rican culture and history, strongly influenced by contemporary ideas about evolution, race, and the environment. Overall, this discourse
depicted Puerto Ricans as poor, illiterate, backward, and unprepared for self-
government. The portrait was based on the belief in the biological and cultural
superiority of the white race, particularly of Anglo-Saxon origin, over other
races and peoples, such as blacks, Asians, and Latins. Temperate zones were
also supposed to be more conducive to civilization than tropical climates (see
Gettleman 1971; Rivera Ramos 2001; Thompson 1995). Anthropologists contributed to this discourse by representing the Other in a state of arrested intellectual, moral, and cultural development (Karp, Kreamer, and Lavine 1992). Such
images had a broad and lasting impact on U.S. public opinion, government
policies, and scholarly research.

The two anthropological projects reviewed in this chapter focused on Puerto
Rico's indigenous and Hispanic traditions, neglecting its African-based traditions. For Fewkes, Puerto Ricans were essentially modern-day Indians; for
Mason, they were predominantly Hispanic folk. Both took the highland town of
Utuado as the Island's archaeological and ethnographic core and the coastal
town of Loíza as emblematic of a peripheral "negro" population. These racialized images of Puerto Rican culture tempered the colonial discourse, especially when compared with the Philippines, whose peoples were considered to
be the most savage of all the newly colonized and hence the ultimate anthropological subjects. As Boas (1916: 716) wrote, "The population of Porto Rico is
derived from three distinct sources—from people belonging to the Mediterranean type of Europe, from West Indian aborigines, and from Negroes." Fewkes
(1902a) put it more bluntly in his diary: "All colors from white to black but
almost all have negroid features." American anthropologists and other contemporary writers (see Hill 1903: 165–69) often depicted Puerto Ricans either as
dark-skinned Mediterranean types or as a racially mixed people, with minor
traces of Indian and black "blood." By highlighting their European and Amer-

indian origins, this racialized portrayal made Puerto Ricans appear more assimilable to Anglo-Saxon civilization than were Filipinos and other conquered peoples.

Anthropological representations of Puerto Rico—as documented by archaeological and ethnographic collections, exhibits, expeditions, monographs, photographs, recordings, notebooks, letters, and diaries—were part of a growing field of ethnographic knowledge about non-European cultures (see Said 1978, 1994; Williams and Chrisman 1994). With the emergence of the United States as an imperial power at the close of the nineteenth century, colonial discourses on Puerto Rico and other outlying possessions—initially Cuba, the Philippines, Hawaii, Alaska, Guam, and Samoa—characterized the new native subjects as uncivilized, immature, and untrained in the art of democracy. Altogether, anthropological research during the first two decades of American rule in Puerto Rico contributed to legitimizing U.S. political, economic, and cultural hegemony by insisting on the underdeveloped state of the Island's culture. Whether they identified closely with imperialist interests and policies—like Fewkes—or with the plight of the common folk—as did J. Alden Mason—American anthropologists tended to represent Puerto Ricans as Other, as racially and culturally inferior to white Anglo-Saxons. In so doing, they bolstered the Island's appropriation by the new metropolis in the name of scientific, cultural, and economic progress.

Postcolonial critics have argued that colonial discourse ultimately rests on a rigid dichotomy between Western and non-Western cultures. From this perspective, colonized peoples in the so-called Third World constitute the inverse image of European and American colonizers (Gandhi 1998). While the former were considered primitive, the latter were thought to be civilized. But this binary opposition is highly problematic in Puerto Rico, where U.S. colonial discourse often recognized the similarities, as well as the differences, between colonizer and colonized. After all, Puerto Rico was initially colonized by Spain, like other Latin American and Caribbean countries, which can legitimately claim to belong to Western civilization. As a result, the representation of a "Westernized" people in Puerto Rico was more complex than in places considered to be part of an oriental tradition, such as the Philippines (Said 1978).

Another common element of colonial history is the domination by white colonizers over nonwhite subjects. Again, Puerto Rico's population of European, African, Indian, and mixed ancestry unsettles such bipolar racial categories (Loomba 1998). As I have shown in this chapter, American anthropologists (such as Fewkes, Mason, and Boas) found it difficult to classify Puerto Ricans as either black or white and assumed an ambivalent position vis-à-vis their "race." At the same time, official counts of the Puerto Rican population found that it was predominantly white. I will elaborate on the practical implications of the American racial classification system on the Island in Chapter 10. For now, I want to underline how it colored anthropological views of Puerto Ricans as a racially heterogeneous population that could not be neatly counterposed to white Americans.

The Puerto Rican case confirms that anthropology was indeed part of the colonial enterprise but that it sometimes othered and racialized people in unpredictable and even contradictory ways. As an archaeologist, Fewkes reinvented contemporary Puerto Ricans as Native Americans, similar to those he had known in the southwestern United States. As a folklorist, Mason romanticized the Hispanic traditions of Puerto Rican peasants, similar to those he had studied in Mexico. Despite their different emphases, both distracted attention from the Island's African heritage, black population, and "primitive" culture. Thus, the two anthropologists systematically whitened and ennobled Puerto Ricans in order to incorporate them into dominant U.S. narratives of race and civilization. Such academic representations of the Island had their popular counterparts in widely circulated visual images, such as the ones analyzed in the next chapter. American views of Puerto Ricans tended to deny their separate national identity and therefore the right to exercise self-rule. This would become a bone of contention for cultural nationalists on the Island, including several prominent anthropologists during the 1950s.

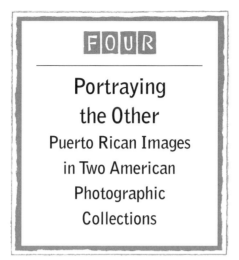

FOUR

Portraying
the Other
Puerto Rican Images
in Two American
Photographic
Collections

Until the 1980s, few anthropologists approached photographs as primary sources of historical and ethnographic documentation on the peoples they studied.[1] Apart from Margaret Mead, Gregory Bateson, and other pioneers in the discipline, most ethnographers used visual images merely as aids to memory, similar to written notes, or as supplementary illustrations of their fieldwork, especially during the early stages (Collier and Collier 1986; Hockings 1995; Ruby 1996). However, visual anthropology has experienced substantial growth, particularly as a result of increased access to video and film technologies. Moreover, a growing number of critical works have examined the visual representation of non-Western cultures from the mid–nineteenth to the early twentieth century (Banks and Morphy 1997; Devereaux and Hillman 1995; Edwards 1992; Scherer 1990). Much of this scholarship has focused on photographic portrayals of other peoples through world's fairs (Breitbart 1997; Brown 1994; Maxwell 1999; Rydell 1998), museum exhibits (Banta and Hinsley 1986), tourist postcards (Alloula 1986; Geary and Webb 1998), and popular magazines (Lutz and Collins 1993, 1994).

Researchers have increasingly turned to the systematic study of photographic collections to unravel European and American colonial discourses. In their analysis of the *National Geographic Magazine*, Catherine Lutz and Jane Collins (1993) found that this publication has tended to depict the peoples of Africa,

Asia, and Latin America as exotic, idealized, naturalized, ritualized, and sexualized others. Since 1888 the magazine has represented non-Western peoples predominantly as male, middle-class, young or middle-aged, rural, and darkskinned noble savages. The magazine's images have usually followed a realistic code, prescribing the literal transcription of the physical and social world. Accordingly, photographers were supposed to be invisible, although their presence was evident in what they decided to include and exclude in the picture. Like other popular forms of photojournalism, National Geographic has frequently promoted the expansion of American economic and political interests abroad (see Spurr 1993).

National Geographic's coverage of Puerto Rico during the first three decades of American rule illustrates its imperialistic rhetoric. In 1902 the magazine published an essay by the American treasurer of Puerto Rico on the problems of administering the new colony. According to William F. Willoughby (1902: 466),[2] the U.S. government proposed "to endow the newly acquired possession with political institutions and systems of law at once conforming to American ideals of individual liberty and political justice and yet adapted to the peculiar local conditions existing and the character of the inhabitants." Soon thereafter, the magazine's editor, Gilbert Hovey Grosvenor (1906: 712), claimed that "the past several years have brought much happiness and prosperity to our little island in the West Indies." William H. Taft, then secretary of war, added triumphantly that "without our fostering benevolence, this island would be as unhappy and prostrate as are some of the neighboring British, French, Dutch, and Danish islands" (Taft 1907: 433).[3] In a lavishly illustrated piece on Puerto Rico, John Oliver La Gorce, a frequent contributor and future editor of the National Geographic Magazine, concluded that "no other nation in history has ever created a finer record in colonial administration than our own United States has written for itself in our beautiful El Dorado of the Antilles" (La Gorce 1924: 651). One of the photographs accompanying that article, showing three halfnaked children, attempted to disguise their poverty by attributing their nudity to "Porto Rico's delightful climate."

The visual representation of the new American possessions after the Spanish-Cuban-American War has received increasing scholarly attention (see Bretos 1996; Díaz Quiñones 2000; Libia González 1998a; McCoy 2000; Ojeda Reyes 1998; Thompson 1995, 1996; Zwick 2000). In his analysis of Our Islands and Their People, a best-selling illustrated book published in 1899, Lanny Thompson (1995) argues that photographic realism was an integral part of U.S. colonial discourse. The book's images stress the negative effects of Spanish colonization in Puerto Rico, while virtually ignoring the existence of a Creole male elite. Furthermore, the photographs highlight the Island's white and indigenous races, children, women, and natural landscapes. Thompson's thesis is that such visual representations bolstered U.S. expansion in Puerto Rico and elsewhere. As Joanna C. Scherer (1992: 33) puts it, "Photography was used extensively in the colonial effort to categorize, define, dominate and sometimes invent, an Other."

Thompson further argues that American political and economic domination of Puerto Rico was predicated on an unequal cultural relation between the two countries. The textual and photographic description of Puerto Ricans helped legitimize U.S. occupation and possession of the Island. Realistic narrative strategies confirmed the observers' avowed objectivity, together with statistical data and government reports. Redefinition of the Puerto Rican people as inferior others was part of a missionary project based on the doctrine asserting the Manifest Destiny of Anglo-Saxon civilization (see White 1898: 16). Accordingly, American travelers often depicted Puerto Ricans as primitive, poor, dependent, childlike, and effeminate. Such imperial representations helped justify the cultural assimilation and political subordination of Puerto Rico to the United States.

Thompson's work unravels a colonial discourse that denied Puerto Ricans the capacity for self-government.[4] American images of Puerto Rico were colored by racist and ethnocentric views prevailing in the early twentieth century. To the new conquerors, Puerto Ricans were the last representatives in America of a decaying Spanish empire and as such belonged to a degraded culture and race. The Island itself was often portrayed as a natural paradise with unlimited opportunities for U.S. investment. The soil's fertility and abundance as well as the natives' supposed innocence and loyalty boded well for the future. The new colonial regime was envisioned as quickly bringing progress and civilization to the Island, paving the way for making Puerto Ricans into good U.S. citizens—or so American leaders thought (see Willoughby 1905).

A key strategy of U.S. colonial domination was symbolic elimination of the Creole elite from these epic narrations. *Our Islands and Their People*, for example, silences the local upper class while emphasizing the natives' oppression by Spanish administrators and merchants. In turn, the Creole elite developed a defensive discourse of Puerto Ricanness to reassert its own cultural hegemony over the Island. What is less clear is why the book highlights the aboriginal elements and downplays the African components among Puerto Ricans. (As I argue in Chapter 10, many other sources insist that the white population predominates on the Island.) Perhaps it is a way of allaying the racial fears of white colonizers who did not want to increase the black population of the United States. Examining other photographic collections will help to assess how representative this view was among American observers. In any case, U.S. colonial discourse often disregarded class and racial differences on the Island, an approach that also characterized nationalist views of identity, although for the opposite purpose—resisting colonialism (see Chapter 1).

In this chapter I analyze two distinct photographic collections on Puerto Rico, assembled during the last years of the nineteenth century and the first decade of the twentieth, the period immediately after the U.S. occupation of the Island, in which a colonial discourse crystallized. Together with museum collections and world's fairs, photographs provided one of the most powerful means through which the American public learned about Puerto Rico. I focus on various kinds of visual images that Americans were commonly exposed to during the period under consideration. The first set of photographs forms part of the Underwood & Underwood Glass Stereograph Collection (1895–1921) at the National Museum of American History (NMAH) in Washington, D.C. Underwood & Underwood was one of the leading American companies specializing in the commercial production and distribution of three-dimensional images about other countries. The second set of images forms part of the Helen Hamilton Gardener Photographic Collection (ca. 1906) at the National Museum of Natural History (NMNH).[5] Gardener was a feminist writer, reformer, and public official who gathered many photographs during a six-year cruise of the world (1902–8). These two contrasting sources of visual images allow one to reconstruct how Americans represented Puerto Ricans around the turn of the twentieth century. To borrow Scherer's words, they document how photography helped "to categorize, define, dominate and sometimes invent" the Puerto Rican people as Other to mainstream American culture.[6]

REPRESENTING THE "HUMBLE HOME LIFE OF OUR PORTO RICAN COUSINS": THE UNDERWOOD & UNDERWOOD COLLECTION

Since the late 1850s, several companies in the United States and Europe mass-produced and marketed stereographs featuring foreign and domestic images of war, history, politics, travel, expeditions, religion, humor, risqué, and urban life.

Stereographs were a pair of photographs taken with camera lenses separated laterally by two and a half inches, roughly the same distance between the pupils of human eyes (Haberstich 1991). The images were then mounted side by side in a standard seven-inch card to be viewed with a stereoscope, an optical instrument with two eyeglasses that created a three-dimensional effect. Stereograph viewing became one of the favorite pastimes of the Victorian era (1837–1903), especially among middle- and upper-class families in Great Britain and the United States. Such images provided detailed visual information about exotic others at home as well as in remote parts of the world to large Western audiences. Thousands of stereocards were distributed free of charge in breakfast cereal boxes or sold en masse to American public schools and colleges (Blum and Barnett 2000; Rosenblum 1984; Zwick 2000). Like television today, stereography was a popular means of entertainment, education, and propaganda from the second half of the nineteenth century through the first two decades of the twentieth century.

During this period, Underwood & Underwood became the largest stereograph publisher in the United States. In 1882 brothers Elmer and Bert Underwood established a small stereograph distribution business in Ottawa, Kansas. They later opened an office in Baltimore and relocated their headquarters to New York City, expanding their coverage to all North America. Beginning in 1890, the company recruited thousands of college students as summer salespersons to peddle its products from door to door. In 1895 Underwood & Underwood began to publish tourist-oriented images, characterized by their stress on action, novelty, personality, and popular appeal. They advertised their stereographs as a unique system based on a "mental" form of travel (Underwood & Underwood 1905, n.d.). The images were sold in boxed sets, usually containing one hundred cards on particular topics, with explanatory text in six languages. A box containing from twenty-four to one hundred stereo views cost between four and twenty-seven dollars in 1908. Coverage ranged from political figures such as Presidents McKinley, Theodore Roosevelt, Taft, and Wilson to foreign countries such as Egypt, Japan, and Australia (Earle 2000).

The Spanish-Cuban-American War stimulated the mass production of stereo views of the war and its aftermath. Underwood & Underwood published more than two thousand images of the war, focusing on the Philippines (McCoy 2000; Zwick 2000). In 1901 the company issued a one-hundred-card set on Cuba and Puerto Rico, at a cost of $16.60 (or $322.47 in 1999 dollars). Some of these views were later grouped under "West Indies" for the H. C. White Company

TABLE 4.1. The Underwood & Underwood and Helen Hamilton
Gardener Collections of Photographs on Puerto Rico (in Percentages)

	Underwood & Underwood (N=98)	Helen Hamilton Gardener (N=155)
Creator		
Underwood & Underwood	91.8	2.0
Helen Hamilton Gardener	0	94.8
Other[a]	8.2	3.2
Date of creation		
1895	1.0	0
1899	1.0	2.6
1900	19.4	1.9
1901	0	9.0
1904	2.0	0
1905	4.1	0
1909	0	30.3
Undated	72.4	56.1
Place of photograph		
Aguadilla	5.1	0
Aibonito	6.1	1.3
Caguas	7.1	0.6
Cayey	3.1	10.3
Coamo	4.1	9.0
Mayagüez	5.1	3.2
Ponce	12.2	14.2
Río Piedras	0	3.2
San Juan	22.4	14.8
Vieques	0	5.2
Yauco	6.1	1.9
Other	5.1	7.7
Unknown	23.5	28.4
Setting of photograph		
Urban	54.1	36.1
Rural	45.9	62.6
Unknown	0	1.3
Presence of persons in photograph		
Yes	68.4	67.1
No	31.6	32.9
Presence of photographer in photograph		
Yes	0	5.2
No	100.0	94.8
Presence of nonnatives in photograph		
Yes	0	14.2
No	100.0	85.8

TABLE 4.1. *continued*

	Underwood & Underwood (N=98)	Helen Hamilton Gardener (N=155)
Presence of animals in photograph		
Yes	24.5	21.9
No	75.5	78.1
Text accompanying photograph		
Includes proper names of places	76.5	53.5
Does not include proper names of places	23.5	46.5
Main subject of photograph		
Buildings and roads	20.4	18.7
Historic sites and monuments	20.4	4.5
Human types	14.3	14.8
Individual portraits	0	9.0
Military activities	1.0	0
Natural landscapes	16.3	7.1
Recreational activities	2.0	3.9
Trees and fruits	0	12.3
Work activities	13.3	18.7
Other	12.2	11.0

Note: Some columns may not add up to 100 percent because of rounding.
[a] Includes R. Y. Young, H. A. Strohmeyer, H. W. Wyman, Selden Allen Day, A. Moscioni, and Paul Beckwith.

catalogue. In 1905 Underwood & Underwood described its fifty-one images of Puerto Rico as follows: "San Juan, Porto Rico. Humble home life of our Porto Rican cousins—their work and their sports. Places made famous by men of four centuries ago and by the men of a few years ago. Crops, industries and social customs" (6). By 1912, when the company discontinued stereograph production, it had printed more than thirty thousand titles on different subjects. Between 1912 and 1921, one of its competitors, the Keystone View Company, acquired all the Underwood & Underwood negatives and remaining stock (Darrah 1977). Keystone continued to reproduce and distribute the images to a mass market.

The Archives Center of the NMAH has nearly twenty-eight thousand glass plates produced by Underwood & Underwood, including ninety-eight images of Puerto Rico, dated between 1895 and 1905. The photographs primarily record the Island's physical structures, such as roads, hotels, houses, cathedrals, forts, and barracks. Few of the images feature Puerto Rican people as their main subject, although they often appear as part of the scenery, as in the case of markets, squares, farms, and cemeteries. The basic purpose of the collection was to furnish a visual inventory of picturesque scenes and locales for potential tourists and investors. Like other Underwood & Underwood sets, the Puerto Rican series was designed to simulate a tour of the country's cities, monuments, industries, natural resources, and people (Darrah 1977).

In the first column of table 4.1 I summarize the main characteristics of the Underwood & Underwood Collection on Puerto Rico. The images were produced by several anonymous photographers as well as three named ones—H. A. Strohmeyer, H. W. Wyman, and R. Y. Young—who did some work for the company. Except for one photograph, all are dated after the American occupation of the Island in 1898. The collection focuses on urban settings, especially the largest cities of Puerto Rico, such as San Juan, Ponce, Caguas, Mayagüez, and Aguadilla. Although more than two-thirds of the images include people, none features the photographer or other nonnative subjects. One out of four images includes an animal, most often a horse, less commonly a donkey, ox, cow, dog, or rooster. More than three-fourths of the places are identified by name, but no individual is named in the captions. The photographs' main subjects consist of buildings and roads, historic sites and monuments, and landscapes.

The first column of table 4.2 describes the basic features of the persons portrayed by Underwood & Underwood. The photographers prefer small groups of adult, dark-skinned, and lower-class men. In this regard the collection resembles other American portraits of non-Western cultures (Lutz and Collins 1993). Subjects usually pose in informal clothes, completely dressed, and standing. While the photographer adopts a naturalistic perspective, subjects tend to look directly at the camera, located frontally to the main figure. This standard pose was the result of technical limitations as well as customary modes of representing socially marginal groups. Nineteenth- and early-twentieth-century photographs of Latin America typically portrayed poor and dark-skinned persons as docile and passive subjects (Levine 1989).

The Underwood & Underwood Collection contains stark images of Puerto Rican poverty in both urban and rural settings. The Island's inhabitants are frequently portrayed barefoot, an emblem of low social status and peasant origin. *National Geographic* reported that the insular police divided the population into two main categories—the urban dwellers who wore shoes and the rural dwellers who couldn't afford them (La Gorce 1924). These socioeconomic differences are visually encoded in many portraits of Puerto Rico during the early twentieth century.

One Underwood & Underwood photograph shows an elderly dark-skinned beggar, probably a blind man, and a small child in the town of Adjuntas, framed by the text, "Human poverty amidst nature's wealth" (figure 4.1). This remark is apparently triggered by the sharp contrast between the subjects' appearance—portrayed barefoot and in rags—and the lush tropical vegetation in the background. Visually, the photograph is built on the play between light and dark colors—the man's dark skin as opposed to his light-colored shirt, as well as his entire figure as distinguished from the trees and bushes in the back. This image forms part of an early-twentieth-century penchant for photographing certain human types, such as beggars, peddlers, old men, and former slaves (Levine 1989). This and other photographs in the Underwood & Underwood Collection document the widespread presence of blacks and mulattoes in the inner highlands of Puerto Rico, in municipalities such as Adjuntas, Aibonito, Yauco, and Cayey, traditionally considered the backbone of the white jíbaro. At the same time, the image suggests that American commercial photographers were primarily interested in portraying the dark-skinned, lower-class inhabitants of the Island as representatives of an Other race and culture.

An ironic caption—"Porto Rican boys in their Sunday dress"—accompanies a picture of two dark-skinned, seminude, barefoot children near Aibonito (figure 4.2). (This image also forms part of Gardener's collection of glass plates.) Both children wear rags, and one of them shows a protruding belly, suggesting malnutrition and perhaps intestinal disease. They both stand against a barren background, with a huge rock rising on one side. They pose for the camera on top of a log bridge, over a dry river or trench. Despite their miserable conditions, they half smile for the photographer. The image of happy natives, notwithstanding their adverse circumstances, is so common in this collection that it may be considered a trope of Puerto Rican conformity with the established order.

In "Rapid transit in Yauco," a racially mixed group of men, women, and children share a crowded oxcart (figure 4.3). Again, the caption is ironic, because this form of transportation compares unfavorably with other Underwood & Underwood images of elevated railways in Germany, for example, but is similar to another view of rural Mississippi. Here, the photographer has placed a dark-skinned, barefoot conductor in front of the two oxen, with two dozen people sitting aboard or standing next to the wagon. The street is unpaved and

TABLE 4.2. Basic Features of Persons Portrayed in the Underwood & Underwood and Helen Hamilton Gardener Collections of Photographs on Puerto Rico (in Percentages)

	Underwood & Underwood (N=98)	Helen Hamilton Gardener (N=155)
Type of portrayal		
Individual	14.3	10.3
Small group (0–5 persons)	32.7	31.6
Large group (6 or more persons)	20.4	24.5
No persons portrayed	31.6	32.9
Unable to determine	1.0	0.6
Gender		
Male	31.6	26.5
Female	7.1	13.5
Both male and female	21.4	26.5
No persons portrayed	31.6	32.9
Unable to determine	8.2	0.6
Age		
Children	1.0	9.0
Adults	37.8	40.6
Children and adults	16.3	16.8
No persons portrayed	31.6	32.9
Unable to determine	13.3	0.6
Skin color		
Mostly light skinned	9.2	25.2
Mostly dark skinned	12.2	13.5
Mixed colors	9.2	16.1
No persons portrayed	31.6	32.9
Unable to determine	37.8	12.3
Social status		
Primarily upper class	1.0	23.2
Primarily lower class	27.6	31.0
No persons portrayed	31.6	32.9
Unable to determine	39.8	12.9
Dress style		
Native costume	1.0	0.6
Informal	37.8	31.0
Formal	14.3	33.5
No persons portrayed	31.6	32.9
Unable to determine	15.3	1.9
Nudity		
Completely nude	2.0	0.6
Partially nude	1.0	1.9
Completely clothed	62.2	64.5
No persons portrayed	31.6	32.9
Unable to determine	3.1	0

TABLE 4.2. *continued*

	Underwood & Underwood (N=98)	Helen Hamilton Gardener (N=155)
Pose		
Standing	52.0	33.5
Sitting	9.2	13.5
Both standing and sitting	6.1	18.1
Other	1.0	1.9
No persons portrayed	31.6	32.9
Style		
Epic	1.0	1.3
Naturalistic	67.3	61.9
Romantic	0	3.9
No persons portrayed	31.6	32.9
Camera gaze		
Direct	31.6	25.8
Indirect	28.6	37.4
Both direct and indirect	4.1	3.9
No persons portrayed	31.6	32.9
Unable to determine	4.1	0
Vantage point of camera		
Frontal	54.1	74.8
Lateral	20.4	14.8
Above eye level	3.1	0.6
Bird's-eye view	22.4	9.7

Note: Some columns may not add up to 100 percent because of rounding.

full of rubbish. The whole image may be taken as a visual metaphor for the undeveloped state of the Puerto Rican economy, especially in light of American insistence on building a good network of roads and railways in the interior of the Island (Austin 1900; White 1898).

In another photograph a large, dark-skinned family in rural Cayey stands in front of a one-room hut, with a dog on one side and a sugar plantation in the background (figure 4.4). Like the previous photographs, this image establishes a strong visual linkage between being poor and having dark skin. Furthermore, the picture dwells on the contrast between the family's low standard of living and the apparent wealth of the surroundings. This image encapsulates Underwood & Underwood's description of the "humble home life of our Porto Rican cousins."

To many Americans, cockfights were bloody symbols of the barbaric customs

FIGURE 4.1. "Human poverty amidst nature's wealth—a beggar in Adjuntas." 1900 glass plate by Underwood & Underwood. Courtesy of the National Museum of American History, Smithsonian Institution.

FIGURE 4.2. "Porto Rican boys in their Sunday dress, near Aibonito." 1900 glass plate by Strohmeyer & Wyman, Underwood & Underwood Collection. Courtesy of the National Museum of American History, Smithsonian Institution.

FIGURE 4.3. "Rapid transit in Yauco." 1899 glass plate by Strohmeyer & Wyman,
Underwood & Underwood Collection. Courtesy of the National Museum of American
History, Smithsonian Institution.

associated with Spanish rule in Puerto Rico as well as in Cuba and the Philippines. According to a Protestant missionary, the Roman Catholic Church had
been an accomplice of Spain's oppressive government in tolerating the igno-
rance and poverty of the Puerto Rican population, as expressed in such popular
pastimes as gambling and cockfighting (Grose 1910). In Underwood & Under-

FIGURE 4.4. "Be it ever so humble, there's no place like home—Cayey." 1904 glass plate by Underwood & Underwood. Courtesy of the National Museum of American History, Smithsonian Institution.

wood's rendering, cockfighting appears as a male-dominated ritual for a racially mixed crowd, although three girls are also featured in the photograph (figure 4.5). Several barefoot boys surround the men who hold two roosters in the center of the image. This and other similar photographs were widely reproduced through stereocards and postcards, including an image preserved in the Gardener Collection.

Several Underwood & Underwood images focus on women, primarily from the lower class, including one of three young, dark-skinned women who pose in

FIGURE 4.5. "Cock fight—a favorite holiday sport at Yauco." Undated glass plate by Underwood & Underwood. Courtesy of the National Museum of American History, Smithsonian Institution.

the street of an unidentified Puerto Rican town (figure 4.6). These women do not strike a provocative pose for the camera but smile as if caught by surprise or perhaps as a sign of modesty. Moreover, the women's bare feet and the humble dwellings in the background suggest their working-class status. Yet their long, light-colored dresses, probably their best formal gowns, give them a dignified air. The title "dusky belles" suggests that, despite racial prejudices, women can be attractive as well as swarthy.

"Amidst the charms of Porto Rico" presents a field of full-grown pineapples in the foreground, with three light-skinned young women and five girls half-hidden in the background (figure 4.7). All the figures stand erect and fully clothed, roughly in chronological order, from youngest to oldest. (One girl's image is partly faded on the left side.) On the back of the stereocard was printed the following text: "These sweet-faced women and girls come of old Spanish stock and their social traditions are modifications of the Spanish." The photograph's composition suggests that its human subjects somehow grow out of the large pineapple groves, which dominate the entire scene. As if to foreground the visual connection between women and pineapples, the central figure holds a pineapple in front of her bosom. Both the caption and the image insinuate that native women, at least those of Spanish stock, are objects of pleasure, like tropical fruits.

The Underwood & Underwood series on Puerto Rico articulates many of the conventional codes for the visual representation of the Other, inherited from a long tradition in Western portrait painting. The photographers tend to adopt a strict realistic approach to document and translate Puerto Rican nature and culture to an American audience. They dwell on the islanders' rustic, rudimentary, and destitute way of life, characterized by sheer misery, undeveloped modes of transportation, primitive technology, and lack of industrial development. The photographers depict Puerto Ricans primarily as blacks and mulattoes, thus placing them at the lower rungs of human evolution in the dominant thinking of their time. In a well-worn, class-coded scheme, the camera approaches most subjects with a frontal shot, suggesting their weak position vis-à-vis the photographers (Lutz and Collins 1994). Visual contrasts between light and dark colors often frame a scene (Geary and Webb 1998).

Furthermore, the captions do not allow viewers to identify individually their subjects, who therefore appear as general human types. Since the mid–nineteenth century, ethnographic photographs tended to illustrate the physical and cultural characteristics of non-European racial groups, especially in

FIGURE 4.6. "Dusky belles, Porto Rico." Undated glass plate by Underwood & Underwood. Courtesy of the National Museum of American History, Smithsonian Institution.

FIGURE 4.7. "Amidst the charms of Porto Rico—delicious pineapples in the fields of Mayagüez." 1899 glass plate by Strohmeyer & Wyman, Underwood & Underwood Collection. Courtesy of the National Museum of American History, Smithsonian Institution.

colonial settings (Edwards 1990). Most of the subjects of these photographs thus become depersonalized representatives of an alien race and culture. When people are portrayed, they always appear full-bodied, never in a close-up. Because the vast majority of the pictures were taken from afar, they suggest a lack of intimacy between photographers and their subjects. After all, Puerto Ricans are nicknamed "cousins," not brothers and sisters, which implies a greater distance in kinship terms.[7]

At the same time, the Underwood & Underwood photographs are primarily set in cities rather than in the countryside, unlike most of the *National Geographic*'s images of African, Asian, and Latin American countries. Moreover, women and children are infrequent objects of the photographers' gaze. Naked views of seductive women are not part of the visual repertoire on Puerto Rico, as they were in such other colonial settings as Algeria, Samoa, or Tahiti. The photographers seldom portray their subjects as noble savages in danger of extinction, like American Indians. Nor do they often depict them engaging in ritual performances, as with many photographs of African cultures (Alloula 1986; Edwards 1992; Geary and Webb 1998; Lutz and Collins 1993; Spurr 1993). Instead, Puerto Ricans are mainly represented as backward, impoverished, uneducated, and dark-skinned people in need of imperial tutelage—Uncle Sam's burden.

CELEBRATING "OUR OUTLYING PORT OF CALL":
THE HELEN HAMILTON GARDENER COLLECTION

In contrast to the Underwood & Underwood Collection, the Helen Hamilton Gardener Photographic Collection was not assembled for commercial but for educational purposes. Unlike the Underwood & Underwood photographers, who were full-time professionals and freelancers, Gardener was an amateur photographer as well as a notable suffragist and progressive freethinker. Unlike the Underwood brothers, who roamed the entire world for visual images, Gardener had a personal link to Puerto Rico. On April 9, 1902, Gardener married Lieutenant Colonel Selden Allen Day, a veteran of the U.S. Civil War who supposedly "commanded the first U.S. troops that entered Porto Rico, and raised the first official American flag that floated in the island" during the Spanish-Cuban-American War (*Washington Post* 1902).[8] As commander of artillery and ordinance officer, Day helped to organize the first battalion of the Puerto Rican regiment under U.S. rule (Hardman 1999). Upon his retirement from active duty in July 1902, Day embarked with Gardener on a world-wide tour.

Gardener took hundreds of pictures of Puerto Rico as part of her comparative survey of twenty countries of the Caribbean, the Pacific, Asia, Africa, and Europe. Some of her photographs document the role of women in different cultures, as well as social class differences within each culture. Upon returning to the United States, she used the images to illustrate her lectures on "ourselves and other peoples" at many universities (Library of Congress 2000). Her lecture notes, preserved at the National Anthropological Archives (NAA), contain twenty-three index cards for Puerto Rico, ranging from its natural resources and tropical agriculture to its form of government and educational system under American rule. In one of her handwritten cards, Gardener noted: "In 5 years PR to be our outlying 'Port of Call' of all nations bound for Panama Canal. Will it be wise to have them antiAmerican [*sic*] then?" (Helen Hamilton Gardener Photographic Collection ca. 1906).

Born in Virginia in 1853 as Mary Alice Chenoweth, Helen Hamilton Gardener died in Washington, D.C., in 1925. A graduate of the Cincinnati (Ohio) Normal School, she studied biology at Columbia University and lectured in sociology at the Brooklyn Institute of Arts and Sciences. She wrote a book on freethinking, *Men, Women, and Gods, and Other Lectures* (1885), in which she criticized Christianity for its subordination of women. In the popular article "Sex in Brain" (1888), she countered the claim by former U.S. surgeon general William Hammond that the female brain was inferior to that of the male. Many of her magazine articles and short stories were gathered in six additional books published during her lifetime. In 1888 she joined the struggle for equal rights for women and was elected vice president of the National American Woman Suffrage Association (NAWSA) in 1917. Thereafter, she served as the chief liaison between NAWSA and the Wilson administration. In 1919 she represented NAWSA at the congressional signing of the Nineteenth Amendment granting American women the right to vote. In 1920 she became the first female member of the U.S. Civil Service Commission, the highest federal post occupied by a woman up to that time, a position she held until her death in 1925. She bequeathed her brain for study at Cornell University to prove that women's mental capacity was equal to that of men (*Encyclopaedia Britannica* 2000; Library of Congress 2000).

The NAA holds about fifteen hundred items in the Helen Hamilton Gardener

Photographic Collection, donated by her niece in 1926. The photographs include scenes from Egypt, Hawaii, Italy, Japan, Malaya, the Philippines, and Singapore, as well as Puerto Rico. The archives have 155 lantern slides on Puerto Rico, including the offshore municipality of Vieques, dated between 1899 and 1909, in addition to numerous photographic prints and albums.[9] Her images capture rare glimpses of daily life in Puerto Rico during the first decade of the twentieth century, featuring farms, schools, hospitals, parades, houses, and modes of transportation. Because of her connections to American civic and military leaders, her photographs also portray influential figures in the Island's colonial administration.[10] Because of her interest in cross-cultural human types, Gardener's collection documents how American travelers imagined Puerto Ricans and other peoples at the height of U.S. expansionism.

The second column of table 4.1 shows an inventory of Gardener's photographs of Puerto Rico.[11] Although Gardener herself took most of the pictures, she included several taken by Underwood & Underwood photographers as well as by her husband, Selden Allen Day; an earlier Smithsonian envoy, Paul Beckwith; and an Italian American photographer who lived in Puerto Rico, Attilio Moscioni.[12] Most of her pictures are dated between August 1901, when she first traveled to Puerto Rico to visit her future husband, and 1909, when they apparently returned as a married couple. Unlike the Underwood & Underwood Collection, Gardener's is set primarily in rural areas, with many scenes from Cayey, Coamo, and Vieques. Like the Underwood & Underwood Collection, about two-thirds of Gardener's photographs include people. Unlike the inconspicuous Underwood & Underwood photographers, Gardener frequently pictures herself and other nonnative men and women. She is also more interested in work activities, individual portraits, and trees and fruits. While the presence of animals is similar in the two cases, Gardener uses fewer proper names for places in her captions. However, she identifies more persons in her portraits, especially members of well-to-do white families such as the Palacios, Domenechs, Morales, Franceschis, Luchettis, McLeans, Vogels, and Wilsons.

Gardener's human subjects differ from those represented by Underwood & Underwood on several counts (second column of table 4.2). Although both collections focus on small groups of people, Gardener includes more children, women, and mixed-gender groups. With regard to skin color and social class, her portraits range more widely than do those of Underwood & Underwood. More people in Gardener's photographs wear formal clothes, but fewer are standing. In both cases, only a very small proportion of the subjects are completely or partially nude, usually infant boys. Although the dominant pose in both collections is naturalistic, subjects gaze indirectly at the camera in Gardener's more frequently than in Underwood & Underwood's. Furthermore, Gardener takes fewer bird's-eye views and more frontal shots.

Unlike commercially oriented photographers, Gardener is much more interested in people than in empty places. Even when she focuses on historical monuments such as the Columbus statue in San Juan, she features a large group of men and women, adults and children, of different colors. Her collection also includes views of the governor's mansion and the San Jerónimo and San Cristóbal Forts in San Juan, the customhouse in Vieques, and the military road between San Juan and Ponce. In most cases, human figures are central to the composition of such tourist and even military sites.

The rugged figure of the jíbaro is the protagonist of a scene misnamed "Military road" (figure 4.8). Here, a barefoot, light-skinned peasant sits on a donkey or mule, carrying two saddle baskets full of cut vegetation, framed on both sides by large trees and smaller bushes. Visually, the wilderness engulfs the small man and his animal, but still the man manages to smile. The photographer's wide-angle shot frames the scene from a long-distance perspective that focuses on the unpaved road. This photograph, which may have been taken by the Smithsonian's Beckwith, fixes the icon of the stoic and noble highland peasant that has inspired so much of the nationalist discourse in Puerto Rico (see Chapters 1 and 6). The image resonates strongly with the beginning of Rafael Hernández's classic song "Lamento borincano" (1929), in which "the little jíbaro departs, beside himself with joy, with his load, for the city."

In a striking image, a dark-skinned boy in rags and without shoes represents a street merchant in Vieques (figure 4.9). This photograph resonates with the caption that an American travel writer composed for another publication: "Street merchants in this island carry about, not only the wares that are common to peddlers in our own cities, but all sorts of peculiar things as strange as the hucksters themselves" (White 1898: 331). The young boy in this picture is selling local drink and food products, probably candies, outside a wooden frame building. He sits comfortably, a hat on his lap and legs crossed. His meager merchandise has been placed atop a barrel and a few boxes. Despite his precarious situation, he offers a contented smile to the camera. This image forms part of an extensive repertoire of urban curiosities, including street eccentrics, blacks, children, vendors, artisans, and indigenous people in native dress (Levine 1989).

FIGURE 4.8. "Military road." Undated photograph, Helen Hamilton Gardener Collection. Courtesy of the National Museum of Natural History, Smithsonian Institution.

FIGURE 4.9. "Street merchant, Viequez." 1901 photograph, Helen Hamilton Gardener
Collection. Courtesy of the National Museum of Natural History,
Smithsonian Institution.

An often-reprinted photograph portrays a dark-skinned woman implausibly
using a sewing machine in the streets of San Juan (figure 4.10). The only one in
the scene who does not look directly at the camera, the young seamstress glances
away to one side, smiling. Sitting on the cobblestone floor, she is surrounded by
barrels, baskets, and crates. The staged scene includes a large group of young
children, presumably related to the woman, in a nearby doorway and on the
street. Their poverty is suggested by their bare feet, crowded housing conditions,
and an infant's nudity. The conspicuous absence of a male head of household is
punctuated by a man who poses defiantly from the next door.

Another photograph shows a large group of poor, dark-skinned people near
the San Juan market (figure 4.11). Several men and children squat near two
chickens and a rooster, while three naked boys look toward the camera. At least
thirty-five people appear in this image, making it one of the most densely
populated in the entire collection. The most striking figure in this photograph
is a well-dressed white man, probably an American, pointing his finger at one of
the children with a serious expression on his face. His standing pose as well as

FIGURE 4.10. "Street scene. San Juan." 1901 photograph, Helen Hamilton Gardener Collection. Courtesy of the National Museum of Natural History, Smithsonian Institution.

his marginal position in the group scene suggest an enormous class, racial, and ethnic distance from the natives. The physical separation between the white man and the other subjects becomes a metaphor for the cultural gap between the colonizer and the colonized (Edwards 1992). However, the well-dressed man occupies the center of attention because of the photograph's composition and perspective: the building's architectural lines point directly toward him, converging around his head. This image was reproduced in another family album (Díaz Quiñones 2000) and may have been taken by an unnamed professional photographer.

Unlike the Underwood & Underwood photographers, Gardener often renders U.S. colonialism in Puerto Rico highly visible. Several of her images record the American political and economic occupation of the Island in the wake of the Spanish-Cuban-American War. Although the U.S. military presence is largely ignored, it is documented in a few photographs. Like Under-

FIGURE 4.11. "The market. San Juan." 1901 glass plate, Helen Hamilton Gardener Collection. Courtesy of the National Museum of Natural History, Smithsonian Institution.

wood & Underwood, Gardener features a standard view with the caption, "First landing place, July 25, 1898. Guanica," but she adds more personal images: "The two who ran up the first flag. (Albezu [*sic*]. Day)" and "The two first settlers, American occupation—Vogel, Day" (figure 4.12). Her photo album includes a picture captioned "Native soldiers drilling. Under American rule," possibly taken by her husband (figure 4.13).

Gardener's lantern slides also contain views of several public schools, founded by the U.S. government on the Island. One such photograph presents the Magüeyes rural school in Coamo, founded in 1908, with an American flag flying on one side. Others depict the McKinley School in San Juan, the Normal School in Río Piedras, and the Industrial School in Ponce. In one of her lecture notes on Puerto Rico, Gardener wrote that public education was "America's one *great* gift to PR," echoing the caption of an Underwood & Underwood photograph (Helen Hamilton Gardener Photographic Collection ca. 1906).

FIGURE 4.12. "The two first settlers, American occupation—Vogel, Day." Undated photograph by Helen Hamilton Gardener. Courtesy of the Center for Historical Research, University of Puerto Rico.

Similarly, Moscioni, who worked freelance for various U.S. government agencies, featured at least thirteen American public schools throughout the Island. The massive expansion of public education was also considered the hallmark of American rule in the Philippines during the first half of the twentieth century (McCoy 2000).

Gardener's vision of Puerto Rico includes a broad spectrum of persons of different classes, colors, ages, and genders. Because of her husband's social

FIGURE 4.13. "Native soldiers drilling. Under American rule." Undated photograph, Helen Hamilton Gardener Collection. Courtesy of the Center for Historical Research, University of Puerto Rico.

networks as well as her own background, Gardener had privileged access to the Island's colonial administrators, including the American governor and his council, and the Creole elite, including prominent families from Ponce, Coamo, and Yauco.[13] In one photograph, she portrayed two light-skinned "native girls" of the upper class, sitting in their comfortable living room, surrounded by family pictures and elegant furnishings. An older woman (presumably their mother) stands behind the girls, while another female figure (probably a maid) is partially suppressed on one side (figure 4.14). Domestic scenes such as this one suggest that Gardener gained more rapport with her upper-class subjects than did most professional photographers.

Like other ethnographic photographs of the time, Gardener's images of Puerto Rico are full of exotic references to the tropical environment. Many of her pictures exalt the Island's abundant flora and fauna, especially the flamboyant, coconut, banana, grapefruit, and breadfruit trees, as well as pineapple, sugar, coffee, and tobacco plants. Two carefully staged still lifes display seventeen varieties of tropical fruits and four coconuts, whole and halved. Together with a host of images featuring landscapes, a sunset, and moonlight, Gardener's

FIGURE 4.14. "Native girls. Upper class." Undated glass plate by Helen Hamilton Gardener. Courtesy of the National Museum of Natural History, Smithsonian Institution.

romantic fascination with the Island's vegetation suggests an unspoiled Eden-like nature. Tributes to Puerto Rico's lavish foliage, ideal climate, and natural beauty were common among American travel writers (La Gorce 1924; White 1898).[14] Like those of Underwood & Underwood, Gardener's photographs show humans and animals in close proximity and harmony, in an economy dominated by agriculture and cattle-raising. In one of her lecture notes she commented that "P.R. is famous in all West India islands for her fine cattle" (Helen Hamilton Gardener Photographic Collection ca. 1906).

Ultimately, the Gardener Collection tends to legitimize American hegemony in Puerto Rico. Despite its poverty, Puerto Rico is represented as a valuable U.S. acquisition and the Island's inhabitants as dignified and hard-working subjects. Gardener devotes more than two dozen photographs to illustrating how natives ply their trades, including plowing sugarcane, harvesting tobacco, drying coffee, winnowing rice, husking coconuts, delivering milk,

FIGURE 4.15. "Milk dealer. The support of two families." Undated glass plate by Helen Hamilton Gardener. Courtesy of the National Museum of Natural History, Smithsonian Institution.

making baskets, and weaving hats (see figures 4.15 and 4.16). Although these work activities were considered exotic from an American standpoint, widespread misery was clearly not the result of lack of native industry. United States colonial officials often attributed the Island's economic woes to inadequate schooling, sanitation, and roads, as well as the evils of Spanish administration (Taft 1907; Willoughby 1905). An American correspondent put it bluntly: "To

FIGURE 4.16. "Weaving 'Panama' hats. Learning the stitch." Undated photograph by
Helen Hamilton Gardener. Courtesy of the Center for Historical Research,
University of Puerto Rico.

nothing but Spanish rule can be charged the primitive conditions of the beautiful island and its backward place in history and in the affairs of the world"
(White 1898: 309). According to a U.S. government official, progress and prosperity would ensue from the application of "American principles" of public
administration (Willoughby 1905: 80), namely, the efficient organization of
human resources and rational planning for physical infrastructure.

As *National Geographic* later noted, "A benevolent government is trying to
do all it can to improve [the jíbaro's] lot, to carry to him whatever it can of the
blessings of health, education, and happiness" (La Gorce 1924: 627). Accordingly, Gardener profiles Puerto Rican children in public schools, youngsters in
industrial schools, and adults in prisons, learning skills and subjects ranging
from embroidery and shoemaking to literature and science. Other photographs

depict St. Luke's Hospital in Ponce, founded by an American, Dr. Vogel, and the Anemia Hospital in Utuado, founded by Dr. Bailey K. Ashford.[15] According to the editor of *National Geographic*, "Perhaps the greatest achievement of American control [of Puerto Rico] is the discovery of Drs Ashford and King, by means of which the people can be cured of tropical anemia" (Grosvenor 1906: 712). Note that the latter quote emphasizes American external agency and passive acceptance by Puerto Ricans, two key rhetorical elements of U.S. colonial discourse.

In sum, Gardener's images portray a colonial administration altruistically concerned with the natives' welfare, much as Taft (1907) and Willoughby (1905) had proclaimed during the same period. From this perspective, American rule over the Island had quickly developed its natural and human resources, especially in agriculture, trade, transportation, education, and health. Unlike other photographic collections, Gardener's does not erase the local upper class from its representations of Puerto Rico; on the contrary, this class becomes one of the main objects of her gaze. Gardener celebrates the presence of a Creole elite of Spanish and Corsican descendants as attractive for well-to-do travelers like herself. Her sympathetic portrait of Puerto Ricans—especially those from lighter-skinned and wealthier families—suggests that they could assimilate into American culture and thereby attain a higher standard of living and civilization. With American capital and technology, Puerto Rico would become a thriving port of call in the Caribbean. In turn, she warned, it would be vital for U.S. security interests to maintain a stronghold in Puerto Rico once the Panama Canal was completed. As Maxwell (1999: 186) argues (citing Sarah Graham-Brown), "The white women who visited foreign places wielding cameras did not necessarily produce images of the colonized that were less condescending than those of men."

CONCLUSION

Analysis of ethnographic photographs as historical documents has shed light on the visual representation of non-Western peoples, especially during the high period of European and U.S. colonialism between 1860 and 1920. Such images helped to construct and divulge racial, class, and gender stereotypes about other cultures, as well as to advance Western imperialism throughout the world. Colonial administrators, missionaries, scientists, journalists, and the general public extensively used photographs to describe, classify, and explain physical and cultural differences (Banta and Hinsley 1986; Edwards 1992; Scherer 1992). Together with other forms of written and visual representation, photographs tended to portray the Other as inferior, primitive, childlike, effeminate, exotic, and erotic. However, not all subject groups were equally othered, nor were they placed in the same stage of human evolution according to Western standards.

The Puerto Rican images assembled by the two American collections examined in this chapter belong to a broader genre of ethnographic photography, but they have their own peculiarities. Neither the Underwood & Underwood Collection nor the Helen Hamilton Gardener Collection characterizes Puerto Ricans as entirely different, savage, exotic, or erotic. Overall, Puerto Ricans appear as content and domesticated colonial subjects, redeemable through hard work, public health, and education. Both collections commemorate the Island's rich Spanish architecture and urban heritage, especially in San Juan and Ponce. Moreover, their photographs show that past human actions have tamed nature, especially how certain export crops—such as sugar, coffee, and tobacco—have transformed the rural landscape. Thus, the Island could not easily be visualized as empty space, virgin territory, or untamed wilderness. Although they depict most Puerto Ricans as poor and dark skinned, the two collections recognize that they live in "places made famous by men of four centuries ago," in the marketing phrase coined by Underwood & Underwood. Neither of the two collections dwell on female nudity, which abounds in photographic collections of other peoples, such as those of the Philippines or Algeria. Gardener's vision of Puerto Rico is notably devoid of any erotic—or, for that matter, androcentric—connotations.

One may speculate about the practical implications of portraying the Other in this manner. Certainly, sympathetic but paternalistic characterizations of "our Porto Rican cousins," "our outlying port of call," "our little island in the West Indies," and "our beautiful El Dorado of the Antilles" help to explain the much longer American presence on the Island than in other former U.S. overseas territories, such as Cuba or the Philippines. The dominant representation of Puerto Ricans as a friendly, polite, hospitable, docile, law-abiding, and industrious people, who welcomed the American occupation of their country, domesticated their otherness and made them exemplary colonial subjects (see, for example, Carroll 1899). Such images endured throughout the twentieth century, especially through advertising campaigns promoting U.S. investment and tourism on the Island. The two photographic collections examined in this chapter suggest that, at least since the Spanish-Cuban-American War, Americans have imagined Puerto Ricans to be different from themselves, both racially and culturally, but not so different as others. Yet, unlike Hawaii or Alaska,[16] Puerto Rico has not become a state of the Union; it is still an unincorporated territory of the United States. Today, colonial encounters between Americans and Puerto Ricans continue to be premised on mutual perceptions of difference as well as identity. After more than a century of U.S. rule, the Island remains outside the imagined community of the American nation, too familiar to be entirely alien, too alien to be entirely familiar.

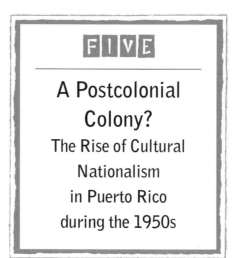

FIVE

A Postcolonial Colony?
The Rise of Cultural Nationalism in Puerto Rico during the 1950s

After World War II, the decolonization movement swept throughout Asia, Africa, and later the Caribbean.[1] One after another, former European and American colonies—beginning with Indonesia, the Philippines, and India in the 1940s and ending with the Marshall Islands in the 1990s—obtained their independence. Today, only a few politically dependent territories remain in the world, especially in the Caribbean and the Pacific. Although the United Nations officially removed Puerto Rico from its list of colonies in 1953, the Island's political status has been intensely contested in international forums as well as in the U.S. Congress and in Puerto Rico itself. Perhaps, to use the paradoxical term suggested by Juan Flores (2000), Puerto Rico has become a "postcolonial colony," in which traditional forms of external domination (such as direct metropolitan control over the Island's government) have been replaced by neo-, late, or *lite* colonialism (in the sense of indirect rule and some measure of local autonomy, especially in cultural and linguistic affairs).

In 1952, Puerto Rico was officially declared an Estado Libre Asociado (Free Associated State) or Commonwealth, as it became known in English, of the United States. The brainchild of Luis Muñoz Marín and the Popular Democratic Party (PDP, founded in 1938), commonwealth was originally supposed to be a transitory, intermediate status between full independence and complete annexation as a state of the Union. Under this arrangement, the Island's electorate would approve its own constitution, select its own government, and pass its own laws, as long as they did not conflict with those of the United States. The Commonwealth would also administer its own programs in education, culture, language, health, housing, and taxation, among other local matters. However, the federal government retained jurisdiction over most state affairs, including citizenship, immigration, customs, defense, currency, transportation, communications, and foreign trade. Although Puerto Ricans elect a resident commissioner to Congress, they do not have their own voting representatives or senators in Washington. Even though Puerto Ricans cannot vote for the president of the United States, they are bound to serve in the U.S. armed forces like any other citizens. While Island residents do not pay federal taxes, they qualify for most federally funded programs, including nutritional assistance and welfare benefits. Such contradictory elements may well warrant the term "postcolonial colony" to describe Puerto Rico's problematic relationship with the United States.

Be that as it may, cultural nationalism became the ideology of the Estado Libre Asociado during the 1950s. The Commonwealth's first legislative acts were to proclaim the national flag and anthem as official symbols of the Island, and an official seal quickly followed. Since 1948, Puerto Rico has participated as a separate country in Olympic sports competitions and later in other international events such as the Miss Universe Beauty Pageant (Morris 1995). In 1955 the establishment of the Institute of Puerto Rican Culture consolidated the project of defining, promoting, and defending national identity. Scholars, writers, and artists were recruited to codify the values, symbols, rituals, and practices that would represent the Puerto Rican nation to itself and to the world. In his 1959 Godkin Lectures at Harvard University, Governor Muñoz Marín used the expression Operation Serenity to describe the government's effort to rescue the Island's traditional culture, as a counterpart to Operation Bootstrap, which promoted the Island's industrialization.

I approach cultural nationalism as a distinct type of political movement, characterized by the moral regeneration of a community imagined as a nation by its leading intellectuals, against the intrusion of foreign values and practices (Hutchinson 1994). Like political nationalists, cultural nationalists emphasize a unique history, culture, language, and geography as the essence of the nation, but unlike political nationalists, they do not necessarily advocate the creation of a sovereign state to embody their ideals. Rather, cultural nationalists typically proclaim the spiritual autonomy of their nation by commemorating their heritage, celebrating their rituals, rescuing their traditions, and educating the people. Cultural nationalism is usually a small-scale movement, primarily appealing to an intellectual minority. At least initially, its major proponents are writers, artists, and other scholars—especially historians, archaeologists, and folklorists—"who combine a 'romantic' search for meaning with a scientific zeal to establish this on authoritative foundations" (Hutchinson 1994: 123). In contemporary Puerto Rico, however, cultural nationalism has acquired a massive following, for reasons that have not been well documented.

In this chapter I examine some of the momentous changes in the dominant representations of national identity on the Island in the postwar period. The leading political figure in Puerto Rico, Luis Muñoz Marín, sought to affirm and preserve the Island's cultural "personality," especially as expressed through the Spanish language, against increasing Americanization. At the same time, Muñoz Marín's PDP deepened the Island's political and economic dependency on the United States. Prominent intellectuals, including anthropologists Ricardo Alegría and Eugenio Fernández Méndez, attempted to reconcile the Commonwealth's official ideology of cultural nationalism with continued association with the United States. Such scholar-activists functioned as intellectual intermediaries between the Creole governing elite and the lower classes in the contested terrain of culture. Cultural nationalism served to ally various sectors of Puerto Rican society to renegotiate the conditions of U.S. colonialism after World War II.

The foundational role of public intellectuals in the construction and representation of national identity has been largely taken for granted on the Island. Much has been written about Muñoz Marín's turn to cultural nationalism and his growing ideological opposition to Albizu Campos's political nationalism during the 1940s and 1950s (Alvarez-Curbelo and Rodríguez Castro 1993; Carrión 1996; García Passalacqua 1998). Much less has been written about the work of a small but influential clique of intellectuals—such as the historian Arturo Morales Carrión, the folklorist Teodoro Vidal, and the anthropologist Ricardo Alegría—who influenced Muñoz Marín's thinking on national identity and helped to put it into practice (see Ramírez 1976, 1985). As a result, prior studies have not fully addressed how various forms of scholarly—especially ethnographic and archaeological—knowledge legitimated the Commonwealth's representation of Puerto Rican identity. Yet, in hindsight, many of the government's cultural policies were informed by concepts of culture, nation, identity, heritage, and patrimony prevalent in the social sciences during the 1950s. Such usually restricted discussions attained much broader public proportions as a result of local scholars' participation in the newly created government.

In this chapter I examine the resonance of Muñoz Marín's discourse on national culture in the work of the two most important Puerto Rican anthropologists of their generation: Ricardo Alegría and Eugenio Fernández Méndez. All three shared a common ideological framework on Puerto Ricanness, largely derived from the canon of the Generation of 1930 (see Chapter 1). However, Alegría and Fernández Méndez added a new twist to cultural nationalism, based on their professional background as anthropologists. Both scholars were consciously reacting to colonial discourses that berated the Island's culture during the first half of the twentieth century. In particular, they contested the negative portrayal of Puerto Ricans by American anthropologists such as Fewkes, whose work I discussed in Chapter 3. At the same time, they continued to privilege the Hispanic and indigenous background of Puerto Rican culture at the expense of its African components.

Anthropological ideas and practices—including the notion of culture, the revaluation of folklore, the preservation of the historical patrimony, the foundation of ethnographic and archaeological museums, and the defense of the vernacular language—became key elements of cultural nationalism in Puerto Rico, as in other colonial and postcolonial countries. Such ideas and practices helped to document and objectify the uniqueness, wealth, and antiquity of Puerto Rican culture vis-à-vis American culture. Hence, anthropology was re-fashioned as part of a larger movement to remove the last vestiges of colonialism on the Island, at least in the cultural sphere. In Puerto Rico as in other countries, the assertion of a separate national identity was one of the multiple forms of struggle against foreign domination (Chatterjee 1995).

AGAPITO'S BAR: PRESERVING PUERTO RICO'S CULTURAL PERSONALITY

Luis Muñoz Marín (1898–1980) was Puerto Rico's foremost political leader during the twentieth century. He was born in San Juan into a prominent autonomist family; his father had been Puerto Rico's minister of grace, justice, and government under the Island's brief autonomy with Spain in 1897 and was later elected resident commissioner in the United States. Muñoz Marín spent most of his childhood and youth commuting between Washington, D.C., New York City, and Puerto Rico. After studying law at Columbia University and journalism at Georgetown University, he became an active supporter of independence and socialism for the Island. During the 1920s, he worked as a journalist and director of the San Juan–based newspaper *La Democracia*, then went back to New York. In 1931 he moved permanently to Puerto Rico and a year later was elected senator from the pro-independence Liberal Party. He founded the PDP in 1938; he was elected president of the Senate in 1940 and became the first elected governor of Puerto Rico in 1948. During the 1940s he abandoned his support for independence, embraced the idea of autonomy, and moved away from political nationalism to cultural nationalism. In 1952 he proclaimed the Commonwealth of Puerto Rico as a noncolonial pact with the United States. After winning four consecutive terms, he retired from the governorship in 1964 and served as senator until 1970. When his party lost the 1976 elections, he retired from public life. Thousands of Puerto Ricans mourned his death in 1980.

In several speeches, essays, and notes written during the 1950s, Muñoz Marín developed his own blueprint for cultural nationalism. First, he thought that the nation was the "natural space" in which a people's identity could flourish in the contemporary world. Second, he believed that it was possible to develop a strong, original, and well-defined personality without resorting to political nationalism. Third, he asserted that Puerto Rico's collective personality was compatible with commonwealth status. Fourth, he held that it was "natural" that some traits of the Island's culture would be modified in contact with the mainland. Finally, he coined the term "Operation Serenity," "which means to have social and spiritual objectives as the goals of the economy, the freedom from tensions due to struggles for social status, a superior scale of values, it also means the ability to adjust to an inevitable system of automation (?), benefitting the personality and good social and spiritual values" (Muñoz Marín n.d.).

Muñoz Marín delivered an impassioned speech at the annual meeting of the Teachers Association of Puerto Rico in 1953. Titled "The Puerto Rican Personality under Commonwealth," it was quickly dubbed "Agapito's Bar speech" because of its memorable reference to a commercial sign in an island town that read "Agapito's Bar" in English. In this speech, Muñoz Marín (1985) outlined his personal views as well as his government's stance toward Puerto Rican identity and its vernacular. Along with the Island's political association with the United States, Muñoz Marín advocated the preservation of a Puerto Rican "personality," the term he preferred to "culture." Muñoz Marín concluded by defending the continued use of the Spanish language in Puerto Rico because, in his own words, "language is the breath of the spirit" (107).

Muñoz Marín's discourse on the Puerto Rican "personality" was a key moment in the development of cultural nationalism on the Island during the

1950s. Under his tutelage, the Commonwealth government sought to buttress its international reputation as a postcolonial arrangement. By promoting Puerto Rican culture from the new state apparatus, Muñoz Marín articulated the concerns of much of the Creole intelligentsia since the mid–nineteenth century and especially since the 1930s (Aguiló Ramos 1987). Thus, many of the Island's leading writers, artists, and teachers supported the Commonwealth's cultural project during the 1950s.

Muñoz Marín's concept of culture was consistently elusive, inclusive, and idealistic. In 1940 he defined it broadly "as the attitude of a community—which can be a world, a hemisphere, or an island—as the bonding together [*trabazón*] of ways of living life" (Muñoz Marín 1975b: 791). In 1952 he continued to describe culture in moral and poetic terms, as "the growth [*cultivo*] that acquires a natural charter in our ideals of life and our ways of achieving them, in the daily conception of good and evil, duty and right, creating and acquiring, giving and taking" (Muñoz Marín 1975a: 805). In the 1953 Agapito's Bar speech, he referred to culture "not in the literary, scientific, artistic sense, but in the broadest [sense], which includes these, of all the attitudes, habits, values of a human community" (Muñoz Marín 1985: 99). The new Commonwealth government, through its cultural institutions, would define more precisely the "attitudes, habits, values" that constituted Puerto Rican identity.

Muñoz Marín's approach included a strong belief in the need to transform national culture. Contrary to the conservative stance of much of the Island's intellectual elite, Muñoz Marín held that some traditional customs and attitudes—especially those impeding economic development—had to be discarded in the name of progress and modernity. In the Agapito's Bar speech, he argued that Puerto Ricans should develop a stricter work discipline, apply more scientific knowledge to the cultivation of land, and create a more efficient commercial distribution system. To this extent, Muñoz Marín departed from the essentialist definition of culture conceived as a static collective property or historical patrimony (Kerkhof 2000). Regarding "spiritual" rather than "material" culture, however, he shared many of the standard nationalistic concerns. For example, Muñoz Marín conceded that the Spanish language was a cornerstone of Puerto Ricanness and, as such, should be cherished and preserved. He also argued that the question of political status should be separated from the development of national culture. As Muñoz Marín wrote in an undated manuscript, asserting the "personality of our people is not in any way contrary to or incompatible with their good and sincere and free association with the U.S."

Since the early 1950s, Muñoz Marín had expressed the concern that growing Americanization brought about by industrialization was undermining the Island's personality. As a result, the governor became increasingly vocal in his public pronouncements on national identity. In 1960 he told an audience of Puerto Rican migrants in New York City that "at no moment whatsoever should you stop feeling Puerto Rican and proud to call yourselves Puerto Rican. The first thing you have to do is to preserve the sense that you're Puerto Rican and that Puerto Rico is worthy" (Muñoz Marín 1960). On the mainland, the Commonwealth government encouraged Puerto Rican migrants to adapt to American culture without surrendering their own national identity (see Chapter 7). On the Island, the government actively promoted such collective pride and sense of worth. The strategy proved immensely popular, as the PDP won all the Island's elections from 1940 to 1968.

In short, Muñoz Marín's espousal of cultural nationalism was an ambivalent but shrewd maneuver. On the one hand, he realized that the Commonwealth had to affirm the Island's cultural autonomy to gain local as well as international support as a noncolonial formula. Thus, he proposed that Puerto Rican identity—especially its Hispanic heritage—should be conserved and promoted, as many pro-independence intellectuals demanded. On the other hand, Muñoz Marín was convinced that the Island's progress depended on continued political association with the United States. Hence, everyday practices and values would undergo increasing Americanization, which many statehood supporters celebrated. These two contradictory impulses in Muñoz Marín's thinking about cultural identity were expressed in his two main projects, Operation Serenity and Operation Bootstrap, in which the latter clearly gained the upper hand, although he often claimed that the former was equally important. Other intellectuals and policymakers, such as Ricardo Alegría, would tease out the practical implications of Operation Serenity.

DECLARING THE DOMAIN OF THE SPIRITUAL AS SOVEREIGN TERRAIN

Born in San Juan in 1921, Ricardo Alegría was raised in an upper-class family with strong patriotic convictions: his father had been one of the founders of the Nationalist Party. After earning a bachelor's degree in history at the University of Puerto Rico, he obtained an M.A. in archaeology from the University of Chicago and a Ph.D. from Harvard University. In 1947 he founded the Center for

Archaeological Research and later directed the Museum of Anthropology, History, and Art at the University of Puerto Rico. In 1955 he became the first executive director of the Institute of Puerto Rican Culture, a post he held until 1973. After directing the Governor's Office for Cultural Affairs, in 1977 he reorganized the Center for Advanced Studies of Puerto Rico and the Caribbean, which he directed until 2001. In 1992 he founded the Museum of the Americas in Old San Juan. In addition to holding multiple administrative positions, Alegría has published widely in the field of anthropology, especially in archaeology. His most important works include a pioneering ethnography of the feast of St. James the Apostle in Loíza (Alegría 1954); a widely read textbook on the history of the Taíno Indians (Alegría 1950); and archaeological essays on the pre-Columbian population of Puerto Rico and the Caribbean (Alegría 1983).

Despite his nationalistic inclinations, Alegría collaborated actively with the PDP and especially with Muñoz Marín. As the founding director of the Institute of Puerto Rican Culture, Alegría played a pivotal role in the formulation and implementation of the Commonwealth's cultural policies. Under his leadership, the institute closely identified the official version of Puerto Rican culture with the autonomist tradition dating back to the second half of the nineteenth century (Díaz Quiñones 1993). Accepting the 1953 United Nations resolution declaring commonwealth a noncolonial form of association with the United States, Alegría (1965) held that Puerto Rican identity could flourish under the present political status, although he personally preferred an independent or associated republic. Nonetheless, he supported the Commonwealth's cultural nationalism, which he helped to put into practice. In a statement prepared for the 1966 United States–Puerto Rico Status Commission, Alegría (1965: 13) argued that "with the creation of the Commonwealth, our Government made clear its firm purpose of favoring the conservation of our national culture. It was clearly established that Puerto Rico's political association with the United States did not imply the country's resignation to its identity. This orientation of our Government was clearly manifested in the creation, in 1955, of the Institute of Puerto Rican Culture, an autonomous institution devoted to the conservation, enrichment, and diffusion of national culture." Muñoz Marín, then a senator and member of the status commission, agreed with the gist of Alegría's presentation, though not with his stance toward political status. According to Muñoz Marín, Puerto Rico was a nation in the cultural but not in the juridical sense, and most Puerto Ricans did not support political nationalism.

Alegría elaborated many of the ideological premises of the official discourse on Puerto Rican identity during the 1950s. First, he deployed a broad anthropological definition of culture, including folk and elite expressions, one centered on the people's intellectual, moral, and spiritual values. Second, he denounced the colonial depreciation of local values, as well as their erosion by "harmful, unnecessary, and superfluous" influences from abroad, especially the United States (Alegría 1971b: 15). Third, Alegría defined the essence of contemporary Puerto Rican culture as the harmonious integration of aboriginal, Spanish, and African traditions, prior to the U.S. invasion of the Island in 1898. Finally, he argued that the basic source of Puerto Rican identity was Hispanic and that the Spanish vernacular should be the primary language of instruction in both public and private schools on the Island (Alegría 1954, 1970 [1963]). Echoing Muñoz Marín, Alegría (1965: 15) wrote that "the soul of every culture is the language in which it manifests itself."

Each of these ideas would be executed through specific programs and activities sponsored by the Institute of Puerto Rican Culture. In its first eighteen years the institute implemented Alegría's two-pronged view of culture, focusing on "high" culture (such as creative literature, concert music, plastic arts, and colonial architecture), while supporting a wide range of popular practices (such as oral traditions, peasant music and dance, folk religious sculpture, and cultural festivals) (Alegría 1996b). Together with public schools and local universities, the institute became one of the privileged sites for the production and dissemination of nationalist narratives of the Island's history and culture. The founding myth of the ethnic and racial triad (Indian, Spanish, and African) was visually encoded in the institute's official seal. The cult of Hispanic heritage, especially the promotion of the Spanish language, became not only the concern of an intellectual minority but also a state-supported project with a broad impact on the population (see Aguiló Ramos 1987; Dávila 1997; García Passalacqua 1998).

Thus, Alegría was the only anthropologist (with the partial exception of Eugenio Fernández Méndez) to hold a powerful government position in postwar Puerto Rico. Alegría's thinking shaped many of the Commonwealth's policies toward national culture, especially language, folklore, and the arts. Much of the state legislation since 1952 has promoted the conservation of the historical patrimony through the creation of public monuments, museums, parks, libraries, archives, publications, and recordings. Many historic sites, such as La Fortaleza in San Juan and the Capá site in Utuado, were developed and preserved during Alegría's tenure at the Institute of Puerto Rican Culture. In 1958 the institute embarked on an ambitious project to restore Old San Juan as a historic zone. By the end of the 1960s, the Puerto Rican people had acquired a clearly defined iconography consisting of a historical patrimony, patriotic commemorations, representative symbols, and foundational myths, which characterize nations everywhere (Smith 1986).

Despite some ideological discrepancies, Alegría and Muñoz Marín shared the basic principles of cultural nationalism. Both believed that Puerto Rican identity (or personality) could be maintained and promoted under commonwealth status. Both held that the Spanish language should be cultivated as a foundation of that identity. Both rejected colonial discourses, which valued all things foreign at the expense of native customs. Finally, both stressed the moral and spiritual values of their people, not just the literary and artistic accomplishments of a small educated elite. Like other anticolonial intellectuals, Muñoz Marín and Alegría "declare[d] the domain of the spiritual [their] sovereign territory and refuse[d] to allow the colonial power to intervene in that domain" (Chatterjee 1993: 6). While Muñoz Marín outlined the broad contours of the Commonwealth's cultural project, Alegría fleshed them out during the first two decades after the 1952 constitution. Another anthropologist, Eugenio Fernández Méndez, was one of the major intellectual authors of that project.

"CULTURALLY PUERTO RICAN, POLITICALLY AMERICAN": CREATING A PUERTO RICAN CIVILIZATION

Eugenio Fernández Méndez (1924–94) was born in Cayey to a distinguished autonomist family. He earned his B.A. degree in economics at the University of Puerto Rico and pursued graduate studies in anthropology at Columbia University. In 1949 he began a long career as professor of social sciences at the University of Puerto Rico. In 1955 Governor Muñoz Marín named him to the first Board of Directors of the Institute of Puerto Rican Culture, over which he presided until 1964. He also served as director of the University of Puerto Rico Press between 1956 and 1964. He continued to teach anthropology until his retirement in 1979. His extensive list of publications includes several polemical essays on Puerto Rican identity (Fernández Méndez 1955, 1959); anthologies of Spanish, Puerto Rican, and American writers on Puerto Rico (Fernández Méndez 1954, 1957, 1973, 1975); a comprehensive cultural history (Fernández Méndez 1964); and a monograph on the art and mythology of the Taíno Indians (Fernández Méndez 1972).

If Alegría was the leading applied anthropologist employed by the Commonwealth government, Fernández Méndez was one of its most influential cultural advisers. Like Alegría, Fernández Méndez was actively engaged in rewriting Puerto Rican history from an autonomist perspective that resonated strongly with the PDP's ideology. Unlike Alegría, Fernández Méndez retained his primary professional identity as a teacher and scholar, rather than as a public official. Also unlike Alegría, he identified closely with commonwealth as the final solution to the Island's colonial status. Still, his personal and ideological ties to Alegría, as well as to Muñoz Marín, were strong and lasting. He too was a convinced cultural nationalist.

One of the recurring themes in Fernández Méndez's work is the binary opposition between American and Puerto Rican cultures. On the one hand, he characterized the contemporary United States as an industrial, financial, and commercial capitalist economy, with a large-scale and mechanized system of production and distribution. Fernández Méndez welcomed the continued importation of material and technological elements from the United States. On the other hand, he described Puerto Rico at the end of the nineteenth century as a rudimentary peasant economy, dominated by coffee and sugar plantations. The clash between these two contrasting modes of production synthesized the major transformations in Puerto Rican society between 1900 and 1950 (Fernández Méndez 1955). Furthermore, Fernández Méndez reiterated the Creole elite's concern that the American occupation had eroded the Island's predominantly Hispanic identity. Like other nationalist intellectuals, he assumed a strong continuity between Spanish and Creole institutions, values, and practices. Unlike other nationalist intellectuals, Fernández Méndez believed that the Island could uphold its own identity under an autonomous, rather than an independent, political status. In his view "a nationality can exist without the political organization of the sovereign State" (Fernández Méndez 1980: 42).

As an anthropologist, Fernández Méndez (1954, 1955, 1964) resorted to an eclectic blending of then current theories of culture. Like functionalists such as Bronislaw Malinowski, he emphasized the systematic integration of social customs, institutions, and values. From his teacher Ruth Benedict, Fernández Méndez borrowed the term "ethos" to characterize the sum of the traits (or configuration) that distinguish one people from another. Following his mentor Julian Steward, he analyzed the ideological as well as the material dimensions of culture, including technological and environmental factors. Echoing Muñoz Marín, Fernández Méndez (1954: 6–7) conceived culture in its broadest possible sense as "man's social heritage taken as a whole or block." Among the most important aspects of this heritage were a people's historical patrimony, spiritual values, literature, and language. For Fernández Méndez (1959: 152), "Nationality is, then, almost exclusively a question of history and feelings." From this perspective, Puerto Ricans had a clearly defined national culture, even though they lacked their own state.

Fernández Méndez's conceptualization of national identity had several practical implications. To begin, he adamantly combated a colonial social psychology based on a sense of Puerto Rican insularity and inferiority vis-à-vis American civilization. One of his earliest newspaper articles was precisely titled "Más allá del insularismo: Hacia una civilización puertorriqueña" (Beyond insularity: Toward a Puerto Rican civilization) (Fernández Méndez 1975 [1954]). At the same time, he shunned the "politics of recalcitrant nationalism" as an "ingenuous blunder" or "pathetic blindness" (Fernández Méndez 1959: 77). Straddling hard-line pro-Americanism (*pitiyanquismo*) and political nationalism, Fernández Méndez charted a middle ideological ground based on the "gradual crystallization of a feeling of affirmation of autochthonous values" (Fernández Méndez 1955: 275). For him, the political formula best suited for cultural autonomy was neither independence nor statehood but the Estado Libre Asociado. Accordingly, "we can be in Puerto Rico, at the same time, culturally Puerto Rican and politically American. What we cannot be is *culturally* Puerto Rican and American at the same time" (Fernández Méndez 1959: 153; emphasis in the original).

Herein lies the crucial paradox of cultural nationalism: the sharp ideological split between statehood and nationality or, to put it otherwise, between citizenship and identity. Although Fernández Méndez proclaimed a separate national culture, he did not advocate a sovereign republic for the Island. Instead, he held that Puerto Rico's main cultural dilemma—the "dissolving" American influence (Fernández Méndez 1955: 278)—could be settled under commonwealth. Ultimately, Fernández Méndez shared with Alegría and Muñoz Marín the utopian project of building the nation without establishing a state. All three believed that Puerto Ricanness could be affirmed, defended, and promoted in a postcolonial colony. The two anthropologists coincided with the statesman in a surprisingly coherent discourse that broke away from political nationalism as the conventional formula to exercise their people's right to self-determination. Puerto Ricans are still struggling with the effects of this conceptual distinction between nation and state.

CONCLUSION

Cultural nationalism was a politically opportune movement in Puerto Rico during the 1950s. It served to carve out a sphere of cultural autonomy for the newly established Commonwealth, projecting its local and international image as a postcolonial pact with the United States. It served to co-opt pro-independence sympathizers, including much of the Island's intellectual elite, who believed in a distinctive national identity. It served to detach the political from the cultural implications of asserting such an identity and thus to allay the fears of pro-statehood supporters. And it served as an effective discursive practice against cultural and linguistic assimilation should the Island become the fifty-first state of the Union. Thus, the adoption of cultural nationalism by the Commonwealth was a clever political strategy by the new ruling elite, in which members of the Creole intelligentsia played a prominent part. Its popular appeal was undeniable, as a way to undo much of the colonial depreciation of local knowledge during the first half of the twentieth century.

Scholar-activists such as Alegría and Fernández Méndez assumed the task of conceptualizing and implementing state interventions in the cultural field. To use Hutchinson's terms (1994), these intellectuals combined a romantic search for identity with claims to scientific authority based on their academic credentials. Like nationalist scholars elsewhere, they helped to objectify those aspects of the historical patrimony and the folk heritage that they deemed typical of an authentic national tradition, such as historic sites, monuments, antiques, ethnographic and archaeological objects, crafts, and works of art (see Handler 1988). Alegría's figure of the "three roots" became consecrated as the official icon of Puerto Rican culture, while Fernández Méndez's vindication of cultural autonomy from the United States became an ideological justification for commonwealth status. Like other Puerto Rican nationalists, both anthropologists privileged the Hispanic heritage, particularly the Spanish language, as the key to national identity, although both were fascinated by its indigenous elements, and Alegría was also interested in its African sources. Both used anthropological concepts, theories, and methods to counter colonial discourses that systematically downgraded native culture. Both defined the spiritual domain as sovereign terrain of the Puerto Rican nation, while allowing the penetration of foreign influences in the material domain. Like cultural nationalists elsewhere, Alegría and Fernández Méndez were primarily interested in the moral and spiritual regeneration of their people, who they thought had been culturally oppressed, especially as a result of the imposition of English as the official language of public instruction. By practically excluding American influences from their conception of Puerto Ricanness, they effectively portrayed the United States as the Other. After World War II, intellectual prestige and scholarly knowledge were therefore instrumental in legitimating new forms of representing national identity on the Island.

Cultural nationalism has had many significant accomplishments in Puerto Rico. As Alegría (1971b, 1996b) has repeatedly claimed, the vast majority of the Puerto Rican people now express a strong pride in their nationality, as evidenced by popular identification with the official symbols of their country (such as the flag, anthem, and participation in international sports competitions and beauty pageants). The Institute of Puerto Rican Culture and other public agencies have sponsored an extraordinary number and variety of cultural activities, ranging from the revival of the folk arts (such as *santería*, the art of carving saints out of wood, or playing the *cuatro*, a small chord instrument) to international artistic expositions and musical concerts to publication of major literary works. The teaching of Puerto Rican history and culture, as well as the Spanish vernacular, has been strengthened throughout the curriculum from the elementary school to the university. Anthropologists, historians, writers, and artists have effectively dismantled much of the colonial discourse depicting Puerto Rico as culturally backward and racially inferior to the United States. In particular, they have salvaged and popularized the traditional values and practices of the peasantry (the legendary jíbaro) as a symbol of Puerto Ricanness. In Puerto Rico as elsewhere, cultural nationalists have contributed to imagine, construct, and represent their people as a unique nation (Hutchinson 1994).

Cultural nationalism has also faced serious ideological and practical limitations on the Island. As several critics have argued (Buitrago Ortiz 1982; Dávila 1997), the founding myth of the three roots provides a partial, incomplete, and biased account of the origins and development of contemporary Puerto Rican culture. To begin, it shuns American culture after 1898 as a "foreign influence" that threatens to corrupt the three main ethnic strands of national identity. Moreover, the Institute of Puerto Rican Culture, as well as other cultural institutions, has often displayed an excessively pro-Hispanic bent that often reifies the Spanish language as the litmus test of Puerto Ricanness. Among other consequences, this restrictive linguistic and territorial definition of Puerto Rican identity has excluded the diaspora in the United States. Finally, cultural nationalism typically underestimates the political and economic dimensions of national identity. Without a sovereign state or an autonomous economy, the people of Puerto Rico have often lacked the political power and material resources to represent themselves under commonwealth status.

In the end, just how postcolonial is contemporary Puerto Rico? Compared with the classic colonialism of the first half of the twentieth century, the Island now enjoys a greater degree of self-government. Culturally, the commonwealth formula has permitted (perhaps even required) a much broader public support for Puerto Rican identity. As Muñoz Marín (n.d.) anticipated, Puerto Ricans have developed a strong, original, and well-defined "personality." But today the Island is even more dependent, economically and politically, on the United States than it was in the 1950s. While Operation Bootstrap successfully transformed Puerto Rico into an urban industrial economy, Operation Serenity had mixed results. Nowadays, the Island's material culture is increasingly American in origin, but dominant ideological representations continue to stress its Hispanic heritage. This contradiction is at the heart of everyday life and cultural politics in contemporary Puerto Rico, a contradiction that cultural nationalism has been unable to resolve.

SIX

Collecting the Nation
The Public Representation of Puerto Rico's Cultural Identity

Recent work in anthropology and cultural studies has been increasingly concerned with the politics of collecting and exhibiting culture in museums and at
festivals, commemorations, folk revivals, and other public rituals (Gillis 1994;
Handler 1988; Henderson and Kaeppler 1997; Karp, Kreamer, and Lavine 1992;
Kurin 1997; Lidchi 1997; Stocking 1985). Museums have served to articulate,
dramatize, and legitimize national identities through ritual and monumental
displays of the historic patrimony (Clifford 1997; García Canclini 1990; Karp
and Lavine 1991). In particular, ethnographic museums have represented traditional popular culture as the essence of the nation. Especially emblematic has
been the romantic figure of the noble peasant as the purest embodiment of the
ancestral customs of the folk. As symbols of rapidly fading cultures, the artifacts
assembled in museums provide the most visible evidence of the spiritual wealth
and political virtue of a people. The creation of museums has been part and
parcel of the process of imagining communities as nations (Anderson 1991).

Since the end of the nineteenth century, one of the dominant discourses of
Puerto Ricanness has centered on highland peasants (jíbaros) and their supposedly Hispanic heritage. As a classic text claims, "The jíbaro represents the
most profound, resistant, and pure element of the Puerto Rican nationality"
(Babín 1986: 14). For many contemporary scholars, this discourse is increasingly
untenable in light of a wide variety of popular practices, identities, and imagi-

naries on the Island. New sources and approaches to the construction and representation of national identity under a continued colonial regime are under exploration. Some authors employ postmodern or poststructuralist theories, as well as the insights gained from cultural, subaltern, and postcolonial studies (see Dávila 1997; J. Duany 1998a; Guerra 1998; Negrón-Muntaner and Grosfoguel 1997; Pabón 1995b). Many intellectuals have distanced themselves from the foundational narrative that takes its point of departure from a Hispanophile, homogeneous, and essentialist view of the Puerto Rican nation. However, no one has yet engaged in a detailed and critical examination of the Island's museological and collecting practices through a case study of a specific collection, such as the one I analyze in this chapter.

In 1997 the Puerto Rican businessman, folklorist, and philanthropist Teodoro Vidal donated more than half of his collection (3,346 objects) to the Smithsonian Institution. The collection documents Puerto Rican culture from the 1600s to the present, including many popular objects used in everyday life, such as games, toys, amulets, personal adornments, musical instruments, and carnival masks. But the hallmark of the Vidal Collection is the series on Catholic devotions, especially the art of woodcarving saints, or *santos* (622 of these images are part of the collection). The Smithsonian now possesses the oldest surviving santo from Puerto Rico—a St. Anne made by an unknown artist in the seventeenth century (Tsang 1998)—as well as a wide sample of items representing popular religiosity on the Island. Other important art objects include half a dozen works by the celebrated eighteenth-century painter José Campeche. No comparable collection exists in Puerto Rico itself.

In this chapter I analyze the public representation of Puerto Rican culture through the Vidal Collection and exhibition at the National Museum of American History. Previous attempts to probe this material include Vidal's own books, several essays published in Puerto Rico, and the Smithsonian's recent efforts (see Quintero Rivera 1998; Smithsonian Institution 1998; Tió 1993; Tsang 1998; T. Vidal 1979, 1983, 1986, 1989, 1994). Still, the collection remains largely an untapped mine of information on popular and elite cultural practices on the Island over the past four centuries. In this chapter I hope to advance the anthropological understanding of the process of constructing and displaying a national identity through popular culture. I also hope to contribute to U.S. Latino studies by clarifying the cultural politics of interpreting and translating Latino cultures to U.S. audiences (see Dávila 1998; Moreno 1997). More specifically, I consider how many Puerto Rican intellectuals—as exemplified by

Vidal—imagined their nation during the second half of the twentieth century. Because the collection was donated to the Smithsonian, its exhibition also shows how U.S.-based curators have attempted to represent Puerto Ricans to Americans.

The significance of this research is threefold. First, it assesses the nationalist project to define, preserve, and promote Puerto Rican folk traditions under increasing Americanization. As I argued in Chapter 5, a leading sector of the Island's intelligentsia has embraced cultural nationalism since World War II (Alegría 1965, 1996b; Morris 1995; Marvette Pérez 1996). As I will show later, Vidal was strategically positioned to articulate the discourse of cultural nationalism because of his influential role as an aide to Governor Muñoz Marín. During the 1950s Vidal participated actively in the struggle to define Puerto Rican identity from various contested sites, such as the Institute of Puerto Rican Culture (see Aguiló Ramos 1987; Flores Collazo 1998; García Passalacqua 1998). Hence, the ideological criteria that led him to document and collect certain objects are widely shared by writers and artists, as well as political leaders, community activists, and ordinary people in Puerto Rico. By exploring how this prominent collector drew the contours of his nation, one might better understand contemporary thinking on Puerto Rican identity.

Second, the research adds to current debates on postcolonialism and nationalism, especially on nationalist discourses in colonial countries (see Anderson 1991; Bhabha 1990; Chatterjee 1993; Hobsbawm 1983; Loomba 1998; Said 1978; Smith 1995; Williams and Chrisman 1994). Paradoxically, Puerto Rico depends politically and economically on the United States, yet it displays a robust cultural nationalism. The Vidal Collection, for example, tends to substantiate the founding myth of "the Great Puerto Rican Family" that has long served to instill a collective sense of common origin and destiny beyond racial and class fissures (see Dávila 1997; Godreau-Santiago 1999; Quintero Rivera et al. 1979; Torres 1998). It also maps out the spiritual terrain (as opposed to the "intrusion" of American material culture) of the Puerto Rican nation, especially in the vernacular language, religion, art, music, and everyday life. At the same time, the virtual absence of the Puerto Rican diaspora from Vidal's materials confirms that nationalist intellectuals have tended to equate the nation with the Island (see Chapter 1). Hence, analyzing the inclusions and exclusions of this collection can offer new ground with which to test and refine recent theories of nationalism.

Finally, this essay contributes to rethinking the public representation of cultural identities through museum displays, expositions, feasts, festivals, fairs, performances, dances, monuments, preservation of historic sites, and other activities (see Cantwell 1993; Gillis 1994; Handler 1988; Henderson and Kaeppler 1997; Karp and Lavine 1991; Kurin 1997). The Vidal Collection documents the use of material culture, particularly arts and crafts, for the construction of collective imaginaries. Locating the collective work of artists and artisans in their larger historical and cultural context helps to understand them as icons of a growing sense of nationality despite centuries of colonial rule. Therefore, this chapter builds on and expands previous interpretations of Puerto Rican culture, which until now had been based largely on literary texts and historical documents (J. Duany 1996). To my knowledge, this is the first time that a collection of material objects is used to reflect on the representation of Puerto Rican identity.

I argue that the Vidal Collection commemorates the Island's historic patrimony as defined by the discourse of cultural nationalism. I use the term "patrimony" in Richard Handler's (1988) sense of objectifying the nation through a unique heritage, including historic buildings and monuments, antiques, ethnographic objects, and works of art. Basically, the Vidal Collection preserves the material culture and traditional practices of a Hispanic, Catholic, rural country against the backdrop of U.S. colonialism, industrialization, urbanization, and migration. Despite the efforts of Vidal and other local intellectuals, the failure to establish a national museum of popular arts and traditions in Puerto Rico led to the collection's expatriation to the United States. Ironically, after its initial showing, most of the collection has been kept off-limits to the general public in one of the museum's storage facilities in suburban Maryland.

Vidal's gift to the Smithsonian coincided with intensive lobbying by U.S. Latino scholars and activists to increase the visibility of Hispanic contributions to American culture. Although the collection makes little reference to the Puerto Rican presence in the mainland, it is one of the largest and most valuable acquisitions documenting the folk art and elite culture of Hispanic origin in the United States. For their part, the curators of the exhibition at the NMAH have attempted to interpret Puerto Rico's national culture to a wide American public. However, they have had to work with the museum's current emphasis on the history of multiculturalism in the United States, in which each ethnic and regional culture contributes its share to constructing the American dream. The colonial history and nationalistic overtones of Puerto Rican identity are often lost in the translation.

RESCUING THE HISTORIC PATRIMONY

Teodoro Vidal was born in San Juan, Puerto Rico, in 1923.[1] He comes from a prominent family of Spanish and Corsican origins, part of which descended from the renowned Ramírez de Arellano family from Cabo Rojo and Mayagüez, on the west coast of the Island. His father was a well-to-do businessman in the import and export trade, himself the son of a coffee hacienda owner in Cayey. A 1914 letterhead preserved at the Archives Center of the NMAH identifies Teodoro Vidal Sr. as a "commission merchant" who bought and sold metals and vegetables in Old San Juan, "specializing in potatoes, onions, hay, and oatmeal."

The young Vidal was the valedictorian of his graduating class at the prestigious St. John's School in Condado. In 1938 he went to study at the N.Y. Military Academy on Hudson, New York. In 1940 Vidal entered the Wharton School of Finance and Commerce at the University of Pennsylvania, earning a bachelor's degree in economics in 1943 and a master's in industrial management in 1945. Ironically, he told me, "I never studied in Spanish. So I had to practice my own language. . . . I learned to be a Puerto Rican patriot over there" in the United States (interview with the author, October 4, 1999). Later, he joined the U.S. Army, served during the Korean War, and attained the rank of captain.

In 1953 Vidal became a military aide and chief of protocol for Governor Muñoz Marín. Vidal was in charge of affairs related to the armed forces, civil defense, fire prevention, state visits, culture, proclamations, and restorations. At one point he was also the governor's liaison with the Department of Agriculture. He wrote numerous letters and speeches for Muñoz Marín during the 1950s and 1960s. He even certified the governor's telegrams as official Commonwealth business (see Fundación Luis Muñoz Marín 1949–64). Vidal helped to found the Institute of Puerto Rican Culture in 1955 and served on its board of directors until 1968. As one of Muñoz Marín's key cultural advisers, Vidal contributed to Operation Serenity, the government's effort to preserve the Island's cultural identity (see Chapter 5).

Vidal's first publication was a protocol manual for La Fortaleza, the governor's executive mansion in Old San Juan (T. Vidal 195?). He soon became involved with the mansion's historic preservation, the first project of its kind on the Island, and wrote a booklet on the topic (T. Vidal 1964). During this period, he authored an official government booklet describing the flag, anthem, seal, and historical background of Puerto Rico (T. Vidal n.d.). He also participated in the first plans to restore the historic zone of Old San Juan. In 1956 he joined the board of directors of the American Association for the Preservation of Historical Monuments and a year later represented Puerto Rico at the Historic Sites Conference in Vermont. Vidal articulated his views on historical monuments in a memorandum to the governor's wife, Inés Mendoza, which she then broadcasted on public television: "These buildings, made largely by industrious Puerto Rican hands, represent various aspects of our history and old life ways of the Puerto Rican people. The profound interest and reverence that they inspire in us as part of our cultural heritage does not come from a mere nostalgia for a romantic past. It comes from our recognition that in the familiarity with our cultural roots lies another force in our resource base [*acervo de fuerzas*] with which we constantly labor to improve ourselves" (Vidal to Mendoza, September 18, 1957).

After leaving La Fortaleza in 1964 (when Muñoz Marín's last term as governor expired), Vidal worked briefly as a government promoter at the Economic Development Administration and as a public relations officer at a local advertising agency, Publicidad Badillo, where he became associate director of his department in 1967. Afterward, he worked on his own as a public relations consultant and devoted more time to his research and writing on Puerto Rican folklore, which he published through his own publishing house, Ediciones Alba.

In the 1950s Vidal began to collect the Island's religious folk sculpture, especially santos. The main inspiration for his collection was none other than Muñoz Marín. "It was his interest in Puerto Rico," noted Vidal years later, "in its history, in the traditions of our Island and the wealth of its culture, that motivated me to initiate [the collection]." Furthermore, he pointed out, "When I arrived in Puerto Rico after studying industrial engineering at the University of Pennsylvania, I was deeply worried upon noticing that part of the representative objects of our traditional culture was disappearing. Some of them were acquired by foreigners and there was no record of them. I first became interested in the *santos*" (Trelles 1993: 18). Later, Vidal's collecting practices expanded to other artifacts, such as *exvotos* or *milagros* (requests for favors by the saints or tokens of gratitude for those granted), as well as prayers, toys, masks, miniature portraits, engravings, paintings, personal adornments, musical instruments, clothing, and furniture. He also gathered many objects from his own family, such as photographs, letters, souvenirs, silver pieces, and jewelry. While traveling abroad, especially in Spain, he purchased rare engravings, maps, and newspapers on Puerto Rico.

In several books and interviews, Vidal has documented how he acquired his extensive collection of Puerto Rican folk art and material culture. During the summer of 1956, he began to travel to the rural areas of the Island, especially the central mountainous region from Barranquitas to Maricao. He conducted fieldwork during his spare time on weekends and vacations. For his research on the Espadas, two prominent folk sculptors of the late eighteenth and early nineteenth centuries, Vidal scoured the countryside (*me tiraba por los campos*), especially in San Germán, Sabana Grande, Yauco, and Mayagüez, asking for personal references to the artisans' work and life "house by house" (interview with the author, October 4, 1999). Initially, he purchased the objects from their former owners, but sometimes he received them as gifts. Eventually, he acquired hundreds of santos and interviewed hundreds of persons, particularly elderly peasants familiar with traditional practices.

"I've tried to build two collections," Vidal has explained. "One is made up of objects. The other is made up of traditions, legends, verses [*coplas*], songs [*décimas*] related to the saints, and popular prayers" (Trelles 1993: 18). More recently, he has added: "An example of an aspect of our nonmaterial culture that I collected is that of the traditions of Puerto Rican witchcraft, which were organized, analyzed, and made public through a book. Of a material character are, for example, the collections of exvotos, masks, and sculptures of the Espadas, which figure in well-illustrated books and with data to document and explain the collected objects." According to Vidal, "The collection isn't typical of contemporary ones, because, unlike the others, this one was made with the specific purpose of donating it for the foundation of a museum. Besides, I collected material to document it, often from firsthand sources, and made an effort to ensure that the objects were not merely beautiful but also representative of a [wider] production. Moreover, I also collected aspects of nonmaterial culture, often about matters unrelated to the objects that were being collected, but it was important to obtain them because of their value for the study of traditional Puerto Rican culture and because of the lack of a systematic and scientific program to gather materials referring to various significant facets of our life as a people" (letter to the author, September 5, 2000).

Since the 1970s, Vidal has published extensively in his two main areas of interest: Puerto Rican material culture and oral literature, including the art of making saints (T. Vidal 1979, 1994, 1998a), miracles (1974), and carnival masks

(1983, 1988a), as well as popular beliefs in witchcraft (1989) and folk healing (1986). In addition, he has authored several essays on José Campeche (1987, 1988b, 2000), Puerto Rico's most important painter during the late eighteenth century. At the time of this writing, Vidal was preparing a book manuscript on popular medical recipes on the Island. Hence, his writing as well as his collecting practices have encompassed both folk and fine arts as traditionally defined.

In many respects, Vidal is a typical collector. For one thing, he is a white, well-educated, upper-class male who devoted much of his leisure time to collecting. For another, he has been primarily interested in preserving his country's historic patrimony through the peasantry's traditional customs, like other leading collectors in Europe, Latin America, and elsewhere. Like other folklorists, he has sought to objectify the most authentic aspects of his national culture. Furthermore, Vidal has always been concerned with maintaining his collection intact and has avoided its sale, dispersal, or destruction (see Johnson and Associates 1992; Pearce 1992). Although he systematically assembled some objects (such as santos and milagros), he accumulated many items haphazardly, especially family heirlooms and memorabilia, which he inserted into the collection as tokens of the Island's national history. Most important, Vidal's chief motivation was to document, rescue, and conserve the material culture of Puerto Rico before "industrialization and modern life, which tend to erase the old customs of peoples" (T. Vidal 1983: 8). He was particularly impressed by the distinctiveness and antiquity of the Island's folk religious sculpture. Like other collectors, Vidal attempted to define, represent, and display national identity through certain emblematic artifacts and cultural practices (see García Canclini 1990; Karp and Lavine 1991).

In other ways, Vidal's trajectory is unique. As a close associate of Muñoz Marín, he played a fundamental role in drafting Puerto Rico's cultural policies during the 1950s, especially the restoration of historic monuments and sites. His private collection is intimately linked with the agenda of public institutions (such as the Institute of Puerto Rican Culture) that sought to conserve and protect the Island's cultural heritage in a period of rapid socioeconomic changes.[2] His ideas on historic preservation deeply influenced Governor Muñoz Marín, his wife, and other powerful figures in postwar Puerto Rico. Ultimately, however, Vidal and his associates were unable to create "a museum that presents the traditional practices [*quehacer*] of our people, highlighting characteristic and distinctive aspects of its culture" (*El Visitante* 1992: 5). Unlike other collectors, Vidal transferred much of his collection to an institution located outside his home country, which, in his view, could best guarantee its preservation and integrity. The following section sketches the collector's dilemmas.[3]

LOSING A NATIONAL TREASURE, OR
HOW THE VIDAL COLLECTION WAS RELOCATED ABROAD

For more than a decade, Vidal and a small group of collaborators made repeated efforts to establish the National Museum of Popular Arts and Traditions in Puerto Rico. In 1983 Vidal formed a consortium to establish the museum, which was incorporated as a nonprofit institution on October 4, 1984. The main purpose of this organization was to find a permanent home for his collection, valued at $6 million in 1990, as well as to attract related collections existing on the Island. Vidal enlisted the cooperation of prominent cultural personalities, including photographer Jack Delano, sculptor Jaime Suárez, art professors Annie Santiago de Curet and Teresa Tió, former judge Angel Martín, and collectors Walter Tischer and Bill O'Connor, who constituted the museum's first board of directors. The members of the board represented the three major political parties on the Island—pro-commonwealth, pro-statehood, and pro-independence.

Vidal and his associates had identified an abandoned structure in Santurce as ideal for the museum. The site was the former Sacred Heart School and Girls' Asylum, a neoclassical Spanish colonial building from the late nineteenth century. Originally, PDP governor Rafael Hernández Colón had expressed interest in the project, granting the use of the building by the museum. Hurricane Hugo seriously damaged the building in 1989, and its roof collapsed. In 1990 PDP senator Velda González submitted a resolution to the legislature to establish the museum. But the government never assigned the $11 million needed to develop the structure into a full-fledged recreational park and community center (Johnson and Associates 1992). In a meeting with the secretary of state, Vidal and his collaborators were told that the Commonwealth lacked the funds to help create the museum or restore the building (*El Visitante* 1992).[4]

Newspaper articles mention several reasons for the lack of state patronage for Vidal's initiatives. According to the editor of the *San Juan Star*, "No government or government agency, commonwealth or municipal, was interested enough to provide shelter or museum for these priceless objects" (Viglucci 1997: 123). The Commonwealth government invested most of its funds for cultural activities in the celebrations of the Columbus Quincentennial in 1992 (especially the construction of the Seville Pavilion) and the Discovery of Puerto Rico in 1993. Vidal himself believes that the Institute of Puerto Rican Culture did not support his proposed museum because its administrators felt that it would compete with the institute's programs (interview with the author, October 4, 1999). In addition, "Banco Popular displayed corporate interest in Vidal's collection by mounting an exhibition in San Juan similar to the one now in Washington, but its top executives said there wasn't much more they could do without a show of government backing" (Friedman 1997: 21).

Journalists had sounded the alarm since 1990. An anonymous newspaper article warned, "We will lose forever a unique collection of its kind, because it is so complete and encompassing, and the possibility of endowing the country with a museum with a national character" (*El Mundo* 1990). In two editorial columns, the writer Rafael Castro Pereda (1990a, 1990b) regretted the absence of a national exposition center on the Island. Calling Vidal's collection a public good, he concluded: "It is scandalous that there isn't in Puerto Rico a clear and definitive cultural policy that retains and esteems our historic and artistic patrimony" (Castro Pereda 1990b: 61). Similarly, the artist Torres Martinó insisted on the need to "allow our people to know more about themselves" and "penetrate joyfully into the soul of Puerto Ricanness" (1991: 60). In another article, Castro Pereda (1990b: 61) wrote: "Puerto Rico is about to lose the most complete collection of popular arts and traditions that now exists in the country."

In January 1992 the museum's board of directors published an open letter to the governor, stating: "We are making arrangements to donate the collection, even if it should be outside Puerto Rico, where the necessary guarantees can be had for the permanent conservation of this notable aspect of our patrimony" (*El Visitante* 1992: 5). By then, Vidal had received offers to house his collection at the Smithsonian Institution in Washington, the International Folk Art Museum of New Mexico, and the Museum of America in Madrid. Finally, the election of a new governor in November 1992 severed any political connections Vidal and his collaborators may have had with the higher echelons of power. As a well-known member of the PDP and ally of Muñoz Marín, Vidal had little clout with Pedro Rosselló's administration, which supported the Island's annexation to the United States as a state of the Union. When the New Progressive Party (NPP) took control of the government in 1993, it showed little interest in reviving Vidal's project and instead embarked on creating another art museum in San Juan. In 1997 Vidal reluctantly gave much of his collection to the

Smithsonian, despite protests by local artists and writers. "I spent eleven years trying to create a Museum of Popular Arts and Traditions," he told a journalist, "but there wasn't enough support" (Mulero 1998b: 81).

In July 2000 the Rosselló administration inaugurated the Arts Museum of Puerto Rico, which could easily have housed the Vidal Collection. But it did not. Although Vidal's original intention was to prevent the dispersion of popular art pieces, his collection was ultimately to travel abroad. As Vidal (1979: 1) wrote decades ago, "We were concerned that the traditions of making those images [the santos] were disappearing, and with their disappearance, some information worth collecting was being forgotten. Our concern increased upon finding out that, for different reasons, above all through selling in the trade in antiquities to persons from outside [the Island], many images were being lost [even though they were] worthy of study and conservation as an invaluable treasure."

The expatriation of this "invaluable treasure" had multiple political ramifications on the Island as well as in the mainland. While some Island artists and writers decried transferring the collection abroad, the Puerto Rican congressman from New York, José Serrano, congratulated Vidal on the floor of the U.S. House of Representatives. Once the collection traveled to Washington, the NPP government enthusiastically supported the exhibition's inauguration at the Smithsonian in July 1998. Governor Rosselló himself attended the opening reception, along with high-ranking members of his cabinet, such as Jorge L. Dávila, director of the Tourism Company, and Jaime Morgan, head of the Economic Development Administration. These two agencies alone spent $354,000 to help subsidize the reception, publication of a catalogue, and travel expenses for several artisans and journalists to Washington (Mulero 1998a: 26).

Vidal's public statements about his Smithsonian gift reveal his disillusionment with public authorities in Puerto Rico: "The most important thing in this affair is the country's indifference to the conservation of the historic and cultural patrimony," he lamented. "The only way to save the collection was to donate it" (Roche 1997: 9). After the transfer was complete, Vidal felt "very pleased with the Smithsonian's efforts to conserve this part of the collection, which is now in the excellent conservation facilities of that institution" (Mulero 1998b: 81). In a personal interview, he reiterated that "the Puerto Rican government is not the site for our patrimony," noting that the ideal model was the Metropolitan Museum of Art in New York, which leases its building from New York City but retains its autonomy (interview with the author, October 4, 1999).

At the same time that he donated the largest part of his collection to the

Smithsonian, Vidal made a smaller gift to the Luis Muñoz Marín Foundation in Trujillo Alto, Puerto Rico. "These are mostly pieces that are not susceptible to damage in our tropical weather," he explained (interview with the author, October 4, 1999). (He also gave a few santos and musical instruments to the Museo del Barrio in New York.) The foundation's inventory of 303 objects donated by Vidal in 1997 estimates its value at $317,095. It includes a wide array of items ranging from lamps, spoons, vases, baskets, hats, and maracas to prayers, milagros, exvotos, and two antique santos worth $65,000 each (Fundación Luis Muñoz Marín 1997). In a letter to the foundation's executive director, Vidal wrote: "I will make the donation in homage to the profound affection and sincere gratitude to don Luis [Muñoz Marín] and doña Inés [Mendoza, his wife] for their great contributions to Puerto Rican culture and their interest in the genuine conservation of our national patrimony" (T. Vidal to Martínez, June 10, 1997). He later underlined: "I am pleased to donate this part of the collection as a homage to don Luis Muñoz Marín for enunciating the concept of Operation Serenity. The main purpose of this collection, which I gathered and documented through the years—as well as the rest of the work I have completed—is to contribute to a better knowledge of the wealth, antiquity, and distinctive aspects of the Country's material culture as a faithful reflection of our national identity" (T. Vidal to Martínez, July 26, 1998).

The prolonged debate over the establishment of a museum of popular arts and traditions in Puerto Rico suggests that the Vidal Collection had become an icon of the "wealth, antiquity, and distinctive aspects" of Puerto Ricanness.[5] On the one hand, the permanent relocation of more than half of the objects reveals the lack of a clear Commonwealth policy toward the protection of the historic patrimony, as well as its relative weakness as a colonial state.[6] According to some critics, it also reveals the collector's lack of faith in his own country's potential to preserve and exhibit the collection. On the other hand, the nearly unanimous condemnation of the loss of a "national treasure" by the Island's intelligentsia suggests a strong ideological consensus around certain emblems of Puerto Rican culture, such as santos, cuatros (the chord musical instruments), or vejigantes (carnival masks). Since the nineteenth century, nationalist discourses coalesced around peasant traditions such as folk art, songs, tales, and costumes deemed worthy of study and conservation, especially as part of anticolonial struggles (see Kurin 1997). The failure to establish a museum of popular arts and traditions in Puerto Rico precisely raised many questions about collecting and exhibiting material culture in a colonial context (see Karp, Kreamer, and

Lavine 1992; Lidchi 1997). "No other country of America needs such a museum more than ours," claimed the board of directors of the ill-fated Museum of Popular Arts and Traditions in Puerto Rico (*El Visitante* 1992: 5). According to Vidal's critics, donating the collection to a U.S. museum only exacerbated the Island's continuing dependence on the metropolitan country. For Vidal himself, "it was dramatic that those pieces had to leave Puerto Rico. . . . I gave them away with great pain [*con dolor en el alma*]" (interview with the author, October 4, 1999). I will now look more closely at their destination.

CULTURAL POLITICS, MUSEUM COLLECTIONS, AND MOMENTOUS OCCASIONS

The Smithsonian Institution is the largest museum and research complex in the world. With its 3.2 million artifacts, the NMAH is one of the largest facilities within the Smithsonian. Originally chartered by Congress in 1955 as the National Museum of History and Technology, the museum adopted its current name in 1980. Many of its collections began with the former U.S. National Museum's anthropological expeditions, expositions, and patent models at the end of the nineteenth century and the beginning of the twentieth. The museum now depends largely on federal funds, supplemented by private gifts, grants, sales, and licensing. Its basic mission is to document U.S. history and its diverse cultures and to make them accessible to the public through various formats, including exhibitions and publications.

Until the 1970s, the NMAH practically excluded African Americans, Native Americans, Latinos, and other ethnic minorities from its collections and exhibitions (Karp, Kreamer, and Lavine 1992). The museum thus contributed to marginalizing the struggles for public recognition of the collective identities of many subaltern groups. Moreover, the museum artificially separated Anglo-Saxon culture and technology from the prehistory and ethnology of Native Americans and other colonized peoples, such as the overseas possessions acquired by the United States after the Spanish-Cuban-American War—Cuba, Puerto Rico, the Philippines, Guam, and Hawaii (Hinsley 1981). Like other public museums, the NMAH did not acquire, preserve, or display significant aspects of the material culture of Native Americans, African Americans, and Latinos until representatives of such communities pressed the museum's administrators to do so (Kurin 1997).

Until the 1990s, the museum—as well as the rest of the Smithsonian—neglected Hispanic contributions to American culture. In 1994 the Smithsonian Institution Task Force on Latino Issues denounced the situation: "The Smithsonian almost entirely excludes and ignores the Latino population of the United States." In 1998 the Center for Latino Initiatives was established to promote research, exhibitions, and public and educational programs on Latino history and culture. The center also sought to increase Latino representation in the activities, workforce, and governance structure of the Smithsonian. One of the first visible programs related to Latinos at the NMAH was precisely the Vidal exhibition, inaugurated in 1997. Acquiring and displaying the collection was a breakthrough in the Smithsonian's efforts to expand its coverage of Hispanic American material cultures. Other more recent Latino-related initiatives include exhibitions on the U.S.-Mexican borderlands, some activities at the annual folklife festival, and a research and public program on Latin music in the United States.

Marvette Pérez, a Puerto Rican curator at the NMAH, first contacted Vidal about bringing his collection to the Smithsonian in 1992. Over the next five years, Smithsonian authorities worked out the practical details of transporting, conserving, and exhibiting the collection in Washington. After concluding the negotiations, Vidal opened up his house in Caparra Heights to twelve curators and other museum staff for five weeks in 1997. The team selected, labeled, packed, and sent more than thirty-two hundred items to the NMAH. In addition, sixty-three santos, paintings, and miniature portraits by Campeche and others, valued at $3 million, went to the National Museum of American Art (NMAA). While the cost of transporting the objects exceeded $150,000, Pérez estimated that the Smithsonian would have to invest more than $600,000 to preserve and display them properly (Mulero 1997; Roche 1997; Smithsonian Institution Research Reports 1998).

In 1997 the NMAA organized an exhibition titled "Colonial Art from Puerto Rico: Selections from the Gift of Teodoro Vidal." It featured twenty-six santos, paintings, and portrait miniatures, carefully chosen for their aesthetic value rather than as historical documents. Hence, the physical division of the Vidal Collection into two museums—an artistic one and an ethnographic one—reproduces the customary distinction between Western art and non-Western material culture (Clifford 1988, 1997; Karp, Kreamer, and Lavine 1992; Price 1989). On the one hand, most of the art objects displayed at the NMAA were created by named individuals or groups (such as Campeche, Felipe and Tiburcio de la

Espada, or the Cabán group), located at specific points in history, mainly the late eighteenth and early nineteenth centuries. On the other hand, most of the ethnographic objects displayed at the NMAH remain anonymous, vaguely dated, and crowded together. While the art museum collected items of permanent aesthetic merit according to its curators, the history museum gathered them as testimonies of cultural traditions in danger of extinction.

Both exhibitions were well-publicized media events. As the *San Juan Star* editorialized, "It will probably take an exhibit in the prestigious Smithsonian for Puerto Rico to appreciate what it lost" (Viglucci 1997: 123). Museum officials were ecstatic about the collection, especially in a period of growing public pressures to collect and exhibit more Latino materials (Smithsonian Institution Task Force on Latino Issues 1994). According to Marvette Pérez, "There has been a lack of representation of Puerto Rican history in museums. The Latino community is hungry for this, and I think we owe it to them to do this kind of exhibit" (Smithsonian Institution Research Reports 1998: 3). Smithsonian secretary I. Michael Heyman spoke of the "magnificent acquisition of an incredible collection," while NMAH director Spencer Crew declared, "We are all excited about this gift" (Friedman 1997: 21). In a letter to Vidal, Heyman stated: "Yours is one of the most significant donations ever made to either the National Museum of American Art or the National Museum of American History. It is a milestone in the history of both museums."[7] Elizabeth Broun, NMAA director, added: "We are honored to give these extraordinary works a home in the nation's capital." Not to be outdone with the superlatives, NMAA curator Andrew Connors concluded: "This is a momentous occasion for the museum" (Friedman 1997: 21; NMAA Press Release 1997).

COLLECTING THE JÍBARO

I now turn my attention to the materials donated by Vidal to the Smithsonian. Table 6.1 provides a summary of the available identifying information for the objects held by the NMAH, most of which are stored at the Smithsonian's warehouses in Silver Hill, Maryland. The data are based on the collection's catalogue, which includes 3,346 items. Identifying information could be obtained for 504 objects, or 15.1 percent of the entire inventory. I noted any available data for each piece in the following categories: the object type, the date it was made, its place of origin, the maker's sex and name, the object's material, and the saint

TABLE 6.1. The Vidal Collection at the Smithsonian: Basic Identifying Information

	Number	Percentage
Main categories		
Agricultural	51	1.5
Clothing	148	4.4
Costume accessory	66	2.0
Fishing	11	0.3
Household	272	8.1
Jewelry	107	3.2
Musical	47	1.4
Religious	2,416	72.2
Text	133	4.0
Toys and games	95	2.8
Object type		
Amulets	6	1.2
Baskets	12	2.4
Candlesticks	4	0.8
Canes and sticks	8	1.6
Children's toys and dolls	6	1.2
Eating implements	19	3.8
Masks	41	8.2
Musical instruments	8	1.6
Other household implements	6	1.2
Other religious objects	9	1.8
Personal objects and adornments	25	5.0
Santos	347	69.8
Work instruments	6	1.2
Date of fabrication		
Before 1749	5	2.9
1750–99	17	9.7
1800–1849	9	5.1
1850–99	85	48.6
1900–1949	23	13.1
1950–97	36	20.6
Place of origin		
Central mountainous region	160	55.7
Barranquitas	6	2.1
Hormigueros	5	1.7
Lares	16	5.6
Las Piedras	7	2.4
Morovis	56	19.5
San Germán	31	10.8
Utuado	14	4.9
Other places	25	8.7

TABLE 6.1. *continued*

	Number	Percentage
Place of origin continued		
Coastal lowlands	127	\44.3
Aguada	5	1.7
Arecibo	15	5.2
Bayamón	5	1.7
Cabo Rojo	8	2.8
Camuy	13	4.5
Loíza	13	4.5
Mayagüez	9	3.1
Ponce	29	10.1
Other places	30	10.5
Sex of maker		
Male	187	93.0
Female	10	5.0
Male and female	4	2.0
Name of maker		
P. Arce	14	4.9
C. Ayala	11	3.8
Cabán group	27	9.4
Cachetón de Lares	15	5.2
J. Cartagena	13	4.5
F. Espada	14	4.9
T. Espada	13	4.5
Espada group	8	2.8
R. García	9	3.1
L. Pagán	9	3.1
G. Rivera	28	9.7
Rivera group	37	12.8
Other	89	30.9
Material used		
Coconut	7	1.8
Gourd	10	2.5
Metal	36	9.1
Paper	26	6.6
Wood	292	73.6
Other	26	6.5
Saint represented		
Child of Prague	6	1.9
Christ crucified	16	5.1
Immaculate Conception	12	3.8
Jesus of Nazareth	5	1.6

TABLE 6.1. *continued*

	Number	Percentage
Saint represented continued		
Lonely spirit	5	1.6
St. Anthony of Padua	44	14.0
St. Blase	6	1.9
St. John Nepomucene	7	2.2
St. Joseph	29	9.2
St. Raphael	11	3.5
St. Raymond	10	3.2
St. Rita	5	1.6
Three Wise Men	13	4.1
Virgin of Carmel	20	6.3
Virgin of Montserrat	40	12.7
Virgin of Sorrows	9	2.9
Other	77	24.4

Source: Velásquez 1999.
Note: Some columns may not add up to 100 percent because of rounding. Total number of artifacts varies as a result of unknown information.

represented. I also tried to specify the object's place of acquisition and former owners, but I discarded these two dimensions for further analysis because the inventory included very few cases. Despite much missing information, a quantitative approach to the collection helps to characterize its contents.

Nearly three-fourths of the artifacts were classified as religious. This category includes santos, milagros, and prayers, which constitute the bulk of the collection. Moreover, all these objects are related to popular Catholic devotions, with the possible exception of a large metal cross, which the curators believe may be associated with spiritualism. Several black rag dolls may also be connected with African-derived practices, but that hypothesis remains to be confirmed. When asked why he focused almost exclusively on Catholic practices, Vidal answered: "The only traditional religion [on the Island] was Catholicism" (interview with the author, October 4, 1999). This is a debatable assertion, given the antiquity and popularity of other religious systems on the Island, such as *espiritismo* or Afro-Cuban *santería*, a Yoruba-based cult. In any case, the Vidal Collection privileges the religious sphere of culture at the expense of work, music, and household implements.

A more detailed list of object types reveals the main characteristics of the sample. Among those artifacts with identifying information, two out of three were santos. Not only are santos overrepresented in the sample, but their places of origin, approximate dates, and makers are better known than for other objects. Masks, personal adornments, and eating utensils are also relatively well documented. Again, the Vidal Collection preserves the spiritual and aesthetic aspects of Puerto Rican history better than other aspects. Conspicuously absent are pre-Columbian religious objects such as *cemíes* and *dujos*, the ceramic figures that are so prominent in archaeological museums on the Island (see Chapter 11).

The artifacts were made primarily in the nineteenth century, especially during the second half. Although the collection includes rare pieces from the eighteenth century, it focuses on a later period when Puerto Rican identity was more clearly defined, according to conventional accounts. For instance, the majority of the santos date from 1850–99, when a distinctive Creole style emerged on the Island (T. Vidal 1998a). Although Vidal also gathered many objects produced during the twentieth century, these tend to illustrate rapidly fading practices, such as wearing pavas, sporting canes, or embroidering handkerchiefs. The assembled materials suggest that the historical roots of Puerto Rican culture lie primarily in the mid–nineteenth century, when the Island was predominantly a rural and agricultural country producing coffee, sugar, and tobacco for export, and before it was ceded to the United States. As a *Washington Post* editor pointed out, "This exhibition [as well as the collection] is historic rather than contemporary, reflecting the island as it was before it was flooded by Yankee military, money, and manners, not to mention tourists" (Burchard 1999).

Vidal's donation to the Smithsonian is highly selective by region of origin, although it contains artifacts from most of the Island's seventy-eight municipios. The central mountainous region dominates the collection, particularly the towns of Morovis, San Germán, Lares, and Utuado, with more than half of all the identified objects. Conversely, the coastal lowlands are greatly underrepresented, except for Ponce, Arecibo, Camuy, and Loíza. Geographically, the Vidal Collection tends to locate the heart of Puerto Rican culture in the inner highlands, where the jíbaros developed a distinctive lifestyle deemed representative of the entire country. Thus, the collection reproduces the binary opposition between the *altura* (highlands) and *bajura* (lowlands) that has prevailed throughout much of Puerto Rican history.

Most of the objects' makers remain anonymous or their personal identity is unclear, as in the case of many santos attributed to the Cabán, Rivera, or Espada groups. Among the known makers, the overwhelming majority are men. This is not surprising because most of these artisans are *santeros*, the makers of santos, who have traditionally been males. (A notable exception is the case of the Ramoses from Aguada, apparently a married couple who worked together.) In addition, female makers often specialized in arts and crafts that did not preserve their names, such as needlework, basket weaving, or doll making. Nonetheless, the predominance of craftsmen—and arguably of their masculine perspective—is striking.

Wood is the most common material in the Vidal Collection, as a result of the large number of santos, which are almost always carved in wood. The inventory sometimes mentions a specific type of local wood, such as *calabazón*, *paloma*, and *guayalote*. Vidal (1994) has written about the native woods—especially Spanish cedar—favored by Puerto Rican santeros because of their natural beauty, softness, and durability. Paper and plaster are also used relatively often, especially to make carnival masks, and metal is employed for many milagros and jewelry. Perhaps most notable is the virtual absence of industrially produced materials from the collection. Plastic appears only three times in the sample, even though it includes many items produced since 1950. Gourd, shell, fibers, and coconut are much preferred to materials imported to the Island. For Vidal, Puerto Rican identity seems to be best embodied in homegrown materials such as wood and other organic sources.

Finally, the collection emphasizes certain religious images. In my sample of documented santos, by far the two most popular figures are St. Anthony of Padua and the Virgin of Montserrat, followed by St. Joseph, the Virgin of Carmel, the Three Wise Men, Christ crucified, the Immaculate Conception, and St. Raphael.[8] Vidal (1998a) and other authors (Quintero Rivera 1998) have explored several reasons for this preference—among them, the popular identification of a racially mixed population with the Montserrat as a mulatto virgin (*la virgen morena*). I would add that the cult of certain saints and apparitions of the Virgin Mary is very localized in Puerto Rico and elsewhere. For instance, the Virgin of Montserrat is most popular in the southwestern region of the Island around Hormigueros, San Germán, and Cabo Rojo, whereas the cult of the Virgin of Candlemas is stronger in the coastal lowlands of the north, and the Virgin of Carmel is better known in the east. Hence, the higher frequency of certain images partly reflects more extensive collecting in some parts of the Island than in others.

EXHIBITING PUERTO RICANNESS

Only a small portion of the entire Vidal Collection—less than 10 percent—was displayed at the NMAH.[9] Looking closely at the exhibition adds another dimension to my analysis: the choices made by the curators from the larger inventory of Puerto Rican artifacts. It also helps to foreground how the Smithsonian represented the Island's cultural identity to the American public.

The Vidal exhibition was located on the first floor of the west wing of the museum. As you entered the building from Constitution Avenue, you turned right and found it tucked in between two larger, high-technology displays, *Information Age* and *Science in American Life*. Nearby was a smaller exhibition titled *Frontier Photographer: Edward S. Curtis*; Curtis specialized in photographing Native Americans in the western United States. Thus, the Vidal exhibition bore little relationship to its immediate surroundings and sat uncomfortably with the museum's stress on American science, technology, and culture.

The display was housed in a former gift shop with a semicircular shape, not in a prominent place within the museum. It was a largely self-enclosed space, isolated from the main hallway. The objects arranged near the glass windows—mostly santos—turned their backs to passersby. A large poster announced the Vidal exhibition in English and Spanish: *A Collector's Vision of Puerto Rico/ Puerto Rico: La visión de un coleccionista*. The poster contained a full-blown color photograph of the exhibition's centerpiece: a carved image of the Virgin of Montserrat, also identified as the Miracle of Hormigueros, referring to the town where the Virgin Mary supposedly appeared in the late sixteenth century. Before entering the exhibition, you heard the sounds of bomba music, later identified as a cut from Rafael Cepeda's compact disc *El roble mayor* (The largest oak tree). Once inside, you constantly heard the drumming.

Contrary to other displays on the same floor, few people entered the Vidal exhibition. The summer morning I took these notes, the main entrance doors were closed, so I had to enter through the exit doors. The display was organized into fifteen sections, with bilingual labels for each one. The first section on the right was called "Spanish Colonial History," featuring Campeche's portrait of José Más Ferrer and the seal of the marquis of Arecibo, Gregorio Ledesma. Another case labeled "Colonial Society" contained Campeche's portrait of Isabel O'Daly and the earrings of the pirate Cofresí, as well as slave chains illustrating "Puerto Rico as a slave society, 1509–1873."

The section on "Puerto Rico and the United States" focused on the teaching of the English language in public schools, noting that the Island's name was officially changed to Porto Rico between 1898 and 1932. (A bottle of bay rum witnessed that change.) On the left stood a large panel titled "Puerto Rican Reflections on the Aftermath of the War," quoting local reactions to the Spanish-Cuban-American War. As an editors' profile for the *Washington Post* (Burchard 1999) notes, "The less-than-perfect relationship between the island and Uncle Sam is gently hinted at here and there" but was not elaborated in the exhibition.

The Palace of Santa Catalina (or La Fortaleza, the governor's executive mansion) was pictured next, with a lamp and a tile from the building. Two panels, titled "Puerto Rican Women: 1880–1930" and "Puerto Rican Men: 1880–1930," displayed everyday objects commonly segregated by sex. Women's activities were represented through coconut cups, lamps, fans, spoons, and a rosary. Men's activities were exemplified through a smoking stand, barber shop implements, coffee cups, and canes. This gendered display helped to counter the predominantly masculine perspective of the collection.

To the left was a section on folk toys, including a wooden car, a toy parrot, rag dolls, a yo-yo maraca, a tricycle, a rooster, and a horse. The section labeled "Objects of Everyday Life" included needlework and other fine textiles. A map of Puerto Rico showed the artifacts' most significant sites of origin: drums from Loíza, cuatros from Morovis and Vega Baja, vejigante masks from Ponce and Loíza, santos from San Germán and Hormigueros. The icons clustered in the central mountainous region. The southwestern town of Maricao was incorrectly located on the map.

The next section, "Catholic Devotions," occupied the most extensive portion of the exhibition. Sixty-five santos of various sizes were displayed, emphasizing the Virgin of Montserrat, St. Joseph, St. Anthony of Padua, and St. John Nepomucene. Two labels highlighted the Espadas from San Germán and the Riveras from Morovis as master craftsmen. Aside from the carved saints, the display comprised rosaries, milagros, prayers, and paintings, including a Campeche portrait of St. John Nepomucene on loan from the NMAA.

"Colonial Cash Economy" was the title of a large case located in the center of this space. This section featured work implements used to grow coffee, tobacco, and sugarcane, along with a huge pava (straw hat) associated with the jíbaro and classic photographs by Jack Delano. An iconic portrait of the noted feminist and labor leader Luisa Capetillo wearing a coat, tie, and pants introduced the practice of reading out loud to tobacco factory workers at the beginning of the twentieth century.

Walking toward the right, you encountered the section on carnival. Twelve vejigante masks hung from the wall, along with four stuffed costumes, including gloves, shoes, and a cane. The labels identified notable mask makers by name, including Leonardo Pagán and Juan Alindato, and singled out Ponce as one of the key sites of carnival activities on the Island. A large Delano photograph of the Ponce carnival occupied a full wall.

Further on, two cases focused on Puerto Rican folk music, including *plena* and bomba, two genres with a strong African component. One case contained musical instruments such as the *güiro* (a gourdlike percussion instrument), drums, and maracas, as well as posters from the Division of Community Education and other government agencies. A separate case labeled "Puerto Rican Music" highlighted "jíbaro music," including the cuatro and *tiple* (two string instruments) and *marímbula* (African thumb piano). Unwittingly, this arrangement suggested that the most authentic form of Puerto Rican music is that of the jíbaros, not that of coastal blacks and mulattoes.

On the wall was a large-scale photographic montage labeled "La Gran Familia Puertorriqueña." These historic pictures, drawn from the National Archives and Records Administration, showed physical types ranging from white to brown to black. Most of the photographs depicted upper- and middle-class whites, despite the curators' intention of showcasing the diversity of the Puerto Rican people and contextualizing the meaning of the terms "Creole" and "mulatto."[10] One of the labels mentioned the massive migration of Puerto Ricans to the United States but incorrectly stated that 3.8 million of them would live in the mainland by the year 2000 (the 2000 census found that 3.4 million Puerto Ricans lived in the mainland and 3.8 million lived on the Island) (U.S. Bureau of the Census 2001).

A small case in the right corner showed a postcard representing cockfighting and objects related to gambling, including a pack of cards and dice. A black fan and jewelry illustrated mourning practices.

A salient part of the exhibition was devoted to Vidal and his family. A full-blown 1957 photograph featured a young Vidal driving a Rolls Royce convertible in the Swiss Alps, while the text highlighted his travels by jeep in the mountains of the Island. Color photographs showed Vidal conversing with a craftsman and a craftswoman. Two television screens intertwined historical images of Puerto Rico with photographs of the Vidal family. A copy of a resolution by the mayor of Ponce, dated 1985–86, dedicated the Ponce carnival to Vidal. One case displayed Vidal's books on Puerto Rican folklore, while another featured the Vidal and Santoni families, including portraits of his grandmother and mother, and personal objects belonging to his relatives.

Muñoz Marín also figured prominently in the exhibition. A photograph from the 1950s showed the governor standing next to the young Vidal, wearing a white U.S. Army uniform. A reproduction of a 1944 *Time* magazine cover celebrated "Puerto Rico's Muñoz Marín."

The last section, titled "Tourism and Souvenirs," displayed a T-shirt, postcards, a machete, a small vejigante mask, maracas, a santo, dolls, and a necklace. The acknowledgments posted on the wall and reprinted in the exhibition's brochure included the Puerto Rican Tourism Company, Banco Popular, and *El Nuevo Día*. If you took the Spanish translation of the exhibition text, you would leave the copy at the main exit or the entrance.

If exhibiting cultures is a political as well as a poetic gesture (Karp and Lavine 1991; Pearce 1992), then the Vidal exhibition provided a public forum for displaying Puerto Rico's national identity. In particular, it articulated the collector's personal vision of the Island as well as the curators' collaborative interpretations of its cultural history. In large measure, the Smithsonian team (Marvette Pérez, Fath Davis Ruffins, and Odette Díaz Schuler) that organized the display appropriated Vidal's discourse of cultural nationalism.[11] The exhibition emphasized the uniqueness and antiquity of Puerto Rican culture as evidenced by historical, ethnographic, and artistic materials. The floor plan led viewers through a quick but informative journey through the Island's distinctive history, economy, religion, music, and politics. Powerful images—visual as well as auditory—evoked a spiritual heritage condensed in the idiom of the Great Puerto Rican Family. Despite the close political and economic ties between Puerto Rico and the United States, the exhibition portrayed the Island as a country with a separate and vibrant identity. The sheer number of objects (more than three hundred) crowded within a small, cloistered space suggested the density, breadth, and wealth of Puerto Rican culture.

UNCOVERING THE ROOTS OF NATIONAL CULTURE

In tandem with an age-old museum tradition, the ethnographic objects displayed in the Vidal exhibition were explained and contextualized through extensive didactic labels. These labels reveal as much about the collector's assumptions, intentions, and worldview as about the curators' (Karp and Lavine 1991; Karp, Kreamer, and Lavine 1992; Kurin 1997; Pearce 1992; Price 1989). The following section provides a close reading of the text accompanying the Vidal exhibition at the NMAH, written by Pérez, Ruffins, and Schuler. This text was available to all visitors as a guide to the collection.

The narrative opens with a general introduction to the collection and a brief historical background of Puerto Rico prior to the Spanish-Cuban-American War. Then it focuses on Spanish colonial history, emphasizing that "Puerto Ricans began to develop their distinctive traditions and practices" during the eighteenth century. The first three centuries of Spanish colonialism, as well as thousands of years of pre-Columbian history, received a cursory treatment. The authors expound the canonized discourse on national identity when they state that "the contemporary culture of Puerto Rico emerged from the blending of European, African, and Native American traditions." Like Vidal himself, the authors have very little to say about the Taíno heritage. Contrary to standard views of the Island's history, however, they highlight the contributions of "African peoples and their mixed descendants to the development of Puerto Rico's creolized society." The text briefly mentions the "change in rule from Spain to the United States" in 1898 but does not dwell on its political, economic, and cultural repercussions.

Instead, the authors spend much time describing the use and meaning of "objects of everyday life" under the "colonial cash crop economy" between 1880 and 1930 (the adjective "colonial" here subtly includes the first three decades of U.S. rule). Their treatment of religion concentrates on "Catholic devotions" at the expense of other manifestations of popular religiosity on the Island, such as spiritualism and Pentecostalism. The sections on carnival and music once again celebrate the mixture of Spanish, African, and "Native American" customs. In a brief note on tourism and souvenirs, the authors acknowledge that Puerto Rican arts and crafts, "aimed at a mass consumer market, are similar to historical objects in the Vidal collection."

The discussion of the Great Puerto Rican Family reiterates that "the Puerto Rican people, no matter what their racial background, are part of a unique Puerto Rican culture born out of a mixture of European, African, and Indian traditions." As a writer for the *Washington Post* (Burchard 1999) notes, "If there is racial or class strife or economic woe on the island, we hear nothing of it here." Finally, the authors of the text praise the collection as "a reaffirmation of *'puertorriqueñidad'*—the identity of Puerto Rico," in Vidal's own words. This identity appears to stand above and beyond any regional, gender, class, color, and ideological distinctions within the Island's population.

What are the underlying premises of this text? I would argue that they follow the basic tenets of the cultural nationalist discourse that Vidal helped to elucidate and institutionalize on the Island since the 1950s. As Arcadio Díaz Quiñones (1985: 82) has noted, "The Hispanic concord of the 'great family' has come to be, for many, the official patriotic discourse, the 'affirmation' of nationality." This discourse, which I and other scholars (Dávila 1997; Godreau-Santiago 1999; Morris 1997) have analyzed elsewhere, represents Puerto Rican culture first and foremost as a racial and ethnic triad, the result of the biological and historical fusion among the Taíno, Spanish, and African peoples. In practice, this discourse has privileged the Hispanic over the indigenous and African sources (Babín 1986; Guerra 1998; Pabón 1995b). Moreover, cultural nationalists have tended to highlight the ancient, unique, and distinctive characteristics of Puerto Rican traditions vis-à-vis American modernity. Nonetheless, most cultural nationalists—at least since the mid–twentieth century—have not embraced the pro-independence movement. Rather, like Vidal, they have been inclined toward an autonomist ideology that seeks to assert Puerto Rico's national identity within a continued political and economic association with the United States (see Chapter 5). In a 1999 interview, Vidal hailed the Commonwealth formula as "a showcase for democracy" that "was able to raise the economy" through Operation Bootstrap.

Returning to the text, note the recurrent theme that Puerto Ricanness derives from the mingling of different cultural traditions, primarily but not exclusively Hispanic and Catholic and definitely barring contemporary American influences. The authors handle the political relations between Puerto Rico and the United States cautiously and indirectly. In any case, they portray the two countries as separate and sometimes opposing entities, as when they write, "Over the years, conflicts arose over what Puerto Ricans should be taught in school—English vs. Spanish, Protestant vs. Catholic beliefs, and yanqui [*sic*] vs. Puerto Rican values." Thus, Puerto Rican culture is systematically characterized as Spanish-speaking, Catholic, and resistant to Americanization. Like many cultural nationalists on the Island, the authors appeal to a multiracial, classless Puerto Rican family as the master metaphor for national identity. Significantly, they employ the term *criollo* in an encompassing sense "to describe music, cuisine, language, arts, people, religion, and other aspects of contemporary island culture." Historically, creolization helped to blur the racial and cultural differences among various ethnic groups in the Caribbean.

The text, as well as the exhibition, speaks volumes through its silences. Following Vidal, the authors restrict their purview of national culture to the Island, although they make two passing references to the Puerto Rican community in the U.S. mainland. They also highlight the Hispanic element in Puerto Rico's founding triad, virtually ignore the Native American component, and make an effort to rescue its African root. Moreover, the curators practically exclude non-Catholic traditions as part of the Island's religious heritage. Like much of the dominant discourse of national culture, their narrative glosses over the racial and class tensions within the so-called Great Puerto Rican Family. As a largely historical retrospective, the text only alludes to the dramatic changes in the Island's material culture after the launching of Operation Bootstrap in 1947. Finally, the complex relationship between contemporary Puerto Rico and the United States is not discussed at great length. Some of these textual practices may be the result of negotiations with the museum's official policies and unofficial stances toward the political status of Puerto Rico, as well as the growing U.S. Latino population.

CONCLUSION

How, then, does the Vidal Collection represent Puerto Rican culture? First, it objectifies the Island's historic patrimony as the material culture and traditional practices that distinguish Puerto Rico as a nation. Second, it documents the Island's long and illustrious past through surviving samples of earlier periods, such as the antique santos from the seventeenth century and Campeches from the eighteenth century. Third, it juxtaposes the popular artifacts of everyday life used by the working classes with the luxurious possessions of the Island's elite (such as the Vidal family's own china, jewelry, and portraits), suggesting that the nation is forged through interclass alliances. Fourth, the collection—and especially the exhibition—depicts Puerto Ricans as a multiracial and multiethnic people who live together harmoniously. Fifth, it enshrines the jíbaro as "the most profound, resistant, and pure element of the Puerto Rican nationality" (Babín 1986: 14). Finally, the Vidal Collection commemorates the Hispanic and Catholic traditions of an agricultural past against a more Americanized,

Protestant, industrial, and urban modernity, rarely documented but always implied in the collection itself.

The exhibition—as well as the larger collection—was organized according to the basic categories of cultural nationalism on the Island. Vidal was one of the key architects of the dominant discourse on Puerto Rican culture after World War II, which holds that "Puerto Rico has all the characteristics of a sovereign nation except sovereignty itself" (United States–Puerto Rico Commission 1966: 140). "I am a patriot from here. . . . I feel very Puerto Rican," Vidal has asserted (interview with the author, October 4, 1999). During the 1990s, Vidal's nationalist project (with regard to Puerto Rico) coincided with the rise of identity politics on the mainland, when Latinos were demanding greater representation in U.S. cultural institutions, such as the Smithsonian. However, the Vidal Collection contains very little material on the Puerto Rican diaspora. For most nationalist intellectuals like Vidal, the Puerto Rican nation is territorially bound to the Island.

Ironically, the most extensive collection of the Island's material culture is now located in the mainland. The Smithsonian tends to treat the Vidal material as a local variant of the American mosaic, much as it does other ethnic and regional collections, such as those related to Native Americans and Mexican Americans in the Southwest or Japanese Americans in Hawaii and African Americans in Washington, D.C. This museological approach tends to dilute the colonial character of the Puerto Rican experience and to transform it into yet another episode in U.S. multiculturalism. Yet the exhibition itself, which highlights that Puerto Rico has its own national identity, cannot be easily accommodated within the museum's overarching American narrative. As the curator of an earlier Smithsonian traveling exhibition of Vidal's collection of votive art has noted, "The persistence of the milagro tradition in Puerto Rico is evidence of the island's success in holding fast to its own customs in the face of pervasive influences from the United States" (Mendelson 1977).

This case study reveals the close links between collecting practices and nationalist discourses in Puerto Rico and other colonial settings. Like folklorists, archaeologists, historians, and collectors elsewhere, Vidal was primarily concerned with preserving and promoting the cultural heritage of his homeland. His project entailed nothing less than collecting the nation: assembling an extensive sample of its traditional objects and practices to document their original, authentic, and lasting value. The collection provides a highly selective reading of the Island's cultural history, marked by certain regional, class, racial, gender, and ideological preferences. Moreover, it seeks to fix the essence of national identity before the postwar socioeconomic changes that ultimately reshaped the country's character. Both the collection and the exhibition suggest that popular religiosity, especially Catholic devotions, still defines much of the Puerto Rican worldview. Although the collector and the curators recognize that traditional Puerto Rican culture derives from the blending of Taíno, Spanish, and African sources, they privilege the Spanish component. Altogether, the Vidal Collection is one of the most concrete and dramatic illustrations of Muñoz Marín's Operation Serenity—the state-led effort to rescue the Island's traditional culture from the onslaught of Americanization.

The failure to establish a national museum on the Island has long-term repercussions for Puerto Rican cultural politics. Can Puerto Ricans imagine their nation without their own museum of popular arts and traditions? Will those living on the mainland recognize themselves in a collection that practically excludes them from the Island's culture? Can the founding myths of the jíbaro and the Great Puerto Rican Family resonate with urban, working-class youth on and off the Island? How will Americans and other visitors to the NMAH respond to this visible assertion of a separate identity in Puerto Rico? To what extent will this exhibition contribute to the decolonization of the Puerto Rican nation? These are some of the questions, fraught with political implications, that should be addressed in future research.

SEVEN

Following Migrant Citizens
The Official Discourse on Puerto Rican Migration to the United States

Cultural nationalists in Puerto Rico have traditionally neglected the diaspora in their definition of the nation. Certainly, the Vidal Collection analyzed in the last chapter overlooks the cultural expressions of migrant communities in New York and elsewhere. Until recently, most Island-based intellectuals have considered emigration to the United States as a serious threat to national identity, particularly with respect to the Spanish language. The nationalist writer René Marqués (1963) dramatized his pessimistic vision of migration in his classic play *La carreta* (The oxcart), the tragic story of a Puerto Rican family that moves from the countryside to San Juan, then to New York City, and finally returns to the homeland. Elsewhere, Marqués (1966) stressed the language barrier between Puerto Rico and the United States, as well as serious differences in the family values, social customs, race relations, and climate of the two countries.

Since the 1950s the Island's social scientists have tended to adopt a nationalist perspective that lamented the inexorable cultural assimilation of Puerto Rican migrants in the United States. Anthropologist Eugenio Fernández Méndez warned that "Puerto Rico, which is now a Hispanic *community*, may cease being one due to the mediate effects of migration" (1959: 151; emphasis in the original). The political scientist Manuel Maldonado-Denis (1972: 134) complained that "our Puerto Rican brothers residing in the United States—but above all the more recent generations—do not have an elementary command of either Spanish or English." Another influential anthropologist, Eduardo Seda Bonilla (1972), wrote that Nuyoricans faced an acute identity problem owing to the loss of their cultural roots and racial discrimination in the United States. From this standpoint, the diaspora represented a cultural and political crisis rather than an enduring solution to the socioeconomic problems of Puerto Rico (see also Vázquez Calzada 1963).

In the 1970s, researchers associated with the Centro de Estudios Puertorriqueños at Hunter College began to question the Island-centered canon of Puerto Rican culture (see Campos and Flores 1979; Cortés, Falcón, and Flores 1976; Flores, Attinasi, and Pedraza 1981). These writers documented the vibrant cultural expressions of Puerto Rican migrants in New York City and elsewhere, especially in music, poetry, and theater. In the 1990s, many intellectuals (especially those residing in the U.S. mainland) reassessed the Island's hard-line positions vis-à-vis the Puerto Rican exodus, particularly in the humanities and above all in literary criticism (Aparicio 1998; Barradas 1998; Díaz Quiñones 1993; Flores 1997; Glasser 1995; C. Hernández 1997; Negrón-Muntaner and Grosfoguel 1997; Sánchez Korrol 1994; Torre, Rodríguez Vecchini, and Burgos 1994; Zentella 1997). Thus, scholars have developed a new appreciation of the literary, musical, and artistic contributions of Puerto Ricans in the diaspora and have highlighted their persistent links with the homeland.

Still, many islanders continue to believe that the emigrants are no longer Puerto Ricans, as if they became Americanized almost automatically upon arriving in the mainland. Socially, the islanders' rejection of the emigrants is expressed in the diffusion of a negative stereotype of Nuyoricans, particularly those who return to the Island; culturally, in the virtual lack of formal study of the diaspora throughout the academic curriculum; and politically, in the popular resistance to allowing mainland Puerto Ricans to participate in local plebiscites on the status of Puerto Rico. In contrast, most Puerto Ricans in the United States continue to identify themselves primarily as Puerto Rican and retain strong ties to their country of origin (see Falcón 1993; Marvette Pérez 1996).

The main theoretical and political problem, then, is how to rethink the nation to include almost half of the Puerto Rican people who currently live outside the insular territory. In the year 2000, the population of Puerto Rican origin in the U.S. mainland represented 47.2 percent of the entire Puerto Rican population, including the Island (Guzmán 2001). In demographic and geographic terms, Puerto Rico increasingly constitutes a nation in the diaspora—that is, a deterritorialized or translocal country (Laó 1997). Yet scholars do not understand well how Puerto Rican migrants have reconstructed their cultural identity; how they maintain links of all kinds with the Island; if their everyday practices appropriate the traditional nationalist discourse; to what extent they redefine the conventional narrative of Puerto Ricanness in the United States; and whether they ultimately perceive themselves as Puerto Ricans, Americans, or both.

In this chapter I examine another angle that has received little scholarly attention: how the sending state approached the migrants' cultural identity. First I describe how the Puerto Rican government has represented Puerto Ricans on the mainland, particularly in New York City after World War II. I ground my analysis of the official view of Puerto Ricanness on the annual and monthly reports of the Migration Division of the Island's Labor Department, which functioned between 1948 and 1989, and its successor, the Department of Puerto Rican Community Affairs in the United States, which operated between 1989 and 1993. The documents of these two agencies provide a unique opportunity to examine the close links between Puerto Ricans on the Island and in the mainland during the period of massive migration. I focus on the ambivalent relation between the Commonwealth government and various grassroots groups in the diaspora, a relation that became increasingly tense during the 1960s when such groups asserted their independence from the government's official discourse. On the one hand, Commonwealth officials constituted diasporic subjects as territorial and symbolic extensions of the Island's citizens on the mainland, based on the discourse of cultural nationalism. On the other hand, leaders of the Puerto Rican community in New York and elsewhere increasingly used that discourse to assert their own claims as an ethnic minority in the United States.

ORGANIZING AND SUPERVISING MIGRATION: THE PUERTO RICAN GOVERNMENT AND THE DIASPORA

Since the first decades of the twentieth century, the Puerto Rican government has assumed an active role in promoting and managing migration (Lapp 1990). In 1919 the Island's Department of Agriculture and Labor began to supervise the recruitment of agricultural contract workers to the United States and other

countries (Sierra Berdecia 1956: 15). In 1930 the government established the
Information and Documentation Office for Puerto Ricans in New York City,
later renamed the Identification and Employment Bureau and, in 1942, the
Office of the Identification Service of the Department of Agriculture and Commerce. The Labor Department created the Bureau of Employment and Migration in 1948, which became the Migration Division in 1951 and the Department
of Puerto Rican Community Affairs in the United States in 1989. After the
proclamation of commonwealth status in 1952, the insular government treated
mainland Puerto Ricans as an outgrowth of the Island's population and lobbied
extensively for their rights and well-being. At this point, it remains unclear
whether U.S. colonial authorities and Commonwealth elected officials handled migrant affairs in a significantly different way. However, the available
evidence suggests that the Migration Division failed to represent the complex
and varied experiences of the Puerto Rican diaspora after World War II.

Michael Lapp (1990) has criticized the Migration Division's attempt to co-
opt the Puerto Rican population in the continental United States to further
the interests of the Commonwealth government. He argues that representatives
of mainland Puerto Rican communities did not play a role in formulating
the agency's policies, which depended exclusively on the Popular Democratic
Party during the period under consideration (1948–68). Throughout the 1950s,
the Migration Division attempted to articulate the interests of Puerto Rican
migrants to the American public as well as to federal, state, and city authorities.
However, new community groups emerged in the late 1950s and early 1960s,
especially in connection with the civil rights movement, often funded by the
federal government. Mainland Puerto Ricans became increasingly alienated
from the Commonwealth's political agenda and organized separately from the
Migration Division, which lost much of its authority over New York's Puerto
Rican community in the mid-1960s. I would add that this loss of hegemony was
largely due to the incapacity of the nationalist discourse adopted by the Puerto
Rican government to capture the cultural identity of the diaspora.

FOLLOWING "MIGRANT CITIZENS":
THE RISE OF THE MIGRATION DIVISION, 1948–1968

The project of organizing and supervising massive emigration from Puerto
Rico to the U.S. mainland was first elaborated by the American sociologist
Clarence Senior, then director of the Social Science Research Center at the

University of Puerto Rico (1945–48) and eventually director of the Migration Division as well (1951–60). Born in Clinton, Missouri, Senior (1903–74) earned advanced degrees in sociology and political science at the University of Kansas and Columbia University. He became a community organizer and national executive secretary of the American Socialist Party (1926–36). In 1945 University of Puerto Rico chancellor Jaime Benítez invited him to teach economics and help organize the new Social Science Research Center in Río Piedras. Senior soon joined a small group of influential American advisers to Puerto Rican political leaders and planners. He played key roles in Puerto Rico as a public official, policy consultant, and academic researcher from the 1940s to the 1960s. He became a personal friend of Muñoz Marín and a lifetime spokesman for the PDP in the continental United States (see Lapp 1990: 79–91; Lauria-Perricelli 1989: appendix 3).

In an influential book, Senior (1947b) advocated the creation of an emigration office, attached to the governor's executive staff and working closely with the Department of Labor. Its main function would be to recruit workers from Puerto Rico to the United States and Latin America. The office would provide migrants with information on job openings, training, transportation, settlement, and insurance, as well as promote further emigration from the Island. Senior included a detailed colonization plan for Venezuela, where he thought "the economic and political situations are quite favorable" (Senior 1947b: 122). Senior's plan to sponsor migration to Latin America proved too expensive (O'Connor to Moscoso, July 22, 1947). But his proposal to find jobs for Puerto Ricans in the United States, especially in New York City, later crystallized in the Migration Division.

Senior's blueprint for planned emigration was well received by Muñoz Marín, then president of the Puerto Rican Senate (1941–48). In a 1946 public forum on Puerto Rico's population problem, Senior had originally asserted that "emigration was possible but not desirable." A memorandum endorsed by Muñoz Marín agreed that "emigration is not a permanent solution to the problem of overpopulation and in the long run is anti-economic. But we concur with Mr. [Salvador] Tió that it is necessary to resort to emigration as a measure for the immediate relief to the problem posed by our surplus population, while we seek permanent solutions in the long run" (Muñoz Marín to Egloff, September 28, 1946). An economist working for the Office of Puerto Rico in Washington, Donald J. O'Connor, also urged the resettlement of Puerto Ricans in the United States and other countries, such as the Dominican Republic or Brazil. According to O'Connor, "Migration can accomplish what economic development programs on the island cannot do quickly"—that is, create jobs and sources of income, while reducing population growth (O'Connor to Piñero et al., August 10, 1948). Although Senior disagreed on the details, he wrote O'Connor, "I agree with you on the need for [the] promotion of emigration" (Senior to O'Connor, March 20, 1947). High-ranking members of the ruling Popular Democratic Party, such as Antonio Fernós-Isern, Teodoro Moscoso, and Rafael Picó, concurred with O'Connor's optimistic assessment. Thus began a government-sponsored program of large-scale migration to the mainland.[1]

Based on the premise that emigration could serve as a safety valve for Puerto Rico's overpopulation, the Island's legislature approved Public Law 25, creating the Employment and Migration Bureau, on May 12, 1947. From the beginning, the Puerto Rican government represented the diaspora as part of its constituency of citizens, but outside its territorial jurisdiction. Public Law 25 defined the official position toward Puerto Ricans in the mainland as follows: "The Government of Puerto Rico does not stimulate or discourage the migration of Puerto Rican workers to the United States or any other foreign country; but it deems its duty to duly orient [them] regarding the occupational opportunities and adjustment problems in ethnologically strange settings." The Island's public policy was "to follow its migrant citizens to facilitate their adjustment and adaptation in the communities in which they chose to live." The agency's administrators believed that their efforts were unprecedented: "The case of Puerto Rico may be unique in that a government, aware of its moral and human duty, follows the migration of a considerable number of its citizens and establishes, to help them, offices in the places where they have settled" (Estado Libre Asociado de Puerto Rico 1972–73: 1; 1975–76: 1–2; 1977–78: 6).

The Migration Division distributed millions of copies of publications orienting Puerto Ricans about American "life and laws," as well as Americans about Puerto Rican culture (Monserrat 1961: 51). In one booklet, the agency advised potential "travelers to the mainland" that "in New York City you and your family will not go together to many places because you don't know English." Another drawing printed by the division illustrated a short story titled "Puerto Rico: Land of Two Christmases" (in English in the original), showing the Three Wise Men and a Christmas tree (Jesús Colón Papers 1901–74: Series VI, Box 1). Marqués's previously cited work (1966) for the Division of Community Education highlighted the cultural conflicts between Puerto Ricans and Americans. Senior (1948) himself wrote about the "many transitions" and "strange contrasts" that Puerto Ricans would face in New York City—from differences in climate and housing to family ties and religion. Puerto Rico's migration policy rested on a semantic equivalence between the United States and "any other foreign country," as well as on its portrayal as an "ethnologically strange setting." Thus, one of the Migration Division's main roles was to bridge the cultural and linguistic gap between Puerto Ricans on the Island and in the mainland.

In several speeches, Muñoz Marín articulated his personal views as well as the Commonwealth's official discourse on Puerto Rican migration. Defining himself as a return migrant to the Island, Muñoz Marín (1958) advised mainland Puerto Ricans to adapt themselves to their new environment, by learning English and registering to vote in local elections. Nonetheless, Muñoz Marín (1960) encouraged the migrants to preserve their cultural identity, assert their pride in being Puerto Rican, and return to the Island, once socioeconomic conditions improved there. As he told a group of Puerto Ricans gathered in Central Park, "How pleasant it is to see, floating in this New York breeze, all those Puerto Rican flags that all of us Puerto Ricans love so much, inside and outside Puerto Rico" (Muñoz Marín 1960: 1).

"THE LOVE OF THE TOWN WHERE YOU WERE BORN": THE MIGRATION DIVISION AND HOMETOWN CLUBS, 1948–1968

To accomplish its mission, the division turned to organizing mainland Puerto Ricans through voluntary associations based on national and regional origin. In the early 1950s the agency's Community Organization Section identified more than two hundred civic, political, social, religious, and recreational organizations among Puerto Ricans in the United States. By the end of the decade, the division supported several confederations of community groups, such as the Council of Spanish-American Organizations of Greater New York, with fifty-eight affiliated groups, and the Federación de Sociedades Hispanas (Federation of Hispanic Societies), with thirty-two groups (Commonwealth of Puerto Rico January 1957; Estado Libre Asociado de Puerto Rico 1953–54). The agency carefully cultivated its relations with these broader organizations in the hope of promoting a united ethnic front. The main model for this kind of community work was the successful experience of European immigrants in the major urban centers of the United States at the turn of the twentieth century.

By far the most common form of association among Puerto Rican migrants— particularly in New York City—was the hometown club, grouping a small

FIGURE 7.1. The Caborrojeños Ausentes at the Puerto Rican Day Parade in New York City. 1968 photograph by Luis R. Díaz. Courtesy of the Archivos Históricos de la Migración Puertorriqueña, Centro de Estudios Puertorriqueños, Hunter College, CUNY.

clique of relatives and friends from the same locality in the Island (Herbstein 1978; Lapp 1990). Most of the groups called themselves *ausentes* (the absent ones) or *hijos* (sons and daughters) of a town back home. The prototype of the hometown club was the Caborrojeños Ausentes, founded in New York in the early 1920s (see figure 7.1). The Migration Division singled out this group as one of its frequent collaborators in the task of maintaining close links between Island and mainland communities. According to one report, the club had "initiated and developed an excursion to Puerto Rico of a group of its members, with the purpose of familiarizing themselves more with the work being done in Puerto Rico by different groups and agencies and also to see if they can initiate stronger links between Puerto Rico's regional (town) groups in New York and the corresponding township in the Island" (Commonwealth of Puerto Rico August 1957).

After World War II, many hometown clubs were created to provide shelter, jobs, financial help, recreation, and other benefits to their members. In 1946 the San Juan Social Club was founded in New York and the Hijos de Borinquen Social Club was established in Brooklyn. Between 1958 and 1963, five new groups from Aguada, Barceloneta, Mayagüez, and Naranjito were organized. By the early 1960s, all of the Island's seventy-seven municipios were represented in El Congreso de los Pueblos (Congress of Hometown Clubs), founded in 1956 in New York City (Estades 1978: 39; Sánchez Korrol 1994: 226). For the Migration Division, hometown clubs represented the backbone of the Puerto Rican community in the United States. Muñoz Marín (1960) himself recognized the resilience of the migrants' places of origin in a speech addressed to Puerto Ricans in New York City.

The division worked closely with dozens of township groups in New York, Chicago, Cleveland, Camden, Boston, Hartford, and other cities. In addition to the Caborrojeños Ausentes, the agency collaborated with the Sociedad Utuadeña Hijos del Viví, Sociedad Cívica Mayagüezana, Canovenses Ausentes, Hijos de Guayanilla, Yauco Social Club, Hijos de Arecibo, Club Fajardeño, and Los Hijos de Barceloneta. Almost every town of some size was represented in the diaspora, including Aguada, Aguadilla, Arroyo, Guánica, Orocovis, Patillas, Peñuelas, Ponce, San Germán, Santa Isabel, and Villalba (see the Justo A. Martí Photographic Collection for a graphic documentation of many of these clubs).

A newspaper article published in New York in the 1950s noted the endurance of regional allegiances among the migrants: "The Puerto Rican, as well as loving his little Island very much, has another love well kept inside his dreamy and romantic soul: the love of the town where he was born" (Marietta 1955: 32). The reporter went on to describe the annual celebrations in honor of *los hijos ausentes* in many of the Island's towns, such as Aguada, Guayama, Arecibo, Aibonito, Camuy, and Humacao. Most of these celebrations took place during the *fiestas patronales*, the traditional feasts in honor of the town's patron saint. (Such ritual practices dedicated to the ausentes are still held in municipios like Cataño, Cidra, and Loíza.) The article thus suggested that strong kinship and friendship networks continued to bind Island hometowns and their daughter communities in the United States.

Early on, the division recognized the value of hometown clubs to ease the transition between the Island and the mainland. After World War II, these associations aided thousands of migrants to find jobs, housing, and social support (Herbstein 1978). The Commonwealth agency noted that "these groups have an enormous attraction for the Puerto Rican. . . . Moreover, they provide a means of expression for social and cultural activities in which the entire family can participate" (Estado Libre Asociado de Puerto Rico 1957–58: 91). The dominant view of the Migration Division (as articulated by Senior in his monthly and annual reports) was that voluntary associations—especially hometown clubs—would hasten Puerto Ricans' assimilation into the American mainstream. As an official report noted, "The major objective of the Migration Division is to speed up and smooth out the temporary problems of adjustment which occur when any group migrates to a new environment with a [sic] different customs" (Continuations Committee 1959: 38).

For Commonwealth planners and administrators, adjustment would lead to upward social mobility. Senior was especially proud that his office had helped to organize "a group of Puerto Rican second generation young adults composed of college graduates, professionals and people of many other walks of life" in New Jersey (Commonwealth of Puerto Rico, September 1955). The office also supported a broad range of professional and civic organizations in New York, from the Spanish-American Bar Owners Association and the Spanish Taxi Drivers Association to the Asociación de Damas Evangélicas (Association of Evangelical Ladies) and the Committee on the Spanish-Speaking Foster Mother of the Year. According to Joseph Monserrat, who succeeded Senior as director of the Migration Division, the logic behind such efforts was unmistakable: "Clearly, our job was to help him [the Puerto Rican migrant] 'integrate' within one generation, we had to plan for the most rapid adjustment possible" to the United States (1968: 204). The large number of Puerto Rican organizations in New York City—an estimated 263 in the early 1960s—was taken as a sign of adjustment to the mainland (Pura Belpré Papers 1897–1985: Series VI, Box 1). As one report boasted, "The Puerto Rican has started to make himself felt in the state of New Jersey and in Philadelphia, Pennsylvania, through his own civic and social activities, carried out on a large scale" (Estado Libre Asociado de Puerto Rico 1962–63: 116).

The Migration Division's annual reports document the rise of voluntary associations among Puerto Ricans in the United States since the early 1950s (see table 7.1). Hometown clubs constituted between one-sixth and one-fourth of all the groups that collaborated with the agency from the mid-1960s to the mid-1970s. At its peak in 1961–62, the agency identified 168 hometown clubs in the mainland. Unfortunately, after 1978 the reports do not distinguish such clubs from other kinds of organizations. Nonetheless, they have continued to play a key role among Puerto Rican migrants. According to the reports, the number of community organizations affiliated with the agency tended to increase until the late 1960s, reached a low point in the early 1970s, and then increased again throughout the 1980s.

This long-term pattern contradicts Lapp's claim (1990) that the Migration Division never developed "a significant constituency" among mainland Puerto Ricans. Although it is difficult to measure how much community support the agency garnered, it survived a critical period in the 1960s. As Judith Herbstein (1978) shows, a distinctive sense of a separate Puerto Rican community in the United States emerged in response to a new ideology of cultural pluralism, antipoverty programs, growing ethnic group awareness, and the civil rights movement. In addition, the rise of the pro-independence, student, antiwar, and feminist movements radicalized many young Puerto Ricans on the Island as well as in the mainland (Torres and Velásquez 1998). The 1960s also witnessed the greatest tension between the Migration Division and representatives of the Puerto Rican diaspora (Estades 1978). However, the division reestablished working relations with Puerto Rican community organizations over the next two decades, as a result of changing leadership, staff, resources, ideologies, and political contexts in both the United States and Puerto Rico.

Part of the clash between the Migration Division and emerging leaders of the Puerto Rican community in New York and elsewhere involved Joseph Monserrat, who directed the division between 1961 and 1969. Born in Bayamón, Puerto Rico, Monserrat was raised in New York City in the 1920s and 1930s. After living in Long Island, his family moved to Spanish Harlem, where he studied Spanish at the school established by the Liga Puertorriqueña e Hispana. Upon finishing his studies at Columbia University and the New School for Social Research, Monserrat worked as a community organizer in New York and joined the U.S. Air Force during World War II. In 1951 Senior recruited him as assistant director of the Migration Division office in New York, and in 1960 Muñoz Marín appointed him national director. Like Senior, Monserrat was closely identified with the PDP. Upon resigning from his office in 1968, he

TABLE 7.1. Puerto Rican Voluntary Associations in the United States Identified by Migration Division, 1953–1988

Year	Number of Associations	Number of Hometown Clubs	As Percentage of Total
1953–54	200	n/a	n/a
1954–55	n/a	n/a	n/a
1955–56	n/a	n/a	n/a
1956–57	n/a	n/a	n/a
1957–58	427	n/a	n/a
1958–59	n/a	n/a	n/a
1959–60	451	n/a	n/a
1960–61	n/a	n/a	n/a
1961–62	n/a	168	n/a
1962–63	102	8	n/a
1963–64	318	n/a	n/a
1964–65	13	n/a	n/a
1965–66	n/a	n/a	n/a
1966–67	n/a	n/a	n/a
1967–68	828	71	8.6
1968–69	1,001	135	13.5
1969–70	779	77	9.9
1970–71	628	86	13.7
1971–72	518	42	8.1
1972–73	84	7	8.3
1973–74	86	10	11.6
1974–75	190	27	14.2
1975–76	259	30	11.6
1976–77	235	55	23.4
1977–78	210	n/a	n/a
1978–79	334	n/a	n/a
1979–80	523	n/a	n/a
1980–81	626	n/a	n/a
1981–82	464	n/a	n/a
1982–83	337	n/a	n/a
1983–84	246	n/a	n/a
1984–85	212	n/a	n/a
1985–86	70	n/a	n/a
1986–87	303	n/a	n/a
1987–88	374	n/a	n/a

Source: Estado Libre Asociado de Puerto Rico 1953–54 to 1987–88.

Note: Between 1953–54 and 1959–60, the figures include civic, political, social, religious, and recreational organizations founded by Puerto Ricans, as well as the public and private agencies of non–Puerto Ricans.

became a member of New York City's Board of Education and was later elected president of the board (Fitzpatrick 1987: 51; *The Rican* 1973).

Under Monserrat's direction, the Migration Division sought "to speak for [*dar voz*] the thousands of Puerto Ricans who come to reside in the cities and towns of the United States" (Estado Libre Asociado de Puerto Rico 1961–62: 182). The division often acted as an unofficial consular office, serving as a liaison between the Puerto Rican community and municipal, state, and federal authorities (Sierra Berdecia 1956: 17). As Monserrat (1961: 57) wrote Muñoz Marín, "When the Migration Division began, we were the 'experts' on Puerto Ricans. We have now become the 'consultants' to the many local experts whom our efforts have created."

But this self-appointed role as spokespersons, experts, and consultants generated resentment in various quarters of the migrant population. One divisive practice involved recruiting islanders to negotiate the problems of New York Puerto Ricans with city officials (Pantoja 1989: 26). Another problem was the perception that the Migration Division was a political arm of the Commonwealth government in the mainland, divorced from the community's interests (Jenkins 1977: 77). Until the mid-1960s, the lack of well-coordinated efforts by grassroots organizations among New York Puerto Ricans contributed to the division's visibility in the United States. Back on the Island, the long hegemony of the PDP between 1940 and 1968 also strengthened the agency's position. However, the rise of new community groups among Puerto Rican migrants and the election of Governor Luis A. Ferré from the New Progressive Party signaled a new period in the relations between the Commonwealth and the diaspora.

REUNITING "THE TWO HALVES OF THE FATHERLAND": CRISIS AND RECOMPOSITION, 1968–1989

During the 1970s, the Migration Division underwent significant reorganization. After a brief hiatus of NPP control over the Island's government (1968–72), the first PDP administration of Governor Rafael Hernández Colón (1972–76) made a stronger claim to represent the Puerto Rican community in the United States. Consequently, the agency began to articulate the idea of a single nation with divided borders, an image long current in the Puerto Rican media in the United States. In the 1950s, one magazine editor asserted that "this country [the United States] is a constitutive part of the fatherland of the children of Borinquen [Puerto Rico]" (*Puerto Rico y Nueva York* 1955: 6). Two decades later, an annual report of the Migration Division echoed those words: "The Puerto Rican people are composed of two parts, almost halves, divided between those who reside in the island-fatherland and those who live in the continental United States . . . both communities maintain affective and material links, which are constant. . . . In summary, they feel like a single people, a single identity, Puerto Ricans all" (Estado Libre Asociado de Puerto Rico 1975–76: 2–3). The author of the report went on to recognize that "in the past, the Division played a paternalistic role, as the leader of the Puerto Rican community" in the United States (3). Henceforth, the agency would support existing local organizations, foster their integration into broader confederations, and strengthen the bonds between Puerto Ricans on the Island and in the mainland. But it would relinquish its pretension to represent the needs and interests of all sectors of the diaspora.

The Migration Division failed to accomplish one of its basic goals: to create a single umbrella organization from a variety of local and special interest groups (Lapp 1990: 273). Instead, the agency's personnel were dismayed at what they perceived as the growing fragmentation of the community since the mid-1960s. In one case, "the Puertorriqueños Unidos de Newburgh desegregated into other bodies such as the Club Social El Caborrojeño, Unidad Católica, Conjunto Los Naturales (artistic), and Club Deportivo Puertorriqueño." Furthermore, the division's report lamented "the dissolution of Puerto Rican groups, associations, and clubs which had formerly met their goals, resulting in the organization of other community action groups in tandem with federal and state economic programs," such as President Johnson's War on Poverty (Estado Libre Asociado de Puerto Rico 1964–65: 124; 1967–68: 189). Many of these new groups dealt directly with employment, housing, education, social services, and civil rights, which the Commonwealth government had handled before (Fitzpatrick 1987: 51). Moreover, the leaders of these groups—many coming from the old hometown clubs—appealed to Puerto Rican nationalism to mobilize their constituencies, rather than promoting their integration into American culture. Such developments forced the Migration Division to reassess its mission, from fostering the migrants' assimilation to asserting their separate cultural identity as Puerto Ricans.

During the 1970s, the agency's community organization program clarified its main objective: "Our service does not pretend to assume a paternalistic attitude in relation to Puerto Rican groups already organized in various communities, but to help them identify and recognize the problems faced in a particular area

and stimulate them to seek solutions by themselves, using all available resources to that end" (Estado Libre Asociado de Puerto Rico 1974–75: 35). But
the accusation that the agency harbored a paternalistic attitude toward the
migrants lingered on and was even accepted by its own administrators (Velázquez 1992). Much of the agency's staff continued to be recruited in Puerto Rico,
and its directors were appointed by the Island's secretary of labor or the governor. New York Puerto Rican leaders often perceived islanders working for the
Migration Division as racist, elitist, and subservient to white Americans (Pantoja 1989: 26).

Gradually, the division abandoned its earlier rhetoric of community organizing and adjustment and instead focused on the migrants' cultural practices and
transnational ties. In 1971 the Department of Puerto Rican Culture was created
within the division with the purpose of "involving the community at large
with knowledge about our folklore, traditions, customs, literature, painting,
music, dances, and songs" (Estado Libre Asociado de Puerto Rico 1971–72:
163). Among other initiatives, the new department organized artistic exhibits
and poetry contests, sponsored academic lectures, collaborated with the Museo
del Barrio and Taller Boricua, and celebrated the Discovery of Puerto Rico and
the founding of the city of San Juan. With the division's support, the Feast of
Saint John the Baptist and the Puerto Rican Folk Festival became key cultural
activities of the migrant community, as did the Puerto Rican Day Parade in
New York City.

The agency's administrators adopted the idiom of cultural nationalism to
justify their new project: "The Migration Division has considered it necessary
to promote activities of a cultural character to help Puerto Ricans adapt to
[new] sociocultural circumstances, unknown to many, and feel proud of their
cultural heritage, at the same time that they contribute to the development of
American culture" (Estado Libre Asociado de Puerto Rico 1973–74: 101). A later
report echoed the same sentiment: "The Puerto Rican community [in the
United States] has lacked various means through which it might expose its
culture in the U.S. mainland" (1976–77: 15).

Party politics in Puerto Rico inevitably spilled over to the diaspora. In 1978–
79, NPP governor Carlos Romero Barceló's administration eliminated the Cultural Affairs Program at the Migration Division, which Governor Hernández
Colón reinstated in 1985 and revitalized (Estado Libre Asociado de Puerto Rico
1985–86). The main purpose of this program was "the dissemination of information to raise the consciousness of Puerto Rican culture in our communities"

(Estado Libre Asociado de Puerto Rico 1987–88: 30). The program actively promoted the visual arts and theater, as well as the establishment of a cultural resource center for Puerto Rican communities in the United States, especially in New York, Chicago, Cleveland, and Philadelphia. Annual reports highlighted the "importance of maintaining our cultural tradition and the Spanish language, based on more than 500 years of a historic cultural tradition." The underlying philosophy was summarized in a poster designed for the Department of Puerto Rican Community Affairs in 1991, with the slogan: "Certainly we are one people, separated by the sea and integrally united by our culture" (Estado Libre Asociado de Puerto Rico 1990–91: 11). Accordingly, the department fostered an intense exchange between individual artists and cultural institutions in Puerto Rico and the United States, such as the Ponce Art Museum, the University of Puerto Rico, the Ford Foundation, and the Museo del Barrio.

APPLYING PUBLIC POLICY IN ANOTHER JURISDICTION?: FROM DIVISION TO DEPARTMENT, 1989–1993

With the transformation of the Migration Division into the Department of Puerto Rican Community Affairs in the United States, the agency underwent another major restructuring. After winning reelection in 1988, the PDP sought to solidify its position in the Puerto Rican diaspora. According to Governor Hernández Colón, Puerto Ricans in the United States and in Puerto Rico were part of a single nation (Falcón 1993: 178). To formalize this proposition, the governor elevated the Migration Division to a full-fledged department of his executive cabinet in 1989.

The secretary of the new department, Nydia M. Velázquez, first eliminated the section on community organization and then created two additional programs: one in cultural promotion to "foster the development of Puerto Rican cultural organizations in the United States," including those concerned with the plastic arts, theater, music, and dance; and another in political orientation and organization to "promote the participation of Puerto Ricans in U.S. electoral processes, principally in New York" (Estado Libre Asociado de Puerto Rico 1989–90: 5, 19). The latter program was known as Atrévete (literally, Dare Yourself). The secretary believed that "the Migration Division lacked credibility and support in the community which it purportedly served. It was perceived as a public relations office of the Government of Puerto Rico, geared toward satisfying the interests of the Island's leaders and not the interests of the Puerto Rican community" in the United States (Velázquez 1992). Thus, the agency needed to establish a more productive relationship with grassroots Puerto Rican organizations in New York City and elsewhere.

Although the department emphasized the persistent ties between the Island and its diaspora to substitute for the paternalistic image of Puerto Rican migrants, it continued to represent the Island as the main source of their collective identity. The Department of Puerto Rican Community Affairs modeled its cultural project on the Commonwealth's Institute of Puerto Rican Culture (Alegría 1996b). Like the institute, the department defined Puerto Rico's cultural heritage primarily as Hispanic, blended with some Taíno and African elements. Both included a broad range of elite and popular practices, such as the poetry of Julia de Burgos and the Puerto Rican Day Parade. According to Secretary Velázquez (1992), the law that created the department "also recognizes [the diaspora's] continuity in cultural identity with Puerto Rico, the nonrupture of social values, and the permanence of affective links with the land of origin." However, the department failed to acknowledge that Puerto Rican communities in the United States had moved away from an exclusive reliance on the Spanish language and other Hispanic cultural traditions, while maintaining a focus on ancestral memories and family background (see Zentella 1997). The department also underestimated the strength of local (as opposed to ethnic or national) allegiances to towns of origin among Puerto Ricans in the United States.

Despite its success in mobilizing mainland Puerto Ricans to register and vote, the Department of Puerto Rican Community Affairs was short lived. In 1992 Nydia Velázquez resigned her position as secretary of the department and was elected to the U.S. House of Representatives from a new electoral district in Brooklyn. The same program she had founded, Atrévete, helped her to obtain votes. However, as Virginia Sánchez Korrol (1994: 238 n. 43) notes, "Her ability to adequately represent New York Puerto Ricans was questioned in light of her island connections." Nonetheless, Velázquez has been twice reelected as one of three Puerto Rican members of Congress from New York.

In 1993 the Rosselló administration eliminated the Department of Puerto Rican Community Affairs. New Progressive Party leaders were well aware that most mainland Puerto Ricans do not support statehood for the Island (Falcón 1993). They also questioned the constitutional right of the Commonwealth government to establish an executive office outside the Island. Majority legislators argued that "it is neither proper nor convenient for a jurisdiction to attempt to apply its own public policy in an overwhelming way in another jurisdiction, when neither its leaders nor the governing program of said leaders have received the electoral endorsement of those whom they purportedly serve" (A. Martínez 1993: 20). Instead, a new law established a New York office affiliated with the Puerto Rico Federal Affairs Administration (PRFAA) in Washington, D.C. Most of the department's staff, budget, and resources were transferred to PRFAA. Thus ended more than six decades of direct state intervention into the resettlement of Puerto Ricans to the United States. However, the Commonwealth government retains a formal presence in several U.S. cities through tourism and trade promotion offices. Although current governor Sila María Calderón has announced plans to restructure these offices, she has not taken any practical measures to do so at the time of this writing. Public policy toward the diaspora remains ill defined on the Island.

CONCLUSION

Since the 1940s, the Puerto Rican government has sought "to follow its migrant citizens" to the U.S. mainland by organizing and supervising their resettlement in an "ethnologically strange setting." This action constitutes one of the earliest examples of a transnational migrant policy by any state, whether colonial or sovereign. Through the Migration Division and later the Department of Puerto Rican Community Affairs, the Commonwealth government extended its reach well beyond the insular territory, first to identify labor shortages and recruit workers, then to organize the migrant community, and finally to preserve its cultural heritage. For decades the Migration Division acted as a go-between for Puerto Ricans on the Island and in the mainland, as well as a liaison with U.S. public and private agencies, while facilitating the migrants' transition from the Island to the mainland. However, the office clashed with emergent organizations and second-generation leaders of a highly mobilized Puerto Rican community, especially in New York City, during the 1960s. The dominant nationalist discourse of the diaspora, elaborated on the Island, neglected the claims of several mainland community institutions, which developed their own agenda within American identity politics. The Migration Division responded to the changing tides by creating a Department of Puerto Rican Culture in the 1970s and abolishing the Community Organization Program in the 1980s. Between 1989 and 1993, under a pro-commonwealth administration, the Department of

Puerto Rican Community Affairs represented official recognition that migrants were still part of a translocal nation, at least rhetorically, but the Island's legislature, then controlled by the pro-statehood party, eliminated the department.

Over time, Commonwealth officials have represented the Puerto Rican diaspora in different ways. Originally, the Migration Division was conceived to identify labor shortages in the continental United States and recruit workers from the Island to address such shortages (Senior and Watkins 1966). During the 1950s, the agency encouraged social, civic, political, religious, and recreational associations among the immigrants. During the 1960s, the agency's community organization program set as its main "objective that the Puerto Rican community identify and know its neighborhood problems and together with other groups . . . obtain the solution to those problems through its own efforts using the existing resources" (Estado Libre Asociado de Puerto Rico 1967–68: 180). From the 1970s onward, the Migration Division strove to preserve what it defined as the historical patrimony of Puerto Ricans in the United States. In the late 1980s, Commonwealth officials rearticulated a cultural nationalist project stressing the Spanish language and other Hispanic traditions as a common denominator for all Puerto Ricans, regardless of their current residence, but continued to privilege the Island over the mainland as the mainspring of collective identity. Hence, the official discourse of the Puerto Rican diaspora had shifted from promoting the migrants' adjustment, adaptation, or integration (read assimilation) to American society, to maintaining close cultural links with the Island. Despite the powerful rhetoric of the "single people" and the "divided nation," Puerto Rican government agencies continued to promote the idea that islanders were more culturally authentic than those who lived in the mainland. To this day, the Island-centered canon has remained contested terrain among Puerto Ricans in the United States. In the next chapter I look more closely at how grassroots Puerto Rican organizations reconstructed the nation in the diaspora.

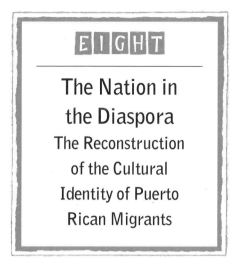

EIGHT

The Nation in the Diaspora
The Reconstruction of the Cultural Identity of Puerto Rican Migrants

Puerto Rican community organizations in the United States both predate and succeed the Migration Division of the Commonwealth's Labor Department and its heir, the Department of Puerto Rican Community Affairs, although their histories intersect for several decades (1948–93). Despite the Puerto Rican government's efforts to contain such organizations within the official discourse on migrants, several diasporic institutions and cultural practices developed outside the parameters of that discourse and represented alternative visions of identity. However, prominent scholars have reiterated that New York Puerto Ricans formed few and weak organizations and that they lacked effective leadership, except for the labor movement (Jenkins 1977: 22; Mills, Senior, and Goldsen 1950: 105, 132; Senior 1948: 81). The pioneering study by Elena Padilla (1958) does not mention a single attempt to establish voluntary associations among Puerto Ricans in Spanish Harlem. This oversight probably stems from a lack of historical perspective and incomplete documentary evidence.[1] Or perhaps scholars could not find the kinds of political interest groups that they studied among other ethnic minorities prior to World War II. Yet, like earlier European immigrants, Puerto Ricans organized themselves to promote their social, cultural, economic, and political interests within American society. They also extended and adapted Island modes of association based on working-class solidarities and hometown origin. Local, regional, and national allegiances were swiftly reconstructed in the diaspora.

Various archival collections at the Centro de Estudios Puertorriqueños of Hunter College provide written and visual support for this claim. The Genoveva de Arteaga, Erasmo Vando, Pura Belpré, and Jesús Colón Papers document the early growth of musical, literary, cultural, and civic organizations among Puerto Ricans in New York—well before the creation of the Migration Division in 1948. Furthermore, the Justo A. Martí Photographic Collection records the multiple ritual activities of Puerto Ricans and other Latinos in New York, including parades, festivals, beauty pageants, religious processions, and family celebrations. These documents allow one to reconstruct—albeit only incompletely—how Puerto Ricans represented themselves in the diaspora, which of their cultural practices traveled better to the north, and how they re-created a sense of national identity against all odds. They also suggest that the migrants' views of themselves sometimes coincided with, but often departed from, official definitions of the Puerto Rican nation. In particular, diasporic narratives of identity tended to move away from exclusive territorial and linguistic criteria to broader cultural and emotional ties to the migrants' communities of origin.

In this chapter I compare the dominant discourse of Puerto Ricanness with the subaltern visions developed by diasporic communities since the beginning of the twentieth century. Furthermore, I explore how migrants maintained strong social and cultural ties to their homeland and developed alternate conceptions of their own identity. Puerto Rican organizations in the United States selectively appropriated the discursive practices traditionally associated with being Puerto Rican, yet they continued to portray themselves as part of a trans-local nation divided between the Island and the mainland. Today, speaking Spanish and living on the Island can no longer be considered to be exclusive identity markers of Puerto Ricanness.

I begin by outlining the history of grassroots Puerto Rican organizations in the mainland during the first half of the twentieth century. I then discuss the proliferation of voluntary associations in the 1940s and 1950s, as well as the emergence of cultural practices representing the Puerto Rican community in the United States, particularly in New York City, such as parades, folk festivals, and other popular feasts. More informal ways of asserting Puerto Ricanness included food, music, and sports. Even in the 1960s, when second-generation immigrants (the Nuyoricans) began to assert their claims as a separate ethnic minority within the United States, they often deployed the rhetoric and tactics of cultural nationalism, rather than define themselves as hyphenated Puerto

Rican–Americans. Thus, the Puerto Rican diaspora nurtured what Anderson (1992) has called "long-distance nationalism" as part of the rise of identity politics after World War II.

EARLY ORGANIZING IN THE DIASPORA:
THE PUERTO RICAN "COLONY" IN NEW YORK

Since the late nineteenth century, Puerto Ricans have established numerous social and political associations in the United States (see Estades 1978; Ribes Tovar 1968; Rodríguez-Fraticelli and Tirado 1989; Sánchez Korrol 1994; B. Vega 1994 [1977]). One of the first labor organizations of Puerto Ricans in New York City was the Alianza Obrera Puertorriqueña (Puerto Rican Workers Alliance). Founded in 1923, the alianza was affiliated with the Puerto Rican Socialist Party headed by Santiago Iglesias Pantín. Its secretary was the Puerto Rican journalist, activist, and labor leader Jesús Colón. Among its founding members were Bernardo Vega, the socialist tobacco worker, and the young Muñoz Marín, then living in New York. The alianza's headquarters were located on East 104th Street, in the heart of Spanish Harlem. The organization proposed "to establish a better intelligence and cooperation among all of us Puerto Ricans living in New York City, principally among the men and women who militate in the ranks of labor." Furthermore, the constitution stated, "differences or divisions engendered in our island, whether of a political, religious, or any other nature, we should forget them." Finally, the alianza's main goal was "to work for the well-being of the Puerto Rican laboring colony in the United States [and] of the working class in Puerto Rico" (Jesús Colón Papers 1901–74: Series V, Box 1). The explicit prolabor orientation of this group contrasts sharply with the Puerto Rican government's policies toward the migrants, which usually took note of their class composition but did not advocate such "radical" causes. However, the alianza was part of a well-established tradition among working-class groups, especially tobacco workers, in the United States and Puerto Rico (see Campos and Flores 1979; B. Vega 1994 [1977]).

In 1923 the Porto Rican League was established in New Jersey to "unite in links of fraternity and mutual protection all Puerto Ricans residing in the United States and those who visit this country." The league was associated with the Democratic Party in the United States but not with any political party in Puerto Rico. One of the group's main objectives was "to develop a cultural program so that those members who so desire may increase their knowledge of the English language and of the political organization of American democracy." It also encouraged its members "to enjoy broadly and freely the rights and privileges offered them by U.S. citizenship" (Jesús Colón Papers 1901–74: Series V, Box 4). Both the Porto Rican League and the Alianza Obrera Puertorriqueña were highly politicized institutions, albeit at different points of the ideological spectrum. Even the names of the two organizations are significant—one in English and the other in Spanish, one accepting the American spelling of the Island (Porto Rico) and the other rejecting it.

In 1926 the Liga Puertorriqueña e Hispana (Puerto Rican and Hispanic League) was founded in Manhattan, with offices on West 113th Street between Lenox and Fifth Avenues. A delegation of the group was soon set up in Brooklyn (see figure 8.1). This organization was essentially civic and cultural in nature, without direct ties to any political party. Its main purpose was "to unite all Hispanics without distinction . . . [and t]o represent the colony before the authorities" (B. Vega 1994 [1977]: 175). Bernardo Vega was one of the founding members and later served as president of the organization. In 1929 the league established a community health clinic in Spanish Harlem, and a year later it organized a small school on Saturdays and Sundays to teach the Spanish language, the history of Puerto Rico, and the history of the Americas. It also published a weekly newspaper, *El Nuevo Mundo*, and sponsored lectures on literary topics. Every year the group organized Mother Day's celebrations, excursions, dances, and contests, where a queen of congeniality (*reina de la simpatía*) was crowned. The league endorsed the creation of the first Employment Office of the Puerto Rican government in New York in 1930. Its first director was also treasurer of the league (Quintero 1963). Although it is uncertain whether the government consulted other community groups, the office enjoyed some local support.

Another early Puerto Rican organization in New York City was Los Jíbaros (The Peasants), a social, cultural, and sports club founded around 1928 and headquartered on West 113th Street in Manhattan. Erasmo Vando, a nationalist actor and community activist, was the leading force behind Los Jíbaros. Years before highland peasants became cult figures on the Island, the group celebrated a public festival "of a regional character," where "anyone who can or wishes to do so may wear the typical costumes of the noble *jíbaros boricuas* [Puerto Rican peasants]." One of the program's highlights was the preparation of *bocaditos criollos* (Creole snacks), such as *chicharrones* (fried pork rinds),

FIGURE 8.1. The Puerto Rican and Hispanic League in Brooklyn during the 1920s. Courtesy of the Jesús Colón Papers, Centro de Estudios Puertorriqueños, Hunter College, CUNY; Benigno Giboyeaux for the Estate of Jesús Colón.

tostones (fried plantains), and *arroz con dulce* (sweet rice). Eating habits were clearly part of the group's definition of what it meant to be a Puerto Rican. The club also sponsored a dance and festival in honor of St. Patrick, the original patron saint of Puerto Rico (Erasmo Vando Papers 1917–88: Series III, Box 2). Perhaps this choice was a way of establishing links with Irish Americans, one of the largest ethnic groups in New York.

The 1920s witnessed a wide range of Puerto Rican associations in the mainland, many with similar goals—such as fostering community solidarity and mutual help—if not the same constituencies or strategies. The Porto Rican Democratic Club was founded in Brooklyn in 1922 (Ribes Tovar 1968: 98). Two other Democratic clubs, the Guaybana and Betances, were organized in the late 1920s. In 1924 a Puerto Rican baseball team from New York's East Side— "the unbeatable San Juan Baseball Club"—played against the Porto Rican Stars from the Island (see figure 8.2). Club Puerto Rico was established on West 116th Street as "a genuinely Puerto Rican group for and by Puerto Rico." The Porto Rican Brotherhood was founded in 1926 "for the protection and aid

BASE BALL

Sunday July 20th, 1924

TWO GAMES   TWO GAMES

—AT—

HOWARD FIELD

Atlantic and Ralph Avenues -

BROOKLYN, N. Y.

FIRST GAME AT 1.30 THE UNBEATABLE

San Juan B.B.C. vs. Porto Rican Stars

The San Juan B. B. C. is another Porto Rican team from New York East Side with Rebollo and Accuedo, the southpaw twirler.

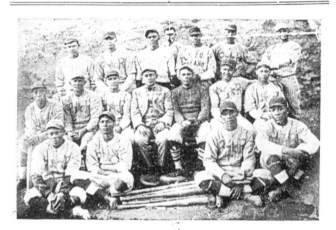

SECOND GAME AT 3.30 THE STRONG

Sheridan Caseys vs. Porto Rican Stars
Knight of Columbus   from Porto Rico

This two teams and our new umpires are members of the Inter-city B. B. A.

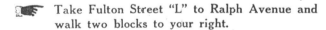 Take Fulton Street "L" to Ralph Avenue and walk two blocks to your right.

FIGURE 8.2. The Unbeatable San Juan Baseball Club from New York City's East Side, 1924. Courtesy of the Jesús Colón Papers, Centro de Estudios Puertorriqueños, Hunter College, CUNY; Benigno Giboyeaux for the Estate of Jesús Colón.

among Puerto Ricans in this city" as an "institution of a benevolent civic, cultural, and political character . . . completely independent of the Island's party politics" (Jesús Colón Papers 1901–74: Series VI, Box 1). One Masonic lodge, Amparo Latino (Latin Relief), was established in Hoboken, New Jersey, in 1919, and another called Faro de las Antillas (Lighthouse of the Antilles) was established in 1928. By the end of the decade, Puerto Ricans had established at least fifteen clubs, brotherhoods, and other social organizations in New York City (Erasmo Vando Papers 1917–88: Series III, Box 2; Jenkins 1977: 24; Jesús Colón Papers 1901–74: Series IX, Boxes 1, 3; B. Vega 1994 [1977]).

The number of community groups continued to grow in the 1930s. Despite its name, the Dutch-American Benevolent Association, founded in 1930, included both the "Curaçaoan and Puerto Rican colony residing in Brooklyn." Also in 1930, the Club Fraternal "Regeneración" started to operate. By 1931, five large Protestant churches catered to Puerto Ricans in New York City. A Puerto Rican Christmas Basket Fund was initiated in 1933. The Lower East Side Hispanic Drum and Bugle Corps performed in the streets of Manhattan in 1937, and the Spanish Merchants Association was established that same year. A Spanish-speaking trade union was formed in 1938 (Jesús Colón Papers 1901–74: Series IX, Boxes 1, 3; Ribes Tovar 1968: 288; Sánchez Korrol 1994: 159; Senior 1948: 50–51). Other groups were based on common origin, occupation, religion, residence, and political ideology. In sum, Puerto Ricans organized themselves well before the first government agencies attempted to supervise their adjustment to mainland life. These associations reflected the migrants' diverse interests and social composition, from trade unions and Masonic lodges to baseball leagues and voting clubs. They suggest the rich texture of social life among Puerto Ricans in the United States during the first half of the twentieth century.

AFTER THE GREAT MIGRATION: "PUERTO RICO LIVES IN NEW YORK"

As New York's Puerto Rican population swelled, so did its community organizations during the 1940s and 1950s (see figure 8.3). By 1940, at least forty Puerto Rican community organizations were operating in New York (B. Vega 1994 [1977]: 242). While some of the preexisting groups disappeared, others were created or incorporated the new arrivals. In 1946 the Puerto Rican Merchants Association—representing *bodegueros*, or grocery store owners—was

FIGURE 8.3. "Passengers disembarking from a steamship in the port of San Juan." 1941
photograph by Jack Delano. Courtesy of the Office of Information for Puerto Rico
Photographic Collection, Centro de Estudios Puertorriqueños, Hunter College, CUNY.

founded in Brooklyn (*El Comerciante* 1964). In 1948 the Congreso de Unidad
Puertorriqueña (Congress of Puerto Rican Unity) was created as an anticolonial
umbrella organization in New York (Jesús Colón Papers 1901–74: Series VI,
Box 1). At least twelve Hispanic, largely Puerto Rican, baseball leagues were
organized in New York after 1950, including teams with such names as Borin-

quen or Puerto Rico. By the early 1960s, New York City's Federation of Hispanic Baseball Leagues boasted 190 teams (*Revista Record* 1957a; Ribes Tovar
1968: 184). According to Senior (1965: 105), Puerto Ricans had established
around three hundred formal associations by that time. The expansion of ethnic organizations and public activities mirrored the migrants' growing numbers
and diversity.

Since the 1950s, New York Puerto Ricans have commemorated the Feast of
Saint John the Baptist, the patron of the city of San Juan (see Díaz-Stevens 1993:
126–34; Fitzpatrick 1987: 130–31; J. Vidal 1994: 94–97). On the Island, *la fiesta
de San Juan* has been a popular religious and secular tradition for decades. In
New York, the feast was first celebrated in Spanish Harlem's La Milagrosa
Parish in 1950 and has been sponsored by New York's archdiocese since 1953.
Over time, the activity has involved many Catholic groups, including the Office of Spanish-American Catholic Action and the *cursillista* (lay Catholic
revivalist) movement.

In 1955 the celebration began with a mass at St. Patrick's Cathedral on June
24, the feast of St. John the Baptist. A local journalist noted that the feast was
"not only for Puerto Ricans but for all Spanish-speaking Catholics. It's like the
celebration of St. Patrick's for the Irish" (*Puerto Rico y Nueva York* 1955: 7). In
1956 more than 30,000 people attended an outdoor celebration at the Bronx
campus of Fordham University (Commonwealth of Puerto Rico July 1956). By
1964, the feast of St. John the Baptist had become "the leading activity of the
Puerto Rican Catholic community" in New York, with more than 60,000 persons attending (Estado Libre Asociado de Puerto Rico 1963–64: 88). In 1971 *El
Diario–La Prensa* called it "the *boricua* heartbeat" and estimated that 75,000
persons had witnessed the previous year's celebration at Downing Stadium on
Randall Island. The 1973 program included a procession, mass, and civic and
religious activities such as a choir, dance groups, and an orchestra. The president of that year's feast, Amalia V. Betanzos, summarized its significance as
follows: "Saint John unites us and Saint John projects us. Thus, although we're
separated by great distances, we form a single people, and thus San Juan de
Puerto Rico unites us to the beloved land and unites us. This is a continuity
with that [the Island], although the sea separates us, a transplant of heritage, of
tradition, of religious faith, of progress, of achievements. . . . Here, in New York,
Puerto Rico lives, hopes, creates, prays, and manifests itself. A beautiful way of
being and saying, of loving and transplanting its spirit" (Justo A. Martí Photographic Collection 1948–85: unprocessed magazines and programs).

FIGURE 8.4. The Puerto Rican Folk Festival in New York City's Central Park. Undated photograph by Luis R. Díaz. Courtesy of the Archivos Históricos de la Migración Puertorriqueña, Centro de Estudios Puertorriqueños, Hunter College, CUNY.

The Puerto Rican Folk Festival (Fiesta Folklórica Puertorriqueña) was first held in New York's Central Park in 1965 (see figure 8.4). Three years later, about 10,000 persons went to the park to enjoy a free program of folk music, including plenas and children's games. By 1974 the festival was attracting more than 80,000 persons (Estado Libre Asociado de Puerto Rico 1967–68: 262–63; 1973–74: 103). A typical program began with religious services, danzas, popular games, songs, and poetry and ended with people eating, drinking, and dancing. Sponsoring organizations included hometown clubs from Arecibo, Arroyo, Orocovis, Ponce, and San Germán. The Sociedad Puertorriqueña de Periodistas y Escritores de Nueva York (Puerto Rican Society of Journalists and Writers of New York) dedicated a literary event to the poet Luis Lloréns Torres. As one program stated, "This Puerto Rican Folkloric Fiesta is a direct approach to all groups that gather in the park." Its main purpose was "to share the [migrants'] values of their cultural heritage" from Puerto Rico (Justo A. Martí Photographic Collection 1948–85: unprocessed magazines and programs). The 1973 and 1976 editions of the festival included a similar combination of religious, musical, literary, and recreational activities (Pura Belpré Papers 1897–1985: Series IV, Box 4).

Like many American ethnic groups, such as the Irish and the Polish, Puerto Ricans have commemorated their heritage through parades, festivals, and other public performances. The Puerto Rican Day Parade (Desfile Puertorriqueño) in New York City became the community's most important public representation in the early 1960s. The parade was first held in 1958 as an offshoot of the short-lived Desfile Hispano, organized in 1956 by a Spanish exile. About 30,000 people marched while another 200,000 watched that first Puerto Rican parade (Estades 1978; Herbstein 1978). The Migration Division worked closely with the parade's organizers from its inception, and the Department of Puerto Rican Community Affairs continued this collaboration in New York and Chicago (Estado Libre Asociado de Puerto Rico 1990–91: 7). Other Puerto Rican parades were held in Hoboken, Camden, Newark, and Paterson, New Jersey, as well as in Philadelphia, Hartford, Boston, and Lorain, Ohio.

The Historical Archives of the Puerto Rican Migration at Hunter College in New York City contain many photographs documenting the Commonwealth government's involvement with the Puerto Rican Day Parade (see figure 8.5). A standard practice was to sponsor a *carroza* (float) with elaborate Puerto Rican motifs, featuring the Puerto Rican flag, folk music, and a beauty queen. Another was to recruit the largest possible number of hometown mayors and politicians from the Island. Many prominent islanders, from San Juan mayor Felisa Rincón de Gautier to Puerto Rican Independence Party president Rubén Berríos and New Progressive Party founder Luis A. Ferré, have served as grand marshals. Historically, the parade has been the most significant display of Puerto Rican identity, power, and solidarity in the United States. In Luis Muñoz Marín's words (1963), "The Puerto Rican Parade is a manifestation of the advancement and progress of Puerto Ricans in New York and of the spirit of improvement of our culture and our people." Today, it is the largest and best attended ethnic parade in New York City (even more so than the West Indian Carnival in Brooklyn) and remains the most visible demonstration of an organized Puerto Rican community (Lapp 1990; Sánchez Korrol 1994: 226).[2]

Another grassroots expression of the Puerto Rican community in New York and elsewhere has been a growing number of evangelical, especially Pentecos-

FIGURE 8.5. The Puerto Rican Day Parade in New York City in the early 1960s.
Courtesy of the Archivos Históricos de la Migración Puertorriqueña, Centro de
Estudios Puertorriqueños, Hunter College, CUNY.

tal, cults. A conference for Lutheran ministers and laypeople was held in New
York City in February 1956, including representatives of the East Harlem Protestant Parish. By that time, the church La Hermosa, affiliated with the Disciples
of Christ, was already operating in the area. In June of that same year, the
Chicago Missionary Society met "to raise the dignity of Puerto Rican Protestantism in this city." In 1957 the Damas Evangélicas established a shelter for
elderly women and unattached girls in New York City. In October 1958 a group
of ministers and other representatives of evangelical churches from Puerto Rico
visited New York. And in 1964 more than forty-five thousand Hispanic children
representing over four hundred Protestant churches participated in the Annual
Parade of Christian Children in New York (Commonwealth of Puerto Rico
February 1956, June 1956, May 1957, October 1958; Estado Libre Asociado de
Puerto Rico 1955–56, 1963–64). The Justo A. Martí Photographic Collection
contains other images of evangelical activities in New York City, Newark, and

other cities. In the early 1960s, New York City alone had 284 Puerto Rican Protestant churches. Pentecostals had established as many as thirty storefront churches (*Asambleas de Dios*) in East Harlem by 1968 (Herbstein 1978: 83; Ribes Tovar 1968: 234). Unfortunately, most academic researchers have not yet accessed the historical records of these homegrown religious groups.

BETWEEN TWO FLAGS: EVERYDAY FORMS OF PUERTO RICAN CULTURE

In addition to formal organizations, Puerto Rican migrants reconstructed their identity in informal ways. Social networks linked people according to kinship and friendship, community of origin, neighborhood residence, eating habits, religious beliefs, musical practices, and sports interests (see Herbstein 1978). Since the 1930s, mainland Puerto Ricans have shown great enthusiasm for prizefighting. During the 1950s, several Spanish periodicals in New York were devoted to sports, especially boxing and baseball. The Athletic Federation of Hispanic Leagues was founded in 1954, and the Miss Hispanic Sport contest was held in 1957 (Chenault 1938: 129; *Revista Record* 1957a; Ribes Tovar 1968: 184; Senior 1965: 105). Baseball became the most popular pastime among Puerto Ricans in New York as well as on the Island. Although athletic leagues have not received much scholarly attention, they played a key role in creating a sense of community solidarity among the migrants. As one commentator put it, "Destiny disunites us but sports unite us" (*Revista Record* 1957b).

The photographers Justo A. Martí and Luis R. Díaz (who worked for the Migration Division) chronicled numerous social activities, such as birthdays, baptisms, weddings, dances, and excursions, among New York Puerto Ricans. Music played a prominent role in these festive gatherings. One journalist reminisced: "A group of Cubans and Puerto Ricans, back in the year 1932, on Lenox Avenue, formed an 'orchestra' in the blink of an eye" (Quintero 1963: 12). Bernardo Vega (1994 [1977]: 128) mentions that many Puerto Rican families owned a Victrola or Pianola and often organized weekend dances in their Spanish Harlem apartments. Ruth Glasser (1995) has shown that Puerto Rican musicians helped to articulate the cultural identity of their New York communities between 1917 and 1940. It was in Spanish Harlem that Rafael Hernández composed Puerto Rico's unofficial anthem, "Lamento borincano" (Puerto Rican lament), in 1929. It was also in New York that Manuel "Canario" Jiménez recorded the first plenas for RCA Victor in the 1920s. Bolero, plena, *guaracha, son,* and later salsa became extremely popular among Puerto Ricans in New York City and other centers of the diaspora.

Singing and dancing punctuated the daily and ritual activities of Puerto Rican migrants. In 1963–64 the Club Familiar Puertorriqueño de New Brunswick organized an annual trip to the countryside (*gira campestre*) "in Puerto Rican style, with typical Puerto Rican music, and dishes from the rural Puerto Rican menu" (Estado Libre Asociado de Puerto Rico 1963–64: 103). On such occasions, Puerto Ricans usually played and listened to folk music (*música jíbara*) from the Island, as well as plena and bomba. They often wore pavas associated with the Puerto Rican peasantry, tropical shirts, and flowery dresses. Their instruments included guitars or *cuatros* (string instruments), *güiros* (gourds), maracas, *panderetas* (tambourines), and sometimes conga drums. *Tríos* and *cuartetos* (three- or four-member ensembles) performed constantly in formal and informal gatherings (Glasser 1995). Few Puerto Rican parties in New York lacked some form of musical entertainment, and many voluntary associations sponsored musical events such as dances, recitals, processions, and festivals.

Food preferences were another popular expression of Puerto Rican culture in everyday life. By the late 1920s, more than 125 Puerto Rican–owned restaurants were operating in New York City (B. Vega 1994 [1977]). A 1927 menu from the Versailles Restaurant featured such traditional Puerto Rican staples as *mofongo* (boiled plantain), *arroz con pollo* (rice and chicken), *beefteak criollo* (steak), and *dulce de coco* (coconut dessert) (Erasmo Vando Papers 1917–88: Series III, Box 2) (see figure 8.6). Restaurants offering Puerto Rican, Cuban, and Spanish food mushroomed throughout the city, especially in the Upper West Side of Manhattan and in East Harlem, with such Spanish names as El Molino Rojo, El Prado, La Nueva Rumba, Mira Palmera, La Concha, and El Mundial. The latter had been established on West 116th Street in 1920 (see *Ecos de Nueva York* 1950). On Lenox Avenue in Spanish Harlem, family-owned cafeterias sold *cuchifritos* (fried fritters) and *matrimonios* and *mixtas* (both of which are combination plates with rice and beans) (Sierra Berdecia 1956: 11). Like other ethnic groups in the United States, Puerto Ricans preserved many of the culinary traditions of their homeland.

Since the beginning of the twentieth century, one of the most common types of Hispanic businesses in New York was the *bodega*, or "grocery store." In 1927 the Porto Rican Brotherhood estimated that Puerto Ricans owned more than two hundred such stores in New York City (B. Vega 1994 [1977]: 179). By the 1950s, bodegas proliferated throughout Manhattan, Brooklyn, and the Bronx,

FIGURE 8.6. New York City's Versailles Restaurant menu, 1927. Courtesy of the Erasmo Vando Papers, Centro de Estudios Puertorriqueños, Hunter College, CUNY.

FIGURE 8.7. A Puerto Rican *bodega* in Newark, N.J. Undated photograph by *Newark News*. Courtesy of the Archivos Históricos de la Migración Puertorriqueña, Centro de Estudios Puertorriqueños, Hunter College, CUNY.

catering to a growing demand for Puerto Rican–style cooking ingredients, such as coffee, malt, *sofrito* (seasoning), rice, beans, and plantains. Over time, the bodega became a center of neighborhood life and information exchange in New York, Newark, and elsewhere (see figure 8.7). Moreover, the proliferation of these grocery stores helped to define the physical and economic landscape of the Puerto Rican barrios (Glasser 1995: 109; Sánchez Korrol 1994: 62). The bodega also served as an effective device for small business development among Puerto Ricans until the 1960s, when Dominican entrepreneurs took over much of the Hispanic food retailing in New York (L. Duany 1987). Together with boardinghouses, barber shops, music stores, and restaurants, grocery stores were a pillar of Puerto Rican settlements in the United States.

La Marqueta, the large open-air market in Spanish Harlem, was formally created in 1936. Located under the train bridge on Park Avenue, the market had

been originally established by Jewish immigrants (B. Vega 1994 [1977]: 37).
With the rising number of Puerto Rican settlers, the area offered many tropical
products imported from the Island and attracted Puerto Ricans from outside
Manhattan. In 1958, 350 Hispanic entrepreneurs established the Park Avenue
Enclosed Market Merchants Association (Quintero 1963: 12; Ribes Tovar 1968:
144). A journalist writing in 1950 noted that Park Avenue between 111th and 116th
Streets had become "the center for vegetables, minor fruits, textiles for retail
sale, and trade in general. In the corners stand those small carts selling toma-
toes, potatoes, beans, and the tasty avocado that creole taste praises so much.
Carts with ripe bananas. The loud small carts with toasted peanuts and sausages
under the wide three-colored umbrella" (Arana 1950). Whatever else they did,
Puerto Rican migrants did not forget their dietary habits in New York City.

Aside from such daily affirmations of their cultural identity, Puerto Ricans
celebrated extraordinary events that gave them a special sense of community. In
1970, when Marisol Malaret was crowned the first Puerto Rican Miss Universe,
she was greeted as a popular heroine by Puerto Ricans in New York. As a local
band played the Island's national anthem, the beauty queen stepped on a
platform prepared by the Open-Air Merchants Association of El Barrio, while
Governor Nelson A. Rockefeller addressed the public. Mayor John V. Lindsay
declared an official holiday to commemorate Marisol's arrival in New York
City. One photograph of the young woman had the following caption: "BE-
TWEEN TWO FLAGS:—Marisol Malaret Contreras, 'Miss Universe,' shows her
beautiful face over the two flags in her life. That of the Motherland, with its
single star, and that of the Stripes and Stars" (El Diario–La Prensa 1970). Back
on the Island, Marisol's election as Miss Universe helped to make participation
in international beauty pageants an important symbol of Puerto Rico's national
identity (see Morris 1995). In New York, the Puerto Rican community celebrated her triumph with great pride and welcomed her as one of its own.

"THE DISTINCTIVE MARK THAT WE ALL CARRY WITH US": RECONFIGURING PUERTO RICANNESS IN THE DIASPORA

Many of the earliest community organizations were explicitly concerned with
preserving and promoting Puerto Rican identity in the United States. The
programs and publications of these organizations tended to represent mainland
Puerto Ricans as culturally linked to islanders. Their predominant use of the

Spanish language and their constant references to the homeland are typical of first-generation migrants. Bernardo Vega (1994 [1977]: 176) wrote about this period: "We were interested in establishing a popular educational center that would counter the general trend among Puerto Ricans to consider their stay in New York as a passing thing, always hoping for an eventual return to the Island. We were aware that before us grew a new generation of Puerto Ricans, born in this city, who deserved our attention." As several scholars have noted, the small Puerto Rican *colonias* in the U.S. mainland did not develop a broad awareness as a separate ethnic minority before World War II (Flores 1997; Herbstein 1978; Sánchez Korrol 1994). Only with the rise of the civil rights movement, which in turn led to the creation of federally funded programs for minorities, did state-side Puerto Ricans mobilize themselves as a special interest group to assert their collective claims vis-à-vis American society.

During the 1950s, community groups increasingly focused on the educational, economic, and political advancement of Puerto Ricans in the United States rather than on the Island. Instead of helping immigrants to adjust to mainland culture, as the Migration Division had done, the new organizations often rejected assimilation as a goal. Some of these groups were primarily civil rights initiatives, such as the Puerto Rican–Hispanic Leadership Forum (1957) and the Puerto Rican Legal Defense and Education Fund (1972). Each in its own way, these groups challenged the Island-centered discourse of national identity by focusing on the immediate concerns of mainland Puerto Ricans, such as poverty, education, and community empowerment. By the early 1960s, community agencies began to displace hometown clubs as the basic form of organization of Puerto Ricans in the United States.

Two groups exemplify this trend. In 1961 ASPIRA became the first Puerto Rican community agency in New York City to receive outside funds to develop young Puerto Rican leaders through educational counseling and occupational training. ASPIRA took its name from the Spanish verb *aspirar* (to aspire) and focused on the educational aspirations of Puerto Rican youth in poverty-stricken areas of inner-city neighborhoods. The Puerto Rican Community Development Project (1964) was a clearinghouse for various self-help efforts, such as child care, bilingual education, drug addiction prevention, technical assistance for local organizations, and financial assistance for small business development. The project also sought to establish an Institute of Puerto Rican Culture to promote artists and artisans in New York City. Its explicit agenda was to affirm and strengthen the cultural identity of the Puerto Rican community, by fostering its indigenous values and promoting voluntary associations (Pantoja 1989; Puerto Rican Forum 1975; Rodríguez-Fraticelli and Tirado 1989).

As noted in Chapter 7, the Migration Division (and, later, the Department of Puerto Rican Community Affairs) encountered resistance among the very groups it helped to organize. Since the late 1950s, leaders of the Puerto Rican communities of New York, Chicago, Philadelphia, Hartford, and elsewhere had questioned the right of the Commonwealth government to manage migrant affairs. Eventually, the division confronted a strong, autonomous infrastructure of organizations that voiced the interests of various sectors of the Puerto Rican diaspora. These organizations represented different ways of being Puerto Rican in the United States, sometimes opposed to the views of the Migration Division. Some developed radical approaches to political struggles in the mainland and on the Island, such as the Young Lords Party, founded in Chicago in 1969, which became the Puerto Rican Revolutionary Workers Organization in 1972 (see Torres and Velásquez 1998). Many groups reflected a shift in leadership from first- to second-generation immigrants in the United States.

Although most young Puerto Ricans, born and raised in the United States, did not adopt militant strategies, they began consciously to distinguish themselves from islanders. The Nuyorican movement in literature and the arts defied the Island-centered canon of Puerto Rican literature, especially through its creative mixture of English and Spanish, or code-switching, pejoratively called Spanglish on the Island (see Algarín and Piñero 1975; Barradas 1998; Cortés, Falcón, and Flores 1976; Flores, Attinasi, and Pedraza 1981; C. Hernández 1997). The New York–based author Nicholasa Mohr (1987) has insisted that Puerto Rican writers in the United States and in Puerto Rico have become culturally distinct and that the separation lies beyond language. In any case, mainland Puerto Ricans have increasingly identified and organized themselves around local issues rather than exclusively around the Island. Many second-generation New York Puerto Ricans now perceive themselves to be different from both Island-born Puerto Ricans and Americans (see Jenkins 1977; Lorenzo-Hernández 1999).

Nonetheless, the definition of Puerto Rican identity espoused by many community organizations on the mainland resonates with the cultural policies of the Commonwealth government. For instance, in 1967 the South Bronx Project of the New York Public Library initiated a series of educational programs featuring the jíbaro, vejigante masks, bomba, and plena. In August 1969 the

United Bronx Parents celebrated Puerto Rican history, music, art, children's games, stories, and poetry. The fiesta highlighted the contributions of José Campeche, Ramón Baldorioty de Castro, Lola Rodríguez de Tió, and Luis Muñoz Rivera, among other canonized writers, artists, and politicians (Pura Belpré Papers 1897–1985: Series IV, Box 6). This partial list of *figuras ilustres* (prominent figures) and cultural activities was repeated in community centers throughout Puerto Rico (Dávila 1997).

Other diasporic groups have approached Puerto Rican history in terms congruent with the official narrative on the Island. The legendary figure of the jíbaro, with his perennial pava, has been an extremely popular symbol of Puerto Ricanness in the United States as well as in Puerto Rico (see figure 8.8). An anonymous author affiliated with the Centro Cultural Aguadillano in Kings County, New York, wrote in 1970: "The mixture of Indian, Negro and Spanish elements in the ethnological and spiritual structure of the people of the island account for the character of its folklore and creative personality." The writer defined Puerto Rican folklore as "the accumulation of the wisdom of the illiterate peasant and the poor dwellers who inhabit certain regions of Puerto Rico." As on the Island, décimas, coplas, aguinaldos, *seis chorreaos*, bombas, and the Juan Bobo stories were singled out as typical examples of traditional Puerto Rican culture. Years later, in 1982, the Casa de la Herencia Cultural Puertorriqueña (Home of Puerto Rican Cultural Heritage) in New York organized folk art contests patterned after similar events held at the Institute of Puerto Rican Culture in San Juan (Genoveva de Arteaga Papers 1913–91: Series IV, Box 1). Thus, the dominant discourse on national culture has been selectively transferred to the diaspora, partly through the efforts of the Commonwealth's Migration Division and the Department of Puerto Rican Community Affairs. Perhaps that discourse was simply appropriating popular practices among Puerto Ricans, such as displaying their flag or asserting their rural origins, even in a metropolis such as New York City. Perhaps the migrants had already been imbued with cultural nationalism before coming to the United States.

Even when their main purpose was not to maintain the migrants' traditional practices in the United States, formal and informal associations tended to strengthen their members' ties to the homeland and among themselves. Many groups represented themselves as outposts of the Puerto Rican nation ("a single people") in another country. Cultural activities such as the Puerto Rican Day Parade or the Feast of Saint John the Baptist recycled many icons of the Island's identity—the pava, the güiro, the mofongo, the cuchifrito, the vejigante mask,

FIGURE 8.8. Puerto Rican children in New York City dressed as *jíbaros*. Undated photograph by Luis R. Díaz. Courtesy of the Archivos Históricos de la Migración Puertorriqueña, Centro de Estudios Puertorriqueños, Hunter College, CUNY.

the fiestas patronales, the flag, the anthem, the Spanish language, the cult of the saints, the love of baseball, or the Puerto Rican Miss Universe. Popular allegiance to these well-recognized symbols of Puerto Ricanness arguably expresses a collective will not to become just another ethnic minority within the American melting pot but to retain a separate nationality. As a 1955 newspaper article put it, "Thousands of *boricuas* [Puerto Ricans] are dispersed around the world and none of them, with very rare exceptions, denies his Puerto Rican homeland or race. That is the seal and the distinctive mark that we all carry with us. That mark or peculiar way of being is what distinguishes us from other races and fellow peoples of the New World. Through his presence, his way of acting or speaking, whether on purpose or unconsciously [*impensadamente*], the Puerto

Rican is easy to identify wherever he may be. And this is markedly so both in the case of the *boricua* with little academic preparation and in nuclei with more education" (Marietta 1955: 32). Or, as a popular saying goes, being Puerto Rican is like carrying the "stain of a plantain" (*la mancha de plátano*).

CONCLUSION

Before World War II, Puerto Rican migrants organized themselves according to common origin, class background, political ideology, and shared interests. The long history of Puerto Rican community organizations in New York and elsewhere includes dozens of self-help groups that catered to the special needs and concerns of a growing immigrant population. Many of these voluntary associations recruited Puerto Ricans as well as other Hispanics, such as Cubans and Spaniards. Labor unions, political clubs, brotherhoods, Masonic lodges, baseball leagues, hometown clubs, and evangelical churches proliferated in the diaspora. In these organized contexts, as well as in more informal ways, migrants reconstructed their identity through such everyday popular practices as eating, drinking, dancing, playing dominoes or baseball, praying, or simply socializing. Caught "between two flags," Puerto Ricans continually reasserted "the seal and the distinctive mark" of their homeland, even as they increasingly found themselves in a transnational context. As the president of the Feast of San Juan put it in 1973, Puerto Rico lived on in New York.

After World War II, Puerto Rican migration to the United States took on massive proportions. With the support of the Migration Division, hometown clubs emerged as the primary form of voluntary association in the diaspora. Despite many efforts to create umbrella organizations, Puerto Ricans continued to identify closely with their locality of origin rather than with a broader conception of national identity. Scholars have not sufficiently recognized the strong regional character of the Puerto Rican diaspora. The fragmentation of the migrant population into small cliques of friends and relatives from the same town on the Island extended well into the 1960s. During this decade, however, a new generation of Puerto Rican leaders matured in New York and other U.S. cities. Larger trends within American society, such as the War on Poverty and the civil rights movement, promoted a growing split between mainland Puerto Ricans and the Commonwealth government. State-sponsored and grassroots representations of Puerto Ricanness often clashed in the diaspora.

Since the 1950s, U.S. Puerto Ricans have organized many mutual aid societies, brotherhoods, hometown clubs, churches, festivals, and parades. Most
voluntary associations continued to identify primarily as Puerto Rican and
secondarily as Hispanic. That the official name of most of these groups was in
Spanish also reveals the migrants' resistance to assimilate completely into the
English language. That they continued to associate largely on a regional basis—
as the persistence of township groups suggests—is also telling. Contrary to the
dominant discourse of the Puerto Rican nation, migrants reproduced many
local distinctions outside the Island. The increasing popularity of evangelical
sects, particularly Pentecostal ones, also contradicts the predominantly Catholic definition of Puerto Rican culture on the Island and in the mainland.

Today, the Puerto Rican nation is still often defined in exclusive terms—
territorially, as an Island unto itself; linguistically, as a Spanish-speaking people;
and culturally, as a Hispanic community.[3] On all three counts, the Puerto
Rican diaspora poses serious challenges to the dominant nationalist narrative.
Perhaps this is why the Department of Puerto Rican Community Affairs was
abolished in 1993, when pro-statehood forces on the Island questioned the
constitutional right of the Commonwealth government to assert its own migration policy in the United States. But the formal demise of this transnational
project was also brought about, at a deeper level, by the popular resistance of
Puerto Rican migrants to incorporation into the canonized view of the Island-
nation. The discourse of Puerto Ricanness needs to be expanded to include
nearly half of the Puerto Rican people, who now live outside the Island, increasingly speak English, and blend Hispanic and American practices in their
daily lives. This is both an urgent research question for scholars and a practical
challenge for policymakers.

Mobile Livelihoods

Circular Migration, Transnational Identities, and Cultural Borders between Puerto Rico and the United States

Migration has traditionally been considered as a single, one-way, and permanent change of residence. The dominant narratives on international migration typically focus on the relocation of surplus workers from poorer to richer countries, as well as on their incorporation into the host society, particularly the United States (see Pedraza and Rumbaut 1996; Portes and Rumbaut 1996). However, an axiom of international migration is that every flow of people generates a corresponding counterflow. Historians have documented the massive reverse movements from North America to southern and eastern Europe—especially Italy and Poland—in the late nineteenth century and the beginning of the twentieth (Hoerder 1985; Rosenblum 1973). Contemporary patterns of return migration have also been studied in Central America, the Caribbean, Southeast Asia, West Africa, and other regions (see Cordell, Gregory, and Piché 1996; Pessar 1997). Less well known is the propensity of some groups of people—such as Mexicans, Puerto Ricans, Dominicans, and Jamaicans—to move back and forth, or circulate, between their places of origin and destination. Such two-way, repetitive, and temporary moves do not fit easily within conventional models of migration (see Chapman and Prothero 1983, 1985; Conway 1988, 1989). As Douglas Massey and his colleagues (1998) point out, current thinking on transnational migration remains largely framed within nineteenth-century concepts and methods.

Circular migration (also known as commuter, swallow, or revolving-door migration) is an increasingly common feature of international population movements. Although back-and-forth movements have long characterized many migrant streams, the current magnitude of circulation is unprecedented. Constant border crossing in both directions has been well established among recent migrants from Mexico, Central America, and the Caribbean to the United States (Basch, Schiller, and Blanc 1994; J. Duany 1994; Hernández Cruz 1985, 1994; O. Martínez 1994; Massey et al. 1987; R. Rouse 1991; Schiller, Basch, and Blanc-Szanton 1992; Smith and Guarnizo 1998; Thomas-Hope 1992). Among other factors, the geographic proximity of countries such as Mexico, Jamaica, the Dominican Republic, and Puerto Rico to North America facilitates circular migration. Although economic, political, and cultural penetration by the United States entices people to move there, migrants often return home when socioeconomic conditions abroad become less attractive—only to move back again when the local situation is unsatisfactory. Moreover, growing access to mass transportation and communications has increased the likelihood that people will engage in repetitive moves across national frontiers throughout their life cycles.

International circulation has been a notable characteristic of the Caribbean region for decades (Conway 1988, 1989; Richardson 1992; Thomas-Hope 1986). At least since the early nineteenth century, Caribbean people have moved frequently in search of jobs and better living conditions, first within the region and later outside the region. During the 1880s and after, circulation became increasingly common through short-term labor contracts in Panama, Central America, Cuba, and the Dominican Republic. The size and range of population movements have increased greatly since World War II. Today, most Caribbean circulators move between their home societies and metropolitan countries in North America and Western Europe, although many continue to move within the region itself. Contemporary population movements between Haiti and the Dominican Republic and between the Dominican Republic and Puerto Rico are cases in point.

As Dennis Conway, Mark Ellis, and Naragandat Shiwdhan (1990: 51) put it, "International mobility has emerged as a major adaptive and survival strategy common to all classes of Caribbean peoples." A particular variant of this strategy is "recycling" or "swallow" migration, in which people move frequently over sustained periods of time. Based on the number of U.S. nonimmigrant visas issued during the mid-1980s, Conway (1989: 41) estimates that 3 to 4 percent of the entire Caribbean population are circulators. Aaron Segal (1996) has outlined several categories of contemporary Caribbean swallows, including temporary migrant workers, professional athletes, entertainers, health sciences personnel, academics, and children. Conway (1988) also includes students as circulators. Furthermore, Segal notes that residents of the nonindependent Caribbean can move freely to and from their metropolises as citizens of those countries (the United States, France, and the Netherlands). This legal status helps to account for high circulation rates among Puerto Ricans, U.S. Virgin Islanders, French Antilleans, and Dutch Antilleans. However, the causes and consequences of circular migration in the Caribbean and elsewhere remain poorly understood.

Murray Chapman and R. Mansell Prothero (1983, 1985) have elaborated a useful conceptual distinction between migration as permanent displacement and circulation as a reciprocal flow of people.[1] From this standpoint, circulation is one of the dominant forms of population movement in the past as well as in the present. However, international circulation in the Caribbean differs from that in other world areas because it is rooted in a long history of forced and induced migrations (Conway 1988). Conway (1989, 1994) believes that some of the principles formulated by Chapman and Prothero for the Melanesian region and other parts of the so-called Third World do not hold well in the Caribbean. Still, he accepts their broad framework to analyze circular movements of people as a time-honored mode of adaptation. Among Conway's propositions is that flexible residential arrangements, multilocal social networks, and continuing commitments to home communities characterize Caribbean circulators.

In this chapter I argue that the emergence of "mobile livelihoods" helps to explain contemporary circulation patterns in the Caribbean and elsewhere (Olwig and Sørensen 1999). By "mobile livelihoods," I mean the spatial extension of people's means of subsistence across various local, regional, and national settings. Circulation is only one, albeit an important, form of physical and social displacement that reflects mobile livelihood practices. People who frequently cross geopolitical frontiers also move along the edges of cultural borders, such as those created by language, citizenship, race, ethnicity, and gender ideology. Thus, the development of mobile livelihoods has serious implications for the construction of labor markets, discourses of citizenship, language policies, and national identities. The concept of mobile livelihoods is especially pertinent to Puerto Ricans, who as U.S. citizens move more easily between their country of origin and the U.S. mainland than do other groups.

Although I focus on the Puerto Rican case, the concept may be profitably applied to other contexts.

I will document the migrants' livelihood practices based on a recent field study of population flows between Puerto Rico and the United States. Specifically, I compare the basic characteristics of multiple movers, one-time movers, and nonmovers in Puerto Rico. More broadly, I assess the implications of circular migration for Puerto Rican communities on and off the Island. As I argue in this chapter and throughout the book, the constant displacement of people—both to and from the Island—blurs the territorial, linguistic, and juridical boundaries of the Puerto Rican nation. As people expand their means of subsistence across space, they develop multiple attachments to various localities. My hypothesis is that circulation does not entail major losses in human capital for most Puerto Ricans but rather often constitutes an occupational, educational, and linguistic gain. At the same time, the constant movement of people between the Island and the mainland requires rethinking how the physical and symbolic borders of national identity are drawn and crossed in Puerto Rico.

A NATION ON THE MOVE

Researchers on Puerto Rican migration traditionally assumed that it was a permanent relocation of low-wage labor from the periphery to the core of the capitalist world system (see History Task Force 1979; Sánchez Korrol 1994; for literature reviews, see Baerga and Thompson 1990; J. Duany 1994–95). Moreover, some scholars believed that large-scale migration from Puerto Rico to the United States had effectively ended after the great exodus between 1945 and 1965 (Hernández Alvarez 1967; Massey et al. 1998). The number of returnees began to surpass those leaving for the United States in the early 1970s, especially as a result of minimum wage hikes on the Island and the industrial restructuring of New York City, the traditional center of the Puerto Rican diaspora (Meléndez 1993a; C. Santiago 1993; Tienda 1989). But mass emigration resumed during the 1980s, at the same time that return migration continued unabated, foreign immigration increased, and circular migration emerged as a significant phenomenon. Between 1991 and 1998, net migration from Puerto Rico to the United States was estimated to be 249,692 persons, compared with 491,361 in the 1980s (Junta de Planificación 1980–98). In 1994–95 alone, 53,164 persons

FIGURE 9.1. "Spectators awaiting inbound passengers at the Isla Grande airport in San Juan." 1946 photograph by Charles Rotkin. Courtesy of the Archivos Históricos de la Migración Puertorriqueña, Centro de Estudios Puertorriqueños, Hunter College, CUNY.

emigrated from the Island, while 18,177 immigrated (Olmeda 1997). In short, contemporary Puerto Rican migration is best visualized as a transient and bidirectional flow (a "revolving-door" movement), rather than as an irrevocable and unilateral displacement.[2]

The massive reverse movement of people from the U.S. mainland to the Island has been well documented since the mid-1960s (Ashton 1980; Bonilla and Campos 1986; Bonilla and Colón Jordán 1979; Cordero-Guzmán 1989; Enchautegui 1991; Hernández Alvarez 1967; Muschkin 1993). Return migrants to Puerto Rico were part of a large-scale, two-way traffic of labor, capital, goods, and information that accelerated after World War II (see figure 9.1). This transnational flow preceded by several decades the current trend toward the globalization of financial and labor markets, facilitated by the lack of formal political barriers between Puerto Rico and the United States. As they move between the Island and the mainland, Puerto Ricans need not carry travel documents or apply for visa permits; the frontier between the two places is more cultural than juridical. But more than simply returning to their homeland (like many other migrants had done before), Puerto Ricans have traced a complex circuit, often involving frequent moves in multiple directions, not necessarily beginning or ending at the same point.[3]

The circular flow between Puerto Rico and the United States challenges conventional views of population movements as linear and irreversible forms of mobility, as permanently disconnected from their sending communities, or as prone to inevitable assimilation into the host societies (see Hernández Cruz 1994; Rivera-Batiz and Santiago 1996; Torre, Rodríguez Vecchini, and Burgos 1994). Such mobile livelihoods subvert dominant discourses of racial, ethnic, class, and gender relations, as well as legal concepts of state and nation, including sedentary notions of place, community, and citizenship. Many Puerto Ricans—such as agricultural contract workers—have learned to live and work in places far away from their homeland, literally and figuratively with their luggage packed (see figure 9.2). Among other results, the large-scale circulation of people, ideas, and practices frequently fractures hard-line positions on national identity, based on clearly bounded territories, languages, or cultures (see Gupta and Ferguson 1997; Kearney 1995; Olwig and Hastrup 1997; Schiller, Basch, and Blanc 1995). As I argued in Chapter 1, Puerto Rico has become a "nation on the move," especially through the relocation of almost half of its population to the United States and the constant flow of people between the Island and the mainland.

Circular migration implies a broader definition of cultural identity for Puerto Ricans in the United States and in Puerto Rico itself. First, it poses the need for functional bilingualism in both places to maintain communication between those who stay and those who move frequently in either direction (Flores 1993; Santiago-Rivera and Santiago 1999; Urciuoli 1996). Rather than being Spanish or English monolinguals, growing numbers of Puerto Ricans are found somewhere along the bilingual continuum. In her study of El Barrio of New York City, Ana Celia Zentella (1997) documents that migrants have redefined Puerto Ricanness to incorporate monolingual English speakers as well as code-

FIGURE 9.2. Luggage of a Puerto Rican migrant worker in Wabash, Indiana. Undated photograph by Tony Rodríguez. Courtesy of the Archivos Históricos de la Migración Puertorriqueña, Centro de Estudios Puertorriqueños, Hunter College, CUNY.

switchers. Although Island-based Puerto Ricans still perceive Nuyoricans as culturally different, the increasing number of people with mainland experience and bilingual skills may well challenge the public perception that moving abroad necessarily implies becoming more American and less Puerto Rican.

Second, circular migration further erodes conventional definitions of citizenship and nationality based on place of birth or residence. Puerto Rican migrants have developed "dual home bases," one in the United States and one in Puerto Rico, which allow them to maintain strong psychological attachments to the Island even when living abroad for long periods of time. As Marixsa Alicea (1989, 1990) argues, frequent movement within expanded communities and households, spread widely across space, has become a common experience for Puerto Ricans since World War II. Such dual or multiple residences allow circular migrants to combine various sources of support from work, family, and the state. Thus, it is increasingly difficult to draw the line between the Island and the diaspora, inasmuch as many Puerto Ricans spend part of their lives at both ends of the migratory circuit. Mobile livelihoods create a porous border zone between communities on and off the Island, which migrants continually traverse and transgress, sometimes several times a year.

Some scholars have argued that circular migration has a negative impact on human capital among Puerto Ricans (Tienda and Díaz 1987; see also Meléndez 1993b). The lack of attachment to local labor markets may confine circular migrants to unskilled blue-collar and service jobs because they cannot accumulate experience and skills either in the United States or in Puerto Rico. Moreover, circular migration can lead to disruptions in schooling and job training as well as in family life (Rivera-Batiz and Santiago 1996: 62). From this standpoint, frequent movement between the Island and the mainland is supposed to be one of the main reasons for the deteriorating living standards of Puerto Rican migrants. Frequent movement has also been cited as a cause for the relatively low Puerto Rican participation in mainland politics (Chavez 1991).

Yet other scholars approach circulation as a flexible survival strategy for Puerto Rican families on and off the Island (Ellis, Conway, and Bailey 1996; Hernández and Scheff 1997; C. Rodríguez 1988, 1994b). In response to shifting economic circumstances, people may seek better employment opportunities elsewhere and maximize their resources by moving constantly. From this perspective, circular migration constitutes a spatially extended livelihood practice. Hence, frequent movement may be interpreted as an effect, rather than a cause, of persistent poverty, low quality of life, and reduced opportunities for advancement on the Island and in the mainland. Until now, the academic controversy over Puerto Rican circular migrants has not been settled because of lack of adequate data, research designs, and conceptual approaches.

RETHINKING PUERTO RICAN CIRCULATION

Although scholars disagree as to the precise terminology, magnitude, and impact of circular migration, most concur that the Puerto Rican diaspora has become a sustained bilateral movement of people. Estimates of the volume of circular migration between the Island and the mainland range from 10 to 45 percent of the total flow, depending on various definitions, sources, methods, and approaches (Ellis, Conway, and Bailey 1996; Hernández Cruz 1985; Ortiz 1994; C. Rodríguez 1994b). According to the 1990 census, 130,335 people moved back and forth between the Island and the mainland—more than 23 percent of those who left Puerto Rico—during the 1980s (Rivera-Batiz and Santiago 1996). Regardless of the exact number, circular movement has become a key feature of contemporary Puerto Rican society.

Current debates on transnationalism help to frame Puerto Rican circular migration in a broader context. "Transnationalism" may be defined as the establishment of frequent and intense social, economic, political, and cultural links between two or more countries (see Portes 1998; Schiller, Basch, and Blanc-Szanton 1992). Applying this definition to Puerto Rico must take into account that the Island is not a sovereign state, and therefore the analytic distinction between state and nation must be made carefully. For example, government authorities do not police Puerto Ricans moving between the Island and the mainland, unlike those who cross international frontiers. However, the subjective experience of migration for many Puerto Ricans as a dual process of deterritorialization and reterritorialization has been well established in the literature (see Hernández and Scheff 1996–97; Laó 1997; C. Rodríguez 1989; Sánchez Korrol 1994). As Puerto Ricans commonly say, moving to the United States involves *irse pa' fuera*, literally "going outside"—their Island-country, that is.

The folk expression *irse pa' fuera* suggests a clear-cut distinction between an outer boundary (*afuera*) and an inner core (*adentro*) of a national sense of place, culture, and identity. Some scholars have written about an inner Puerto Rican community (meaning those living on the Island) and an outer community (those living in the mainland).[4] In everyday conversation, Puerto Ricans seldom talk about migrating as such but often refer to living outside the Island. Thus, such popular phrases as *estudiar afuera* (to study abroad) or *venir de afuera* (to come from outside) are understood to be located in the United States. As the literary critic Hugo Rodríguez Vecchini (1994: 53) has argued, the contemporary Puerto Rican situation cannot be contained within the conventional meanings of the academic term "migration." For most Puerto Ricans, moving abroad does not entail permanently settling in another country or moving temporarily in a seasonal fashion; rather, people come and go as circumstances change here and there. Although describing the entire Puerto

Rican people as a "commuter nation" (Torre, Rodríguez Vecchini, and Burgos 1994) may be exaggerated, this term captures the constant oscillation between points of departure and destination that characterizes the movement of thousands of Puerto Ricans.

The Puerto Rican diaspora has usually been represented as a unique, special, or anomalous case because of the Island's dependence on the United States, the legal nature of the migrant flow, and the free movement of labor and capital in both directions. Another notable aspect of the Puerto Rican presence in the United States is the recruitment of more than 200,000 Puerto Ricans by the U.S. armed forces since 1917. At least 18,000 Puerto Ricans were drafted for military service during World War I, 65,000 during World War II, 61,000 during the Korean War, and 38,000 during the Vietnam War. Many Puerto Ricans first moved abroad, returned to the Island, and relocated again as part of U.S. military engagements (see Cruz 2000).

A further distinctive characteristic often mentioned by researchers has been the active role of the sending state in exporting workers and controlling population growth on the Island (Bonilla and Campos 1986; Lapp 1990). Since the mid-1940s, migration has been a key element of the Puerto Rican government's development strategies, especially Operation Bootstrap, which promoted the exchange of U.S. capital for Puerto Rican surplus labor. In this vein, Frank Bonilla (1993: 183) has noted the "anomaly" "that a plan intended to capitalize on the island's most abundant resource, its labor power, instead has cast a majority of the population into forced idleness, underemployment, and a restless circulation between colony and metropolis."

Scholars have disputed whether mainland Puerto Ricans are actually "international" migrants. Some authors believe that Puerto Rican migration to the United States should be classified as an internal population movement, similar to, say, the relocation of residents of New York to Florida (see, for example, Ashton 1999). After all, the absence of a legal frontier between the Island and the mainland precludes any strict government control over population movements between the two territories. From a different perspective, Puerto Ricans have been characterized as colonial immigrants similar to Africans and West Indians in their English, French, and Dutch metropolises (Grosfoguel 1994–95; C. Rodríguez 1989). Being a citizen of the metropolitan country and holding a subordinate position within its class and racial systems are elements common to colonial immigrants. Furthermore, the Puerto Rican experience has striking parallels to that of Native Americans, African Americans, Mexican Americans, Hawaiians, Filipinos, and other "conquered peoples" in the United

States. All these groups lost control of their homeland as a result of war and occupation; all have suffered massive displacements throughout their history (J. Hernández 1994).

In my view, the Puerto Rican case represents a special but not "anomalous" form of transnationalism, despite the absence of a sovereign nation-state on the Island. Strictly speaking, Puerto Rican migrants are not international because they do not cross a major political frontier between the Island and the mainland,[5] yet they may be considered transnational in the broader sense that they move from one national culture to another. The similarities and differences between the transnational practices of Puerto Ricans and other migrant groups such as Mexicans or Dominicans merit further reflection. For instance, more often than not migrants relocate to diasporic communities with similar sociocultural characteristics to their country of origin.

Many of the findings and interpretations of transnational migration are relevant to the Puerto Rican case. Dense kinship networks characterize the transnational circuit between Puerto Rico and the United States as much as they do in the case of Mexico and other Caribbean countries (Conway 1988; Massey et al. 1987; R. Rouse 1991). The rites of passage, such as the elaborate welcome and farewell parties, associated with going abroad (irse pa' fuera) and coming back home do not differ substantially in Puerto Rico and the Dominican Republic. Moreover, moving between the Island and the mainland entails crossing significant cultural, linguistic, and geographic frontiers (Massey et al. 1998: 70). For instance, Puerto Ricans who resettle in the United States have to learn some English, while those returning home must maintain their competence in Spanish. In turn, studying Puerto Rican circular migrants may help to conceptualize different types of border crossings, depending on people's citizenship status. In Michael Kearney's terms (1991: 53), Puerto Rican migrants cross borders—understood as geographic and cultural contact zones—but not boundaries—the legal spatial markers of nations.

From this standpoint, revisiting the Puerto Rican case shows that border crossing is hardly confined to movements across state frontiers. Rather, people may create fluid fields of social, economic, and political relations in various settings—local, regional, national, and transnational. Constant movement in multiple directions suggests the spatial expansion of personal and familial livelihood practices to geographically distant but socially connected areas (Olwig and Hastrup 1997; Olwig and Sørensen 1999). Under such shifting conditions, it is difficult to site Puerto Rican culture in a particular landscape, either in the Island or in the mainland. The frequent mobility of the Puerto Rican population tends to collapse conventional distinctions between points of origin and destination, between places of birth and residence. Consequently, examining transnational flows to and from Puerto Rico can contribute to contemporary debates on the relation among peoples, cultures, places, and identities (see Gupta and Ferguson 1997). In particular, circular migrants test the limits of spatially localized images of life, work, and homeland.

My basic argument is that the constant displacement of people—both to and from the Island—blurs the territorial, linguistic, and juridical boundaries of the Puerto Rican nation. More specifically, the mobile livelihoods of circular migrants defy fixed and static conceptions of cultural identity. As people expand their means of subsistence across space, they develop multiple attachments to various localities. In the Puerto Rican situation, such mobile livelihoods are easier to establish than in other places because of the free movement of labor, capital, and goods between the Island and the mainland. I hypothesize that circulation does not entail major losses in human capital for most Puerto Ricans but, rather, often represents an occupational, educational, and linguistic asset.

The remainder of this chapter documents the mobile livelihood practices of circular migrants and challenges conventional thinking about contemporary Puerto Rican migration. To begin, I show that many Puerto Ricans continue to move back and forth between the Island and the mainland, for relatively long periods of time. Second, I describe how multiple movement differs between Island communities with recent histories of migration to the United States and those with more established migrant traditions. Third, I determine whether circulating Puerto Ricans have geographically broadened their subsistence strategies to a larger number of destinations than in the past. Fourth, I draw a sociodemographic profile of circulators between the Island and the mainland. Fifth, I demonstrate that frequent movement is associated with having many relatives living in the mainland. Finally, I substantiate my claim that circulation tends to improve a person's occupational and educational status, as well as English-language skills.

STUDYING CIRCULATION

SAMPLE

Four communities were surveyed in Puerto Rico during July and August 1998.[6] (One community was partially surveyed between July and September 1996.)[7] A

TABLE 9.1. Characteristics of Sample, by Place of Origin

	Cataño-Guaynabo (N=863)	Cidra (N=615)	Loíza (N=607)	San Juan (N=904)	Total (N=2,989)
Sex					
Male	48.1	47.8	44.0	46.1	46.6
Female	51.9	52.2	56.0	53.9	53.4
Median age (number of years)	35	38	36	41	37
Education (number of years of schooling)					
Median	11	12	11	11	11
Mean	9.5	9.4	9.6	9.4	9.5
Birthplace					
United States	5.6	6.5	7.2	8.3	6.9
Puerto Rico	89.1	88.0	91.4	82.8	87.5
Other countries	0.5	0.5	0.2	1.4	0.7
Unknown	4.9	5.0	1.2	7.4	4.9
Employment status					
Unemployed or out of labor force	70.6	74.7	57.7	68.1	67.7
Employed	29.4	25.3	42.3	31.9	32.3
Current occupation[a]					
Managers and administrators	1.0	1.6	0.1	2.5	1.7
Professionals and technicians	14.8	34.9	14.9	19.7	19.4
Administrative support and sales workers	36.9	22.2	9.5	34.5	25.4
Craft and repair workers	27.1	25.4	11.6	22.7	20.8
Operators and laborers	5.4	5.6	53.1	8.9	20.6
Service workers	14.8	10.3	9.5	11.3	11.5
Agricultural workers	0	0	0.1	0.5	0.6

Note: In percentages, unless otherwise indicated. Some columns may not add up to 100 because of rounding.
[a] Of all employed persons with a known occupation.

variety of municipios—the basic administrative units of local government on the Island, roughly equivalent to counties in the U.S. mainland—was sampled to provide a basis for comparison and generalization. Prior research has found important differences in the rates and characteristics of transnational migration from various communities (Massey, Goldring, and Durand 1994). Among other factors, the frequency of circulation depends on the degree of integration of the community of origin to larger sociocultural and political systems (Chapman and Prothero 1983). For example, Puerto Rico's rural areas sent a disproportionate number of migrants to the United States and, to a lesser extent, the San Juan metropolitan area during the 1940s and 1950s. By the 1980s, San Juan had become one of the major exporters of residents to the mainland and the rest of the Island (see Cruz Báez and Boswell 1997: chap. 5).

The communities chosen for this study represent a range of population sizes, regions, ethnic compositions, and economic bases. The sample covered neighborhoods in the municipios of San Juan, Cataño-Guaynabo, Cidra, and Loíza; it included the Island's largest urban center, two contiguous urban fringes within the San Juan metropolitan area, a medium-size town in the inner highlands, and a small town on the northeast coast. By local standards, Loíza is a predominantly black community and Cidra is primarily white, while racial mixture is more common in San Juan and Cataño-Guaynabo.[8]

The sample size ranged between 100 and 200 households for each community, for a total of 650 households or 2,989 individuals. Each community was censused on a house-by-house basis, and households were selected using simple random methods. To qualify for an interview, household heads had to be born in Puerto Rico or in the U.S. mainland of Puerto Rican descent. The main characteristics of the sample are summarized in table 9.1.

Because the sample was drawn in Puerto Rico, it underrepresents migrants currently residing in the United States. However, previous research suggests that migrants who return to the Island do not differ substantially from those who leave for the mainland, with regard to basic characteristics such as gender and occupation (Godoy et al. 2000; Meléndez 1993a, 1994; Olmeda 1997). Some studies have found that return migrants differ from nonmigrants in age and education (Rivera-Batiz and Santiago 1994, 1996). Moreover, circular migrants in the middle of their stay in the United States may have different experiences from current residents of Puerto Rico. Also, the sample probably overrepresents certain kinds of people, such as those who moved alone and more recent migrants. Therefore, the results of this study should not be generalized to the entire migrant population. The present analysis focuses on Island dwellers who circulate to the United States.[9]

INSTRUMENT

The instrument for this study was an adapted version of the ethnosurvey designed by the Mexican Migration Project (MMP) at the University of Pennsylvania and the University of Guadalajara. Developed by Douglas Massey and his colleagues, the ethnosurvey was originally employed to collect information on migration between Mexico and the United States (Massey et al. 1987; Massey and Zenteno 1998; Mexican Migration Project 1999). It was later extended to fieldwork in Puerto Rico, the Dominican Republic, Argentina, and other countries (Latin American Migration Project 2001). The questionnaire followed a semistructured format to generate a flexible, unobtrusive, and nonthreatening interview schedule. Although identical information was obtained for each person, question wording and ordering were left to the interviewers' judgment.

The Puerto Rican version of the MMP instrument contained fourteen tables with variables arranged in columns and rows referring to persons, events, years, and other categories. The first tables recorded the social, economic, and demographic characteristics of the household head, the spouse, their living and nonliving children, and other persons residing in the household. The following tables gathered information on each person's first and last trips within Puerto Rico and the United States. Next, the instrument focused on household heads and their spouse's business ownership and labor histories, beginning at age fifteen or the first job, whichever came first. Another table recorded the migratory experiences of the head's relatives and friends in the United States. Finally, detailed information was compiled about the head's most recent trip to the United States, including social ties with U.S. citizens of various ethnic origins, English-language ability, and job characteristics.

PROCEDURE

Four local research assistants, supervised by a field coordinator, conducted interviews in Spanish, with the household head serving as the principal respondent for all persons in the sample. The questionnaires were applied in three phases. In the first phase, interviewers gathered basic data on all members of the household, including age, birthplace, marital status, education, and occupation. The interview began by identifying the household head (as defined by the respondents) and systematically enumerating the spouse and children, whether or not they lived at home. If a son or daughter was a member of another household, this fact was recorded as well. A child was considered to be living in a separate household if he or she was married, maintained a separate house or kitchen, and organized expenses separately. After listing the head, spouse, and children, other household members were enumerated and their relationship to the head was clarified.

An important task in the first phase of the fieldwork was the identification of people with prior migrant experience in either Puerto Rico or the United States. For those individuals with migrant experience, interviewers recorded the total number of trips within Puerto Rico, as well as information about the first and most recent trips, including the year, duration, destination, occupation, and wage. This exercise was then repeated for the first and most recent migrations to the United States. If necessary, households were revisited to complete or clarify information.

The project's criteria for determining the number of trips included the respondent's motive, duration, and activity. For example, if a person intended to work in the United States for several months and moved with her household from Puerto Rico, that was counted as one trip. Short-term visits for family reunions or recreational purposes (*de paseo*) were excluded from consideration. Thus, a trip was considered to be a round-trip journey between the Island and the mainland if the intention was to settle in either place for the purpose of working or reuniting with other family members.

"CROSSING THE POND":
THE MOVEMENT BETWEEN THE ISLAND AND THE MAINLAND

Table 9.2 summarizes the total number of trips made by all persons in the sample. More than 77 percent had never moved to the U.S. mainland, nearly 20 percent had traveled once, and 3 percent had completed two or more trips. (The latter is used as the operational definition of multiple movers or circular migrants in this chapter.)[10] Of those who had lived abroad, 13.4 percent were multiple movers (not shown in table). This figure is slightly higher than some earlier estimates of circular migrants (Conway, Ellis, and Shiwdhan 1990; Ellis, Conway, and Bailey 1996; Ortiz 1994; C. Rodríguez 1994b) and is much lower than others (Hernández and Scheff 1997; Hernández Cruz 1985; Rivera-Batiz and Santiago 1996). At the same time, it coincides with Conway's appraisal (1989) of circular migration for the Caribbean region as a whole and with a study based on the 1990 census of Puerto Rico (Godoy et al. 2000). As mentioned before, differences in the estimates of circular migration are probably due to the methodologies used by various authors, especially their sampling frames. Still, the circulation of people between Puerto Rico and the United States is a substantial component of a much larger migrant stream.

TABLE 9.2. Number of Trips to the United States, by Place of Origin

	Cataño-Guaynabo	Cidra	Loíza	San Juan	Total
No trips	81.7	75.0	72.3	78.1	77.3
One trip	15.6	22.8	21.7	19.9	19.6
Two or more trips	2.7	2.3	5.9	2.0	3.0
Still on current trip	26.1	23.4	37.7	39.6	32.3
Mean number of trips	0.22	0.27	0.44	0.25	0.29

Note: In percentages, unless otherwise indicated. Some columns may not add up to 100 because of rounding.

Migration rates ranged from a low of 18.3 percent in Cataño-Guaynabo to a high of 27.6 percent in Loíza. The mean number of trips taken by *loiceños* was double that of residents of Cataño-Guaynabo. Moreover, Loíza had the highest incidence of multiple movement (5.9 percent), while San Juan had the lowest (2 percent). Not surprisingly, Loíza has the highest unemployment and poverty rates in the sample, whereas Guaynabo has the lowest (U.S. Bureau of the Census 1993b). As Massey et al. (1998) propose, people are more likely to move abroad if they live in a community with a high prevalence of out-migration, because they are better connected socially to people who have been abroad. For members of economically deprived communities such as Loíza, mobile livelihoods have become a well-established survival strategy. Loiceños, in particular, have been moving in and out of the town within Puerto Rico for decades.

Furthermore, the proportion of household members still on their current trip to the United States varies from one municipio to another. San Juan and Loíza have relatively high percentages of persons living abroad, while Cataño-Guaynabo and Cidra have much lower proportions. Altogether, 32.3 percent of all household members were living in the mainland at the time of the ethnosurvey.[11] This figure is much lower than the 45 percent obtained for Mexicans interviewed in the Mexican Migration Project (1999).

Table 9.3 compares the dates of departure for the first trip to the United States from the four Puerto Rican communities. About a third of the residents of San Juan made their first trip in the 1940s and 1950s, while more than half of Loíza's residents made their first trip in the 1970s and 1980s. The median year of first departure ranged from 1968 in San Juan to 1978 in Loíza. Hence, large-scale out-migration proceeded first from San Juan, then from Cidra and Cataño-

TABLE 9.3. Year of First Trip to the United States of All Movers in Sample,
by Place of Origin (in Percentages)

Year	Cataño-Guaynabo	Cidra	Loíza	San Juan	Total
1940–49	5.1	5.3	0.6	7.7	4.8
1950–59	19.1	19.7	11.3	25.8	19.2
1960–69	15.9	23.7	16.7	20.1	19.1
1970–79	26.8	18.4	26.8	14.4	21.3
1980–89	24.8	17.8	28.6	20.6	23.0
1990–98	8.3	15.1	16.1	11.3	12.7
Median year	1973	1971	1978	1968	1973

Guaynabo, and finally from Loíza. According to the ethnosurvey, more people left the Island during the 1980s than any other decade. This finding coincides with aggregate data showing that current population movements from the Island to the mainland have already surpassed the numbers reached during the 1940s (Junta de Planificación 1980–98). The increase in recent migration is probably related to the exhaustion of various development strategies employed by the Puerto Rican government since the onset of the industrialization program in 1947 (Dietz 1986; Pantojas-García 1990).

Of the four areas under study, San Juan has a much longer history of out-migration. This finding is related to the incidence of internal migration to San Juan, as witnessed by its high proportion of residents born in other municipios (32.3 percent). Throughout the twentieth century, the capital has served as a stepping-stone to the United States. It is unquestionably the area with more transportation and other links to New York City and to other major points of the continent. Furthermore, many migrants who were born outside San Juan have resettled there on returning to the Island (Hernández Alvarez 1967). Hence, the city also has the highest proportion in the sample of residents born in the United States (8.3 percent). However, multiple movement is more common in communities with recent migrant traditions (such as Loíza) than in those with well-established histories of migration to the mainland (such as San Juan). Although this pattern requires further research, it may be related to higher unemployment and poverty rates in Loíza and Cidra than in San Juan and Cataño-Guaynabo. Furthermore, according to the results of this study, the Island's rural areas continue to send a proportionately larger number of migrants to the mainland than do urban areas.

TABLE 9.4. Major Metropolitan Areas of Destination of Multiple Movers on
First and Last Trips to the United States (in Percentages)

Destination	First trip	Last trip
Boston, Mass.	6.2	10.9
Buffalo, N.Y.	10.8	4.7
Chicago, Ill.	6.2	4.7
Cincinnati, Ohio	0	3.1
Hartford, Conn.	3.1	6.3
Los Angeles, Calif.	3.1	1.6
Miami, Fla.	3.1	1.6
New Haven, Conn.	7.7	6.3
New York, N.Y.	32.3	25.0
Philadelphia, Pa.	10.8	9.4
Providence, R.I.	0	6.3
Syracuse, N.Y.	1.5	4.7
Other places	15.0	16.0

The duration of residence in the United States also varies among the four
municipios. Overall, the average stay abroad increased slightly between the
first and most recent trips—from 136.7 to 137.4 months. Residents of San Juan
tended to remain abroad much longer than those from other places—over
fourteen and a half years. In contrast, residents of Loíza stayed in the mainland
for only nine years on their first trip. Except for residents of San Juan, migrants
spent roughly the same or more time on their last trips as compared with their
first. Many Puerto Ricans are apparently postponing the return from the mainland to the Island. This trend may be related to continuing economic insecurity
on the Island, especially after the 1996 elimination of Section 936 of the U.S.
Internal Revenue Code, which provided tax exemption for American corporations operating in Puerto Rico (see Baver 2000).

Much has been written about the increasing dispersal of the Puerto Rican
population in the United States. Analysis of recent census data has suggested a
movement away from traditional areas of settlement in large urban centers of
the Northeast and Midwest and toward smaller cities of the Northeast and
Southeast, especially in states such as Florida (Navarro 2000; Rivera-Batiz and
Santiago 1994). However, when one compares the place of destination for the
first and last trips among multiple movers, their concentration in New York City
and other cities in the Northeast remains extreme (table 9.4). Nearly one-third
of all multiple movers traveled to New York City on their first journey to the

United States, as did one-fourth on their second journey. On their first trip abroad, the migrants' secondary concentrations were Buffalo, Philadelphia, and New Haven. On their most recent journey, they went more often to Boston, Hartford, and Providence, as well as Philadelphia. Thus, Puerto Ricans are still moving primarily to New York City, but they have also established other centers in the diaspora.

Since 1980, a growing number of Puerto Ricans have migrated to central and southern Florida, as well as to medium-size cities along the northeast coast of the United States, rather than to large metropolitan areas such as New York, Chicago, and Philadelphia. Surprisingly, very few respondents had traveled to Orlando, Miami, Tampa, and other cities in Florida—all of which have experienced a boom in their Puerto Rican populations since 1980. The table does not show the proportions for those who had moved to Orlando and Tampa because they were fewer than 3 percent of the sample. This finding is probably related to the recency of this migration; hence, most people who moved to Florida (and other states in the South and the West, such as Texas and California) have not yet returned to the Island and would not be counted as multiple movers in the ethnosurvey.

The data suggest strong linkages between particular municipios in Puerto Rico and certain cities in the United States (table 9.5). The leading destination for residents of Loíza is now Boston, while New York City dominates for people from Cataño-Guaynabo and San Juan. For Cidra's residents, Chicago, Hartford, and Newark are important secondary destinations; residents of Loíza travel more frequently to Philadelphia and New Haven. Migrants from Cataño-Guaynabo also move to Philadelphia and Miami, while many *sanjuaneros* settle in Chicago and various places not contained in metropolitan areas. Each of the municipios has tended to form its own "daughter communities" (Massey et al. 1987) in the United States, especially in New York City, Chicago, and Boston. In sum, each sending community has developed a distinct migratory circuit that connects it to several points of the diaspora.

Table 9.6 presents a comparison of the sociodemographic characteristics of multiple movers, one-time movers, and nonmovers. Men were more likely than women to move once or more frequently. On average, multiple movers were five years older than one-time movers and thirteen years older than non-movers.[12] The median education of recurrent and one-time migrants was one year higher than for nonmigrants. Calculated as a mean, schooling levels were also higher for those who moved than for those who did not. A higher percent-

TABLE 9.5. Major Metropolitan Areas of Destination of All Movers on Last Trip to
the United States, by Place of Origin (in Percentages)

Destination	Cataño-Guaynabo	Cidra	Loíza	San Juan	Total
Allentown, Pa.	0	3.4	0	0	0.7
Boston, Mass.	1.8	2.3	31.0	4.0	12.4
Buffalo, N.Y.	1.8	1.1	4.4	3.0	2.8
Chicago, Ill.	5.4	23.9	0	6.0	7.2
Cleveland, Ohio	0	0	0.6	3.0	0.9
Greensboro, N.C.	0	3.4	0	0	0.7
Hartford, Conn.	0	13.6	0.6	1.0	3.5
Los Angeles, Calif.	0.9	1.1	3.8	0	1.7
Miami, Fla.	6.3	0	0.6	5.0	2.8
Newark, N.J.	0	11.4	1.9	0	2.8
New Haven, Conn.	0	0	7.6	0	2.6
New York, N.Y.	64.9	22.7	25.9	58.0	42.0
Philadelphia, Pa.	9.0	1.1	9.5	0	5.7
Springfield, Mass.	0	6.8	0	0	1.3
Syracuse, N.Y.	0	0	5.1	0	1.7
Worcester County, Mass.	3.6	0	0	0	0.9
Other places	6.3	8.9	8.7	20.0	7.0

age of multiple movers than of the rest of the sample were born in Puerto Rico rather than abroad. More than half were unemployed or outside the labor force, especially housewives and retired persons. Of those who were employed, the vast majority were operators, laborers, and craft and repair workers. Thus, the data suggest that circulation is most common among middle-aged men with a high school education and a blue-collar job.

The finding that respondents with one trip were more likely to be unemployed than those with two or more trips is revealing. On the one hand, it suggests that multiple movement is an efficient livelihood strategy, insofar as it is associated with finding work in various places. This interpretation fits well with the profile of circular migrants outlined before. On the other hand, the characteristics of one-time movers—especially their gender, age, and birthplace—are correlated with unemployment status. Unfortunately, the small size (90 persons) of the sample of circular migrants does not permit controlling for these differences in a statistically valid fashion.

Table 9.7 compares multiple movers' occupations during their first and last trips to the United States. Note that the proportion of persons who were unemployed or out of the labor force decreased considerably between the two trips.

TABLE 9.6. Sociodemographic Characteristics of Nonmovers, One-Time Movers, and Multiple Movers

	No Trips	One Trip	Two or More Trips
Sex			
Male	45.2	50.8	56.0
Female	54.8	49.2	44.0
Median years of age	35	43	48
Education (number of years of schooling)			
Median	11	12	12
Mean	9.5	10.4	10.1
Birthplace			
Puerto Rico	92.0	91.2	97.7
United States	7.3	8.1	2.3
Other countries	0.7	0.7	0
Employment status			
Unemployed or out of labor force	69.4	62.4	55.7
Employed	30.6	27.6	44.3
Current occupation			
Professionals and technicians	20.2	20.9	12.9
Managers and administrators	1.4	2.5	0
Administrative support and sales workers	29.0	18.4	16.1
Craft and repair workers	18.6	16.6	22.6
Operators and laborers	18.4	26.4	45.2
Service workers	11.5	14.7	3.2
Agricultural workers	0.9	0	0

Note: In percentages, unless otherwise indicated.

The main shift (from 31.4 to 8.6 percent of the total) occurred among students and other persons under fifteen years of age who did not study or work during their first trip and were working during the second trip. Among the employed, the proportion in white-collar and skilled jobs increased significantly, especially among craft and repair workers and administrative support workers. Inversely, the proportion of agricultural and service workers decreased substantially. The evidence suggests that moving back and forth between the Island and the mainland tends to improve the occupational status of Puerto Ricans.

The social networks of all household heads who had lived in the United States are summarized in table 9.8. Multiple movers had proportionally more relatives—such as parents, older siblings, uncles, aunts, nieces, and nephews—in the United States than did one-time migrants. Only on one count—cousins—

TABLE 9.7. Employment Status and Occupation of Multiple Movers during First
and Last Trips to the United States (in Percentages)

	First Trip	Last Trip
Employment status in the U.S.		
Unemployed or out of the labor force	50.0	36.2
Employed	50.0	63.8
Occupation in the U.S.		
Professionals and technicians	2.9	5.4
Managers and administrators	0	0
Administrative support and sales workers	0	8.1
Craft and repair workers	11.4	21.6
Operators and laborers	25.7	27.0
Service workers	17.1	5.4
Agricultural workers	42.9	32.4

did one-time movers have more relatives abroad than multiple movers. Both one-time movers and multiple movers had developed close relations with Nuyoricans at work and at home. However, multiple movers had proportionally fewer friends abroad than those who had moved only once, perhaps because circulation makes it difficult to maintain nonkin ties. In any case, the data show that recurrent migration is associated with close-knit kinship networks in the United States. Such social ties help migrants to secure jobs, housing, and financial and emotional support on the Island and in the mainland. Family obligations are also one of the major reasons why people—especially women—move back and forth, in addition to looking for a job, improving one's economic situation, studying, and retiring.

The frequency and meaning of mobile livelihood practices differ significantly by gender. Prior studies have characterized female circulation between Puerto Rico and the United States as "tied-circulation" because it depends largely on others' decision to move, especially male partners, parents, and other relatives (Conway, Ellis, and Shiwdhan 1990; Ellis, Conway, and Bailey 1996). Most Puerto Rican women migrate not to work outside the home or search for employment but to "attend to their home or family group" (Olmeda 1997)—that is, to sustain the mobile livelihoods of transnational households. Circulating women do much of the unpaid labor—such as babysitting and taking care of the sick and elderly—required to maintain kinship networks across wide distances. Thus, they help to construct transnational communities through the

TABLE 9.8. Social Networks of All Household Heads Who Moved to the
United States (in Percentages)

	One Trip	Two or More Trips
Mother resides in the U.S.	17.8	21.3
Father resides in the U.S.	9.7	27.7
Older sibling resides in the U.S.	55.7	72.3
Uncle or aunt resides in the U.S.	21.8	25.5
Cousin resides in the U.S.	54.6	51.1
Niece or nephew resides in the U.S.	57.8	66.0
Has one or more friends in the U.S.	75.7	47.1
Related to Nuyoricans at work and at home	44.8	44.1

subsistence and caring work involved in organizing family gatherings, celebrations, meals, and other major rituals. Female mobility tends to concentrate in certain critical points of the life cycle, such as marriage, divorce, and retirement (Alicea 1989, 1997; C. Rodríguez 1994b).

Table 9.9 reports language use among migrant heads of households while they were living abroad. As expected, multiple movers had a larger percentage of persons who spoke English frequently or always at home, at work, among friends, and in the neighborhood. The results show that multiple movers use English more commonly and in more settings than those who move only once. As argued before, circular migrants need to be fully bilingual in English and Spanish to succeed in the United States as well as in Puerto Rico. This pattern has long-term effects on Puerto Rican cultural identity; among others, it may contribute to erode the long-standing assumption that being Puerto Rican is equivalent to speaking Spanish. In New York City, the Puerto Ricanness of English-speaking children raised in the mainland is rarely questioned as it is on the Island; family origin and cultural traditions are the key markers of identity for most migrants (Zentella 1997). Perhaps circular migration will expand the monolingual Spanish definition of Puerto Rican culture on the Island as well.

The results of this study question commonly held beliefs about Puerto Rican circular migration. Most Puerto Ricans do not "commute" regularly between the Island and the mainland but remain settled in one of the two places; others move frequently in both directions for short visits. Those who circulate do so mainly between their communities of origin on the Island and a few cities of the northeastern United States, such as New York, Boston, Philadelphia, Hartford,

TABLE 9.9. English-Language Use among All Household Heads Who Moved to the United States (in Percentages)

	One Trip	Two or More Trips
Spoke English at home		
Never	57.8	56.7
Sometimes	28.9	20.0
Frequently	6.3	16.7
Always	7.0	6.7
Spoke English at work		
Never	19.5	20.0
Sometimes	44.5	23.3
Frequently	9.4	23.3
Always	26.6	33.3
Spoke English among friends		
Never	39.8	36.7
Sometimes	43.8	26.7
Frequently	14.1	33.3
Always	2.3	3.3
Spoke English in neighborhood		
Never	23.4	23.3
Sometimes	57.8	40.0
Frequently	10.9	23.3
Always	7.8	13.3

New Haven, and Providence. Certain kinds of people are more likely to move frequently, such as middle-aged, better-educated men employed as blue-collar workers. Contrary to a popular assumption, back-and-forth movement usually has a positive effect on a person's occupational status. Multiple movers have a larger network of relatives in the United States, are more proficient in English, and use it in more situations than those who have traveled abroad only once. Thus, the mobile livelihoods of many Puerto Ricans expand their economic opportunities, social relations, and cultural practices.

CONCLUSION

Much of the existing knowledge on transnational population movements is based on the premise that people move only once, in a single direction, and settle permanently in another country. In the last two decades, scholars have contributed to rethinking transnational flows that do not conform to the classic pattern of international migration (see Chapman and Prothero 1985; Conway 1989; Massey et al. 1998; Schiller, Basch, and Blanc 1995; Smith and Guarnizo 1998). People often return home after spending time abroad and, less frequently, move again to the first or a different destination. The strategy of recurrent migration from Mexico to the United States has been well documented, especially among seasonal farmworkers, since the beginning of the twentieth century (Massey et al. 1987). Within the Caribbean, international circulation has been a common practice since the late nineteenth century (Conway 1989; Richardson 1992). Circular migration has more recently become a viable livelihood strategy for thousands of Puerto Ricans.

The finding that frequent mobility among Puerto Ricans tends to improve their socioeconomic position runs against conventional wisdom. A recurrent problem with prior research was that it did not distinguish clearly between the causes and effects of circulation. Hence, it was difficult to know if people moved frequently in search of a better livelihood or if, alternatively, the spatial expansion of their means of subsistence led them to move constantly. The results of this study provide empirical support for the second proposition. That is, many Puerto Ricans move back and forth between the Island and the mainland because their subsistence strategies have broadened geographically to include several labor markets, multiple home bases, extended kinship networks, and bilingual and bicultural practices as a result of transnational migration. When economic opportunities are unequally distributed in space—as they are in the case of Puerto Rico and the United States—people develop mobile livelihood practices through circulation and other forms of physical, social, and economic mobility.

The results also substantiate the need to expand scholarly treatments of transnational mobility to include circulation and other movements of varying durations (Conway 1994). The Puerto Rican case demonstrates the significance of repetitive movements between "home" and "abroad," although such distinctions have become increasingly artificial. It also confirms that the reciprocal flow of people is an integral part of the exchange of capital, commodities, technology, and information now occurring on a global scale (see Chapman and Prothero 1983). Last, it calls for a detailed analysis of how circulation draws on and broadens the social networks between communities of origin and their places of destination, including but not limited to kinship and friendship ties.

Three main implications can be drawn from this study's findings. First, circulation by itself cannot account for the continuing poverty and deprivation among Puerto Ricans in the continental United States (see Meléndez 1993b; Tienda 1989). Rather, the fluidity of population movements is a productive survival strategy for many households on and off the Island, in view of the incapacity of local labor markets to absorb additional workers, especially in the declining manufacturing sector (Ellis, Conway, and Bailey 1996; C. Rodríguez 1994b). Circulation is a way of mobilizing personal and family resources spread widely in space and transcending geocultural boundaries. It constitutes a set of mobile livelihood practices in two or more localities (Olwig and Sørensen 1999). For most people, multiple movement is a form of acquiring skills and education and improving their occupational status. Bilateral displacement is one of the key transnational links between their communities in Puerto Rico and the United States, especially along the northeastern seaboard. More than for other migrants, the daily lives of circular migrants depend on dense and multiple social networks across national borders (Schiller, Basch, and Blanc 1995).

Second, circular migration mobilizes cultural identities beyond neatly bounded categories of language, territory, or citizenship. Circular migrants have to acquire bilingual and bicultural skills to survive in both a Puerto Rican and an American setting. In developing dual or perhaps multiple "home bases" (Alicea 1990), they also defy the standard criterion of defining permanent residence as living in a single place for a long time. United States citizenship appears as a practical convenience, rather than an emotional identity marker, for those who travel frequently between the Island and the mainland. That so many Puerto Ricans have lived abroad, many more than once; that most have relatives and friends abroad; and that they maintain close ties to Nuyorican communities suggest that Puerto Rico itself has been thoroughly transnationalized over the last five decades through migration, circulation, and other social processes. For many Puerto Ricans, the Island no longer represents a well-bounded national entity, an exclusive homeland, but rather one point in an extensive migratory circuit, a pole in a geographic and cultural continuum of interconnected places of residence and work.

Third, traversing formal geopolitical frontiers may actually *increase* the likelihood of moving back and forth, at least between bordering regions such as western Mexico and the southwestern United States. Contrary to my original expectation, recurrent migration is much more common among Mexicans (44 percent of all migrants interviewed in the ethnosurvey), although many of them are undocumented (Mexican Migration Project 1999), than among Puerto Ricans (13 percent), who are U.S. citizens. The Mexican sample also had a much larger percentage of household members currently residing in the United States (45 percent) than the Puerto Rican sample (32 percent). Returning to Kearney's intriguing distinction (1991) between borders and boundaries, Mexicans cross legal boundaries more frequently than Puerto Ricans cross the cultural border to the United States. For Puerto Ricans, moving abroad seems to be a more prolonged and definitive decision than for Mexicans, many of whom have been accustomed to frequent travels north and south of the Rio Grande for generations. Because of lack of research, it is unclear whether Puerto Ricans circulate more often than other Caribbean people such as Martinicans or Arubans, who also have free access to their metropolises. In any case, the mobile livelihoods of many Puerto Ricans on and off the Island undermine the highly localized images of space, culture, and identity that have dominated nationalist discourse and practice in Puerto Rico and elsewhere. Although much work remains to be done on this topic, "irse pa' fuera" represents a radical decentering of the Puerto Rican nation.

For further inquiry, I would advocate rethinking the abstract image of a "deterritorialized nation-state" that permeates current writing on transnationalism (Schiller, Basch, and Blanc 1995). Although Puerto Rico is not a sovereign state, its migrants experience extensive deterritorialization (and reterritorialization) in the United States, similar to other transnational migrants. Hence, people may circulate across national borders without ever crossing state boundaries. Moreover, this study suggests the need to engage in systematic comparisons between Puerto Rican and other Latin American and Caribbean migrations. In particular, elaborating a typology of transients and settlers may help to locate Puerto Rican circulators in their regional context (Segal 1996; Thomas-Hope 1986). Finally, fieldworkers should gather comparable data in both the United States and Puerto Rico, including more representative samples of Puerto Rican households currently residing in the mainland. Such research would shed more light on the mobile livelihoods of Puerto Ricans on and off the Island.

Neither White nor Black

The Representation of Racial Identity among Puerto Ricans on the Island and in the U.S. Mainland

How is racial identity represented in an Afro-Hispanic Caribbean nation like Puerto Rico? And how do racial and ethnic categories shift in the diaspora? In 1990 I directed an ethnographic study of the sociocultural causes of the census undercount in Barrio Gandul, a poor urban community in San Juan (Duany, Hernández Angueira, and Rey 1995). At the beginning of our fieldwork, my colleagues and I asked our informants, "What race do you consider yourself to belong to?" Responses to this seemingly innocuous question ranged from embarrassment and amazement to ambivalence and silence: many informants simply shrugged their shoulders and pointed to their arms, as if their skin color were so obvious that it did not need to be verbalized. When people referred to others' race, they often used ambiguous euphemisms (such as "he's a little darker than I"), without committing themselves to a specific racial label. Sometimes they would employ diminutive folk terms such as *morenito* or *trigueñita* (referring to dark-skinned persons), which are difficult to translate into U.S. categories. For the purposes of this research, it seemed culturally appropriate to collect our impressions of people's phenotypes as coded in Hispanic Caribbean societies such as Puerto Rico and the Dominican Republic. However, this procedure left open the question as to what extent the researchers' racial categories coincided with the subjects' own perceptions.

My field notes for that project are full of references to the intermediate physical types of many residents of Barrio Gandul, including *moreno* and *trigueño*. For statistical purposes, these terms are usually grouped under the generic label "mulatto," but Puerto Ricans make finer social distinctions in their daily lives. For instance, our informants used the terms *grifo*, *jabao*, and *colorao* to refer to various combinations of hair types and skin tones. At least nineteen different racial categories are commonly used in Puerto Rico (see table 10.1; see also Godreau 2000). Contrary to the collapsing of racially mixed persons in the United States into the nonwhite category, residents of Barrio Gandul recognized several intermediate groups. In American racial terminology, most of our subjects would probably classify themselves as "other," that is, neither white nor black.

As table 10.1 suggests, popular racial taxonomies in Puerto Rico cannot easily be reduced to the white/black antithesis prevalent in the United States. Puerto Ricans usually group people into three main racial groups—black, white, and brown—based primarily on skin pigmentation and other physical traits, such as facial features and hair texture, regardless of their ancestry. In the United States, the dominant system of racial classification emphasizes a two-tiered division between whites and nonwhites deriving from the principle of hypodescent—the assignment of the offspring of mixed races to the subordinate group (Davis 1998; Harris 1964). According to the "one-drop rule," anyone with a known African ancestor is defined as black, regardless of his or her physical appearance. This clear-cut opposition between Puerto Rican and American conceptions of racial identity has numerous repercussions for social analysis and public policy, among them the appropriate way to categorize, count, and report the number of people by race and ethnicity.

The problem of representing the racial identity of Puerto Ricans, both on the Island and in the U.S. mainland, has troubled American scholars, census enumerators, and policymakers since the end of the nineteenth century. Two key issues have pervaded academic and public debates on race in Puerto Rico. On the one hand, the proliferation and fluidity of racial terms have puzzled outside observers. On the other hand, census tallies report a growing proportion of whites in Puerto Rico between 1899 and 1950 and then again in the year 2000. Even though the census's racial categories changed several times during this period, the white category remained intact, and the number of persons counted as white increased from one census to another. I discuss both these issues later in the chapter.

TABLE 10.1. Major Folk Racial Terms Used in Puerto Rico

Term	Approximate Meaning
Blanco(a)	White
Blanquito(a)	Literally, little white; figuratively, elitist, upper class
Colorao(a)	Redheaded, reddish skin
Rubio(a)	Blond
Cano(a)	Blond, fair skinned
Jincho(a)	Pale skinned; sometimes used pejoratively
Blanco(a) con raja	Literally, white with a crack; white with some visible black features
Jabao(a)	Fair skinned with curly hair
Trigueño(a)	Literally, wheat colored or brunette; usually light mulatto
Moreno(a)	Dark skinned; usually dark mulatto
Mulato(a)	Mixed race; rarely used in public
Indio(a)	Literally, Indian; brown skinned with straight hair
Café con leche	Literally, coffee with milk; tan or brown skinned
Piel canela	Literally, cinnamon skin; tan or brown skinned
Prieto(a)	Dark skinned; usually derogatory
Grifo(a)	Dark skinned with kinky hair; usually derogatory
De color	Euphemism for black; usually meaning black
Negro(a)	Black; rarely used as a direct term of reference
Negrito(a)	Literally, little black; often used as a term of endearment

In the United States, Puerto Rican migrants do not fit well in the conventional white/black dichotomy and therefore challenge the hegemonic discourse on race and ethnicity (C. Rodríguez 1994a, 2000). Recent research efforts by the U.S. Bureau of the Census have focused on determining why so many mainland Puerto Ricans, as well as other Hispanics, choose the "other" category when asked about their racial identity. In the 2000 census, 42.2 percent of all Hispanics in the United States declared that they belonged to "some other race" besides white, black or African American, American Indian and Alaska Native, Asian, or Native Hawaiian and other Pacific Islander (U.S. Bureau of the Census 2001). The existence of a large and growing segment of the U.S. population that perceives itself ethnically as Hispanic or Latino, while avoiding the major accepted racial designations, is a politically explosive phenomenon. It is no wonder that the federal government has so far resisted public pressures to include a separate multiracial category (as opposed to "more than one race") in the census and other official documents. So have many African American, Latino, and Asian American lobbying groups, which perceive a threat to their numbers by creating further divisions within racial minorities. For these groups, checking more than one race in the census questionnaire means reducing their influence on public policymaking (see Schemo 2000).

In this chapter I examine how Americans have represented the racial identity of Puerto Ricans, as well as how Puerto Ricans have represented themselves racially, both at home and in the diaspora. First I review census data on the racial composition of the Island's population between 1899 and 1950 and then again in 2000. Next I analyze estimates of the racial composition of Puerto Rican migrants between 1940 and 1999. I show that U.S. racial categories have historically been at odds, and continue to be so, with prevailing self-concepts among Puerto Ricans. My premise is that the changing racial categories used by the census in Puerto Rico and in the diaspora articulate the hegemonic discourse on race in the United States. However, Puerto Ricans continue to represent themselves differently from official views on race and ethnicity, both on the Island and in the mainland. Whereas Americans tend to draw a rigid line between white and black people, Puerto Ricans prefer to use a fluid continuum of physical types. In essence, different and competing racial discourses have produced incompatible portraits of racial identity on the Island and in the U.S. mainland. On the Island, the vast majority of Puerto Ricans regard themselves as white. In the mainland, most consider themselves to be neither white nor black but members of some other race. To many Americans, Puerto Ricans occupy an ambiguous position between white people and people of color.

THE MYTH OF RACIAL DEMOCRACY IN PUERTO RICO AND THE DIASPORA

During the 1940s, anthropological and sociological interest in race relations boomed on the Island, especially on the part of U.S. academics.[1] This growing interest was related to the "American dilemma" centered on black-white tensions and persistent racial inequality in socioeconomic opportunities, despite the dominant creed of equality and justice for all (Myrdall 1944). For many scholars, Puerto Rico (along with Brazil) seemed to be a racial paradise, especially because of the prevalence and popular acceptance of racial mixture on the Island. Compared with the southern United States, Puerto Rico appeared to be a racial democracy where blacks, whites, and mulattoes lived in harmony. Racial prejudice and discrimination seemed less pervasive and destructive on the Island than in the mainland.

Racial questions were not purely intellectual but utterly political, as American legislators and policymakers who visited Puerto Rico during the 1950s recognized. Arkansas senator J. W. Fulbright declared that the Island was "an example of a racial solution" through education, while George William Culberson, director of Pittsburgh's Commission on Human Relations, reported that "there are no racial prejudices in the public life" of Puerto Rico (*El Mundo* 1958, 1959). Governor Muñoz Marín (1960) believed that racial tolerance was one of the greatest spiritual contributions of Puerto Rican migrants to New York City. The myth of racial democracy in Puerto Rico was often deployed as an alternative to the American apartheid under Jim Crow laws, which enforced the strict separation between whites and blacks in education, housing, transportation, recreation, and marriage.

During the 1940s, several scholars contrasted the social construction of race in Puerto Rico and the United States (see, for instance, T. Blanco 1985 [1942]; Rogler 1940; Siegel 1948). One of the recurrent themes of this early literature was that the Island's history and culture promoted racial integration rather than segregation, as in the United States and South Africa. Outsiders were surprised that Puerto Ricans of different colors mingled freely in public activities and that many married across color lines. In particular, light mulattoes (known locally as "trigueños") mixed with lower-class whites and were often accepted as white, even by the local elite (Rogler 1972b [1944]). Social distance between whites and blacks also seemed less marked on the Island than in the mainland.

According to these studies, the main difference between the Puerto Rican and American models of racial stratification was not the treatment of blacks—who were accorded a subordinate status in both societies—but rather the treatment of the mixed group. In Puerto Rico, trigueños could often pass for whites, whereas in the United States, an intermediate racial category (such as mulattoes) had not formally existed since the 1930 census. Although racial mixture also occurred in the mainland, the federal government did not officially recognize it, except as part of the black population (Davis 1998). The symbolic boundaries between whites and mulattoes were apparently more porous in Puerto Rico than in the United States.

An important subtheme of this literature was whether color distinctions in Puerto Rico were better interpreted as a racial or class hierarchy. The Puerto Rican writer Tomás Blanco (1985 [1942]: 128) represented the dominant view that prejudice was "more of a social than a racial character in Puerto Rico" (see also Mintz 1966; Sereno 1947). According to Blanco, whatever racial prejudice may have been present on the Island was primarily a recent importation from the United States. Others, however, recognized the long history of racial prejudice and discrimination in Puerto Rican society, as expressed through folklore, occupations, religion, courtship, marriage, and voluntary associations.

Although different from the American system of racial classification, the Puerto Rican system still assigned blacks and mulattoes a lower rank than whites (see Gordon 1949, 1950; Rosario and Carrión 1951). A consensus emerged from these classic studies that Puerto Rican society is stratified in both class status and color gradations ranging from white to brown to black. Whether race or some other variable such as occupation, education, or residence determines one's life chances continues to be debated.

Researchers have long been concerned with how Puerto Ricans define "race" or "color"; much of the literature treats the two terms as synonyms. Color distinctions on the Island involve a complex inventory of such physical traits as skin pigmentation, hair texture, nose shape, and lip form (Ginorio 1971; C. Rodríguez 1996; Seda Bonilla 1968; Zenón Cruz 1975). More than descent, phenotype defines one's racial identity in Puerto Rico, as in much of the Caribbean and Latin America. Socioeconomic variables such as occupational prestige and family connections can also alter a person's "race." Contrary to the United States, ancestry is not the most significant variable in assessing race in Puerto Rico. Rather, as the American sociologist Charles Rogler (1972a [1946]) noted long ago, Puerto Ricans place most emphasis on visual evidence of race as an individual's anatomic feature.

The proliferation, elasticity, and ambiguity of Puerto Rican racial terms have fascinated American social scientists. Rogler (1972b [1944]) was one of the first to write about the "confusion" among race, color, and class in Puerto Rico. He was frustrated by the weak correlation between racial terms and social interaction on the Island. The anthropologist Morris Siegel also perceived widespread confusion about the racial constitution of the Island's population. Siegel (1948: 187) recognized that Puerto Ricans are "terribly color-conscious" and that they pay much attention to visual cues to determine if a person is white, black, or an in-between type such as trigueño or jabao. Furthermore, many scholars found that "money whitens" on the Island: the wealthier a person is, the more likely she will be classified as light skinned or simply as white, regardless of her physical appearance. Like Brazil and other Latin American societies, Puerto Rico developed a "mulatto escape hatch" that allowed some persons of mixed ancestry upward social mobility (Degler 1971; Wade 1997).

Based on fieldwork conducted during the late 1950s and 1960s, Eduardo Seda Bonilla (1968, 1973) confirmed that most Puerto Ricans use phenotype rather than hypodescent as the main criterion for racial identity. Like many Latin Americans, Puerto Ricans tend to distinguish three basic physical types—

white, black, and brown—defined primarily by skin color, facial features, and hair texture. Furthermore, whereas Americans pay close attention to national and ethnic background in defining a person's identity, Puerto Ricans give a higher priority to birthplace and cultural orientation. Among other features of the Puerto Rican discourse on race, Seda Bonilla noted the public recognition of racially intermediate types, the reduced social distance among contiguous categories, and the frequency of racial mixture.

Another common practice on the Island is a strong desire to whiten oneself (*mejorar la raza*), a tendency also known as "bleaching" (*blanqueamiento*). For decades, local enumerators have classified the vast majority of the Puerto Rican population as white, despite the high incidence of *mestizaje* (racial mixture). As Maxine Gordon (1949) pointed out long ago, census statistics since the mid–nineteenth century show the continuous rise of the white sector of the Island's population, at the expense of the black and mulatto sectors. These statistics are open to debate because of the flexible boundaries between racial groups as well as the lack of fit between local and U.S. concepts of race. However, they suggest that most Puerto Ricans perceive themselves as white rather than as black or mulatto and that this trend is increasing.

The generalized view about the virtual absence of racial prejudice and discrimination has made race a difficult research topic in Puerto Rico. As José Colombán Rosario and Justina Carrión (1951: 88) put it, "The discussion of the problem of the black [has] been kept in a humid and unhygienic obscurity." Most authors agreed with Rogler's assessment (1972b [1944]: 55) that "race competition, tension, and conflict are not conspicuous processes in most Puerto Rican situations," as they are in the United States. In a famous turn of phrase, Blanco (1985 [1942]: 103) compared racial prejudice in Puerto Rico to "an innocent children's game." According to Siegel (1948: 3), "The island is one of the few places in the world where interracial harmony has been achieved in high degree . . . the more overt and vicious forms of racism are largely absent." More recent writers have continued to downplay racial prejudice and discrimination in Puerto Rico (see Arana-Soto 1976; Davis 1998; Fitzpatrick 1987; Hoetink 1967; Mintz 1966; C. Rodríguez 1974; Wolfson 1972). It is still extremely difficult to break through the "conspiracy of silence" that surrounds racial politics in Puerto Rico—what one author called "the prejudice of having no prejudice" (Betances 1972, 1973).

One of the earliest critics of standard views of race relations in Puerto Rico was the American sociologist Maxine Gordon (1949, 1950). She argued that historical and cultural factors—such as the absence of racial violence and the prevalence of racial intermarriage over several generations—fostered the belief that no racial prejudice existed on the Island. However, she found instances of racism in various Puerto Rican institutions, such as college fraternities and upper-class private clubs. Unfortunately, her thesis was poorly documented, having been based largely on anecdotal evidence from secondary sources, not on systematic fieldwork. As a result, Gordon's work could not seriously undermine the established discourse on race in Puerto Rico.

In the mid-1960s, Puerto Rican social scientists began to question the conventional wisdom that racial prejudice was absent on the Island. Juan Rodríguez Cruz (1965: 385) cautiously acknowledged "the existence of [racial] discriminatory practices in certain spheres of Puerto Rican society," such as private schools, the University of Puerto Rico, private enterprises, voluntary associations, and residential neighborhoods. Seda Bonilla's cited work was part of an emerging academic consensus that racism did indeed persist on the Island. Reviewing the literature from the United States, Samuel Betances (1972, 1973) sharply criticized the myth of racial integration in Puerto Rico. But the most sustained attack on Puerto Rican racism came from the literary critic Isabelo Zenón Cruz, whose two-volume treatise denounced the "constant and systematic marginalization" (1975: 23) of black Puerto Ricans as second-class citizens in elite and folk poetry, as well as in other areas of national culture. Although his work provoked an intense polemic on the Island, it did not foster new ethnographic or sociological fieldwork on race relations. It did, however, spark a new wave of revisionist research on the history of Puerto Rican slavery (see Díaz Quiñones 1985; Kinsbruner 1996; Scarano 1984).

Although the empirical evidence on racial politics in contemporary Puerto Rico is still scanty, several studies have documented that blacks are a stigmatized minority on the Island; that they suffer from persistent prejudice and discrimination; that they concentrate in lower classes; and that they are subject to an ideology of whitening through intermarriage with lighter-skinned groups and a denial of their cultural heritage and physical characteristics (Kantrowitz 1971; Picó de Hernández et al. 1985; Seda Bonilla 1973, 1980; Zenón Cruz 1975). The latter ideology helps to explain why an increasing proportion of Puerto Ricans have reported their race to be white over time, despite the absence of massive immigration to the Island during the first decades of the twentieth century. Many authors have noted the unreliable nature of census data on the racial composition of the Puerto Rican population (T. Blanco 1985 [1942];

Cabranes 1979; Fitzpatrick 1987; Rodríguez Cruz 1965; Rogler 1940; Siegel 1948). No published studies have yet explored the congruence between popular representations of race in Puerto Rico and the official racial categories of the United States.[2] Recent ethnographic fieldwork on racial issues has concentrated on Afro–Puerto Rican coastal communities and their cultural contributions to national identity (Godreau-Santiago 1999; Moira Pérez 1998; Torres 1998).

In addition, scholars have questioned whether the dominant white/black dichotomy can capture the complex racial situation of the Puerto Rican diaspora. Since World War II, massive migration from Puerto Rico to the mainland has pitted two racial classification systems against each other: the Puerto Rican one, based largely on physical appearance, and the American one, based largely on ancestry. Thus, when Puerto Ricans move abroad, they confront a different construction of their racial identity (Fitzpatrick 1987; Ginorio 1979; Montero Seplowin 1971; C. Rodríguez 1974; Seda Bonilla 1980). In the 1940s, C. Wright Mills, Clarence Senior, and Rose Kohn Goldsen (1950) found that one of the main problems of Puerto Ricans in New York City was racial prejudice and discrimination. They noted that adaptation was particularly difficult for racially intermediate types (such as the so-called *indios*) and blacks, who were more prone to return to the Island than whites.

The dominant opposition between whites and nonwhites in the United States eludes many Puerto Rican migrants, who have African as well as European backgrounds and range phenotypically across the entire color spectrum from black to brown to white. As a result of their racial heterogeneity, mainland Puerto Ricans are often lumped together with blacks. Those with mixed racial ancestry lose their intermediate status in a white/nonwhite dichotomy. Light-skinned immigrants are sometimes called "white Puerto Ricans," whereas dark-skinned immigrants are often treated like African Americans. In New York City, many are simply classified as "Pororicans," as if this were a distinct racial category.[3] Like other ethnic minorities, Puerto Ricans have been thoroughly racialized in the United States (see V. Rodríguez 1997; Rodríguez-Morazzani 1996).

The work of New York–based Puerto Rican sociologist Clara Rodríguez has dominated academic discussions about race among Puerto Rican migrants. Based on the analysis of the Public Use Microdata Sample of the 1980 census as well as her own survey results, Rodríguez reports that many members of the Puerto Rican community in New York resist being classified as either black or white and prefer to identify themselves as "other." In the 1980 census, 48 percent of New York City's Puerto Ricans chose this category, sometimes adding terms such as Hispanic, Latino, Spanish, and Boricua (C. Rodríguez 1989, 1990, 1992; Rodríguez and Cordero-Guzmán 1992). In 1990 nearly 46 percent of all Puerto Ricans in the United States classified themselves as "other" (C. Rodríguez 2000). Hence, many Puerto Ricans and their descendants continue to employ a tripartite rather than a dual scheme of racial classification. Contrary to Seda Bonilla's (1980) prediction that they would split along color lines, most migrants reject their indiscriminate labeling as members of a single race (see also Ginorio 1979). Rather than splintering themselves into white and black, Puerto Ricans recognize that they are a multiracial people.[4]

Rodríguez's work points to the need for further research and reflection on the conflicts and negotiations between popular and official representations of Puerto Rican identity. Víctor Rodríguez (1997) has argued that Puerto Ricans in the United States have been racialized through close association with African Americans. From a different perspective, Roberto Rodríguez-Morazzani (1996) suggests that mainland Puerto Ricans have avoided identification as black to escape their negative racialization. I would argue that a similar process took place on the Island, where the U.S. government has attempted to impose its bipolar view of race on the Puerto Rican population. This effort has mostly failed, as witnessed by the continued use of a folk system of racial classification that differs markedly from the one prevailing in the mainland (compare tables 10.1 and 10.2).[5] How does one translate the multiple and fluid racial labels popular on the Island into the smaller number of categories used by the U.S. census?

In sum, the Puerto Rican model of race relations has several distinguishing features. Unlike Americans, most Puerto Ricans do not consider race primarily a question of descent. Like other Caribbean and Latin American people, Puerto Ricans emphasize physical appearance in representing racial identity (Hoetink 1967; Seda Bonilla 1968). As a result, a person of mixed racial background is not automatically assigned to the black group in Puerto Rico. Rather, racial classification depends largely on skin color and other visible characteristics such as the shape of one's mouth and nose and hair texture. Social status (including income, occupation, and education) is also taken into consideration. Unfortunately, Puerto Ricans have developed an elaborate racist vocabulary to refer to racially stereotyped characteristics—especially the idea that kinky hair is "bad" (*pelo malo*). Furthermore, Puerto Ricans usually distinguish blacks from mulattoes, whereas Americans tend to view both groups as nonwhite. In contrast to the U.S. model, which tends to be dichotomous, the Puerto Rican racial model is based on a threefold scheme.

Finally, because of the proliferation of intermediate physical types, Puerto Rico has not established a two-tiered institutionalized system of racial discrimination such as that of the United States. For example, lower-class urban settlements in San Juan, such as Barrio Gandul, are not strictly segregated by color but primarily by class (Duany, Hernández Angueira, and Rey 1995). Nonetheless, racial prejudice on the Island is expressed in myriad forms—such as folk humor, beauty contests, media portrayals, and political leadership. In all these areas, whites are usually depicted as more intelligent, attractive, refined, and capable than are blacks. As Seda Bonilla (1968: 592) has underlined, both the Puerto Rican and U.S. models "commit the inhuman error of assigning intellectual, moral, or social superiority to some racial categories over others." In Puerto Rico, as well as in the United States, an ideology of white supremacy and black inferiority has prevailed since the days of colonial slavery.

"THE WHITEST OF THE ANTILLES": REPRESENTING RACE IN PUERTO RICO

One of the first official acts of the U.S. government in Puerto Rico after acquiring the Island in 1898 was to conduct a census of its population. The War Department assumed that task in 1899. Since 1910, the Department of Commerce has been in charge of the census in Puerto Rico as well as in the U.S. mainland. Until 1950, the Bureau of the Census attempted to quantify the racial composition of the Island's population, while experimenting with various racial taxonomies. In 1960 the census dropped the racial identification question for Puerto Rico but included it again in the year 2000 (see table 10.2). The only category that remained constant over time was white, even as other racial labels shifted greatly—from colored to black, mulatto, and other; back to colored and other races; then to nonwhite; again to Negro and other races; and finally to black or African American and other races. Regardless of the precise terminology, the census reported that the bulk of the Puerto Rican population was white from 1899 to 2000.

From the beginning of the twentieth century, American observers remarked on the "surprising preponderance of the white race" on the Island (*National Geographic Magazine* 1900: 328). One travel writer called Puerto Rico "the

TABLE 10.2. Racial Categories Used in the Census of Puerto Rico, 1899–2000

Year	Category	Number of Persons	Percentage
1899	White	589,426	61.8
	Colored	363,817	38.2
1910	White	732,555	65.5
	Black	50,245	4.5
	Mulatto	335,192	30.0
	Other	20	0
1920	White	948,709	73.0
	Black	49,246	3.8
	Mulatto	301,816	23.2
	Other	38	0
1930	White	1,146,719	74.3
	Colored	397,156	25.7
	Other races	38	0
1935	White	1,313,496	76.2
	Colored	411,038	23.8
1940	White	1,430,744	76.5
	Nonwhite	438,511	23.5
1950	White	1,762,411	79.7
	Negro	446,948	20.2
	Other races	1,344	0.1
2000	White	3,064,862	80.5
	Black or African American	302,933	8.0
	Other	440,815	11.5

Sources: Administración de Reconstrucción de Puerto Rico 1938; Departamento de la Guerra 1900; U.S. Bureau of the Census 1913, 1921, 1932, 1943a, 1953a, 2001.

whitest of the Antilles" (White 1898). In a widely distributed piece, a geologist (Hill 1899c: 93) wrote that the Island was "notable among the West Indian group for the reason that its preponderant population is of the white race." In a more academic book, he reiterated that "Porto Rico, at least, has not become Africanized, as have all the other West Indies excepting Cuba" (Hill 1903: 165). Such authoritative reports helped to allay the common racist fear that the U.S. government had annexed a predominantly black population after the War of 1898. Such a view still surfaces in contemporary debates about the Island's political status, albeit indirectly.

Table 10.3 compiles the available census statistics on the proportion of whites and nonwhites in Puerto Rico between 1802 and 2000. The Spanish censuses show that Puerto Ricans were about evenly divided between whites and non-whites until the mid–nineteenth century. Since 1860, the proportion of the

TABLE 10.3. Racial Composition of the Puerto Rican Population, as Reported
in the Census, 1802–2000 (in Percentages)

Year	White	Nonwhite[a]
1802	48.0	52.0
1812	46.8	53.2
1820	44.4	55.6
1827	49.7	50.3
1830	50.1	49.9
1836	52.9	47.1
1860	51.1	48.5
1877	56.3	43.7
1887	59.5	40.5
1897	64.3	35.7
1899	61.8	38.2
1910	65.5	34.5
1920	73.0	27.0
1930	74.3	25.7
1935	76.2	23.8
1940	76.5	23.5
1950	79.7	20.3
2000	80.5	19.5

Sources: Administración de Reconstrucción de Puerto Rico 1938; Departamento de la Guerra 1900;
U.S. Bureau of the Census 1913, 1921, 1932, 1943a, 1953a, 2001.
[a] Includes black, colored, mulatto, mixed-blood, and other races.

Island's population classified as white has increased steadily, except for the
year 1899, when the first U.S. census registered a small decrease. Correspond-
ingly, the proportion of people reported as nonwhites (including blacks and
mulattoes) has diminished, again except for 1899. In the 2000 census, 80.5 percent of the Island's residents classified themselves as white, with only 8 percent
black and 11.5 other races. According to these statistics, the Puerto Rican population has become increasingly whiter, especially during the first half of the
twentieth century.

What social factors account for this dramatic transformation in the official
representation of Puerto Rico's racial composition? To some extent, the gradual
lightening of the Island's population was due to European immigration, especially during the second half of the nineteenth century (Hoetink 1967). But the
number of white immigrants was not large enough to produce such a significant
shift in racial groups during the first half of the twentieth century. Nor was there
a massive outflow of blacks to the United States or other countries at this time.

Barring major population movements into and out of the Island until the 1940s, scholars have proposed several additional hypotheses.

Rogler (1940: 16) put forth one of the most popular explanations: "The Census includes as colored both full-blooded and mixed. The census estimate is probably low because many who are known to have colored blood are counted as white. . . . Because of the absence of marked race prejudice, and also because of the tendency to deal with color as a class rather than a race phenomenon, the attitude of the community as a whole operates to reduce materially the percentage classified as colored and to classify many quadroons and octoroons as white." While Rogler points out that light mulattoes are often accepted as whites in Puerto Rico, he fails to acknowledge that "passing" also takes place in the United States, although it operates differently there and without official approval. Moreover, the whitening of the Puerto Rican population is hardly due to the absence of racial prejudice but rather to its very presence: many people prefer to identify as white to avoid racial stigmatization. Nor is it a question of conflating color and class, although the two factors are closely linked. As elsewhere, Puerto Ricans clearly distinguish a person's physical appearance and socioeconomic status. Finally, racial categories such as quadroons and octoroons are meaningless in contemporary Puerto Rico, precisely because it is practically impossible to determine the degree of racial mixture in much of the population (see Fitzpatrick 1987).

Rogler (1972a [1946]: 62) provides a second explanation: "This apparent decline [in the nonwhite population] is probably the consequence of changing race conceptions or, more specifically, the social definition as to who is a person of color. In other words, these percentages would suggest that many persons of color are moving into the white race." I would accept the first premise of this proposition—that census categories reflect changing discourses on race—but would reject its second implication—that Puerto Ricans jumble together white and black people. On the contrary, the Puerto Rican scheme of racial classification is primarily concerned, perhaps even obsessed, with distinguishing various shades of skin color. However, such definitions of race clash with the categories imposed by the U.S. Bureau of the Census. Hence, the problem is not, as Siegel (1948: 189) believed, that "the reliability of Puerto Rican racial classifications is open to serious criticisms." *All* such classifications are historically contingent, culturally relative, politically contestable, ultimately arbitrary, and of dubious scientific value (see Omi and Winant 1994).[6]

The Bureau of the Census itself has offered a third explanation for the apparent increase in Puerto Rico's white population: "The percentage of the population which was colored, according to the census returns, declined from 38.2 percent in 1899 to 23.8 percent in 1935. A part of this nominal decline, however, was without doubt the result of the gradual change in the concept of the race classification as applied by the census enumerators" (Administración de Reconstrucción de Puerto Rico 1938: 17). I doubt that Puerto Rican census takers substantially altered their racial concepts during this period and therefore counted more people as white. Since 1899, enumerators have been recruited from the Island's population and have presumably applied local standards of racial classification. According to the *National Geographic Magazine* (1901: 80), "The facts presented in the reports were gathered in all cases by the [Puerto Rican] people themselves, as the most intelligent of the better classes were induced to compete for positions as census-takers by the relatively handsome salaries offered by the U.S. government." Until the 1960 census, enumerators in Puerto Rico as well as in the U.S. mainland usually judged their informants' physical appearance as a visual cue of racial identity (Ruggles et al. 1997; Torres Aguirre 2000). Only in the 2000 census was the racial question based on self-classification in Puerto Rico.

My own interpretation of the Island's changing racial statistics focuses on the transactions between state-supported and popular representations of race. From the beginning, the U.S. government attempted to divide the Puerto Rican population neatly into "two main classes, pure whites and those who are not" (Departamento de la Guerra 1900: 57). In turn, Puerto Ricans insisted on distinguishing blacks from mulattoes and blurring the boundaries between "pure whites" and "mixed blood." In 1930 the Bureau of the Census dropped mulattoes from its count of the Puerto Rican population and lumped them together with blacks under "colored." This change paralleled the collapsing of blacks and mulattoes into a single category in the mainland (Davis 1998; Domínguez 1998). Between 1900 and 1930, the U.S. census counted persons of mixed black and white ancestry as a separate group. But in 1940, such persons were considered Negro (see table 10.4). On the Island, census enumerators tended to avoid the "colored" and "black" labels altogether and to identify their informants as white. Thus, the official disappearance of racially intermediate types accelerated the movement from nonwhite to white categories on the Island.

In short, the U.S. government sought to apply a binary race model to a fluid multiracial situation in Puerto Rico. As an official report to the local House

TABLE 10.4. Major Racial Categories Used in the Census of the
United States, 1900–2000

Year	Categories
1900	White, black, mulatto, Indian, Chinese, Japanese, Filipino, Hindu, Korean, Mexican
1910	White, black, mulatto, Chinese, Japanese, Indian
1920	White, black, mulatto, Indian, Chinese, Japanese, Filipino, Hindu, Korean
1930	White, black, mulatto, Indian, Chinese, Japanese, Filipino, Hindu, Korean, Mexican
1940	White, Negro, Indian, Chinese, Japanese, Filipino, Hindu, Korean
1950	White, Negro, Indian, Chinese, Japanese, Filipino
1960	White, Negro, American Indian, Japanese, Chinese, Filipino, Hawaiian, Part Hawaiian, Aleut, Eskimo
1970	White, Negro or black, Indian (Amer.), Japanese, Chinese, Filipino, Hawaiian
1980	White, Negro or black, Japanese, Chinese, Filipino, Korean, Vietnamese, Indian (Amer.), Asian Indian, Hawaiian, Guamanian, Samoan, Eskimo, Aleut
1990	White, black or Negro, Indian (Amer.), Eskimo, Aleut, Asian or Pacific Islander
2000	White, black or African American, American Indian or Alaskan Native, Asian, Native Hawaiian or other Pacific Islander

Sources: Office of Management and Budget 1997; Ruggles et al. 1997.

of Representatives noted, "The population is extremely mixed and there are not just two colors but rather an infinite number of hues" (*El Mundo* 1945). Although the census recognized that most "colored" people were mulattoes rather than "pure blacks" (the terms used by the census), the dominant discourse on race silenced that trend after 1930 (see table 10.5). From an American standpoint, only two distinct races existed in Puerto Rico—white and black (variously called Negro, colored, or nonwhite). Well into the 1940s, the Bureau of the Census claimed that racial terms "probably need no definition" (U.S. Bureau of the Census 1946: 2). However, it instructed local enumerators to classify persons of mixed ancestry as "colored" rather than white (U.S. Bureau of the Census 1943a: 100). As a Bureau of the Census (1963: ix) report understated, "It is likely that the commonly held conceptions of race among Puerto Ricans in Puerto Rico, among Puerto Ricans in the United States, and among other persons in the United States are somewhat different, and there was a considerable variation in the classification." For instance, the 1950 census categorized persons of mixed ancestry according to the race of the nonwhite parent, following the rule of hypodescent (U.S. Bureau of the Census 1953a: 53-V). In contrast, Puerto Ricans classified them primarily according to their physical

TABLE 10.5. Mulatto and Black Populations of Puerto Rico, as Reported in the
Census, 1899–1920 (in Percentages)

	1899	1910	1920
Mulattoes	83.6	86.9	85.9
Blacks	16.4	13.1	14.1
Total "colored"	100	100	100

Sources: Departamento de la Guerra 1900; U.S. Bureau of the Census 1913, 1921.

appearance. Whereas the census insisted on distinguishing only two groups, white and nonwhite, Puerto Ricans continued to use three or more categories, including trigueño, moreno, indio, and other folk terms. Many people in Puerto Rico contested the racial practices articulated by the Bureau of the Census.

The racial politics of census enumeration in Puerto Rico reveal a sharp discrepancy between self-representations and representations by others. In 1899 nearly two-thirds of all Puerto Ricans were considered white. In 2000 more than four-fifths classified themselves as white. However, many Americans— including visiting scholars and public officials—mistrusted such statistics, believing instead that the Island's "colored" population was much larger than suggested by the census. Some Puerto Rican authors granted that the majority of the local population was composed of mulattoes (T. Blanco 1985 [1942]; Rodríguez Cruz 1965). In 1960 the federal government eliminated any references to race or color from the census of Puerto Rico, apparently because it considered them to be unreliable and practically useless. A brief note in the 1950 census reads: "There is considerable evidence which indicates that color is misreported [in Puerto Rico]. The comparison of the 'white' and 'nonwhite' total from census to census reveals the tendency of the enumerator to report persons with varying amounts of Negro blood as 'white'" (U.S. Bureau of the Census 1952: viii). Racial statistics on the Island did not generate a portrait compatible with the dominant discourse on race in the United States.

For its own reasons, the Puerto Rican government attempted to eliminate references to race from most public documents on the Island. According to the director of the Office of the Census of the Puerto Rican Planning Board, Lillian Torres Aguirre (letter to the author, January 21, 2000), the race question was dropped because the Commonwealth's constitution prohibits discrimination by race or color and because the local government is not required by law to collect racial statistics in order to provide public services. In 1978 an attorney working for the Office of Legal Affairs of the Puerto Rican Planning Board recommended that "the most adequate and convenient solution for our economic, social, and cultural reality is not to include the question about racial determination in the 1980 census questionnaire" (Mercado Vega 1978: 3). Between 1960 and 1990, the census questionnaire in Puerto Rico did not ask about race or color. Racial categories therefore disappeared from the official discourse on the Puerto Rican nation.

However, the 2000 census included a racial self-identification question in Puerto Rico and, for the first time ever, allowed respondents to choose more than one racial category to indicate mixed ancestry. (Only 4.2 percent chose two or more races.) With few variations, the census of Puerto Rico used the same questionnaire as in the U.S. mainland. This decision was a response to intense lobbying by former governor Pedro Rosselló's administration to include Puerto Rico in federal census statistics, along with the fifty states (see Mulero 1999). According to census reports, most islanders responded to the new federally mandated categories on race and ethnicity by insisting on their "whiteness"; few declared themselves to be black or some other race (U.S. Bureau of the Census 2001). Clearly, many of the census's racial categories—such as American Indian, Alaska Native, Asian, Hawaiian, or Pacific Islander—are irrelevant to most of the Puerto Rican population.

WHITE, BLACK, OR OTHER?:
THE RACIAL REPRESENTATION OF PUERTO RICAN MIGRANTS

If classifying the race of Puerto Ricans on the Island was complicated, the task became even more daunting to government authorities in the U.S. mainland. Since the beginning of the twentieth century, the Bureau of the Census has frequently altered its racial designation of Puerto Rican and other Hispanic immigrants. For instance, the census counted Mexicans as a separate (non-white) race in 1930, white between 1940 and 1970, and of any race they reported between 1980 and 2000. Until 1970, most Puerto Ricans living in the United States were considered white, "unless they were definitely Negro, Indian, or some other race" (Domínguez 1998). In 1980, the census introduced two separate self-identification questions, one on Hispanic origin and one on race, based on the premise that Hispanics could be of any race. Consequently, the federal government encouraged Puerto Ricans to classify themselves primarily as Hispanics rather than as white or black.

Table 10.6 presents census data on the racial composition of Puerto Ricans in the United States from 1940 to 1990.[7] First, the proportion of mainland Puerto Ricans who were reported to be white decreased drastically after 1970, largely as a result of the inclusion of the new Hispanic category. In 1990 the proportion of Puerto Ricans who classified themselves as white (nearly 46 percent) was slightly more than half the 1940 figure (87 percent). Second, the proportion of black Puerto Ricans has remained extremely low since 1950 (between 4 and 8 percent). Third, those reporting other races jumped from less than 2 percent in 1970 to more than 47 percent in 1990. Thus, over the past several decades, Puerto Ricans in the United States have changed their racial self-perception from a predominantly white population to a hybrid one. Contrary to the dominant trend among Puerto Ricans on the Island, fewer of those residing in the mainland reported that they were white between the 1970 and 1990 censuses.

Let me review some possible reasons for this change and then offer my own explanation. Several authors have argued that Puerto Ricans in the United States tend to reject their labeling as black, because that would mean accepting an inferior position within American society. From this perspective, the migrants assert a separate cultural identity to evade rampant prejudice and discrimination against African Americans (Fitzpatrick 1987; Montero Seplowin 1971; Rodríguez-Morazzani 1996; Seda Bonilla 1968; Wolfson 1972). Although this argument may help to explain why many dark-skinned Puerto Rican migrants do not align themselves with African Americans, it misses two basic points. First, about the same proportion of Puerto Ricans on the Island and in the mainland (8 percent, according to the census) classify themselves as black rather than white or other races. Second, proportionally fewer Puerto Ricans in the mainland than on the Island classify themselves as white when offered an opportunity to declare other races. The key question then becomes why so many U.S. Puerto Ricans chose the "other" category—neither white nor black—in the last two censuses.

Clara Rodríguez believes that Puerto Ricans in New York City continue to define their racial identity according to a color continuum from white to black. As in Puerto Rico, this continuum is based on phenotypic categories ranging in pigmentation, hair form, and facial features. Surprisingly, few of her Puerto Rican interviewees reported that they were "other" because of racial mixture as

TABLE 10.6. Racial Composition of Puerto Ricans in the United States, as Reported in the Census, 1940–1990 (in Percentages)

Year	White	Nonwhite[a]	Other
1940	86.8	13.2	n/a
1950	92.0	8.0	n/a
1960	96.1	3.9	n/a
1970	92.9	5.3	1.8
1980	48.3	4.3	47.5
1990	45.8	7.1	47.2

Sources: Almaguer and Jung 1998; U.S. Bureau of the Census 1953b, 1963, 1973.
Note: For 1940, refers only to persons of Puerto Rican birth; for other years, includes persons of Puerto Rican birth or parentage. Until 1970, "race" was based on the census enumerators' judgment; since then, it has been based on the respondents' self-reports.
[a] Includes Negro or black, Native American or American Indian, and Asian and Pacific Islander.

such. The majority stated that they had chosen the "other race" option because of their culture, family, birthplace, socialization, or political perspective. However, most respondents placed themselves in racially intermediate positions between black and white. They rarely used conventional U.S. terms to describe their racial identity and preferred to say that they were Spanish, Puerto Rican, Boricua, or trigueño (C. Rodríguez 1990, 1992, 2000; Rodríguez and Cordero-Guzmán 1992). From this perspective, the growing use of the term "other" among Puerto Rican and other Hispanic immigrants reflects their disapproval of the American racial classification system.[8]

Despite its eloquence, this thesis raises some unresolved issues. As Rodríguez (1997) recognizes, the meaning of census racial categories has shifted greatly for Puerto Ricans and other Latinos in the United States. Thus, it is difficult simply to juxtapose American and Latin American discourses of race and to suggest that the latter are more attuned to large-scale racial mixture and conceptual fuzziness. Both types of discourses may be converging: American black/white relations have been complicated by the growth of "brown" groups such as Asian Americans or Latinos, while Latin American race relations, at least in Brazil, are increasingly polarized between whites and nonwhites (Winant 1994).

Furthermore, the rise of new ethnic/racial labels, such as "Hispanics" and "Latinos," has affected the self-definition of Puerto Ricans and other Latin American immigrants in the United States (see Latin American Perspectives 1992; Oboler 1995). Among other repercussions, the official adoption of the

Hispanic label by the Bureau of the Census and other federal government bureaucracies often treats Puerto Ricans as racially distinct from both non-Hispanic whites and blacks. The quasi-racial use of the term "Hispanic" has led Puerto Ricans to move away from the black/white dichotomy in the United States.

Finally, many Puerto Ricans choose the catchall "other" as a proxy for brown or tan—that is, as neither white nor black but an in-between color (Fitzpatrick 1987). As several researchers have found, migration to the mainland tends to produce a "browning effect" (Ginorio 1979; A. R. Martínez 1988; C. Rodríguez 1996), as opposed to the whitening of the Island's population. The contemporary self-representation of Puerto Ricans in the United States may therefore constitute a rupture, rather than a continuity, with the dominant racial discourse on the Island. However, most migrants have not adopted the U.S. racial model wholesale but have adapted it to their particular situation of racial mixture and heterogeneity.

Recent studies by the Bureau of the Census provide empirical support for this alternative conception of the othering trend among Puerto Rican migrants (Tucker et al. 1996). The 1995 Current Population Survey supplement included four versions of the race and Hispanic origin questions, with and without a multiracial category. More than 70 percent of Puerto Ricans in the United States identified as Hispanic in a combined race and ethnicity question. Only 7 percent chose the multiracial category in the separate race and Hispanic origin panel, while less than 3 percent did so in the combined panel. However, more than 32 percent of the respondents classified themselves as "all other" when they were asked separate race and ethnicity questions, as currently formulated in the decennial census. In short, "other" seems to be increasingly used as a racialized synonym for Hispanic.

The Current Population Survey, conducted annually in March by the Bureau of the Census, allows one to construct a brief time series on this issue (see table 10.7). Between 1992 and 1995, the proportion of U.S. Puerto Ricans who classified their race as "other" increased from less than 5 percent to more than 15 percent. However, when the Bureau of the Census eliminated the "other" category, the proportion of whites rose from less than 80 percent in 1995 to nearly 91 percent in 1999. The percentage of blacks rose from less than 5 percent to almost 8 percent during this period. Throughout the 1990s, only between 1 and 2 percent classified themselves as American Indian or Asian. These data confirm that an increasing number of Puerto Ricans prefer not to label

TABLE 10.7. Racial Self-Identification of Puerto Ricans in the United States in the Current Population Survey, 1992–1999 (in Percentages)

Race	1992	1993	1994	1995	1996	1997	1998	1999
White	89.0	89.1	81.5	79.3	91.8	88.9	90.9	90.6
Black	6.4	4.4	6.1	4.8	7.0	10.7	7.4	7.9
American Indian[a]	0.1	0.5	0.2	0.2	0.3	0.1	0.7	0.3
Asian[b]	n/a	0.4	0.4	0.4	0.9	0.3	1.0	1.2
Other	4.5	5.6	11.8	15.3	n/a	n/a	n/a	n/a
Total	100	100	100	100	100	100	100	100

Source: U.S. Bureau of the Census 1999.
[a] Includes Eskimo or Aleut.
[b] Includes Pacific Islander.

themselves as either white or black when they have another option presumably indicating mixed descent.

In sum, census figures suggest two main trends in the racial self-identification of Puerto Ricans in the United States. On the one hand, mainland Puerto Ricans classify their "racial" identity primarily as Hispanic, regardless of federal government policy stating that Hispanics can be of any race. Most Puerto Ricans prefer to place themselves in an intermediate position between white and black, even when offered a multiracial option. On the other hand, if forced to separate their Hispanic origin from their racial identity, many Puerto Ricans choose to call themselves "other." This option seems to provide a third alternative, conceptually equivalent to brown, which eludes the white/black dichotomy altogether. Either as Hispanics or as others, Puerto Ricans in the United States are increasingly racialized. Rather than repudiating the dominant American scheme of group classification, as Rodríguez claims, mainland Puerto Ricans may be assigning new meanings to existing racial and ethnic categories.[9]

CONCLUSION

During the twentieth century, the problem of defining, classifying, and representing the racial identity of Puerto Ricans was officially addressed in two main ways. On the Island, the Bureau of the Census did not collect any racial statistics between 1950 and 2000, largely because they were incompatible with the dominant U.S. scheme of racial classification. Furthermore, Commonwealth officials were not interested in dividing the Puerto Rican population by race but in uniting it under a common nationality. In the mainland, the 1980 census asked people to identify themselves as either Hispanic or not Hispanic, and then as white, black, American Indian, Asian, or other. Whereas most islanders describe themselves as white, most mainland Puerto Ricans now consider themselves to be neither white nor black but other. Many use Hispanic, Latino, or Spanish origin as racial self-designators. The increasing racialization of such panethnic terms has numerous implications for American society, such as the possible broadening of a bipolar racial order into a tripartite color scheme including white, black, and brown (see Winant 1994).

The study of race relations in Puerto Rico (as in Brazil and other Latin American countries) traditionally counterposed the Island's racial discourses and practices to those of the United States. Whereas Puerto Ricans defined race phenotypically, Americans used the principle of hypodescent. While the Puerto Rican system recognized physically intermediate types, the American system dwelled on the dichotomy between white and black. In contrast to a high degree of racial mixture and integration in Puerto Rico, segregation and conflict characterized race relations in the United States. This binary opposition led many scholars to minimize racial prejudice and discrimination on the Island prior to the importation of the U.S. racial model (see T. Blanco 1985 [1942]; Mintz 1966; Rogler 1940; Sereno 1947; Siegel 1948). After an initial wave of studies celebrating Puerto Rico as a racial democracy in the 1940s, a critical perspective emerged in the late 1960s and early 1970s denouncing racial inequality and exclusion on the Island (Betances 1972, 1973; Picó de Hernández et al. 1985; Seda Bonilla 1968, 1973; Zenón Cruz 1975; see also Gordon 1949, 1950; Rosario and Carrión 1951). However, academic discourse on Puerto Ricans and race has been limited during the past two decades, both in the Island and on the mainland (C. Rodríguez 1997). The "conspiracy of silence" continues today as a result of the paucity of fieldwork and official data on racial distinctions among Puerto Ricans (Routté-Gómez 1995).

Between 1899 and 1950, the U.S. Bureau of the Census computed the number of white and nonwhite people in Puerto Rico. In spite of changing racial categories, as well as their popular contestation, the census reported that Puerto Ricans were becoming whiter over time. This trend continued with the 2000 count. The "bleaching" of the Island's population is partly due to the propensity to incorporate light mulattoes (trigueños) into the white category, as well as the common belief in "improving one's race" through intermarriage with lighter-skinned persons. But the main reason for the transformation of Puerto Rico's racial statistics was the growing polarization between whites and nonwhites in the census. The American scheme of racial classification diverged from local discourses and practices, which paid more careful attention to gradations in skin color and recognized multiple physical types between white and black, such as trigueño, indio, and jabao, as well as the more exotic café con leche, piel canela, and blanco con raja. A bipolar racial model could not capture such fine social distinctions.

Since 1940, the Bureau of the Census has faced the challenge of counting a growing number of Puerto Ricans in the continental United States. At first, the U.S. government considered most Puerto Ricans to be whites whose mother tongue happened to be Spanish. By 1980, the census had adopted "Hispanic" as a quasi-racial term and encouraged Puerto Ricans and other Latin American immigrants to identify with that category, rather than with non-Hispanic whites or blacks. In 1990 and 2000, an even larger proportion of Puerto Ricans, Mexicans, Dominicans, and other Hispanics reported that they belonged to other races (Latin American Perspectives 1992; C. Rodríguez 1992, 2000). For U.S. Puerto Ricans, "other" has multiple semantic connotations, including trigueño, tan, brown, Spanish, Hispanic, Latino, Boricua, or simply Puerto Rican. Contrary to the whitening of the Island's population during the first half of the twentieth century, mainland Puerto Ricans underwent a browning tendency during the second half of the century.

Throughout this chapter, I have argued that the popular racial categories used by Puerto Ricans on the Island and in the diaspora depart from dominant American racial codes. Although the official racial terminology in the United States has changed over time, the two main categories—white and black—have remained relatively stable, distinct, and opposed to each other (Domínguez 1998). The presumed purity and homogeneity of the white and black races, however, clashed against the prevalence of racial mixture among Puerto Ricans. The multiplicity of physical types, produced by seemingly endless combinations of skin color, facial features, and hair texture, could not easily be accommodated within the U.S. hegemonic racial taxonomy. From the standpoint of the federal government, Puerto Ricans on the Island had to be labeled according to discrete racial groupings—or not at all. But most islanders insisted that they were white, even if they knew they had some African ancestry. In contrast, migrants to the mainland evaded the bipolar racial order by choosing a third alternative, "other," which increasingly mirrored their Hispanic identity.

The contested representation of the racial identity of Puerto Ricans has wider theoretical and practical implications. This case study confirms that all racial classification systems are scientifically invalid as representations of human biological diversity. They are even less appropriate as explanations for social and cultural differences. Although some group variations related to skin, hair, and eye pigmentation, stature, and body form are hereditary, such variations are difficult if not impossible to categorize in a reliable way. Phenotypically, Puerto Ricans display the full range of characteristics traditionally associated with both whites and blacks. According to American standards, they should be counted as people of color because of their mixed ancestry. According to Puerto Rican standards, they should be considered white if they have light skin color, thin lips, elongated noses, and straight hair. It is sterile to argue that one scheme is right and the other wrong, or that one is morally superior to the other. Instead, both systems are historically and culturally grounded in racist ideologies originating in colonialism and slavery (see Omi and Winant 1994).

The practical implications of this analysis are ominous, especially for racial counting efforts such as the census. Allowing respondents to choose more than one racial category did not change substantially the proportion of Puerto Ricans on the Island or in the mainland who classified themselves as whites or blacks. Instead, the racial self-identification question has opened a Pandora's box in Puerto Rico. Most islanders—more than 80 percent—checked the "white" box on the 2000 census questionnaire because local standards of race allow them to consider themselves white even though some of them might not be accepted as such according to American standards. Like Hispanics in the mainland, islanders could have chosen "other," or they might have opted for both "black" and "white." Then again, Puerto Ricans could have defined themselves according to multiple racial categories, but most did not. In the 1998 status plebiscite, island residents had to choose among four alternatives: the current Commonwealth, free association, independence, or statehood. The largest proportion of voters supported "none of the above." Perhaps, to recycle that formula, the best response to the racial question in the 2000 census would also have been "none of the above."[10]

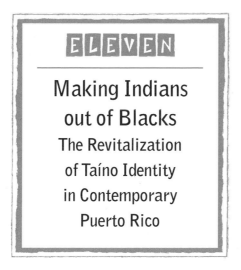

ELEVEN

Making Indians out of Blacks
The Revitalization of Taíno Identity in Contemporary Puerto Rico

The quest for ancestral native origins is a common discursive practice to narrate the nation by including certain autochthonous ideological elements and excluding foreign ones (Bhabha 1990).[1] In colonial societies, the search for indigenous roots acquires a specific symbolism with political repercussions. Perhaps the best-known case is that of pre-1947 India, where nationalist discourse articulated a series of moral values, rooted in the native land, history, and religion, against the onslaught of British imperialism (see Bhabha 1994; Chatterjee 1993, 1995; Harasym 1990). As Partha Chatterjee (1993) has shown, Indian elites developed a patriotic consciousness based on the spiritual regeneration of their native culture. In other cases, such as Puerto Rico, cultural nationalism has served to define and crystallize a counterhegemonic movement against colonial rule. Recent writing in postcolonial studies has begun to unpack the various strategies of resistance, negotiation, and accommodation to British, French, Dutch, U.S., and other imperialisms in Asia, Africa, Latin America, and the Caribbean (see Chambers and Curti 1996; Loomba 1998; Thomas 1994; Williams and Chrisman 1994). A frequent gesture of anticolonial projects everywhere has been to recover, reappraise, and commemorate the historical patrimony prior to European and U.S. colonization.

In Puerto Rico, the nativistic movement has historically faced several challenges. First, the Island's original inhabitants were decimated during the first half of the sixteenth century, although their cultural and biological characteristics influenced the local population. Second, Puerto Rico changed colonial masters in 1898, from Spain to the United States, so that nationalists first turned to Spanish, not indigenous, culture as a form of resistance against Americanization. Third, the massive importation of African slaves throughout most of the Spanish colonial period complicates any search for the pure pre-Columbian or European origins of Puerto Rican culture.

In this chapter I trace the historical background of the current interest in the Island's indigenous population. The turn to aboriginal culture is primarily the result of five decades of activities by the Commonwealth government, as well as the Creole intellectual elite since the late nineteenth century. Both factors help to explain the revitalization of Taíno identity on the Island and in the diaspora, which provides an alternative view of Puerto Ricanness, based on pre-Columbian physical appearance, ancestry, and heritage. Although the "Taíno nation" movement still represents a small minority of Puerto Ricans on the Island and in the continental United States,[2] it is a significant by-product of the cultural nationalism promoted by various Commonwealth agencies. However, rather than espouse the official rhetoric of the "three roots" as the ethnic foundations of the Puerto Rican nation, members of the Taíno nation claim that their indigenous background takes precedence over their Spanish or African ancestry. This position constitutes a surprising twist in contemporary representations of Puerto Ricanness.

I interpret the revival of indigenous elements as symbols of cultural identity, as a result of the growing appeal of cultural—as opposed to political—nationalism on the Island and in the diaspora after World War II. I show how nationalist intellectuals—particularly anthropologists, archaeologists, and historians—appropriated and elaborated the imagery of the Taíno, the Island's pre-Columbian population, as "the first root" of Puerto Ricanness. I argue that the indigenous heritage has been canonized through state-sponsored institutions such as museums, monuments, festivals, contests, crafts, and textbooks, at the expense of "the third root," as African culture is commonly called. This is what I mean by the title of this chapter, "Making Indians out of Blacks": the symbolic displacement of the African by the Taíno in many scholarly analyses and public representations of Puerto Rican identity on the Island and in the mainland.

CONSTITUTING AN ARCHAEOLOGICAL PATRIMONY:
INTELLECTUAL DISCOURSES ON THE TAÍNO INDIANS

The scholarly recovery of the Taíno Indians in Puerto Rico has undergone five distinct phases. The first serious efforts to study the pre-Columbian peoples of the Island began in the mid–nineteenth century, under the influence of the Romantic movement, closely linked with the *indigenista* and *costumbrista* schools of literature, which turned to indigenous customs as the most authentic sources of local culture (Alegría 1978, 1996a; López de Molina 1980). Since 1847, Puerto Rican writers had cultivated the Indian theme as part of their patriotic exaltation of New World natives vis-à-vis Spanish conquistadors (Corchado Juarbe 1993). Much of the renewed interest in the Taíno Indians was fueled by the efforts of Creole elites to distinguish themselves from *peninsulares* (those born in the Iberian peninsula). As in the rest of Latin America, *criollo* in Puerto Rico came to be identified with everything native, local, or typical of the land and people of the Americas, as opposed to the Old World. In his classic study of racial prejudice in Puerto Rican culture, Isabelo Zenón Cruz (1975: 256) has documented that local "poets have generally criticized the extinction of the Indian and orient themselves toward *mestizaje*, that is, toward conceiving the Puerto Rican people as a product of the Indian and Spanish elements, which means an indirect rejection of blacks."

The founders of Puerto Rican prehistory were trained in other fields of study, such as the zoologist Agustín Stahl, the historians Cayetano Coll y Toste and Salvador Brau, and the literary critic and poet Luis Lloréns Torres. Leading amateurs and private collectors included George Latimer, José Julián Acosta, Robert L. Junghanns, and José María Nazario. This early stage in the reconstruction of the Taíno heritage was marked by debates concerning the proper place of the indigenous cultures of the Caribbean in a larger evolutionary scale; the ideological influence of biological and geographic determinism; and the growing recognition of "the remarkable beauty and finish of the stone implements of Porto Rico and others of the Antilles," as Otis T. Mason (1877: 372) put it. The romantic rediscovery of the indigenous roots of Puerto Rican culture might be an apt phrase to summarize this first trend.

A second moment in the development of the Taíno heritage as cultural capital on the Island involved the gradual accumulation of highly technical data on the pre-Columbian peoples of the Caribbean. This stage was characterized by the growing professionalization of archaeological research on the subject. Roughly between 1898 and 1945, most archaeologists (primarily from the United States) focused on the detailed historical reconstruction of the Taíno Indians and their predecessors (see J. Duany 1987 and I. Rouse 1992 for summaries of this research). American archaeologists such as Jesse Fewkes, Froilich Rainey, and Irving Rouse contributed significantly to this stage of the Taíno revival (see Chapter 3). By the 1930s, the dominant paradigm in anthropology worldwide had shifted from evolutionism to historical particularism and diffusionism. Stripped from the bluntest forms of racial thinking, scholars pursued their interests in Taíno art and mythology and explored the cultural contacts between the circum-Caribbean and South America in prehistoric times.

Pablo Morales Cabrera (1932), a self-proclaimed aficionado, and Adolfo de Hostos (1941), then the official historian of Puerto Rico, wrote extensively on the traditional beliefs and customs of the Island's aborigines. Both essays, each in its own way, offer glimpses into the state of knowledge on the Taíno Indians during the first half of the twentieth century. Both display a fascination with indigenous art, particularly sculptures made of stone, clay, wood, and bone. This aesthetic appreciation is a recurrent theme in the contemporary use and elaboration of visual images from the pre-Columbian past. A distinctive iconography referring to indigenous motifs was thus identified and widely circulated.

The third moment in the Taíno revival began shortly after World War II and extends into the present. A nationalist reappropriation of the indigenous legacy captures the essence of this phase. In 1947 Ricardo Alegría founded the Center for Archaeological Research and directed the Museum of History, Anthropology, and Art at the University of Puerto Rico in Río Piedras. Although Alegría (1954) conducted pioneering ethnographic fieldwork on the descendants of African slaves, he specialized in archaeological research on the pre-Columbian populations of Puerto Rico. Alegría, Eugenio Fernández Méndez, and other Puerto Rican scholars were inspired by nationalist concepts of cultural identity based on indigenismo and mestizaje, such as those developed in Mexico during the 1920s and 1930s by Manuel Gamio and José Vasconcelos (see Martínez-Echazábal 1998).

The definitive statement on the Taíno Indians from a cultural nationalist perspective is precisely Alegría's *Historia de nuestros indios (versión elemental)* (1950). This short text reveals the deployment of "our Indians" as one of the foundations of contemporary Puerto Rican identity. Here Alegría synthesizes the available archaeological and historical evidence to provide a sympathetic account of indigenous values and practices. His portrait highlights the Taínos' happiness, simplicity, tranquillity, peacefulness, and innocence prior to the arrival of Columbus. The graphic illustrations by his wife, Carmen Pons de Alegría, represent everyday scenes from the Indians' lifestyle, from sleeping in hammocks and rowing in canoes to playing in their ball courts and dancing *areítos*, the ritual commemorations of their ancestors. This essay and its accompanying images have become one of the most widely disseminated texts of indigenista discourse on the Island.

Another key work of the cultural nationalist project dominant during this period is Eugenio Fernández Méndez's *Art and Mythology of the Taíno Indians of the Greater West Indies* (1972). Although more specialized than Alegría's "elementary version," *Art and Mythology* depicts the Taínos in a similar light. The author argues that the original inhabitants of Puerto Rico had developed a distinctive artistic style prior to conquest by the Spanish. He focuses on the Taínos' religious icons—the *cemíes*—to reconstruct their worldview and show that they had a relatively advanced aesthetic sense of life, similar to that of the Maya. Along with Alegría, Fernández Méndez contributed to the consolidation of Taíno imagery as a token of the Island's national culture.

Although the latter trend continues today, the fourth stage in the intellectual discourse on the Taíno Indians (initiated during the mid-1970s) was the criticism of established knowledge. Contemporary archaeologists and historians such as Diana López (López Sotomayor 1975, López de Molina 1980), Jalil Sued Badillo (1978, 1995b), Miguel Rodríguez (1984), and Francisco Moscoso (1986, 1999) have distanced themselves from the official treatment of "the first root." A good example of this trend is Sued Badillo's work (1978) on the Carib Indians, who he claims were a fable invented by Spanish conquistadors to justify warfare and enslavement (see also Sued Badillo 1995a). Rather than romantically search for the lost link of Puerto Rican culture, many scholars are now engaged in the painstaking documentation and reassessment of the pre-Columbian past, often employing insights from historical materialism.

Although archaeological studies are still commonly framed in terms of the need to preserve the Island's national patrimony, they tend to concentrate on highly specialized issues with little practical relevance for cultural nationalism (see, for example, Chanlatte Baik 1976, 1986, 1990; Instituto de Cultura Puertorriqueña 1997). Now that the indigenous heritage has become a public asset, so to speak, many scholars have retreated into an academic posture that tends to take for granted the dominant representation of the Taíno Indians as an icon of Puerto Ricanness. Since the 1980s, archaeological research on the pre-

Columbian populations of the Island has been stimulated by federal legislation mandating excavations prior to developing real estate, locally known as *arqueología de contrato*, or contract archaeology (see Alegría 1996a; Asociación Puertorriqueña de Antropólogos y Arqueólogos 1990). With the upsurge in contract archaeology, the idea of rescuing the Taíno heritage has receded in importance, and the concept of cultural resource management has gained wider currency. This label might be used to characterize the fifth and contemporary phase in the study of the indigenous populations of Puerto Rico.

During the 1990s, culture wars at the Institute of Puerto Rican Culture, especially as a result of administrative and policy shifts, softened the nationalist rhetoric of local archaeology. In part, these wars derive from contending definitions of the Puerto Rican nation and its cultural identity within the context of the Island's relations with the United States. During this period, the pro-statehood party (NPP) attempted to dismantle much of the cultural apparatus developed by the pro-commonwealth party (PDP) since the 1950s, in an effort to promote the Island's annexation to the United States. Note the subdued tone of the following introduction to a 1997 collection of archaeological essays: "The dissemination of the nature and value of our archaeological patrimony holds great importance for the development of the study of our history and the enrichment of our artistic-cultural heritage" (Instituto de Cultura Puertorriqueña 1997: i). The adjective "national" seems to have disappeared from the author's vocabulary. It is no coincidence that the NPP controlled the Commonwealth government—including the Institute of Puerto Rican Culture—between 1993 and 2000. Thus, the Indian theme has become a contested terrain among annexationists, autonomists, and statehooders. The issue is part of a wider struggle to define the nation from various ideological perspectives (see Flores Collazo 1998).

"AWAKENING THEIR IMAGE IN THE MEMORY OF MEN": LESSONS FROM THE INDIGENOUS PAST

This brief genealogy of Taíno studies on the Island suggests several patterns. First, the rapid decimation of the native people of Puerto Rico during the Spanish colonial period has forced scholars to rely primarily on incomplete archaeological and historical sources of information, and secondarily on cross-cultural and linguistic evidence, such as related ethnographic research on

Amazonia (López-Baralt 1985). Large gaps in anthropological knowledge have often been filled with wild speculation, fantasy, and myth. The virtual absence of prehistoric monuments—comparable to the Maya pyramids of Chichén Itzá or the Inca city of Machu Picchu—has led cultural nationalists to look else-where in their reconstruction of the indigenous past in Puerto Rico. At the same time, the dearth of ethnohistorical data has proven convenient for those en-gaged in the invention of tradition.

From the beginning, the most useful remains of Taíno material culture were their abundant and prodigious ceramics, including a large number and variety of pieces of pottery, beads, amulets, collars, masks, and stools. Archaeological collections of these artifacts were repeatedly canvassed to show that the Taínos were not savages (O. T. Mason 1877: 391); that they had attained a higher stage of culture than the Caribs or the Ciboneys (Coll y Toste 1979 [1897]); and that they were actually "quite developed" in their socioeconomic integration and religious beliefs (Fernández Méndez 1972: 43). The survival of Taíno art thus encouraged their retrieval as a relatively advanced indigenous people prior to their European "discovery." This was a necessary step in their retrospective reassessment for contemporary nationalistic purposes.

A common thread in the Taíno revival has been the romantic impulse. The standard treatment of the Indians as a symbol of Puerto Rican (as op-posed to Spanish) identity first emerged in creative literature—especially in poetry—toward the end of the nineteenth century through such major figures as Eugenio María de Hostos. In the twentieth century, leading writers such as Enrique Laguerre, Juan Antonio Corretjer, and René Marqués employed the Taíno figure as an inspiration in the unfinished quest for the Island's freedom, now from the United States (Ayala-Richards 1995; Corchado Juarbe 1993). Al-though not all scholars succumbed to the temptation of idealizing the in-digenous heritage, most converged with the nationalist canon in literature and politics.

Stahl initiated a long tradition in the recovery of the Taínos when he wrote, "I propose in this work to awaken their image [*despertar su recuerdo*] in the memory of men of learning and of the *borincanos* who have replaced them" (1889: v). Moreover, Stahl's exalted rhetorical tone is typical of indigenista writing of his period: "That desire [to know the Indians] . . . sprouts spontane-ously from the soul that loves the memories of this land where one's eyes first saw the brilliant light of the tropical sun, where one's cradle once rocked and the happy days of one's pleasant youth drifted, and where one's ashes will probably rest" (Stahl 1889: 3). Lloréns Torres's classical statement (1967 [1898]: 84–85) is also worth quoting here: "Without any kind of commodities and means to develop their well-being, as befitted their semi-savage life, [the Taíno Indians] passed the happy days of their existence, without hate or rancor, without intestine struggles, and enjoying the delights of the agreeable paradise under whose leafy trees another people will not drift as united by fortune, by happiness, by affection, and by the most fervent love that their small fatherland inspired in them."

Most nationalist intellectuals since then have shared Stahl's and Lloréns Torres's enthusiasm for the Indians, from Adolfo de Hostos's reevaluation of Taíno art for its "pristine innocence" (1941: 89), to Fernández Méndez's characterization of Taíno ceramics as "superior" to all the ceramics of northern South America (1972: 72). Furthermore, scholars have tended to claim the Taínos as "ours," while recognizing that they settled throughout the Greater Antilles. Even today, detailed maps of the wider Caribbean are notably scarce in archaeological museums in Puerto Rico. Finally, most studies have focused specifically on the Taíno heritage rather than on the full range of pre-Columbian cultures, including the *igneri*, the so-called archaic peoples of the Island.

A recurrent theme in the indigenista literature since the late nineteenth century has been the glowing portrayal of the Taíno character. From Stahl to Alegría, the pre-Columbian inhabitants of Borinquen have been typified as "sweet, affable, serviceable, peaceful, and hospitable" (Stahl 1889: 119), terms that keep appearing in contemporary descriptions of Puerto Ricans. In contrast to the Caribs, usually depicted as "warlike and adventuresome, bloodthirsty and cruel cannibals" (Coll y Toste 1979 [1897]: 57), the Taínos become the prototype of a Rousseauistic "noble savage." The constant recitation of the same adjectives—docile, sedentary, indolent, tranquil, chaste—from one author to another acquires ritual and mythical connotations. Such traits have become basic elements in standard portraits of Puerto Rico's "national character" (see, for instance, Marqués 1977).

Since the end of the nineteenth century, Puerto Rican scholars have represented the Taíno as an essentially good figure, with a peaceful and generous nature, a relatively simple but respectable way of life, and a spiritual innocence uncontaminated by Western civilization. The Island's environment itself— Lloréns Torres's "agreeable paradise"—has typically been depicted as fertile, abundant, placid, and benevolent to human settlement, if not especially conducive to intellectual or moral progress. This Eden-like characterization of indigenous culture and nature has had enormous ideological value for writers engaged in the construction of a national identity on the Island, especially in the second half of the twentieth century. Nothing can be more useful for nationalists than the founding myth of a land and people spoiled by foreign invasion. As Sued Badillo (1995b: 27) points out, "This [national] consciousness expresses that the reality of Puerto Rico is rooted in its mythical geography, a sacred past that is Amerindian in origin and meaning and geographic in its present attributes."

Another discursive practice of Puerto Rican intellectuals has been to over-stress the physical traits of the Taíno Indians, primarily to distinguish them from (but also to blur the differences with) those of black slaves.[3] Brau (1972 [1894]) was at pains to clarify the original meaning of the folk term *cobrizo* (copperlike or tanned) as opposed to *moreno* (dark skinned, a euphemism for black in Puerto Rico) when applied to the Taíno phenotype. As J. Alden Mason wrote to Franz Boas (April 24, 1915), "An individual of a ruddy or coppery tinge of complexion is commonly known as 'indio,' the name referring to color rather than to race." More recently, the literary critic María Teresa Babín (1986: 48) noted that "in the physical type of numerous 'Indian-looking' Puerto Ricans [*aindiados*] there sometimes seems to reincarnate the beautiful and straight black hair, the pale and lusterless [*mate*] skin, and the slanted eyes with an unfathomable gaze that form our ancestral memory of the physical traits of the *borincano* Indian." Note the rhetorical whitening of the indigenous population in these passages, as well as its romanticization in the third quote.

Until the mid–twentieth century, anthropological thought usually characterized the Taínos as an "inferior race" compared with Europeans, but superior to Africans. Stahl, Brau, Coll y Toste, and Lloréns Torres all shared the viewpoint that the Indians' "racial" characteristics made them physically and intellectually subordinate to the "brave," "indomitable," and "imperturbable" Spaniards (Brau 1972 [1894]: 82). But they also shared the conviction that Africans (or Ethiopians, as they were often called then) were even more "primitive" and "savage" than the Taínos. A similar evolutionary logic ranked the Taínos higher than the Caribs. As Peter Hulme (1986) and other scholars have shown, the retrospective valorization of the Taíno reproduced binary colonial representations of the native peoples of the New World.

Although contemporary authors avoid such blatantly ethnocentric and racist terms, many still imply that the Indians were neither white nor black but brown or "copperlike" and that their intermediate phenotype placed them between

Europeans and Africans in moral and aesthetic terms. Few standard descriptions of the Taíno Indians fail to mention their skin color, physical stature, bodily constitution, hair texture, and facial features (see, for example, Alegría 1950). The current social studies curriculum from elementary school to the college level highlights such physical features as "essential" to an understanding of Puerto Ricanness; any nine-year-old child on the Island can easily recite them. For example, a third-grade textbook widely used in Puerto Rico today (Vizcarrondo 1994: 57) lists the following "characteristic traits of the Taíno race": medium height, copper-tone skin, black and straight hair, prominent cheekbones, slightly slanted eyes, long nose, and relatively thick lips. These features are sharply contrasted with the phenotypes of both Spaniards and Africans.

The idea that "the indigenous element is alive and persists" (Babín 1986: 48) in the contemporary Puerto Rican population has gained wide currency. A pseudoscientific study of University of Puerto Rico students even went so far as to classify one-fifth of its sample as "Indianic" (*indiado*), ten times the number of blacks in the sample (Rodríguez Olleros 1974). In a promotional brochure for the Museo del Indio in Old San Juan, Alegría underlined "the typically Indian physical traits that characterize Puerto Ricans: copper-colored skin, straight hair and prominent cheekbones, among others" (Alegría n.d.). The above-cited textbook asks students to think about people they have met in Puerto Rico with "the same or similar physical traits to those of the Taínos," as well as those of Spaniards, but not those of Africans (Vizcarrondo 1994: 57). A more recent study found that 70 percent of a sample of people from the Indieras region of Maricao, in the central area of the Island, had a DNA identified as Indo-American. According to a journalistic report, "Traces of Taíno blood still flow in the veins of modern Puerto Ricans" (Ferrer 1999).

The racialization of the Taíno is a key to the symbolic displacement from the African to the indigenous sources of Puerto Rican culture. Throughout Latin America, nationalist discourses have privileged the European and indigenous sources of cultural identity over the African Other (see, for example, Radcliffe and Westwood 1996; Wade 1997). By pitting the Indian and African "races" against each other, nationalist intellectuals have traditionally blended their physical and cultural traits. Historically, this strategy resulted in the overextension of the folk term *indio*, rather than *negro* or *mulato*, to refer to dark-skinned people throughout the Hispanic Caribbean (Roberts 1997, 1999). For instance, the Dominican government officially classifies most of its citizens into one of two categories—*indio claro* or *indio oscuro*—but reserves *negro* for the much-despised Haitians. The semantic equation between Indian and black has served to camouflage the African origins of a large share of the Cuban, Dominican, and Puerto Rican populations.

The confusion between Indians and blacks has produced endless debates about the origins of musical instruments, culinary traditions, linguistic expressions, and other cultural practices. An academic example of this trend is Babín's *La cultura de Puerto Rico* (1986), which easily attributes an exclusive indigenous origin to such Creole foods as *alcapurrias*, *mofongo*, and *pasteles*, which probably have some African influence as well (see Alvarez Nazario 1974). On a popular level, a local television commercial for a food distributing company during the 1980s represented three moments in the development of Puerto Rican cuisine: indigenous, Spanish, and modern (that is, American), but not African. Such discursive practices literally render blacks invisible.

In their effort to rescue the Taíno heritage, some Puerto Rican scholars have tended to downplay the African contribution to their culture. This gesture is evident in Manuel Alvarez Nazario's monumental history (1992) of the Spanish language in Puerto Rico, which claims that the Taínos contributed many more words than any African language to the local dialect. Unfortunately, the largely positive attempt to recover the first root is often predicated on a denial of the third root of Puerto Rican culture. As Dávila (1994) has argued, the symbolic elaboration of the Indian has all too often been a way of dismissing the Island's African legacy. The natives' relatively light skin color, in addition to their physical disappearance as a people and the dearth of reliable information on many crucial aspects of their culture, has helped to mythologize them and overstate their current impact, usually at the expense of blacks.

"A SYSTEMATIC REDISCOVERY OF OUR CULTURAL PATRIMONY": INSTITUTIONALIZING THE TAÍNO HERITAGE

By the mid-1970s, when the anthropologist Ronald Duncan (1978) surveyed college students in San Germán, the Taíno had attained canonical status in Puerto Rico. Most of those interviewed believed that the Indians constituted one of the historical "roots" of contemporary Puerto Rican culture. Although many respondents could not specify what beliefs and customs had an indigenous origin, most could mention a few Taíno words and other tokens of their material culture, such as the *cemíes* (the small stone idols) or the *bateyes* (the ceremonial ball courts). Duncan concluded that the Taínos had become an important icon of Puerto Ricanness, despite incomplete archaeological and historical knowledge. Between World War II and the 1970s, the pre-Columbian Indian legacy was consolidated as a cornerstone of national culture. How did this indigenous emblem transcend the narrow confines of an intellectual elite in a colonial society?

The answer to this question lies in the political and cultural history of the Island, especially since the creation of the Estado Libre Asociado in 1952, the constitutional formula for limited self-government under colonial rule by the United States (see Chapter 5). The meteoric rise to power of the PDP between 1940 and 1968 meant, among other things, the ideological displacement of political nationalism by a new autonomist project with a strong populist orientation, fostering economic development through industrialization while preserving close political ties with the United States (Alvarez-Curbelo and Rodríguez Castro 1993). This project also entailed the selective appropriation of nationalist symbols and practices (such as the national flag and anthem) through Operation Serenity. Former governor Muñoz Marín (1985 [1953]) himself defended the need to assert and preserve Puerto Rico's own personality in the midst of sweeping socioeconomic changes. Cultural nationalism became increasingly strong on the Island after the establishment of the Institute of Puerto Rican Culture in 1955 (see Aguiló Ramos 1987; Alegría 1978; Dávila 1997; Flores Collazo 1998).

The institute's founder and director for eighteen years, Ricardo Alegría, was the author of the canonical text on the Taíno Indians in Puerto Rico. He also developed and applied the most influential model of national culture on the Island to date: the notion that Puerto Rican culture was the result of the harmonious integration of three roots—the Indian, Spanish, and African (Aguiló Ramos 1987; Ramírez 1985). Under Alegría's leadership, the institute initiated "a systematic rediscovery of our cultural patrimony," including the indigenous peoples of the Island (Alegría 1978: 382). Local government funds sponsored a comprehensive series of lectures, conferences, documentaries, exhibits, recitals, publications, courses, seminars, and research projects. Perhaps the most relevant initiative, for the present purposes, was the acquisition and development of archaeological collections on the aboriginal population of Puerto Rico.

By the early 1970s, the institute had established a major museum in Utuado devoted exclusively to the Indians (Centro Ceremonial Caguana) and a smaller one in San Juan (Museo del Indio). In addition, Alegría proposed the creation of the Museum of Aboriginal Cultures to display a growing number of pre-Columbian clay and stone pieces owned by the institute. All these institution-building efforts were part of a larger agenda of "providing Puerto Rico with new museums where our compatriots can rediscover their history and culture and feel proud of their nationality" (Alegría 1971a: 1). In practice, most of the museums have focused on the Spanish colonial heritage, especially the military and religious architecture and art of the nineteenth century, particularly in Old San Juan (although smaller museums throughout the Island did not specialize as much on Hispanic traditions as on local history and culture). The Taíno legacy played a secondary but important role in the public representation of Puerto Ricanness through museums, textbooks, and other cultural activities such as festivals and crafts.

The Island's first museum was the University of Puerto Rico's Museum of History, Anthropology, and Art, located at the Río Piedras campus. Founded in 1951, the museum later moved to its present building, designed by the architect Henry Klumb, at the entrance to the campus. Today, the museum is divided into three main sections: the Egyptian Hall, Archaeology Hall, and Francisco Oller Hall. The Archaeology Hall houses one of the most extensive selections of Taíno and pre-Taíno artifacts in the Caribbean, including the collections of Adolfo de Hostos and José Leandro Montalvo Guenard. The Center for Archaeological Research, long devoted to the study of the native peoples of the region, is affiliated with the museum. Beyond the accidental reasons for the acquisition and development of its three disparate collections (ancient, "primitive," and impressionistic art), their inclusion in the same space tends to equate Taíno culture with Egyptian and French cultures. Thus, Puerto Rican visitors to the museum can feel justifiably proud of their ancestral roots, as much as they may be impressed by Oller's monumental painting *El velorio* (The wake), or the mummy of a long-dead Egyptian queen.

Over the past four decades, the Institute of Puerto Rican Culture has developed an extensive network of museums and parks throughout the Island. At this writing, the institute administers thirteen museums and is restoring seven additional ones. Of these, three are devoted to the indigenous theme: the Museo del Indio and the Museo Puertorriqueño in San Juan and the Centro Ceremonial Indígena near Utuado. The Museo del Indio documents the indigenous peoples of Puerto Rico from their arrival on the Island thousands of years ago through their disappearance during the Spanish colonial period. The Museo

Puertorriqueño was projected to provide a panoramic view of the Island's culture but was merged with the institute's Indian collection because of a shortage of funds and administrative restructuring.

The Caguana Ceremonial Center is the most important of its kind in the Antilles because of its eleven large ball courts (bateyes) lined with ancient monoliths. The site had originally been identified by Franz Boas and excavated by J. Alden Mason and Robert T. Aitken in 1914–15 (see Chapter 3). The Institute of Puerto Rican Culture expropriated and developed the site as a historical monument in the 1950s. The institute has also preserved the adjacent area as a botanical garden that re-creates the plants used for food and building materials by the indigenous peoples of Puerto Rico. Thus, visitors to the site make a strong visual connection between the native soil and the aboriginal population. This is undoubtedly the centerpiece of the institute's indigenista project. An official promotional brochure holds that here "the collective soul of Puerto Rican Indians expressed itself through sports and religious rituals." Note the spiritual emphasis of this quote as well as the attempt to commemorate a sacred landscape for the origins of contemporary Puerto Rican culture.

In addition to the institute's museums throughout the Island, two important exhibits of Taíno art are located in Ponce and San Juan. (Smaller collections have been founded at the Catholic University in Ponce and Turabo University in Caguas.) After Caguana, Tibes is the second most important indigenous ceremonial center of the Caribbean, according to a semiofficial promotion (L. Rodríguez 1998). The archaeological site was accidentally discovered in 1975 by a local resident and was later studied and preserved by a regional group of archaeologists, historians, engineers, and geologists called Sociedad Guaynía. Although considered part of the national patrimony, the Tibes Ceremonial Center was acquired by the Ponce municipal government. Tibes provides a forceful example of how the nationalist discourse is played out in a regional context.

Local authorities administer the museum, exhibit hall, and surrounding landscape, whose overall design and function are very similar to the structures administered by the Institute of Puerto Rican Culture. The entrance to the archaeological site holds a botanical garden with indigenous plants reminiscent of those found at Caguana. At Tibes, tour guides also make an explicit connection between "our Indians" and "our indigenous plants." A small Indian village (*yucayeque*) in both Tibes and Caguana re-creates the sites' original atmosphere. At Tibes, employees frequently dress themselves in Indian garb to reenact the Taínos' everyday life, complete with their own version of the native ball game. Schoolteachers throughout the Island encourage their students to draw, paint, carve, and write about the pre-Columbian past to commemorate the Spanish "discovery" of Puerto Rico. Their work is then showcased in the Tibes museum and exhibit hall.

The institutionalization of Taíno imagery has gone hand in hand with its growing commercialization. Over the last few decades, indigenous motifs have become increasingly fashionable in Puerto Rico—from naming practices to T-shirts and tourist merchandise. Every year, the town of Jayuya celebrates a national indigenous festival in which a "Taíno-looking" woman is crowned queen (Dávila 1997). Folk dance groups constantly dramatize native areítos for both foreign and local consumption. Artisans and engravers have incorporated Taíno themes in their crafts, posters, and murals. Since the 1970s, transnational corporations such as those which manufacture Mazola cooking oil and Winston cigarettes have featured indigenous references in their advertising campaigns. A local insurance agency, GA Life, has issued a photographic calendar on the Taíno heritage. Puerto Rico's official tourist magazine, *Qué Pasa*, usually showcases the indigenous heritage—especially in arts and crafts—but downplays African culture as an integral part of the Island's history. Native folklore, especially the omnipresent cemí, has become a marketable commodity in Puerto Rico. The Taíno heritage has even been diffused on the Internet, through a museum that showcases and sells more than two hundred replicas of indigenous objects.

THE FIRST ROOT: THE CULTURAL POLITICS OF TAÍNO SYMBOLISM

It seems, then, that the intellectual discourse on national identity, with its strong emphasis on the recovery of the Island's indigenous roots, has been popularized in contemporary Puerto Rico. On the one hand, this trend is a positive and necessary step in the construction of an imagined community. Growing awareness of their pre-Columbian heritage has provided Puerto Ricans with a longer and more complete view of their past, apart from their colonial histories under Spain and the United States. The widespread cult of the "first root" has instilled local pride and collective identification, which have helped to defend, promote, and even invent traditions. The mythical image of Borinquen as a tropical paradise uncorrupted by Western civilization has sustained several generations of Puerto Ricans on the Island and in the diaspora. Today, various grassroots movements in the United States and Puerto Rico claim descent from the "Taíno nation."[4]

On the other hand, the revitalization of the Taíno Indians has helped to erase symbolically the racial and cultural presence of blacks in Puerto Rico. In the past, anthropologists, archaeologists, and historians explicitly compared Taínos and Africans, invariably concluding that the Indians were physically more attractive, intellectually more capable, and culturally more developed than blacks. While the Taínos were vindicated as noble savages, blacks were despised as primitive others, along with Carib Indians. Evolutionary thinking typically relegated African peoples to the lowest ranks of cultural development. Racialized images of Indians and Africans have dominated how Puerto Ricans imagined their ethnic background.

Although most contemporary scholars have abandoned such racial doctrines, many continue to overrate the pre-Columbian past while downgrading the African contribution to Puerto Rican culture, thus making Indians out of blacks. As I have argued before, such discursive practices have their institutional impact on lived experiences. The Commonwealth government did not support a proposal by Alegría (1971b) to create the Museum on the Legacy of African Cultures decades ago. A recent inventory of museums and monuments mentions no historical sites commemorating the black presence on the Island, while indigenous objects are displayed in Barranquitas, Caguas, Coamo, Jayuya, Ponce, San Juan, Utuado, Vieques, and Yabucoa (Departamento de Educación 1992). A major exhibit on the "third root," cosponsored by the Institute of Puerto Rican Culture, was quickly dismantled after the Quincentennial Commemoration of the Discovery of Puerto Rico in 1993 (see Lydia González 1993). In 1999 the institute finally inaugurated the Museo de Nuestra Raíz Africana, the Museum of Our African Root, in Old San Juan. In 2000 Alegría succeeded in opening a permanent exhibit on the Island's African heritage at the Museum of the Americas.

As I showed in Chapter 5, under Alegría's direction, the Institute of Puerto Rican Culture implemented the dominant cultural project of the Estado Libre Asociado. Like Fernández Méndez (1980) and other local intellectuals, Alegría believed that Puerto Rico could maintain its own national culture while remaining politically and economically tied to the United States. Both anthropologists defined culture as a spiritual configuration of moral values compatible with an autonomous government. As Fernández Méndez (1980: 42) wrote, "A nationality can exist without the political organization of the sovereign State." Alegría's (1996b: 11) view of national culture closely paralleled Fernández Méndez's idealistic approach: for him, "culture is, above all, a concept and a way of life; it is a spiritual state that defines the physiognomy of a people, of a nationality."

As cultural nationalism became state policy, the Institute of Puerto Rican Culture enshrined the organic metaphor of the three roots: "From the beginning we defined national culture as the product of the integration that in the course of four centuries and a half had taken place in Puerto Rico among the respective cultures of the Taíno Indians that inhabited the Island at the time of the Discovery, of the Spaniards who conquered and colonized it, and of the black Africans who since the first decades of the sixteenth century began to incorporate into our population" (Alegría 1996b: 9; see also Babín 1986: 36). This long quote from Alegría reveals the chronological and ideological ranking of the three main ethnic groups on the Island—first Indians, then Spaniards, finally Africans. It also suggests how cultural nationalists have represented each of these groups: the Taínos as the Island's original inhabitants, the Spaniards as conquerors and colonizers, and Africans as late arrivals to be incorporated into "our" culture. Note also that the only racially marked group in this passage is the "black" Africans, not Indians or Spaniards, who thereby appear colorless or equally light skinned.

This ethnic/racial hierarchy is graphically encoded in the official seal of the Institute of Puerto Rican Culture. The seal represents a well-dressed Spaniard in the center with a grammar book in his hand and three Catholic crosses in the background; to his right stands a seminude Taíno with a cemí and a corn plant, and to his left, a topless African holds a machete and a drum, with a vejigante mask lying at his feet and a sugarcane plant on one side. This visual representation has multiple symbolic connotations, among them the suggestion that the main contribution of African slaves in Puerto Rico was less cultural than economic—that is, their labor power as cane cutters. The image also suggests that Catholicism was one of the foundations of Puerto Rican culture, represented by the lamb directly underneath the Spanish man. (Note that all the images are masculine.) In principle, the three figures are on an equal footing, thus evoking the myth of peaceful coexistence among separate races and cultures (see Buitrago Ortiz 1982).

In practice, the institute has assigned different priorities to each of the three roots. Most of the institute's programs have focused on the preservation, restoration, and promotion of the Island's Hispanic heritage, particularly in architecture, history, painting, popular arts, folk music, theater, and poetry. Perhaps its most notable achievement has been the conservation and recuperation of the colonial district of Old San Juan as part of the Island's national patrimony. The institute has also sponsored historical, archaeological, and folklore research and publications. Furthermore, it has spearheaded the commemoration of historical figures (*hombres ilustres*)—mostly upper-class white males—as well as naming public places in their honor. As a result of its numerous initiatives, Alegría claims (1996b), the institute has fostered growing national pride among Puerto Ricans.

A secondary focus of the institute has been the study, collection, and display of pre-Columbian artifacts. Rediscovering and exhibiting the indigenous roots of Puerto Rican culture became a top priority on the institute's research agenda and in its museum-building efforts and educational projects. The institute acquired a valuable archaeological collection, second only to that held by the University of Puerto Rico's Museum of History, Anthropology, and Art. Indigenous designs, such as the now famous petroglyphs, were actively promoted through the institute's graphic arts program. An entire folk arts industry producing beads, shells, and bracelets has developed around Taíno icons as widely recognized symbols of national identity. These cultural objects are marketed by a well-organized system linking state officials in San Juan, regional centers throughout the Island, and local communities and artisans (Dávila 1997).

Unfortunately, the third root of Puerto Rican culture has not received as much official attention as the first two roots, the Taíno and the Spanish. As mentioned before, the lack of interest in documenting the cultural legacy of African slaves and their descendants contrasts sharply with the proliferation of museums and parks consecrated to Spanish and Taíno traditions in Puerto Rico. Compared with more than a dozen museums showcasing Spanish and indigenous traditions, only one focuses on the African heritage. (In 1998 an itinerant exhibition on African art, organized with the New York International African Institute, was held at the University of Puerto Rico's museum. However, the foreign and temporary nature of this display suggests that Africans are still represented as external to Puerto Rican culture.) A promising development has been the emergence of a grassroots movement to establish in Humacao a Museum on the African Man and Woman. Only recently has a growing group of scholars begun to question the established "conspiracy of silence" surrounding the persistence of racial prejudice and discrimination on the Island (Routté-Gómez 1995).

CONCLUSION

In keeping with the official discourse on national identity, Puerto Rican museums have represented the Island's historical patrimony primarily as the Spanish colonial heritage and secondarily as the pre-Columbian indigenous tradition. In their efforts to resist American cultural penetration, many nationalist intellectuals have elaborated a coherent but incomplete image of the Island's cultural identity based on a selective reading of its history, which tends to exclude the African component and celebrate the Indian heritage (Zenón Cruz 1975: 235). From a conventional nationalist standpoint, the political value of recovering the black legacy seems minor compared with the need to establish the ideological link between the pre-Columbian past and the present. The black "root" has been systematically "uprooted" from the main "trunk" of the Puerto Rican nation.

Since the 1950s, the telluric metaphor of the three roots has organized much of the dominant representation of Puerto Rican culture, thanks largely to the influence of Ricardo Alegría and other intellectuals and artists working with the Institute of Puerto Rican Culture. Alegría's vision of the historical patrimony as constituted primarily by the defense of the Spanish vernacular, the commemoration of national heroes and foundational events, and the development of the arts in their elite and popular manifestations permeated standard views of Puerto Ricanness in the second half of the twentieth century (see Aguiló Ramos 1987). Scholars have confirmed the strong ideological consensus on these core symbols across political parties and social classes (Morris 1995; Rivera 1996). Alegría's own archaeological and historical research on the Taíno heritage illustrates the use of the Island's native roots to strengthen the sense of continuity between the present and the pre-Columbian past. Following a long-standing literary tradition in the Spanish Antilles, nationalists have drawn on the Taíno Indians as a symbolic resource to reaffirm patriotic values in Puerto Rico (see Ayala-Richards 1995). As I argued in Chapter 5, after World War II the local intellectual elite was able to consolidate its cultural nationalist project without creating a state.

The official adoption of cultural nationalism by the Commonwealth government has had an enormous impact on the revival of the Taíno heritage in Puerto Rico. On the positive side, the Institute of Puerto Rican Culture and other cultural institutions such as the Ateneo Puertorriqueño and the University of Puerto Rico have promoted the study, appreciation, and dissemination of the Island's rich and diverse cultural traditions, including the Taíno. Cultural (and especially linguistic) nationalism has created a strong ideological front against colonialism, even though it has not undermined the political and economic bases of the colonial discourse. The search for indigenous roots has added historical depth to national culture, apart from Spanish and U.S. influences. In the diaspora, Taíno symbolism has served to reassert Puerto Rican identity in a hostile environment. Today, most Puerto Ricans identify strongly, if somewhat superficially, with the Island's original inhabitants. Many use the native terms Borinquen, *borinqueño*, *borincano*, and *boricua* in a highly emotional way.

On the negative side, the dominant image of the Puerto Rican nation as a harmonious integration of three cultures and races is problematic on both theoretical and political grounds. As Dávila (1997) and others have argued, the official view of national culture on the Island glosses over inner conflicts and bolsters the myth of a racial democracy based on *mestizaje*. According to this view, the Taínos and Africans fused together with the Spanish to form a new cultural amalgam that overcame racial and ethnic fissures. Yet a close analysis of both the hegemonic discourse and institutional practices on Puerto Rican identity reveals the systematic overvaluation of the Hispanic element, the romanticization of Taíno Indians, and the underestimation of African-derived ingredients. In constructing their image of Puerto Ricanness, many cultural nationalists have symbolically made Indians out of blacks. That is, they have often exaggerated the indigenous roots while neglecting the African contribution to the Island's largely mulatto population and hybrid culture. I hope that future versions of the nationalist discourse will develop more inclusive ways of narrating the Puerto Rican nation.

Conclusion

Nation, Migration, Identity

During the first half of the twentieth century, U.S. colonial discourse denied the existence of a separate Puerto Rican nation. Part of the American rationale for occupying the Island was precisely its avowed incapacity for self-government and its lack of a well-defined cultural identity (Thompson 1995). For most U.S. government officials as well as for numerous American travelers, journalists, and scholars, Puerto Rico was unfit for independence after the Spanish-Cuban-American War. The Island's inhabitants were often depicted as racially and culturally inferior to Anglo-Saxons in world's fairs and museum exhibits; in the letters, diaries, and notebooks of American anthropologists; in academic journals and popular magazines; in the photographs taken by professionals and amateurs; and in official census reports. Such textual and visual forms of representation projected a paternalistic image of Puerto Rico as an undeveloped tropical paradise, ripe for American investment and in dire need of American tutelage.

After World War II, following a worldwide wave toward decolonization, Puerto Rico obtained a greater degree of autonomy from the United States. In 1952 a large majority of the Puerto Rican electorate supported the Estado Libre Asociado. Although commonwealth status did not alter the basic contours of the colonial situation, it permitted the adoption of cultural nationalism as a state policy on the Island. Since the mid-1950s, the Institute of Puerto Rican Culture and other government agencies have promoted a distinctive national identity based on powerful images and practices such as the Spanish language, the jíbaro, the Taíno heritage, and the folk art of carving santos. Like other nations, Puerto Rico has developed its own set of collective myths, rituals, and symbols, such as the flag, anthem, and seal, as well as representation in Olympic sports and international beauty contests. Such icons have been widely diffused among the Puerto Rican population on the Island and in the mainland and have strengthened the sense of being Puerto Rican as opposed to American. Their popular appeal, however, has not translated into massive support for independence or even free association with the United States. Cultural nationalism has been practically divorced from political nationalism on the Island.

One of the key impediments to a radical rupture with the current political status of Puerto Rico is the diaspora. Demographically, Puerto Rico is a divided nation in which nearly half of its members live outside the Island. Since the beginning of the twentieth century, the Puerto Rican government has sponsored large-scale migration to the U.S. mainland as a safety valve for the Island's overpopulation and unemployment problems. During the 1940s and 1950s, public officials and planners conceived Puerto Ricans in the United States as "migrant citizens" in need of assistance, orientation, and organization. For decades, Commonwealth leaders treated the Puerto Rican community abroad as a symbolic extension of the Island's culture rather than as an independent entity. In turn, migrant grassroots groups constructed their own identity primarily as Puerto Rican but did not accept wholesale the traditional discourse of Puerto Ricanness, especially its exclusive definition of the nation on linguistic and territorial grounds. Those who move back and forth between the Island and the mainland are likely to be bilingual and bicultural, as well as unbound by a fixed location in either place; yet most perceive themselves to be as Puerto Rican as those who move less frequently.

As I have documented throughout this book, political nationalism is a minority position today, whereas cultural nationalism is firmly entrenched among Puerto Ricans on the Island and in the diaspora. Across a broad spectrum of social classes, political affiliations, and racial groups, Puerto Ricans identify themselves primarily as Puerto Rican, not American, Hispanic or Latino, even though they value the material and symbolic benefits of U.S. citizenship. I have argued that Puerto Ricans on the Island and in the mainland assert a strong national, not just ethnic, identity, even though most of them do not support independence. Like Quebec, Scotland, or Catalonia, Puerto Rico remains a stateless nation, rather than simply another ethnic minority within an imperial state. As the historian César Ayala puts it (letter to the author, March 11, 2001), the Puerto Rican case suggests that "the idea of the nation has to be understood not as a territorially organized nation state, but as a translocal phenomenon of a new kind."

As a result of massive migration, Puerto Ricans have become members of a translocal or deterritorialized nation "whose boundaries shift between the archipelago of Puerto Rico and its U.S. diaspora" (Laó 1997: 171). Among all recent Latino migrants to the United States (including Mexicans, Cubans, and Dominicans), only Puerto Ricans insist on calling themselves simply Puerto Ricans, rather than Puerto Rican–Americans, which speaks volumes about their persistent stress on national origin and their adamant rejection of a hyphenated ethnicity. Many contemporary representations of Puerto Ricanness on the mainland are thoroughly diasporic notions based on long-distance nationalism. Unlike well-established nation-states, Puerto Rico cannot be imagined from any fixed location as a sovereign community, exclusively tied to a single territory or language, and characterized by a sense of deep, horizontal comradeship (Anderson 1991). Rather, it is a geographically, politically, linguistically, and culturally splintered country.

Is the Puerto Rican case unique, or does it suggest any broader "lessons"? Today, the Island is one of the few remaining colonies in the world. Within Latin America, Puerto Rico is the only country (with the partial exception of Cuba) that did not stage a successful independence movement against Spain, its former metropolis. Even in its immediate Caribbean context, the Island's dependence on the United States is anomalous given the strong decolonization movement in the region since the 1960s. Unlike other parts of the world, where political nationalism and ethnic separatism have reemerged with a vengeance, Puerto Rico has quietly experienced a growing economic and political integration with its metropolis. Compared with other Latin American and Caribbean people, the Puerto Rican diaspora seems exceptional because it takes place within the geopolitical borders of the United States.

At the same time, Puerto Rico's predicament resonates strongly with the struggles of other peoples in other places. Perhaps most clearly, the Island's continuing colonial dilemma invites comparisons with the dependent territories of the Caribbean, such as the Dutch and French Antilles, and the Pacific, such as Guam and American Samoa. Since 1898, U.S. colonial discourses on Puerto Rico developed under the framework of the American "imperial archipelago," which included Cuba, the Philippines, and Hawaii (Thompson 1998). Even more broadly, American images of Puerto Rican Others shared much of the "rhetoric of empire," common to British and French colonialism (Spurr 1993). Expressions of local resistance to American domination—such as the assertion of a separate Puerto Rican "personality" despite decades of political and economic penetration or the avowed moral superiority of indigenous values and practices over foreign ones—are typical of anticolonial movements in the so-called Third World (Chatterjee 1995). Nor is the growing split between political and cultural nationalism solely a Puerto Rican phenomenon: it has recurred at various times and in various parts of the world (Hutchinson 1994). Without suggesting that Puerto Rico represents identical trends in other countries, I would argue that the Island encapsulates many parallel and sometimes contradictory forces, such as transnationalism and nationalism, deterritorialization and reterritorialization, alterity and identity.

This case study of the multiple representations of Puerto Rican identity provides theoretical insights about colonialism, nationalism, and transnationalism. My analysis suggests that the strength of political nationalism tends to decline with the deterritorialization of national boundaries through massive migration and the emergence of a new (*lite*) form of colonialism. Diasporic communities often depart from the dominant nationalist canon by stressing their cultural and affective ties to an ancestral homeland, rather than their linguistic and territorial borders. Cultural nationalism may be a more useful ideology than political nationalism where a large portion of the population has become transnational. It can also help to advance the multiple economic and political interests of various sectors of a society, such as intellectuals, politicians, entrepreneurs, and even migrant workers, without necessarily establishing a sovereign state. Thus, colonialism, nationalism, and transnationalism can coexist uneasily at the same time and in the same place, as they do in contemporary Puerto Rico, a nation on the move.

No country in recent history has undergone a more dramatic, prolonged, and massive displacement of its people than Puerto Rico. Recalling Ireland's experience during the second half of the nineteenth century, Puerto Rico has exported almost half of its population to the United States since World War II. Unlike Ireland and other major sending countries in Europe during the heyday of emigration, Puerto Rico has received a growing number of returning and circulating migrants since the 1960s, as well as a substantial influx of foreign immigrants from neighboring countries such as the Dominican Republic and Cuba. Such dizzying nomadism—a constant dislocation and relocation of peoples, practices, imaginaries, and identities—has been posited as one of the defining moments of a global, transnational, or postmodern age (Chambers 1994). That may well be so. But regardless of one's theoretical preferences, representing nations on the move remains a difficult task. In this book, I have explored alternative approaches to the problem by mobilizing the object of study through time and space, as well as by looking at it from various method-ological standpoints and identifying multiple social actors and ideological posi-tions. Although much work remains to be done, I hope to have conveyed a sense of the fluidity—and, at the same time, tenacity—of national identities across many kinds of borders, both territorial and symbolic.

Notes

INTRODUCTION

1. Conventional historical accounts in the United States have usually called the War of 1898 simply the "Spanish-American War," thus omitting that Cubans had been struggling for independence from Spain since 1895 (and even earlier, between 1868 and 1878). Some historians now prefer the cumbersome expression "Spanish-Cuban-Filipino-American War" to include the insurrection in the Philippines. Because I am emphasizing the long-term consequences of the war in the Caribbean, I will use the term "Spanish-Cuban-American War" throughout this book.

2. Since 1898, Puerto Rico has occupied a juridical limbo within the framework of the U.S. Constitution. For analyses of the legal doctrine establishing that the Island "belongs to but is not part of the United States," see Burnett and Marshall (2001) and Rivera Ramos (2001).

3. The following paragraphs incorporate my previous writing on the subject (J. Duany 1996).

CHAPTER ONE

1. This chapter was first published in 2000 as "Nation on the Move: The Construction of Cultural Identities in Puerto Rico and the Diaspora," *American Ethnologist* 27 (1): 5–30.

2. For a critical review of the concepts of *lite* colonialism and nationalism as they apply to Puerto Rico, see Flores 2000, chap. 2.

3. Richard Handler (1994) asks the rhetorical question, "Is identity a useful cross-cultural concept?" and concludes that it is not. Instead of identity, he proposes the term "affiliation."

4. As Juan Manuel Carrión notes (letter to the author, August 25, 2000), this modification of Anderson's well-known definition of the nation is problematic. Eliminating sovereignty from the definition subverts the modern political equation of nations with states and aligns nations more closely with ethnic groups, commonly understood as culturally distinctive units within a state. But that is precisely my point: the case of Puerto Rico (like those of Scotland, Quebec, and Catalonia), where cultural nationalism is stronger than political nationalism, does not fit the dominant view of nations as "free" and completely self-determined communities. Few Puerto Ricans can now imagine their nation apart from some form of political association with the United States.

5. In the 2000 gubernatorial elections, more than 95 percent of the voters supported either the pro-statehood or the pro-Commonwealth candidate.

6. A 1998 volume edited by Juan Manuel García Passalacqua examines Muñoz Marín's embrace of cultural nationalism during the 1950s, particularly his support for the Institute of Puerto Rican Culture.

7. Pedro Albizu Campos (1891–1965) was elected president of Puerto Rico's Nationalist

Party in 1930. A radical nationalist, Albizu defended the right to resort to armed struggle to wrest the Island's independence from the United States. Albizu has been recognized as the shrewd inventor of a nationalist Puerto Rican project in opposition to U.S. imperialism. For more details on his life, thought, and practice, see Carrión, Gracia Ruiz, and Rodríguez Fraticelli 1993; Ferrao 1990.

8. For a sensitive reassessment of the relationship between anthropology and literature, see Behar 1997.

9. Unless otherwise noted, all translations are my own.

10. The Second Conference of the Puerto Rican Studies Association (PRSA) witnessed numerous attempts to revisit the cultural links between the Island and its diaspora. The meeting was held in San Juan, Puerto Rico, on September 26–29, 1996, under the central theme "Transcending Boundaries: Fostering Dialogues between the Island and Its Diaspora." The gathering attracted prominent scholars, writers, and artists from Puerto Rico and the United States, including Arcadio Díaz Quiñones, Rosario Ferré, Juan Flores, Tato Laviera, Iris Morales, Angel Quintero Rivera, and Juan Sánchez.

11. A partial exception to this trend is Esmeralda Santiago's autobiography, *When I Was Puerto Rican* (1994), which was published almost simultaneously in English and Spanish and was well received by literary critics on the Island.

12. The publication of a letter by Rosario Ferré in the *New York Times* (1998) stating her new political position sparked many critical commentaries on the Island, centering on the question of language and identity. Ferré has chosen to write in English in order to reach a wider audience in the United States, which has also generated much controversy in Puerto Rico. See, for instance, the heated exchange between Juan López Bauzá (1999) and Juan Duchesne Winter (1999).

13. This paragraph is based on the conclusions of a workshop that I organized at the Universidad del Sagrado Corazón in Santurce, Puerto Rico, on September 24–25, 1996, with the financial support of the Social Science Research Council. It gathered leading scholars on circular migration from the U.S. mainland and the Island, including Marixsa Alicea, Frances Aparicio, David Hernández, Juan Hernández Cruz, Edwin Meléndez, Vilma Ortiz, and Clara Rodríguez.

14. I should also note the existence of a nonnationalist critique of U.S. colonialism in Puerto Rico since the early twentieth century, associated with such leading intellectuals as Rosendo Matienzo Cintrón (see Bernabe 1996), as well as with labor leader Ramón Romero Rosa. However, the dominant anticolonial narrative on the Island since the 1930s has been strongly nationalistic in the sense described in this chapter.

CHAPTER TWO

1. The Smithsonian's interest in Puerto Rico dates at least to the last third of the nineteenth century. According to the historian Luis Martínez-Fernández (letter to the author, February 8, 2000), Henry Bryant, who died in Arecibo in 1867, represented the Smithsonian on the Island. Also connected to the Smithsonian was the American Frederick Ober, who first traveled to the Island in 1880 and returned as West Indian Commissioner for the Columbian Exposition in Chicago in 1893. He obtained permission to exhibit a local collection of Puerto Rican antiquities "owned by a learned doctor residing in Bayamon [sic]," probably Agustín Stahl (Ober 1893: 403). He subsequently published *Puerto Rico and Its Resources* (Ober 1899).

2. According to the historian Francisco Scarano (conversation with the author, March

18, 2000), President William McKinley was mortally shot briefly after visiting the Puerto Rican exhibit at Buffalo on September 6, 1901. According to contemporary accounts, the president had a light lunch in the U.S. government building and then had a public reception at the Temple of Music, where he was gunned down by the anarchist Leon Czolgosz.

3. Between 1898 and 1950, Puerto Rico experienced a remarkable Spanish revival in architecture, especially the California Mission style and Florida's Spanish Renaissance Revival. The American government on the Island built numerous schools, hospitals, and other public structures in the latter two styles (see Vivoni Farage and Alvarez Curbelo 1998).

4. This phrase is apparently a mistranslation of "Puerto Rico," which literally means "rich port," not "rich gate." The latter expression was also the title of La Gorce's 1924 article on Puerto Rico for *National Geographic*.

5. Toward the end of this period, Puerto Rico's participation in colonial exhibits arranged by the U.S. government became a source of increasing friction with the local elite. In 1931 the Puerto Rican House of Representatives passed a bill forbidding the Island's representation at the International Colonial Exposition in Paris, but American officials ignored the bill and included Puerto Rico in that fair, along with the Philippines, Hawaii, Alaska, Samoa, and the U.S. Virgin Islands (Greenhalgh 1988; Rydell 1993). I would speculate that the growing strength of Puerto Rican nationalism during the 1930s led to unconformity with colonial representations in international exhibitions.

6. In contrast, early-twentieth-century American images of Samoans usually depicted them as innocent and charming. For instance, the Keystone View Company published a stereocard titled "People and Home in the Samoan Islands, Pacific Ocean, Oceania." The text printed on the back of the card asked, "Are the natives handsome or ugly?" and responded, "The natives are of a light brown color, and have handsome features, splendid physical bodies, and alert minds."

CHAPTER THREE

1. American war correspondents, travel writers, and juvenile novelists produced an extensive literature on Puerto Rico during the first two decades of the twentieth century (see Matos-Rodríguez 1999).

2. Although the Island's name was the object of public controversy after the Spanish-Cuban-American War (see Hilgard 1900; Hill 1899c; Hyde 1900), most government and journalistic reports on the Island retained the American spelling until 1932, when the U.S. Congress passed a resolution accepting the official name of Puerto Rico.

3. Mason was also a stammerer (Mason to Boas, March 6, 1916), which may have contributed to the close attention he paid to collecting Puerto Rican folk stories verbatim (see Lastra 1999). A street has been named in Mason's honor in the town of Utuado, Puerto Rico, where he conducted most of his fieldwork.

4. As Mason wrote Boas (November 2, 1916), "I always was and am a Maderista," referring to one of the early leaders of the Mexican Revolution, Francisco Madero, a moderate reformer and ousted president of Mexico (1911–13).

5. At the time, geographic determinism was a widely shared doctrine beyond the field of anthropology. For instance, Ober (1899: 24) wrote for a popular audience: "It is in the temperate regions that man has made his greatest development—in the arts, literature, science; in everything that makes for progress and well-being, and this is doubtless owing to

the difference of environment. In the tropics his energies are dissipated; in the temperate zone he is thrown upon himself, as it were, and becomes resourceful, self-reliant." Similarly, Willoughby (1905: 79) held the common belief that the "tropical climate [was] but illy suited for permanent occupation by American men and women." Writing on the Philippines, Foreman (1906: 10) argued that "it is quite impossible for a race born and living in the Tropics to adopt the characteristics and thought of a Temperate zone people."

6. In an earlier incident, Spanish military authorities had convicted the American correspondent of the *New York Herald*, William Freeman Halstead, of spying for the U.S. government in Puerto Rico.

7. Vall Spinosa was the second Protestant minister to serve in Puerto Rico during the Spanish colonial period. He was rector of the Church of the Holy Trinity in Ponce, before moving on to San Juan with his family and retiring from the ministry (Luis Martínez-Fernández, letter to the author, February 8, 2000).

8. One of the best-selling descriptions of Puerto Rico and the other American colonies in the Caribbean and the Pacific, published in 1899, was titled *Our Islands and Their People*. Other contemporary publications were *Our New Possessions* (White 1898), *Myths and Legends of Our New Possessions and Protectorate* (Skinner 1900), and *Photographic Views of Our New Possessions* (Willets, Hamm, and McIntosh, n.d.).

9. Mason initiated a long series of studies on the survival of Hispanic oral traditions on the Island after the American occupation. Later collections of Puerto Rican folklore include Cadilla de Martínez 1938, Garrido 1952, Ramírez de Arellano 1926, and Tió Nazario 1979 [1921].

10. Junghanns (1875–1947) was an American of German descent who settled in Puerto Rico in 1898. His extensive folklore collection and a smaller one of archaeological objects on the Island were acquired by the Institute of Puerto Rican Culture.

11. This counterpoint is historically based on the prevalence of subsistence farming and coffee haciendas in the center of the Island and slave sugar plantations in the coastal plains. To this day, "African" elements (as in popular music, dance, and cuisine) are more visible in such coastal towns as Loíza, Guayama, or Ponce than in highland towns such as Utuado, Jayuya, or Lares.

12. By the mid–nineteenth century, the privileging of the Island's "white" peasant culture was evident in the work of local intellectuals, some of which was read by such American anthropologists as Mason and Fewkes. According to official accounts, the Island's Creole literature began with the publication of Manuel Alonso's *El Gíbaro* (1849), a romantic re-creation of the peasant dialect and customs.

13. Decades later, Mason's (1960) collection of riddles, published by the Institute of Puerto Rican Culture, was confiscated by the U.S. customhouse in San Juan because it considered the collection pornographic.

14. Six weeks earlier Boas had undergone oral surgery to extirpate a cancer that had attacked a facial nerve and permanently paralyzed the left side of his face (Boas to Mason, July 12, 1915). After a long illness, Boas found life in Utuado "rather strenuous" (Boas to Britton, June 13, 1915), but he was "feeling better" when he returned to the mainland (Boas to Espinosa, July 12, 1915).

CHAPTER FOUR

1. This chapter was first published in 2001 as an article in *Discourse* 23 (1): 319–53.

2. Willoughby had been the first president of the governor's Executive Council, later

served as secretary of state in Puerto Rico, and wrote a book about the public administration of the newly acquired territories of the United States (see Willoughby 1905).

3. Taft had been the first American civil governor (1901–4) of the Philippines after the Spanish-Cuban-American War.

4. In 1898 President McKinley commissioned the Protestant minister Henry K. Carroll to investigate the social, economic, and political conditions of Puerto Rico. Carroll (1899) reported that Puerto Ricans had had little opportunity to demonstrate their capacity for self-government under Spanish rule. Although Carroll recommended the concession of self-government to the Island, the U.S. Congress decided that Puerto Rico would remain an unincorporated territory. In 1900 Congress approved the Foraker Act, which limited the political participation of Puerto Ricans to voting for members of the House of Delegates, while legislative and executive power was highly centralized in a presidentially appointed governor and his Executive Council.

5. The National Anthropological Archives contain another important collection of photographs taken in Cuba by Charles Edward Doty between 1899 and 1902. Like Underwood & Underwood, Doty focused on buildings, fortifications, streets, and city squares. For a perceptive analysis, see Bretos 1996.

6. It would be equally interesting to explore how Puerto Rican photographers have represented their own culture, as well as American culture. A good starting point for this research would be Osvaldo García's compilation (1989) of historical photographs from various private and public sources. Teodoro Vidal has also donated a large photographic collection to the Smithsonian Institution (see Chapter 6). For more recent photographic albums on Puerto Rico, see Delano 1990 and Méndez Caratini 1990.

7. I thank Héctor Méndez Caratini for these insights.

8. Day's claim to fame as the first to raise the American flag in Puerto Rico is disputable. According to a former officer of the Spanish army in Puerto Rico, two other soldiers from the USS *Gloucester* carried the star-spangled banner to Guánica on July 25, 1898 (Rivero 1973). An American correspondent noted that others hoisted the American flag during an official ceremony at El Morro Castle on the final day of occupation, October 18, 1898 (White 1898). Day's military biographer writes that he ran up a ship's flag on the Ponce customhouse on July 28 and hoisted another flag over El Morro on October 18 of that same year (Hardman 1999). In any case, Gardener's niece donated an American flag to the Smithsonian in 1926. Last flown in 1901 at the San Jerónimo fort in San Juan, the flag may have been the one that Colonel Day first took to the Island.

9. Many reprints of Gardener's photographs are available at the Center for Historical Research at the University of Puerto Rico, Río Piedras, catalogued as Collections 97 and 98, Box 3.

10. Four decades later, Jack Delano came to Puerto Rico as a photographer working for the federal government's Farm Security Administration. Delano was also interested in documenting living conditions on the Island and established close ties to American and Puerto Rican leaders. It would be interesting to compare Gardener's and Delano's perspectives, although this comparison lies beyond the scope of this chapter (for suggestive analyses of Delano's work, see Baldrich 1999; Martínez–San Miguel 1996).

11. Because many of her printed photographs were repeated or had insufficient identifying information, I focused on Gardener's lantern slides on Puerto Rico for this inventory. These were the images that she presented in her public lectures comparing various cultures.

12. Moscioni was one of the first professional photographers to set up his studio in San

Juan after arriving on the Island with the U.S. Army during the Spanish-Cuban-American War. He lived in Puerto Rico between 1898 and 1917, married a Puerto Rican, and died in New York in 1950 (*El Mundo* 1950). A still unprocessed collection of his photographs and postcards is housed at the Puerto Rican Collection of the Library of the University of Puerto Rico, Río Piedras. Moscioni's basic project was to document the material improvements in the Island's infrastructure under American rule (Alvarez Sánchez 2000).

13. The governor of Puerto Rico during Gardener's second visit was Regis H. Post (1907–9); he appears in several of her photographs.

14. Moscioni's collection of photographs of Puerto Rico also features pineapples, oranges, bananas, coconuts, coffee, tobacco, and sugar—all exotic tropical species from an American viewpoint.

15. Colonel Ashford (1873–1934) came to Puerto Rico in 1898 as part of the U.S. military forces. In 1900, together with Drs. Pedro Gutiérrez Igaravidez and Walter W. King, he discovered that hookworm was one of the main causes of widespread anemia on the Island. He remained on the Island until his death.

16. Among other factors, the collapse of the indigenous population and the rise in the number of white settlers in Hawaii and Alaska facilitated their incorporation into the union. Conversely, the presence of a dense population with its own cultural and linguistic practices has prevented Puerto Rico's total assimilation by the United States.

CHAPTER FIVE

1. Here I focus on the 1950s as a key decade in the emergence and consolidation of cultural nationalism in Puerto Rico. However, many of the ideological premises of this movement were laid out by the Generation of 1930, which has been the topic of extensive research and discussion elsewhere. For more information on the contributions of this generation to the debate on national identity on the Island, see Alvarez-Curbelo and Rodríguez Castro 1993 and Gelpí 1993.

CHAPTER SIX

1. The following biographical details were culled from several journalistic sources and corroborated in an interview with Vidal (October 4, 1999).

2. See Ricardo E. Alegría's position paper (1965) on political status and national culture. As I noted in Chapter 5, the Institute of Puerto Rican Culture has sponsored activities ranging from the conservation and restoration of archaeological, historic, and artistic objects and sites to research and publication on Puerto Rican folklore, literature, and music.

3. Vidal was aware of the historical significance of his dilemmas. He gave me a copy of a 1932 article decrying the expatriation of prior archaeological, historical, and art collections, such as Latimer's gift to the Smithsonian, Fewkes's acquisition of the Neumann collection, and Stahl's donation to the American Museum of Natural History (see E. Blanco 1932). J. Alden Mason's archaeological materials were also deposited at the latter museum as part of the Boas collection on Puerto Rico. Vidal further noted that several collectors, including Alan Moss, Angel Botello, and Dorothy Pike, had sold many santos in the arts' collector market.

4. At the time of this writing, in February 2001, the building was being restored as a conservatory of music, at a cost of $53.8 million.

5. In January 2000 another controversy focused on the partial dismantling of the Vidal

exhibition from the NMAH. A letter-writing campaign organized by Puerto Ricans in the Washington area asked the museum's administration to continue the exhibition. As the author of one letter argued, "It is important that Puerto Rico is portrayed in the National Museum of American History and that our contributions to American history are acknowledged at this level" (Ilia Vélez, letter to the author, January 11, 2000). The museum's director, Spencer R. Crew, responded that "the continued display of many of the objects may put them in jeopardy" because they include "rare and fragile carvings and instruments" (letter to the author, February 11, 2000). As a compromise, all santos were removed for conservation purposes, while the remainder of the exhibit remained on view at the museum.

6. In 1955, Alegría had proposed a bill "to end the continuous and progressive loss of our cultural patrimony" (Alegría to Mendoza, February 16, 1955).

7. Vidal provided me with a copy of the letter, dated January 2, 1998.

8. According to Vidal (letter to the author, September 5, 2000), the four most popular santos in Puerto Rico were the Three Wise Men, the Virgin of Carmel, the Virgin of Montserrat, and Saint Anthony of Padua. Admittedly, his collection does not adequately represent these popular preferences because he chose to assemble more exemplars of some figures than others.

9. An electronic version of the Vidal exhibition may be accessed through the NMAH's Web site: ⟨http://americanhistory.si.edu/vidal⟩. The complete exhibition was on view at the museum from July 1998 to January 2000.

10. The photograph, preserved at the Archives Center of the NMAH, was taken at the christening of Olga Hernández Vázquez in Miramar, an upper-class neighborhood of San Juan. The girl was the granddaughter of the president of the Puerto Rican Supreme Court.

11. Nonetheless, one of the curators, Marvette Pérez, has publicly distanced herself from the official discourse on Puerto Rican identity (see Lassalle and Pérez 1997).

CHAPTER SEVEN

1. Mayra López (1998) has analyzed Muñoz Marín's discourse on migration, which emphasized the need to export Puerto Rico's surplus population in order to promote economic development, as well as to foster the migrants' adaptation to American society. On many public occasions in New York, Muñoz Marín defined himself as a return migrant.

CHAPTER EIGHT

1. Bernardo Vega's memoirs (1994), first published in Spanish in 1977, helped to fill in the gaps in the history of the Puerto Rican community in New York between the last third of the nineteenth century and the first half of the twentieth century. Although Jesús Colón's collection (1982) of newspaper articles had been published in English in 1961, it did not focus on the migrants' organizational activities. Colón himself was an active member in many voluntary associations founded by Puerto Ricans in New York City.

2. In 2000 the organizers of the Puerto Rican Parade in New York dedicated the parade to the nationalist leader Pedro Albizu Campos, sparking a wave of protests and boycotts from pro-statehood leaders in Puerto Rico. In turn, the organizers responded that their decision was based on cultural, not political, considerations. The event was also dedicated to the peace movement in Vieques.

3. As I show in Chapter 10, race does not figure explicitly in the official narrative on

Puerto Rican identity on the Island and in the mainland. That narrative generally assumes that Puerto Ricans are a racially heterogeneous population, predominantly white and of Spanish origin.

CHAPTER NINE

1. Murray Chapman (letter to the author, August 3, 2000) argues that the term "circular migration" is nonsense because it joins two discrete concepts about people's behavior over time. In his view, migration should be restricted to the geographic redistribution of population, whereas circulation does not alter its long-term distribution. In this chapter I retain the term "circular migration" to underline its difference from other types of "linear" movement from one place to another.

2. Some scholars have called contemporary immigrants "transmigrants" insofar as they maintain multiple linkages to their homelands (see Schiller, Basch, and Blanc 1995). However, as Alejandro Portes (1998) has noted, the neologism "transmigration" occupies the same semantic space as migration, and little is gained analytically by substituting one term for the other.

3. Many Puerto Ricans do not follow the standard definition of circulation as a population movement that ultimately terminates in the community in which it originated (Chapman and Prothero 1983; Conway 1988). The travel itineraries of Puerto Rican migrants often reproduce a triangular or even zigzag form.

4. The phrase *los de afuera* (those from the outside) is currently applied to return migrants and Dominican immigrants as well as other persons who do not conform to local norms of dress, speech, and demeanor in Puerto Rico. In contrast, *los de aquí* refers to people who practice native customs. For an excellent ethnographic analysis of this discourse as it operates in a small Puerto Rican highland town, see G. Pérez 2000.

5. Traveling from Puerto Rico to the mainland is distinct from traveling within the fifty states in two main ways: first, all baggage must be inspected by the U.S. Department of Agriculture at the airport, and second, passengers may be asked if they are U.S. citizens by officers from the Immigration and Naturalization Service. For other practical purposes, travel between the Island and the mainland is considered an internal move within U.S. territory. Still, some airline, train, and courier companies, as well as banks and retail businesses, classify Puerto Rico as an international or overseas destination.

6. The study reported in this chapter was directed by Douglas S. Massey, of the University of Pennsylvania, and Jorge Durand, of the University of Guadalajara. The survey was part of the Latin American Migration Project (LAMP), supported by the National Institute of Child Health and Human Development. LAMP personnel have recently interviewed Puerto Ricans in the U.S. mainland. The database is available online at ⟨http://www.pop.upenn.edu/lamp/⟩.

7. In 1996 Rafael Zapata conducted sixty interviews in Loíza. In 1998 Moira Pérez completed the sample of one hundred households in the same area.

8. According to the 2000 census, the black population ranged from 57.9 percent in Loíza to 4.1 percent in Cidra (U.S. Bureau of the Census 2001).

9. Analysis of 1990 census data on Puerto Rico has found that circular migrants tended to be males with a high school education and employed in service, technical, and sales occupations (Godoy et al. 2000). This sociodemographic profile coincides with the results of the study reported in this chapter.

10. Using multiple movement as a proxy for circular migration may be problematic for some purposes—for instance, to calculate the velocity with which people travel back and forth between the Island and the mainland. However, imposing an arbitrary time limit on the category of circular migrant, as some authors have done before, is artificial and unnecessary. I prefer a minimal definition of circulation as the completion of two full migrant cycles, that is, at least two round-trip journeys between the Island and the mainland.

11. Given the sample design, only migrants with families who still consider them members of their households are included in this estimate. Entire families who have moved abroad or individuals who are no longer counted as part of the household remaining in Puerto Rico are omitted.

12. Based on the available evidence, it is difficult to determine if older people were more likely to move frequently because they had a longer period during which to move or because the frequency of moves has changed over time. Future studies of circular migration should tease out whether such differences are due to aging or time period.

CHAPTER TEN

1. This section draws on and expands an earlier review of the literature on race in Puerto Rico; see J. Duany 1998b.

2. Between July and October 2000, the Bureau of the Census commissioned an evaluation of the high nonresponse rate to the 2000 census of Puerto Rico. According to a personal conversation with one of the fieldworkers, Isar Godreau, the study found that many islanders were puzzled by the race and ethnicity questions on the census questionnaire. Unfortunately, the results of this research have not yet been made public.

3. In the 1950s an official New York City report made headlines in Puerto Rico because it distinguished Puerto Ricans as a racial type, separate from whites and nonwhites (*El Mundo* 1954).

4. The memoirs of Bernardo Vega (1994 [1977]) document that Puerto Rican settlements in New York City at the turn of the twentieth century were not strictly segregated by color. The residents of today's barrios continue to be racially heterogeneous.

5. A current application form to the Teaching Practicum at the College of Education of the University of Puerto Rico, Río Piedras, inquired about "ethnic origin" and included the following categories: "White," "Black," "Trigueño Claro," "Trigueño Oscuro," and "Other." I thank Isar Godreau for providing me a copy of this document.

6. Virginia Domínguez (1998) has reviewed changing racial taxonomies in the United States, as reflected in Hawaiian censuses during the twentieth century. She found much categorical flip-flopping in U.S. concepts of race since the first census of 1790. Since 1900 the census has used twenty-six different terms to identify the racial composition of the American population.

7. Before 1940 it is practically impossible to obtain separate cross-tabulations for Puerto Ricans and race in the United States. At the time of this writing, the U.S. Bureau of the Census had not yet released separate data for the race of mainland Puerto Ricans in 2000.

8. Similarly, Benjamin Bailey (1999) found that young Dominican Americans in Providence, Rhode Island, describe their race as Spanish, Hispanic, Dominican, or Latino, but never as black or white.

9. As Angela Ginorio (1979: 107) argues, the recognition of a third racial group such as brown or other to designate Native Americans, Chicanos, Puerto Ricans, and other Latinos

does not fundamentally challenge the American system of racial classification. Rather, it merely adds another discrete category based on ethnic background.

10. The racial implications of the various status options for Puerto Rico lie beyond the scope of this chapter. However, many black Puerto Ricans have traditionally supported the Island's annexation to the United States, while the pro-independence movement has been predominantly white. The impact of racial distinctions on local elections remains unknown as a result of lack of research.

CHAPTER ELEVEN

1. An earlier version of this chapter appeared in Haslip-Viera 1999: 31–55.

2. In the 2000 census, only .4 percent of the Island's population defined itself as "American Indian and Alaska Native" (U.S. Bureau of the Census 2001).

3. This rhetorical strategy has long been shared by non–Puerto Ricans and nonacademics as well. For instance, the Keystone View Company published an early-twentieth-century stereocard titled "America's Greatest Gift to Porto Rico—The Public School, Caguas" (a reprint from the Underwood & Underwood Collection). The text printed on the back of the card claimed that "in 1899 one-third of the inhabitants of Puerto Rico were Spanish, and the rest were half-breeds, negroes and Chinese. The Indian blood of the old Caribs is plainly evident in the natives. They are light in color and have little of the physical or mental characteristics of the negroes. They are generally small of stature and slight of build."

4. The Taíno revival in the United States is attracting increasing scholarly attention. The United Confederation of Taíno People, based in New York, lists eight affiliated organizations in the U.S. mainland. In addition, a Taíno Inter-Tribal Council has been established in New Jersey. For more information on these groups, see Bonilla 2000, Borrero 1999, Dávila 1999, Jiménez Román 1999, and United Confederation of Taíno People 1998.

Works Cited

Abad, José Ramón. 1885. *Puerto-Rico en la feria-exposición de Ponce en 1882*. Ponce, P.R.: El Comercio.

Administración de Reconstrucción de Puerto Rico. 1938. *Censo de Puerto Rico: 1935. Población y agricultura*. Washington, D.C.: Government Printing Office.

Aguiló Ramos, Silvia. 1987. Idea y concepto de la cultura puertorriqueña durante la década del '50. Ph.D. diss., Centro de Estudios Avanzados de Puerto Rico y el Caribe, San Juan.

Aitken, Robert T. 1917. Puerto Rican Burial Caves. In *Proceedings of the Nineteenth International Congress of Americanists*, 224–28. Washington, D.C.: n.p.

———. 1918. A Porto Rican Burial Cave. *American Anthropologist* 20:296–309.

Alegría, Ricardo E. 1950. *Historia de nuestros indios (versión elemental)*. San Juan: Departamento de Instrucción.

———. 1954. *La fiesta de Santiago Apóstol en Loíza Aldea*. San Juan: Colección de Estudios Puertorriqueños.

———. 1955. Letter to doña Inés [Mendoza], February 16. Section V: Governor of Puerto Rico, 1949–1964; Series I: General Correspondence; Folder 173: "Instituto de Cultura Puertorriqueña." Fundación Luis Muñoz Marín, Trujillo Alto, P.R.

———. 1965. El status político y la cultura nacional. Section V: Governor of Puerto Rico, 1949–1964; Series I: General Correspondence; Folder 173: "Instituto de Cultura Puertorriqueña." Fundación Luis Muñoz Marín, Trujillo Alto, P.R. Partly reproduced in the Statement of Ricardo E. Alegría (1966). In *Status of Puerto Rico: Hearings before the United States–Puerto Rico Commission on the Status of Puerto Rico*. Volume 2, *Social-Cultural Factors in Relation to the Status of Puerto Rico*, ed. United States–Puerto Rico Commission on the Status of Puerto Rico, 243–76. Washington, D.C.: Government Printing Office.

———. 1970 [1963]. No es necesario resolver el status para enseñar en el vernáculo de la Isla. In *Politics and Education in Puerto Rico: A Documentary Survey of the Language Issue*, ed. Erwin H. Epstein, 130–36. Metuchen, N.J.: Scarecrow Press.

———. 1971a. *Los museos del Instituto de Cultura Puertorriqueña*. San Juan: Instituto de Cultura Puertorriqueña.

———. 1971b. *Puerto Rico y su cultura nacional: Discurso pronunciado en la colación de grados de la Universidad Católica de Puerto Rico, en Ponce, el 23 de mayo de 1971, en ocasión de investirle dicha Universidad con el grado de Doctor Honoris Causa*. Ponce: Universidad Católica de Puerto Rico.

———. 1978. Introducción: Los estudios arqueológicos en Puerto Rico. *Revista/Review Interamericana* 8 (3): 380–85.

———. 1983. *Ball Courts and Ceremonial Plazas in the West Indies*. New Haven: Department of Anthropology, Yale University.

———. 1996a. Archaeological Research in the Scientific Survey of Puerto Rico and the

Virgin Islands and Its Subsequent Development on the Island. In *The Scientific Survey of Puerto Rico and the Virgin Islands: An Eighty-Year Reassessment of the Island's Natural History*, ed. Julio C. Figueroa Colón, 257–64. New York: New York Academy of Sciences.

———. 1996b. *El Instituto de Cultura Puertorriqueña, 1955–1973: 18 años contribuyendo a fortalecer nuestra conciencia nacional.* 2d ed. San Juan: Instituto de Cultura Puertorriqueña.

———. N.d. *The Museum of the Puerto Rican Indian.* San Juan: Institute of Puerto Rican Culture.

Algarín, Miguel, and Miguel Piñero, eds. 1975. *Nuyorican Poetry: An Anthology of Words and Feelings.* New York: William Morrow.

Alicea, Marixsa. 1989. The Dual Base Phenomenon: A Reconceptualization of Puerto Rican Migration. Ph.D. diss., Northwestern University.

———. 1990. Dual Home Bases: A Reconceptualization of Puerto Rican Migration. *Latino Studies Journal* 1 (3): 78–98.

———. 1997. "A Chambered Nautilus": The Contradictory Nature of Puerto Rican Women's Role in the Social Construction of a Transnational Community. *Gender and Society* 11 (5): 597–626.

Alloula, Marek. 1986. *The Colonial Harem.* Minneapolis: University of Minnesota Press.

Almaguer, Tomás, and Moon-Kie Jung. 1998. The Enduring Ambiguities of Race in the United States. Working paper no. 573, Center for Research on Social Organization, University of Michigan, Ann Arbor.

Alvarez-Curbelo, Silvia, and María Elena Rodríguez Castro, eds. 1993. *Del nacionalismo al populismo: Cultura y política en Puerto Rico.* Río Piedras, P.R.: Huracán.

Alvarez Nazario, Manuel. 1974. *El elemento afronegroide en el español de Puerto Rico.* San Juan: Instituto de Cultura Puertorriqueña.

———. 1992. *Historia de la lengua española en Puerto Rico.* San Juan: Academia Puertorriqueña de la Lengua Española.

Alvarez Sánchez, Belisa L. 2000. Estudio fotográfico colección A. Moscioni. Unpublished manuscript, Department of Sociology and Anthropology, University of Puerto Rico, Río Piedras.

Anderson, Benedict. 1991. *Imagined Communities: Reflections on the Origin and Spread of Nationalism.* 2d ed. London: Verso.

———. 1992. *Long-Distance Nationalism: World Capitalism and the Rise of Identity Politics.* Amsterdam: Center for Asian Studies.

Anonymous. 1871. *Programa de la Quinta Feria y Exposición Públicas que se han de celebrar en esta isla en el mes de junio de 1871. Aprobado por el Superior Gobierno de esta Provincia.* Puerto Rico: Imprenta del Comercio.

Anonymous. 1901. *Puerto Rico and Its Resources: The Puerto Rican Exhibit at the Pan-American Exhibit at Buffalo, N.Y., May–November 1901, and Charleston, South Carolina, December 1901–May 1902.* Washington, D.C.: n.p.

Anonymous. 1913, Letter to the Governor of Porto Rico, November 6. Franz Boas Papers, American Philosophical Society, Philadelphia.

Aparicio, Frances. 1996. Circular Migration and Puerto Rican Cultural Identity. Paper presented at the workshop "Circular Migration between Puerto Rico and the United States: A Transnational Approach," Universidad del Sagrado Corazón, Santurce, P.R., September 24–25.

——. 1998. *Listening to Salsa: Gender, Latin Popular Music, and Puerto Rican Cultures.* Hanover, N.H.: University Press of New England.

Aponte-Parés, Luis. 1996. Pequeñas Patrias: Appropriating Place in the American City. Paper presented at the Second Conference of the Puerto Rican Studies Association, San Juan, September 26–29.

Appadurai, Arjun. 1996. *Modernity at Large: Cultural Dimensions of Globalization.* Minneapolis: University of Minnesota Press.

Arana, Felipe. 1950. Los hispanos de Harlem. *Ecos de Nueva York*, February 2, 10–13.

Arana-Soto, S. 1976. *Puerto Rico: Sociedad sin razas y trabajos afines.* San Juan: Asociación Médica de Puerto Rico.

Asad, Talal, ed. 1973. *Anthropology and the Colonial Encounter.* Atlantic Highlands, N.J.: Humanities Press.

Ashton, Guy T. 1980. The Return and Re-Return of Long-Term Puerto Rican Migrants: A Selective Rural-Urban Sample. *Revista/Review Interamericana* 10 (1): 27–45.

——. 1999. Professor's Report on Travel Patterns Fails to Surprise. *San Juan Star*, September 30, 78.

Asociación Puertorriqueña de Antropólogos y Arqueólogos, ed. 1990. *Arqueología de rescate: Cinco ponencias.* San Juan: Asociación Puertorriqueña de Antropólogos y Arqueólogos.

Austin, O. P. 1900. Our New Possessions and the Interest They Are Exciting. *National Geographic Magazine* 11 (2): 32–33.

Ayala-Richards, Haydée. 1995. La presencia de los taínos en la literatura puertorriqueña. Ph.D. diss., University of Nebraska.

Baatz, Simon. 1996. Imperial Science and Metropolitan Ambition: The Scientific Survey of Puerto Rico, 1913–1934. In *The Scientific Survey of Puerto Rico and the Virgin Islands: An Eighty-Year Reassessment of the Island's Natural History*, ed. Julio C. Figueroa Colón, 1–16. New York: New York Academy of Sciences.

Babín, María Teresa. 1986. *La cultura de Puerto Rico.* 2d ed. San Juan: Instituto de Cultura Puertorriqueña.

Baerga, María del Carmen, and Lanny Thompson. 1990. Migration in a Small Semi-Periphery: The Movement of Puerto Ricans and Dominicans. *International Migration Review* 24 (4): 656–83.

Bailey, Benjamin. 1999. Language and Ethnic/Racial Identity of Dominican American High School Students in Providence, Rhode Island. Ph.D. diss., University of California, Los Angeles.

Baker, Lee D. 1998. *From Savage to Negro: Anthropology and the Construction of Race, 1896–1954.* Berkeley: University of California Press.

Baldrich, Juan José. 1999. Jack Delano, ¿un expatriado al servicio del Estado? *Revista Mexicana del Caribe* 4 (7): 36–63.

Balibar, Etienne, and Immanuel Wallerstein. 1991. *Race, Nation, Class: Ambiguous Identities.* London: Verso.

Banks, Marcus, and Howard Morphy, eds. 1997. *Rethinking Visual Anthropology.* New Haven: Yale University Press.

Banta, Melissa, and Curtis M. Hinsley. 1986. *From Site to Sight: Anthropology, Photography, and the Power of Imagery.* Cambridge: Harvard University Press.

Barradas, Efraín. 1998. *Partes de un todo: Ensayos y notas sobre literatura puertorriqueña en los Estados Unidos.* Río Piedras, P.R.: Editorial de la Universidad de Puerto Rico.

Basch, Linda, Nina Glick Schiller, and Cristina Szanton Blanc. 1994. *Nations Unbound: Transnational Projects, Postcolonial Predicaments, and Deterritorialized Nation-States*. New York: Gordon and Breach.

Baver, Sherri L. 2000. The Rise and Fall of Section 936: The Historical Context and Possible Consequences of Migration. *Centro* 11 (2): 45–55.

Behar, Ruth. 1997. *The Vulnerable Observer: Anthropology That Breaks Your Heart*. Boston: Beacon.

Bender, Lynn-Darrell, ed. 1998. *The American Presence in Puerto Rico*. Hato Rey, P.R.: Publicaciones Puertorriqueñas.

Benedict, Burton. 1983. *The Anthropology of World's Fairs: San Francisco's Panama Pacific International Exposition of 1915*. London: Scolar Press.

Bernabe, Rafael. 1996. *Respuestas al colonialismo en la política puertorriqueña, 1899–1929*. Río Piedras, P.R.: Huracán.

Betances, Samuel. 1972. The Prejudice of Having No Prejudice in Puerto Rico. Part 1. *The Rican* 2:41–54.

———. 1973. The Prejudice of Having No Prejudice in Puerto Rico. Part 2. *The Rican* 3:22–37.

Bhabha, Homi K. 1994. *The Location of Culture*. London: Routledge.

———, ed. 1990. *Nation and Narration*. London: Routledge.

Blanco, Enrique T. 1932. Campeche. III. Su obra. *Alma Latina* 23 (June): 19–27.

Blanco, Tomás. 1985 [1942]. *El prejuicio racial en Puerto Rico*. 3d ed. Río Piedras, P.R.: Huracán.

Blum, Ron, and Stephen Barnett. 2000. A Window into the Past: A Short History of the Stereo Photograph. Electronic document. ⟨http://www.txt.de/spress/foto/museum/galleries/beginnings/albumen/stereos/history.htm⟩.

Boas, Franz. 1915a. Letters to N. L. Britton. Franz Boas Papers, American Philosophical Society, Philadelphia.

———. 1915b. Letters to Aurelio M. Espinosa. Franz Boas Papers, American Philosophical Society, Philadelphia.

———. 1915c. Letters to J. Alden Mason. Franz Boas Papers, American Philosophical Society, Philadelphia.

———. 1916. New Evidence in Regard to the Instability of Human Types. *Proceedings of the National Academy of Sciences* 2 (12): 713–18.

———. 1917. Letter to Ezequiel Chávez, August 7. Franz Boas Papers, American Philosophical Society, Philadelphia.

———. 1919. Scientists as Spies. Letter to the Editor, *The Nation*, December 20. Franz Boas Papers, American Philosophical Society, Philadelphia.

———. 1921. Letter to Ezequiel Chávez, February 15. Franz Boas Papers, American Philosophical Society, Philadelphia.

———. 1925. Letter to N. L. Britton, November 7. Franz Boas Papers, American Philosophical Society, Philadelphia.

———. 1940. Letter to J. Alden Mason, August 5. Franz Boas Papers, American Philosophical Society, Philadelphia.

Bonilla, Frank. 1993. Migrants, Citizenship, and Social Pacts. In *Colonial Dilemma: Critical Perspectives on Contemporary Puerto Rico*, ed. Edwin Meléndez and Edgardo Meléndez, 181–88. Boston: South End.

Bonilla, Frank, and Ricardo Campos. 1986. *Industry and Idleness*. New York: Centro de
    Estudios Puertorriqueños, Hunter College.
Bonilla, Frank, and Héctor Colón Jordán. 1979. "Mamá, Borinquen Me Llama!" Puerto
    Rican Return Migration in the 70s. *Migration Today* 7 (2): 1–6.
Bonilla, Yarimar. 2000. Taíno Renaissance: The Cultural Politics of "Indigenismo"
    among Puerto Ricans at Home and in the Diaspora. Paper presented at the XXII
    International Congress of the Latin American Studies Association, Miami, Fla.,
    March 16–18.
Borrero, Roberto Mucaro. 1999. Rethinking Taíno: A Taíno Perspective. In *Taíno Revival:
    Critical Perspectives on Puerto Rican Identity and Cultural Politics*, ed. Gabriel
    Haslip-Viera, 109–27. New York: Centro de Estudios Puertorriqueños, Hunter
    College.
Brau, Salvador. 1972 [1894]. *Puerto Rico y su historia*. 2d ed. San Juan: Editorial IV
    Centenario.
Breitbart, Eric. 1997. *A World on Display, 1904: Photographs from the St. Louis World's
    Fair*. Albuquerque: University of New Mexico Press.
Bretos, Miguel. 1996. Imaging Cuba under the American Flag: Charles Edward Doty in
    Havana, 1899–1902. *Journal of Decorative and Propaganda Arts* 22:83–103.
Britton, N. L. 1917. Memorandum to Boas, Crampton, Berkey, Poor, and Tower, October
    13. Franz Boas Papers, American Philosophical Society, Philadelphia.
——. 1919–22. History of the Survey. *Scientific Survey of Porto Rico and the Virgin Islands*
    1:1–10.
——. N.d. Memorandum to Kemp, Crampton, Boas, and Poor. Franz Boas Papers,
    American Philosophical Society, Philadelphia.
Brown, Julie K. 1994. *Contesting Images: Photography and the World's Columbian
    Exposition*. Tucson: University of Arizona Press.
Buchanan, William I. 1899. Letter to J. H. Brigham, December 5. RU 70, Series 14, Box
    52, Folder 26, Smithsonian Institution Archives, Washington, D.C.
Buel, J. W., ed. 1904. *Louisiana and the Fair: An Exposition of the World, Its People, and
    Their Achievements*. 10 vols. St. Louis: World's Progress Publishing Co.
Buitrago Ortiz, Carlos. 1982. Anthropology in the Puerto Rican Colonial Context:
    Analysis and Projections. In *Indigenous Anthropology in Non-Western Countries*, ed.
    Hussein Fahim, 97–111. Durham, N.C.: Carolina Academic Press.
Burchard, Hank. 1999. A Collector's Vision of Puerto Rico. Electronic document.
    ⟨http://yp.washingtonpost.com//E/E/WASDC/oooo/66/18/cs1.html⟩.
Burnett, Christina Duffy, and Burke Marshall, eds. 2001. *Foreign in a Domestic Sense:
    Puerto Rico, American Expansion, and the Constitution*. Durham: Duke University
    Press.
Cabán, Pedro A. 1999. *Constructing a Colonial People: Puerto Rico and the United States,
    1898–1932*. Boulder, Colo.: Westview.
Cabranes, José A. 1979. *Citizenship and the American Empire: Notes on the Legislative
    History of the United States Citizenship of Puerto Ricans*. New Haven: Yale
    University Press.
Cadilla de Martínez, María. 1938. *Costumbres y tradicionalismos de mi tierra*. San Juan:
    Imprenta Venezuela.
Campos, Ricardo, and Juan Flores. 1979. Migración y cultura nacional puertorriqueñas:
    Perspectivas proletarias. In *Puerto Rico: Identidad nacional y clases sociales*

(coloquio de Princeton), by Angel G. Quintero Rivera, José Luis González, Ricardo
    Campos, and Juan Flores, 81–146. Río Piedras, P.R.: Huracán.

Cantwell, Robert. 1993. *Ethnomimesis: Folklore and the Representation of Culture.*
    Chapel Hill: University of North Carolina Press.

Carr, Carolyn Kinder, and George Kurney, eds. 1993. *Revisiting the White City: American
    Art at the 1893 World's Fair.* Washington, D.C.: National Museum of American Art.

Carrión, Juan Manuel. 1980. The Petty Bourgeoisie and the Struggle for Independence in
    Puerto Rico. In *The Puerto Ricans: Their History, Culture, and Society,* ed.
    Adalberto López, 233–56. Rochester, Vt.: Schenkman.

——. 1996. *Voluntad de nación: Ensayos sobre el nacionalismo en Puerto Rico.* San Juan:
    Nueva Aurora.

——. 1999. El imaginario nacional norteamericano y el nacionalismo puertorriqueño.
    Revista de Ciencias Sociales, n.s., 7:66–101.

Carrión, Juan Manuel, Teresa C. Gracia Ruiz, and Carlos Rodríguez Fraticelli, eds. 1993.
    La nación puertorriqueña: Ensayos en torno a Pedro Albizu Campos. Río Piedras,
    P.R.: Editorial de la Universidad de Puerto Rico.

Carroll, Henry K. 1899. *Report on the Island of Puerto Rico: Its Population, Civil
    Government, Commerce, Industries, Productions, Roads, Tariff, and Currency.*
    Washington, D.C.: Government Printing Office.

Castro Pereda, Rafael. 1990b. Un bien público. *El Nuevo Día,* October 12, 49.

——. 1990b. Peligra un gran proyecto. *El Nuevo Día,* October 5, 61.

Centro: Journal of the Center for Puerto Rican Studies. 1996. Race and Identity. Thematic
    issue. 8 (1–2).

Chambers, Iain. 1994. *Migrancy, Culture, Identity.* London: Routledge.

Chambers, Iain, and Linda Curti, eds. 1996. *The Post-Colonial Question: Common Skies,
    Divided Horizons.* London: Routledge.

Chanlatte Baik, Luis A. 1976. *Cultura igneri: Investigaciones arqueológicas en Guayanilla,
    Puerto Rico.* Santo Domingo: Museo del Hombre Dominicano y Fundación García
    Arévalo.

——. 1986. *Cultura ostionoide: Un desarrollo agroalfarero antillano.* San Juan: n.p.

——. 1990. *Nueva arqueología de Puerto Rico: Su proyección en las Antillas.* Santo
    Domingo: Taller.

Chapman, Murray, and R. Mansell Prothero. 1983. Themes on Circulation in the Third
    World. *International Migration Review* 17 (4): 597–632.

——. 1985. Circulation between "Home" and Other Places: Some Propositions. In
    *Circulation in Population and Movement: Substance and Concepts from the
    Melanesian Case,* ed. Murray Chapman and R. Mansell Prothero, 1–12. New York:
    Routledge and Kegan Paul.

Chatterjee, Partha. 1993. *The Nation and Its Fragments: Colonial and Postcolonial
    Histories.* Princeton: Princeton University Press.

——. 1995. *Nationalist Thought and the Colonial World: A Derivative Discourse?* 2d ed.
    Minneapolis: University of Minnesota Press.

Chavez, Linda. 1991. *Out of the Barrio: Toward a New Politics of Hispanic Assimilation.*
    New York: Basic Books.

Chenault, Lawrence R. 1938. *The Puerto Rican Migrant in New York City.* New York:
    Columbia University Press.

Clifford, James. 1988. *The Predicament of Culture: Twentieth-Century Anthropology,
    Literature, and Art.* Cambridge: Harvard University Press.

——. 1997. *Routes: Travel and Translation in the Late Twentieth Century*. Cambridge: Harvard University Press.

Clifford, James, and George Marcus, eds. 1986. *Writing Culture: The Poetics and Politics of Ethnography*. Berkeley: University of California Press.

Cobas, José A., and Jorge Duany. 1997. *Cubans in Puerto Rico: Cultural Identity and Ethnic Economy*. Gainesville: University Press of Florida.

Coll y Toste, Cayetano. 1979 [1897]. *Prehistoria de Puerto Rico*. 2d ed. Cataño, P.R.: Litografía Metropolitana.

Collier, John, Jr., and Malcolm Collier. 1986. *Visual Anthropology: Photography as a Research Method*. Albuquerque: University of New Mexico Press.

Colón, Jesús. 1982. *A Puerto Rican in New York and Other Sketches*. 2d ed. New York: International Publishers.

El Comerciante: The Voice of the Puerto Rican Merchants Association. 1964. 1 (1).

Commonwealth of Puerto Rico, Department of Labor, Migration Division. May 1955–July 1962. Monthly Reports. Archivos Históricos de la Migración Puertorriqueña, Centro de Estudios Puertorriqueños, Hunter College, New York.

Continuations Committee. 1959. First Report of Continuation Committee, June 12. Third Migration Conference, San Juan, P.R., January 19–26, 1958. Mimeographed copy.

Conway, Dennis. 1988. Conceptualizing Contemporary Patterns of Caribbean International Mobility. *Caribbean Geography* 3 (2): 145–63.

——. 1989. Caribbean International Mobility Traditions. *Boletín de Estudios Latinoamericanos y del Caribe* 46:17–48.

——. 1994. The Complexity of Caribbean Migration. *Caribbean Affairs* 7 (4): 96–119.

Conway, Dennis, Mark Ellis, and Naragandat Shiwdhan. 1990. Caribbean International Circulation: Are Puerto Rican Women Tied-Circulators? *Geoforum* 21 (1): 51–66.

Corchado Juarbe, Carmen. 1993. *El indio en la poesía puertorriqueña: Desde 1847 hasta la generación del sesenta. Antología*. 2d ed. Río Piedras, P.R.: ESMACO.

Cordell, Dennis D., Joel W. Gregory, and Victor Piché. 1996. *Hoe and Wage: A Social History of a Circular Migration System in West Africa*. Boulder, Colo.: Westview.

Cordero-Guzmán, Héctor. 1989. The Socio-Demographic Characteristics of Return Migrants to Puerto Rico and Their Participation in the Labor Market, 1965–1980. Master's thesis, University of Chicago.

Corretjer, Juan Antonio. 1977. *Obras completas*. San Juan: Instituto de Cultura Puertorriqueña.

Cortés, Dharma, and Rodolfo R. Vega. 1996. The Meaning of Puerto Rican Identity and Acculturation among New York City Puerto Ricans. Paper presented at the Second Conference of the Puerto Rican Studies Association, San Juan, September 26–29.

Cortés, Félix, Joe Falcón, and Juan Flores. 1976. The Cultural Expression of Puerto Ricans in New York: A Theoretical Perspective and Critical Review. *Latin American Perspectives* 3 (2): 117–52.

Coss, Luis Fernando. 1996. *La nación en la orilla (respuesta a los posmodernos pesimistas)*. San Juan: Punto de Encuentro.

Cox, William V. 1899. Notes on Remarks of Mr. Wm. I. Buchanan, November 27. RU 70, Series 14, Box 52, Folder 26, Smithsonian Institution Archives, Washington, D.C.

Cruz, José E. 2000. Nosotros, puertorriqueños: Contribuciones a la política, los movimientos sociales y las fuerzas armadas. In *"Adiós Borinquen Querida": La diáspora puertorriqueña, su historia y sus aportaciones*, ed. Edna Acosta-Belén et al., 39–59. Albany, N.Y.: CELAC.

Cruz Báez, Angel David, and Thomas D. Boswell. 1997. *Atlas Puerto Rico*. Miami: Cuban American National Council.

Darrah, William C. 1977. *The World of Stereographs*. Gettysburg, Pa.: W. C. Darrah.

Dávila, Arlene. 1994. The Historical Development of the Taíno Indians as a Symbol of National Identity in Puerto Rico. Lecture to a course on Puerto Rican Culture, Universidad del Sagrado Corazón, Santurce, P.R.

——. 1997. *Sponsored Identities: Cultural Politics in Puerto Rico*. Philadelphia: Temple University Press.

——. 1998. Latinizing Culture: Art, Museums, and the Politics of U.S. Multicultural Encompassment. *Cultural Anthropology* 14 (2): 180–202.

——. 1999. Local/Diasporic Taínos: Towards a Cultural Politics of Memory, Reality, and Imagery. In *Taíno Revival: Critical Perspectives on Puerto Rican Identity and Cultural Politics*, ed. Gabriel Haslip-Viera, 11–30. New York: Centro de Estudios Puertorriqueños, Hunter College.

Dávila-López, Grace. 1996. Más allá de la nostalgia tropical: La construcción de la identidad en el teatro nuyorriqueño. Paper presented at the Second Conference of the Puerto Rican Studies Association, San Juan, September 26–29.

Davis, F. James. 1998. *Who Is Black? One Nation's Definition*. University Park: Pennsylvania State University Press.

Degler, Carl N. 1971. *Neither Black nor White: Slavery and Race Relations in Brazil and the United States*. New York: Macmillan.

Delano, Jack. 1990. *Puerto Rico Mío: Four Decades of Change*. Washington, D.C.: Smithsonian Institution Press.

Departamento de Educación (Puerto Rico). 1992. *Puerto Rico: Museos, monumentos y lugares históricos*. San Juan: Departamento de Educación.

Departamento de la Guerra, Dirección del Censo. 1900. *Informe sobre el censo de Puerto Rico, 1899*. Washington, D.C.: Imprenta del Gobierno.

Devereaux, Leslie, and Roger Hillman, eds. 1995. *Fields of Vision: Essays in Film Studies, Visual Anthropology, and Photography*. Berkeley: University of California Press.

El Diario–La Prensa. 1970. NY celebra Día de Marisol, August 28. Series VI, Box 1, Pura Belpré Papers, Centro de Estudios Puertorriqueños, Hunter College, New York.

——. 1971. Fiesta de San Juan Bautista es latir de corazón boricua, June 20. Series VI, Box 1, Pura Belpré Papers, Centro de Estudios Puertorriqueños, Hunter College, New York.

Díaz Quiñones, Arcadio. 1985. Tomás Blanco: Racismo, historia, esclavitud. Introduction and preliminary study to *El prejuicio racial en Puerto Rico*, by Tomás Blanco, 13–91. Río Piedras, P.R.: Huracán.

——. 1993. *La memoria rota*. Río Piedras, P.R.: Huracán.

——. 2000. *El arte de bregar: Ensayos*. San Juan: Callejón.

Díaz-Stevens, Ana María. 1993. *Oxcart Catholicism on Fifth Avenue: The Impact of Puerto Rican Migration upon the Archdiocese of New York*. Notre Dame: University of Notre Dame Press.

Dietz, James. 1986. *Economic History of Puerto Rico: Institutional Change and Capitalist Development*. Princeton: Princeton University Press.

Domínguez, Virginia. 1998. Exporting U.S. Concepts of Race: Are There Limits to the U.S. Model? *Social Research* 65 (2): 369–400.

Duany, Jorge. 1987. Imperialistas reacios: Los antropólogos norteamericanos en Puerto Rico, 1898–1950. *Revista del Instituto de Cultura Puertorriqueña* 26 (97): 3–11.

——. 1994. *Quisqueya on the Hudson: The Transnational Identity of Dominicans in Washington Heights*. New York: Dominican Studies Institute, City University of New York.

——. 1994–95. Common Threads or Disparate Agendas? Research Trends on Migration from and to Puerto Rico. *Centro* 7 (1): 60–77.

——. 1996. Imagining the Puerto Rican Nation: Recent Work on Cultural Identity. *Latin American Research Review* 31 (3): 248–67.

——. 1998a. Después de la modernidad: Debates contemporáneos sobre cultura y política en Puerto Rico. *Revista de Ciencias Sociales*, n.s., 5:218–41.

——. 1998b. Reconstructing Racial Identity: Ethnicity, Color, and Class among Dominicans in the United States and Puerto Rico. *Latin American Perspectives* 25 (3): 147–72.

——. 1999. Two Wings of the Same Bird? Contemporary Puerto Rican Attitudes toward Cuban Immigrants. *Cuban Studies* 30:26–51.

Duany, Jorge, Luisa Hernández Angueira, and César A. Rey. 1995. *El Barrio Gandul: Economía subterránea y migración indocumentada en Puerto Rico*. Caracas: Nueva Sociedad.

Duany, Luis A. 1987. Fostering Puerto Rican Small Business as a Device for Economic Development. Unpublished manuscript. New York Area Undergraduate Research Program, Columbia University.

Duchesne, Juan, Chloé Georas, Ramón Grosfoguel, Agustín Laó, Frances Negrón, Pedro Angel Rivera, and Aurea Sotomayor. 1997. La estadidad desde una perspectiva democrática radical. *Diálogo*, February, 30–31.

Duchesne Winter, Juan. 1999. Escritor, idioma, literatura: Las "defensas" que no ayudan. *Palique*, March 5, 44–45.

Duncan, Ronald J. 1978. The Taínos as a Symbol of Cultural Identity. *Revista/Review Interamericana* 8 (3): 500–510.

Earle, Edward W. 2000. On the Stump: Theodore Roosevelt in Stereographs. Electronic document. ⟨http://www.cmp.ucr.edu/essays/edward_earle/tr⟩.

Ecos de Nueva York. 1950, February 20. Periodicals collection, Centro de Estudios Puertorriqueños, Hunter College, New York.

Edwards, Elizabeth. 1990. Photographic "Types": The Pursuit of Method. *Visual Anthropology* 3:235–58.

——, ed. 1992. *Anthropology and Photography, 1860–1920*. New Haven: Yale University Press.

Ellis, Mark, Dennis Conway, and Adrian J. Bailey. 1996. *The Circular Migration of Puerto Rican Women: Towards a Gendered Explanation*. Working Paper no. 98-5, Population Institute for Research and Training, Indiana University.

Enchautegui, María E. 1991. *Subsequent Moves and the Dynamics of the Migration Decision: The Case of Return Migration to Puerto Rico*. Ann Arbor: Population Studies Center, University of Michigan.

Encyclopaedia Britannica. 2000. Gardener, Helen Hamilton. Electronic document. ⟨http://www.women.eb.com/women/articles/Gardener_Helen_Hamilton.html⟩.

Erasmo Vando Papers. 1917–88. Series III: New York (1922–1950); Series VI: Photographs. Centro de Estudios Puertorriqueños, Hunter College, New York.

Espinosa, Aurelio M. 1917–20. Letters to Franz Boas. Franz Boas Papers, American Philosophical Society, Philadelphia.

——. 1918. Romances de Puerto Rico. *Revue Hispanique* 43:1–56.

Estades, Rosa. 1978. *Patterns of Political Participation of Puerto Ricans in New York City.* Río Piedras, P.R.: Editorial Universitaria, Universidad de Puerto Rico.

Estado Libre Asociado de Puerto Rico, Departamento de Asuntos de la Comunidad Puertorriqueña en los Estados Unidos. 1989–90 to 1990–91. Informe anual. Archivos Históricos de la Migración Puertorriqueña, Centro de Estudios Puertorriqueños, Hunter College, New York.

Estado Libre Asociado de Puerto Rico, Departamento del Trabajo, División de Migración. 1953–54 to 1987–88. Informe anual. Archivos Históricos de la Migración Puertorriqueña, Centro de Estudios Puertorriqueños, Hunter College, New York.

Fahim, Hussein, ed. 1982. *Indigenous Anthropology in Non-Western Countries.* Durham, N.C.: Carolina Academic Press.

Falcón, Angelo. 1993. A Divided Nation: The Puerto Rican Diaspora in the United States and the Proposed Referendum. In *Colonial Dilemma: Critical Perspectives on Contemporary Puerto Rico*, ed. Edwin Meléndez and Edgardo Meléndez, 173–80. Boston: South End.

Fernández Méndez, Eugenio. 1955. Reflexiones sobre 50 años de cambio cultural en Puerto Rico. *Historia* 5 (2): 257–79.

———. 1959. *La identidad y la cultura: Críticas y valoraciones en torno a Puerto Rico.* San Juan: El Cemí.

———. 1964. *Historia cultural de Puerto Rico, 1493–1968.* San Juan: El Cemí.

———. 1972. *Art and Mythology of the Taíno Indians of the Greater West Indies.* San Juan: El Cemí.

———. 1975 [1954]. Más allá del insularismo: Hacia una civilización puertorriqueña. In *Antología del pensamiento puertorriqueño*, ed. Eugenio Fernández Méndez, 1:842–48. Río Piedras, P.R.: Editorial Universitaria.

———. 1980. *Puerto Rico: Filiación y sentido de una isla (cuatro ensayos en busca de una comunidad auténtica).* 2d ed. San Juan: Ariel.

———, ed. 1954. *Unidad y esencia del ethos puertorriqueños: Antología del pensamiento puertorriqueño sobre el problema de nuestra cultura.* 3 vols. Río Piedras, P.R.: Universidad de Puerto Rico.

———. 1957. *Crónicas de Puerto Rico: Desde la conquista hasta nuestros días.* San Juan: Ediciones del Gobierno, Estado Libre Asociado.

———. 1973. *Portrait of a Society: Readings on Puerto Rican Sociology.* Río Piedras, P.R.: Editorial Universitaria.

———. 1975. *Antología del pensamiento puertorriqueño.* 2 vols. Río Piedras, P.R.: Editorial Universitaria.

Ferrao, Luis Angel. 1990. *Pedro Albizu Campos y el nacionalismo puertorriqueño.* Río Piedras, P.R.: Cultural.

Ferré, Rosario. 1997. Blessing of Being Ambidextrous. *Venue: The San Juan Star Sunday Magazine*, January 10, 8–9.

———. 1998. Puerto Rico, U.S.A. *New York Times*, March 19, A21.

Ferrer, Melba. 1999. Students to Seek Hair for Taíno Study. *San Juan Star*, August 22, 5.

Fewkes, Jesse Walter. 1901. Notebook 43, Manuscript 4408, National Anthropological Archives, National Museum of Natural History, Smithsonian Institution, Washington, D.C.

———. 1902a. Diary, April 26–May 26. Puerto Rico trip. Notebook 44, Manuscript 4408,

National Anthropological Archives, National Museum of Natural History, Smithsonian Institution, Washington, D.C.

——. 1902b. Diary, May 27–June 30. Puerto Rico trip. Notebook 45, Manuscript 4408, National Anthropological Archives, National Museum of Natural History, Smithsonian Institution, Washington, D.C.

——. 1902c. Prehistoric Porto Rico. In *Proceedings of the American Association for the Advancement of Science. Fifty-first Meeting Held at Pittsburgh, PA, June–July, 1902*, 487–512. Washington, D.C.: Gibson Bros.

——. 1903. Diary and Drawings of Pictographs. Notebook 45b, Manuscript 4408, National Anthropological Archives, National Museum of Natural History, Smithsonian Institution, Washington, D.C.

——. 1904. Diary, March–April. Puerto Rico. Notebook 47a, Manuscript 4408, National Anthropological Archives, National Museum of Natural History, Smithsonian Institution, Washington, D.C.

——. 1970 [1907]. *The Aborigines of Porto Rico and Neighboring Islands*. New York: Johnson Reprint Corp.

Fitzpatrick, Joseph P. 1987. *Puerto Rican Americans: The Meaning of Migration to the Mainland*. 2d ed. Englewood Cliffs, N.J.: Prentice-Hall.

Flores, Juan. 1993. *Divided Borders: Essays on Puerto Rican Identity*. Houston: Arte Público Press.

——. 1997. *La venganza de Cortijo y otros ensayos*. Río Piedras, P.R.: Huracán.

——. 2000. *From Bomba to Hip Hop: Puerto Rican Culture and Latino Identity*. New York: Columbia University Press.

Flores, Juan, John Attinasi, and Pedro Pedraza, Jr. 1981. "La Carreta Made a U-Turn": Puerto Rican Language and Culture in the United States. *Daedalus* 110 (3): 193–217.

Flores Collazo, Margarita. 1998. La lucha por definir la nación: El debate en torno a la creación del Instituto de Cultura Puertorriqueña, 1955. *Op. Cit.: Revista del Centro de Investigaciones Históricas* 10:175–200.

Foreman, John. 1906. *The Philippine Islands: A Political, Geographical, Ethnographical, Social, and Commercial History of the Philippine Archipelago, Embracing the Whole Period of Spanish Rule, with an Account of the Succeeding American Insular Government*. 3d ed. London: T. Fisher Unwin.

Friedman, Robert. 1997. P.R.'s Art Exhibition Opens at Smithsonian. *San Juan Star*, October 11, 21.

Fundación Luis Muñoz Marín. 1949–64. Section V: Governor of Puerto Rico; Series I: General Correspondence; Folders 95–107: "Gobierno de Puerto Rico: Autocrítica e ideas, Asistentes, Teodoro Vidal." Fundación Luis Muñoz Marín, Trujillo Alto, P.R.

——. 1997. Inventario de piezas antiguas donadas por Teodoro Vidal el 9 de junio de 1997. Unpublished manuscript, Fundación Luis Muñoz Marín, Trujillo Alto, P.R.

Gandhi, Leela. 1998. *Postcolonial Theory: A Critical Introduction*. New York: Columbia University Press.

García, Gervasio. 1997–98. El otro es uno: Puerto Rico en la mirada norteamericana del 1898. *Fundamentos: Cuaderno de la Variante Fundamentos del Conocimiento en las Ciencias Humanas* 5–6:3–25.

García, Osvaldo. 1989. *Fotografías para la historia de Puerto Rico, 1844–1952*. Río Piedras, P.R.: Editorial de la Universidad de Puerto Rico.

García-Calderón, Myrna. 1998. *Lecturas desde el fragmento: Escritura contemporánea e imaginario cultural en Puerto Rico*. Berkeley: Latinoamericana Editores.

García Canclini, Néstor. 1990. *Culturas híbridas: Estrategias para entrar y salir de la modernidad*. Mexico City: Grijalbo.

García Passalacqua, Juan Manuel. 2000. The "National Question" Again on the Table. *San Juan Star*, May 7, 26.

———, ed. 1998. *Vate, de la cuna a la cripta: El nacionalismo cultural de Luis Muñoz Marín*. San Juan: Editorial LEA.

García Ramis, Magali. 1995. Retrato del dominicano que pasó por puertorriqueño y pudo emigrar a mejor vida a Estados Unidos. In *Las noches del riel de oro*, 107–12. Río Piedras, P.R.: Cultural.

Garrido, Pablo. 1952. *Esoteria y fervor populares de Puerto Rico: Contribución al estudio y análisis de la conducta mística del pueblo en sus aspectos intuitivos, tradicionales y vulgares*. Madrid: Cultura Hispánica.

Geary, Christraud M., and Virginia-Lee Webb, eds. 1998. *Delivering Views: Distant Cultures in Early Postcards*. Washington, D.C.: Smithsonian Institution Press.

Gellner, Ernest. 1983. *Nations and Nationalism*. Oxford: Blackwell.

Gelpí, Juan G. 1993. *Literatura y paternalismo en Puerto Rico*. Río Piedras, P.R.: Editorial de la Universidad de Puerto Rico.

Genoveva de Arteaga Papers. 1913–91. Series IV: Subject File; Series V: Photographs and Scrapbooks. Centro de Estudios Puertorriqueños, Hunter College, New York.

Gettleman, Marvin E. 1971. John H. Finley y el Caribe, 1900–1903: Contribuciones a un consenso imperialista. *Revista de Ciencias Sociales* 15 (3): 303–16.

Gillis, John R., ed. 1994. *Commemorations: The Politics of National Identity*. Princeton: Princeton University Press.

Ginorio, Angela Beatriz. 1971. A Study in Racial Perception in Puerto Rico. Master's thesis, University of Puerto Rico.

———. 1979. A Comparison of Puerto Ricans in New York with Native Puerto Ricans and Native Americans on Two Measures of Acculturation: Gender Role and Racial Identification. Ph.D. diss., Fordham University.

Glasser, Ruth. 1995. *My Music Is My Flag: Puerto Rican Musicians and Their New York Communities, 1917–1940*. Berkeley: University of California Press.

Go, Julian. 2000. Chains of Empire, Projects of State: Political Education and U.S. Colonial Rule in Puerto Rico and the Philippines. *Comparative Studies in Society and History* 42 (2): 333–62.

Godoy, Ricardo, Irineu Carvalho, Thomas Hexner, and Glenn P. Jenkins. 2000. Review of Quantitative Studies of Puerto Rican Migration. Unpublished manuscript, Sustainable International Development Program, Brandeis University, Waltham, Mass., October 12.

Godreau, Isar P. 2000. La semántica fugitiva: "Raza," color y vida cotidiana en Puerto Rico. *Revista de Ciencias Sociales*, n.s., 9:52–71.

Godreau-Santiago, Isar Pilar. 1999. Missing the Mix: San Antón and the Racial Dynamics of "Nationalism" in Puerto Rico. Ph.D. diss., University of California, Santa Cruz.

González, Libia M. 1998a. La ilusión del paraíso: Fotografías y relatos de viajeros sobre Puerto Rico, 1898–1900. In *Los arcos de la memoria: El '98 de los pueblos puertorriqueños*, ed. Silvia Alvarez Curbelo, Mary Frances Gallart, and Carmen I. Raffucci, 273–304. San Juan: Oficina del Presidente de la Universidad de Puerto

Rico, Comité del Centenario de 1898, Asociación Puertorriqueña de Historiadores, and Postdata.

——. 1998b. Progreso y modernidad: Las ferias de fin de siglo y los hombres de letras en Puerto Rico. In *La nación soñada: Cuba, Puerto Rico y Filipinas ante el 98*, ed. Consuelo Naranjo Orovio, Miguel Angel Puig, and Luis Miguel García, 539–46. Madrid: Doce Calles.

González, Lydia M., ed. 1993. *La tercera raíz: Presencia africana en Puerto Rico*. San Juan: Centro de Estudios de la Realidad Puertorriqueña.

González Díaz, Emilio. 1991. *La política de los empresarios puertorriqueños*. Río Piedras, P.R.: Huracán.

Gordon, Maxine. 1949. Race Patterns and Prejudice in Puerto Rico. *American Sociological Review* 14 (2): 294–301.

——. 1950. Cultural Aspects of Puerto Rico's Race Problem. *American Sociological Review* 15 (3): 382–92.

Greehalgh, Paul. 1988. *Ephemeral Vistas: The Expositions Universelles, Great Exhibitions, and World's Fairs, 1851–1939*. Manchester: Manchester University Press.

Grose, Howard B. 1910. *Advance in the Antilles: The New Era in Cuba and Porto Rico*. New York: Eaton and Mains.

Grosfoguel, Ramón. 1994–95. Caribbean Colonial Immigrants in the Metropoles: A Research Agenda. *Centro* 7 (1): 82–95.

Grosvenor, Gilbert Hovey. 1906. Prosperous Porto Rico. *National Geographic Magazine* 17 (12): 712.

Guerra, Lillian. 1998. *Popular Expression and National Identity in Puerto Rico: The Struggle for Self, Community, and Nation*. Gainesville: University Press of Florida.

Gupta, Akhil, and James Ferguson, eds. 1997. *Culture, Power, Place: Explorations in Critical Anthropology*. Durham: Duke University Press.

Guzmán, Betsy. 2001. The Hispanic Population 2000. Census 2000 Brief. Electronic document. ⟨http://www.census.gov/population/www/cen2000/briefs.html⟩.

Haberstich, David. 1991. Stereo Photographers—Stereographs, 1893–1904, #414. Electronic document. ⟨http://www.americanhistory.si.edu/archives/d6414a.htm⟩.

Haeberlin, Hermann K. 1917. Some Archaeological Work in Porto Rico. *American Anthropologist* 19:214–38.

Hall, Stuart. 1994. Cultural Identity and Diaspora. In *Colonial Discourse and Postcolonial Theory: A Reader*, ed. Patrick Williams and Laura Chrisman, 392–403. New York: Columbia University Press.

——, ed. 1997. *Representation: Cultural Representations and Signifying Practices*. London: Sage.

Handler, Richard. 1988. *Nationalism and the Politics of Culture in Quebec*. Madison: University of Wisconsin Press.

——. 1994. Is "Identity" a Useful Cross-Cultural Concept? In *Commemorations: The Politics of National Identity*, ed. John R. Gillis, 27–40. Princeton: Princeton University Press.

Harasym, Sarah, ed. 1990. *The Post-Colonial Critic: Interviews, Strategies, Dialogues. Gayatri Chakravorty Spivak*. London: Routledge.

Hardman, Larry. 1999. Civil War Units: 7th Ohio Volunteer Infantry, USA. Electronic document. ⟨http://www.ehistory.com/uscw/features/regimental/ohio/union/7thOhio/BiogC.c fm⟩.

Harris, Marvin. 1964. *Patterns of Race in the Americas*. New York: Norton.

Haslip-Viera, Gabriel, ed. 1999. *Taíno Revival: Critical Perspectives on Puerto Rican Identity and Cultural Politics*. New York: Centro de Estudios Puertorriqueños, Hunter College.

Helen Hamilton Gardener Photographic Collection. Ca. 1906. Photo lot 98, drawer 55. National Anthropological Archives, National Museum of Natural History, Smithsonian Institution.

Henderson, Amy, and Adrienne L. Kaeppler, eds. 1997. *Exhibiting Dilemmas: Issues of Representation at the Smithsonian*. Washington, D.C.: Smithsonian Institution Press.

Herbstein, Judith F. 1978. Rituals and Politics of the Puerto Rican "Community" in New York City. Ph.D. diss., City University of New York.

Hermandad de Artistas Gráficos, ed. 1998. *Puerto Rico: Arte e identidad*. Río Piedras, P.R.: Editorial de la Universidad de Puerto Rico.

Hernández, Carmen Dolores. 1997. *Puerto Rican Voices in English: Interviews with Writers*. Westport, Conn.: Praeger.

Hernández, David, and Janet Scheff. 1996–97. Puerto Rican Geographic Mobility: The Making of a Deterritorialized Nationality. *Latino Review of Books* 2 (3): 2–8.

———. 1997. Puerto Rican Ethnicity and U.S. Citizenship on the Puerto Rico–New York Commute. Paper presented at the XX International Congress of the Latin American Studies Association, Guadalajara, Mexico, April 17–19.

Hernández, José. 1994. *Conquered Peoples in America*. 5th ed. Dubuque, Iowa: Kendall/Hunt.

Hernández Alvarez, José. 1967. *Return Migration to Puerto Rico*. Berkeley: Institute for International Studies, University of California.

Hernández Cruz, Juan. 1985. ¿Migración de retorno o circulación de obreros boricuas? *Revista de Ciencias Sociales* 24 (1–2): 81–112.

———. 1994. *Corrientes migratorias en Puerto Rico/Migratory Trends in Puerto Rico*. San Germán, P.R.: Centro de Publicaciones, Universidad Interamericana de Puerto Rico.

Hilgard, E. W. 1900. Geographic Nomenclature. *National Geographic Magazine* 11 (1): 36–37.

Hill, Robert T. 1899a. Mineral Resources of Porto Rico. *U.S. Geological Survey, Annual Report for 1898–99* (20): 771–78.

———. 1899b. *Notes on the Forest Conditions of Porto Rico*. Bulletin no. 25, U.S. Department of Agriculture, Division of Forestry. Washington, D.C.: Government Printing Office.

———. 1899c. Porto Rico. *National Geographic Magazine* 11 (3): 93–112.

———. 1903. *Cuba and Porto Rico, with the Other Islands of the West Indies*. 2d ed. New York: Century.

Hinsley, Curtis W. 1981. *The Smithsonian and the American Indian: Making a Moral Anthropology in Victorian America*. 2d ed. Washington, D.C.: Smithsonian Institution Press.

———. 1991. "The World as a Marketplace": Commodification of the Exotic at the World's Columbian Exposition, Chicago, 1893. In *Exhibiting Cultures: The Poetics and Politics of Museum Display*, ed. Ivan Karp and Stephen D. Lavine, 344–65. Washington, D.C.: Smithsonian Institution Press.

History Task Force, Centro de Estudios Puertorriqueños. 1979. *Labor Migration under Capitalism: The Puerto Rican Experience*. New York: Monthly Review Press.

Hobsbawm, Eric. 1983. Introduction: Inventing Traditions. In *The Invention of Tradition*, ed. Eric Hobsbawm and Terence Ranger, 1–14. Cambridge: Cambridge University Press.

———. 1990. *Nations and Nationalism since 1790: Programme, Myth, Reality*. Cambridge: Cambridge University Press.

Hockings, Paul, ed. 1995. *Principles of Visual Anthropology*. New York: Mouton de Gruyter.

Hoerder, Dirk, ed. 1985. *Labor Migration in the Atlantic Economies: The European and North American Working Classes during the Period of Industrialization*. Westport, Conn.: Greenwood.

Hoetink, Harmannus. 1967. *Caribbean Race Relations: A Study of Two Variants*. London: Oxford University Press.

Holmes, W. H. 1907. *Twenty-fifth Annual Report of the Bureau of American Ethnology to the Secretary of the Smithsonian Institution, 1902–1903*. Washington, D.C.: Government Printing Office.

Hostos, Adolfo de. 1941. *Anthropological Papers*. San Juan: Office of the Historian, Government of Puerto Rico.

Hulme, Peter. 1986. *Colonial Encounters: Europe and the Native Caribbean, 1492–1797*. London: Methuen.

Hutchinson, John. 1994. Cultural Nationalism and Moral Regeneration. In *Nationalism*, ed. John Hutchinson and Anthony D. Smith, 122–31. Oxford: Oxford University Press.

Hutchinson, John, and Anthony D. Smith, eds. 1994. *Nationalism*. Oxford: Oxford University Press.

Hyde, John. 1900. Puerto Rico, Not Porto Rico. *National Geographic Magazine* 11 (1): 37–38.

Instituto de Cultura Puertorriqueña, ed. 1997. *Ocho trabajos de investigación arqueológica en Puerto Rico*. San Juan: Instituto de Cultura Puertorriqueña.

James, Arthur. N.d. *Twenty Years in Porto Rico: A Record of Presbyterian Missionary Work since the American Occupation*. New York: Board of Home Missions, Presbyterian Church in the U.S.

Jenkins, James. 1977. *Puerto Rican Politics in New York City*. Washington, D.C.: University Press of America.

Jesús Colón Papers. 1901–74. Series V: Organizational Activities; Series VI: New York Organizations; Series IX: Photographs. Centro de Estudios Puertorriqueños, Hunter College, New York.

Jiménez Román, Miriam. 1999. The Indians Are Coming! The Indians Are Coming! The Taíno and Puerto Rican Identity. In *Taíno Revival: Critical Perspectives on Puerto Rican Identity and Cultural Politics*, ed. Gabriel Haslip-Viera, 75–108. New York: Centro de Estudios Puertorriqueños, Hunter College.

Johnson, E. Verner, and Associates. 1992. Folk Arts and Traditions Museum: San Juan, Puerto Rico. Feasibility Report. Unpublished manuscript, Boston, Mass., November 17.

Junta de Planificación de Puerto Rico. 1980–98. *Balanza de pagos*. San Juan: Junta de Planificación de Puerto Rico.

Justo A. Martí Photographic Collection. 1948–85. Series II: Photographs. Unprocessed
    magazines and programs. Centro de Estudios Puertorriqueños, Hunter College,
    New York.
Kantrowitz, Nathan. 1971. Algunas consecuencias raciales: Diferencias educativas y
    ocupacionales entre los puertorriqueños blancos y no blancos en los Estados Unidos
    continentales, 1950. *Revista de Ciencias Sociales* 15 (3): 387–97.
Karp, Ivan, Christine Mullen Kreamer, and Stephen D. Lavine, eds. 1992. *Museums and
    Communities: The Politics of Public Culture.* Washington, D.C.: Smithsonian
    Institution Press.
Karp, Ivan, and Stephen D. Lavine, eds. 1991. *Exhibiting Cultures: The Poetics and
    Politics of Museum Displays.* Washington, D.C.: Smithsonian Institution Press.
Kearney, Michael. 1991. Borders and Boundaries of the State and Self at the End of
    Empire. *Journal of Historical Sociology* 4 (1): 52–74.
——. 1995. The Local and the Global: The Anthropology of Globalization and
    Transnationalism. *Annual Review of Anthropology* 24:547–65.
Kedourie, Elie. 1993. *Nationalism.* 4th ed. Oxford: Blackwell.
Kennedy, Richard. 1998. Rethinking the Philippine Exhibit at the 1904 St. Louis World's
    Fair. In *1998 Smithsonian Folklife Festival,* 41–44. Washington, D.C.: Smithsonian
    Institution.
Kerkhof, Erna. 2000. Contested Belonging: Circular Migration and Puerto Rican
    Identity. Ph.D. diss., University of Utrecht, Holland.
Kinsbruner, Jay. 1996. *Not of Pure Blood: The Free People of Color and Racial Prejudice in
    Nineteenth-Century Puerto Rico.* Durham: Duke University Press.
Kramer, Paul. 1999. Making Concessions: Race and Empire Revisited at the Philippine
    Exposition, St. Louis, 1901–1905. *Radical History Review* 73:74–114.
Kurin, Richard. 1997. *Reflections of a Culture Broker: A View from the Smithsonian.*
    Washington, D.C.: Smithsonian Institution Press.
La Gorce, John Oliver. 1924. Porto Rico, the Gate of Riches: Amazing Prosperity Has
    Been the Lot of Ponce de León's Isle under American Administration. *National
    Geographic Magazine* 46 (12): 599–651.
Laó, Agustín. 1997. Islands at the Crossroads: Puerto Ricanness Traveling between the
    Translocal Nation and the Global City. In *Puerto Rican Jam: Essays on Culture and
    Politics,* ed. Frances Negrón-Muntaner and Ramón Grosfoguel, 169–88.
    Minneapolis: University of Minnesota Press.
Lapp, Michael. 1990. Managing Migration: The Migration Division of Puerto Rico and
    Puerto Ricans in New York City, 1948–1968. Ph.D. diss., Johns Hopkins University.
Lassalle, Yvonne M., and Marvette Pérez. 1997. "Dis-"Locating Puerto Rican-ness and Its
    Privileged Sites of Production. *Radical History* 68:54–78.
Lastra, Sarai. 1999. Juan Bobo: A Folkloric Information System. *Library Trends* 47 (3).
    Electronic document. ⟨http://www.northernlight.com⟩.
Latin American Migration Project. 2001. Population Studies Center, University of
    Pennsylvania. World Wide Web site. ⟨http://www.pop.upenn.edu/lamp/⟩.
Latin American Perspectives. 1992. The Politics of Ethnic Construction: Hispanic,
    Chicano, Latino. . . ? Thematic issue. 19 (4).
Lauria, Antonio. 1964. Respeto, Relajo, and Interpersonal Relations in Puerto Rico.
    Anthropological Quarterly 3:53–67.
Lauria-Perricelli, Antonio. 1989. A Study in Historical and Critical Anthropology: The
    Making of the People of Puerto Rico. Ph.D. diss., New School for Social Research.

Lesser, Alexander. 1985. Franz Boas and the Modernization of Anthropology. In *History, Evolution, and the Concept of Culture*, ed. Sidney W. Mintz, 15–33. Cambridge: Cambridge University Press.

Levine, Robert. 1989. *Images of History: Nineteenth and Early Twentieth Century Latin American Photographs as Documents*. Durham: Duke University Press.

Leymarie, Isabelle. 1994. Salsa and Migration. In *The Commuter Nation: Perspectives on Puerto Rican Migration*, ed. Carlos Antonio Torre, Hugo Rodríguez Vecchini, and William Burgos, 343–64. Río Piedras, P.R.: Editorial de la Universidad de Puerto Rico.

Library of Congress. 2000. Helen Hamilton Gardener (Alice Chenoweth Day), 1853–1925. Electronic document. ⟨http://www.rs6.loc.gov⟩.

Lidchi, Henrietta. 1997. The Poetics and the Politics of Exhibiting Other Cultures. In *Representation: Cultural Representations and Signifying Practices*, ed. Stuart Hall, 151–222. London: Sage.

Lloréns Torres, Luis. 1967 [1898]. *América: Estudios históricos y filosóficos sobre Puerto Rico*. 2d ed. Hato Rey, P.R.: Cordillera.

Loomba, Ania. 1998. *Colonialism/Postcolonialism*. London: Routledge.

López, Mayra I. 1998. Adaptación sin imitación: Luis Muñoz Marín y el discurso de la migración (1947–1960). In *Vate, de la cuna a la cripta: El nacionalismo cultural de Luis Muñoz Marín*, ed. Juan Manuel García Passalacqua, 247–71. San Juan: Editorial LEA.

López-Baralt, Mercedes. 1985. *El mito taíno: Lévi-Strauss en las Antillas*. 2d ed. Río Piedras, P.R.: Huracán.

López Bauzá, Juan. 1999. Rosario Ferré: El debate del idioma, los escritores de ayer y hoy. *Palique*, February 19, 32–34.

López de Molina, Diana. 1980. La arqueología como ciencia social. In *Crisis y crítica de las ciencias sociales en Puerto Rico*, ed. Rafael R. Ramírez and Wenceslao Serra Deliz, 81–96. Río Piedras, P.R.: Centro de Investigaciones Sociales, Universidad de Puerto Rico.

López Sotomayor, Diana. 1975. Vieques: Un momento de su historia. Master's thesis, Universidad Nacional Autónoma de México.

Lorenzo-Hernández, José. 1999. The Nuyorican's Dilemma: Categorization of Returning Migrants in Puerto Rico. *International Migration Review* 33 (4): 988–1013.

Lutz, Catherine, and Jane Collins. 1993. *Reading National Geographic*. Chicago: University of Chicago Press.

——. 1994. The Photograph as an Intersection of Gazes: The Example of National Geographic. In *Visualizing Theory: Selected Essays from V.A.R., 1990–1994*, ed. Lucien Taylor, 363–84. New York: Routledge.

McCoy, Alfred W. 2000. Orientalism of the Philippine Photograph: America Discovers the Philippine Islands. Electronic document. ⟨http://www.library.wisc.edu/etext/seait/instruct.html⟩.

Maldonado-Denis, Manuel. 1972. *Puerto Rico: A Socio-Historic Interpretation*. New York: Vintage.

——. 1984. *Puerto Rico y Estados Unidos: Emigración y colonialismo*. 4th ed. San Juan: Compromiso.

Marietta, Manuel. 1955. La celebración del Día de los Hijos Ausentes en los Pueblos de Puerto Rico. *Puerto Rico y Nueva York: Magazine Mensual Ilustrado* 2 (2): 32.

Marqués, René. 1963. *La carreta*. Río Piedras, P.R.: Cultural.

——. 1977. *El puertorriqueño dócil y otros ensayos (1953–1971)*. San Juan: Antillana.

——, ed. 1966. *Emigración*. 2d ed. San Juan: División de Educación de la Comunidad, Departamento de Instrucción Pública.

Martínez, Andrea. 1993. Eliminarán la Oficina de Asuntos de la Comunidad Puertorriqueña. *El Nuevo Día*, January 14, 20.

Martínez, Angel R. 1988. The Effects of Acculturation and Racial Identity on Self-Esteem and Psychological Well-Being among Young Puerto Ricans. Ph.D. diss., City University of New York.

Martínez, Oscar J. 1994. *Border People: Life and Society on the U.S.-Mexico Borderlands*. Tucson: University of Arizona Press.

Martínez-Echazábal, Lourdes. 1998. Mestizaje and the Discourse of National/Cultural Identity in Latin America. *Latin American Perspectives* 25 (3): 21–42.

Martínez–San Miguel, Yolanda. 1996. Puerto Rico mío: Mitificación y crisis del proyecto desarrollista en las fotografías de Jack Delano. *Postdata* 12:42–51.

——. 1997a. ¿Confederación caribeña? Migraciones de cubanos y dominicanos a Puerto Rico y la formación de fronteras intranacionales en la representación cultural. Paper presented at the XX Congress of the Latin American Studies Association, Guadalajara, Mexico, April 17–19.

——. 1997b. Deconstructing Puerto Ricanness through Sexuality: Female Counternarratives on Puerto Rican Identity (1894–1934). In *Puerto Rican Jam: Essays on Culture and Politics*, ed. Frances Negrón-Muntaner and Ramón Grosfoguel, 127–39. Minneapolis: University of Minnesota Press.

Mason, J. Alden. 1914–20. Letters to Franz Boas. Franz Boas Papers, American Philosophical Society, Philadelphia.

——. 1916. Porto-Rican Folk-Lore: Riddles. Edited by Aurelio M. Espinosa. *Journal of American Folk-Lore* 29:423–504.

——. 1918. Porto-Rican Folk-Lore: Décimas, Christmas Carols, Nursery Rhymes, and Other Songs. Edited by Aurelio M. Espinosa. *Journal of American Folk-Lore* 31:289–450.

——. 1920. Spanish Romance from Porto-Rico. Edited by Aurelio M. Espinosa. *Journal of American Folk-Lore* 33:76–79.

——. 1921. Porto-Rican Folk-Lore: Folk-Tales. Edited by Aurelio M. Espinosa. *Journal of American Folk-Lore* 34:143–208.

——. 1922. Porto-Rican Folk-Lore: Folk-Tales. Edited by Aurelio M. Espinosa. *Journal of American Folk-Lore* 35:1–61.

——. 1924. Porto-Rican Folk-Lore: Folk-Tales. Edited by Aurelio M. Espinosa. *Journal of American Folk-Lore* 37:247–344.

——. 1925. Porto-Rican Folk-Lore: Folk-Tales. Edited by Aurelio M. Espinosa. *Journal of American Folk-Lore* 38:507–618.

——. 1926. Porto-Rican Folk-Lore: Folk-Tales. Edited by Aurelio M. Espinosa. *Journal of American Folk-Lore* 39:227–369.

——. 1927. Porto-Rican Folk-Lore. Edited by Aurelio M. Espinosa. *Journal of American Folk-Lore* 40:313–414.

——. 1929. Porto-Rican Folk-Lore. Edited by Aurelio M. Espinosa. *Journal of American Folk-Lore* 42:85–156.

——. 1941. A Large Archaeological Site at Capá, Utuado, with Notes on Other Porto

Rican Sites Visited in 1914–1915. *Scientific Survey of Porto Rico and the Virgin Islands* 18 (2): 207–72.

——. 1956. Letters to Aurelio M. Espinosa. J. Alden Mason Papers, American Philosophical Society, Philadelphia.

——. 1956–57. Letters to Ricardo Alegría. J. Alden Mason Papers, American Philosophical Society, Philadelphia.

——. 1960. *Folklore puertorriqueño.* Vol. 1, *Adivinanzas.* Edited by Aurelio M. Espinosa. San Juan: Instituto de Cultura Puertorriqueña.

Mason, Otis T. 1877. *The Latimer Collection of Antiquities from Porto Rico in the National Museum at Washington, D.C.* Washington, D.C.: Government Printing Office.

——. 1898. Letter to Frederick W. True, October 1. RU 70, Series 14, Box 52, Folder 17, Smithsonian Institution Archives, Washington, D.C.

——. 1899. *The Latimer Collection of Antiquities from Porto Rico in the National Museum and the Guesde Collection of Antiquities in Pointe-a-Pitre, Guadeloupe, West Indies.* Washington, D.C.: Smithsonian Institution.

Massey, Douglas S., Rafael Alarcón, Jorge Durand, and Humberto González. 1987. *Return to Aztlan: The Social Process of International Migration from Western Mexico.* Berkeley: University of California Press.

Massey, Douglas S., Joaquín Arango, Graeme Hugo, Ali Kouaouci, Adela Pellegrino, and J. Edward Taylor. 1998. *Worlds in Motion: Understanding International Migration at the End of the Millennium.* Oxford: Clarendon Press.

Massey, Douglas S., Luin Goldring, and Jorge Durand. 1994. Continuities in Transnational Migration: An Analysis of Nineteen Mexican Communities. *American Journal of Sociology* 99 (6): 1492–1533.

Massey, Douglas S., and René Zenteno. 1998. A Validation of the Ethnosurvey: The Case of Mexico-U.S. Migration. Unpublished manuscript, Population Studies Center, University of Pennsylvania.

Matos-Rodríguez, Félix V. 1999. Their Islands and Our People: U.S. Writing about Puerto Rico, 1898–1920. *Centro* 11 (1): 33–50.

Maxwell, Anne. 1999. *Colonial Photography and Exhibitions: Representations of the "Native" and the Making of European Identities.* London: Leicester University Press.

Meléndez, Edwin. 1993a. *Los que se van, los que regresan: Puerto Rican Migration to and from the United States, 1982–1988.* Political Economy Working Paper Series no. 1. New York: Centro de Estudios Puertorriqueños, Hunter College.

——. 1993b. Understanding Latino Poverty. *Sage Race Relations Abstracts* 18 (2): 1–42.

——. 1994. Puerto Rican Migration and Occupational Selectivity, 1982–88. *International Migration Review* 28 (1): 49–67.

Meléndez, Edwin, and Edgardo Meléndez, eds. 1993. *Colonial Dilemma: Critical Perspectives on Contemporary Puerto Rico.* Boston: South End.

Mendelson, Johanna. 1977. *Divine Favors, Human Vows: Milagros from Puerto Rico.* Exhibition script. Washington, D.C.: Smithsonian Institution Traveling Exhibition Service.

Méndez, José Luis, ed. 1980. *La agresión cultural norteamericana en Puerto Rico.* Mexico City: Grijalbo.

Méndez Caratini, Héctor. 1990. *Tradiciones: Álbum de la puertorriqueñidad.* San Juan: Brown, Newson and Córdova.

Mercado Vega, César A. 1978. Memorandum to Rosendo Miranda Torres, November 13. Xeroxed copy. Junta de Planificación de Puerto Rico, San Juan.

Mexican Migration Project. 1999. Population Studies Center, University of Pennsylvania. World Wide Web site. ⟨http://www.pop.upenn.edu/mexmig⟩.

Mills, C. Wright, Clarence Senior, and Rose Kohn Goldsen. 1950. *The Puerto Rican Journey: New York's Newest Migrants*. New York: Harper.

Mintz, Sidney W. 1966. Puerto Rico: An Essay in the Definition of a National Culture. In *Selected Background Studies Prepared for the U.S.-P.R. Commission on the Status of Puerto Rico*, ed. U.S.-P.R. Commission on the Status of Puerto Rico, 339–434. Washington, D.C.: Government Printing Office.

Mohr, Nicholasa. 1987. Puerto Rican Writers in the United States, Puerto Rican Writers in Puerto Rico: A Separation beyond Language. *Américas* 15 (2): 87–92.

Monserrat, Joseph. 1961. Suggestions for a New Approach to Migration. Confidential Memorandum to Luis Muñoz Marín, February 9. Section V: Governor of Puerto Rico, 1949–1964; Series I: General Correspondence; Departments, 9: Labor—Migration Division. Fundación Luis Muñoz Marín, Trujillo Alto, P.R.

——. 1968. Planeamiento comunal para la integración del puertorriqueño en los Estados Unidos. In *El libro puertorriqueño de Nueva York*. Vol. 1. Ed. Federico Ribes Tovar, 201–8. New York: Plus Ultra.

Montero Seplowin, Virginia. 1971. Análisis de la identificación racial de los puertorriqueños en Filadelfia. *Revista de Ciencias Sociales* 15 (1): 143–48.

Moore-Gilbert, Bart. 1997. *Postcolonial Theory: Contexts, Practices, Politics*. London: Verso.

Morales Cabrera, Pablo. 1932. *Puerto Rico indígena: Prehistoria y protohistoria de Puerto Rico*. San Juan: Imprenta Venezuela.

Moreno, María José. 1997. Identity Formation and Organizational Change in Nonprofit Institutions: A Comparative Study of Two Hispanic Museums. Ph.D. diss., Columbia University.

Morris, Nancy. 1995. *Puerto Rico: Culture, Politics, and Identity*. Westport, Conn.: Praeger.

——. 1997. Nosotros y ellos: Reflexiones de activistas políticos sobre la identidad puertorriqueña. *Revista de Ciencias Sociales*, n.s., 2:42–67.

Moscoso, Francisco. 1986. *Tribus y clases en el Caribe antiguo*. San Pedro de Macorís, Dominican Republic: Universidad Central del Este.

——. 1999. *Sociedad y economía de los taínos*. Río Piedras, P.R.: Edil.

Mulero, Leonor. 1997. Una santa colección. *Revista Domingo, El Nuevo Día*, December 28, 5–6.

——. 1998a. Fondos del gobierno para una exhibición boricua. *El Nuevo Día*, July 30, 26.

——. 1998b. Habla Vidal. *El Nuevo Día*, July 31, 81.

——. 1999. Ingresa la Isla a las estadísticas del censo federal. *El Nuevo Día*, January 9, 10.

El Mundo. 1945. Comité Bell preocupado con gobierno insular. May 2, 5.

——. 1950. Attilio Moscioni murió en New York. Vino a la isla en 1898, con tropas de los E.U. March 22, 2.

——. 1954. Estudio población NY: Distingue a boricuas de blancos. November 24, 1, 16.

——. 1958. Senador J. W. Fulbright: Afirma la isla es ejemplo solución racial. April 15, 1.

——. 1959. George William Culberson: Impresionado por ausencia de prejuicios raciales aquí. October 19, 17.

———. 1990. La nota negativa de la década. January 1, n.p.

Muñoz Marín, Luis. 1946. Foro público sobre el problema poblacional de Puerto Rico. Resumen de las soluciones ofrecidas por los ponentes en la sesión de julio 19, 1946. Memorandum to Max Egloff, September 28. Section IV: President of the Senate, 1941–1948; Series 2: Insular Government; Subseries 1: Fortaleza; Box 1B: Office of Information; Folder 16. Fundación Luis Muñoz Marín, Trujillo Alto, P.R.

———. 1958. Celebration of the Tenth Anniversary of the Migration Division of Puerto Rico's Department of Labor. Section V: Governor of Puerto Rico, 1949–1964; Series 9: Speeches; Box 13: Status; Folder 8. Fundación Luis Muñoz Marín, Trujillo Alto, P.R.

———. 1960. Discurso a los puertorriqueños en Nueva York pronunciado por el Gobernador Muñoz Marín el 10 de abril de 1960. Section V: Governor of Puerto Rico, 1949–1964; Series 9: Speeches; Box 16: Status; Folder 7. Fundación Luis Muñoz Marín, Trujillo Alto, P.R.

———. 1963. Mensaje para el anuario del Desfile Puertorriqueño. Section V: Governor of Puerto Rico, 1949–1964; Series 9: Speeches; Box 21: Status; Folder 5. Fundación Luis Muñoz Marín, Trujillo Alto, P.R.

———. 1975a [1952]. El buen saber del jíbaro puertorriqueño. In *Antología del pensamiento puertorriqueño*, ed. Eugenio Fernández Méndez, 1:797–807. Río Piedras, P.R.: Editorial Universitaria.

———. 1975b [1940]. Cultura y democracia. In *Antología del pensamiento puertorriqueño*, ed. Eugenio Fernández Méndez, 1:790–96. Río Piedras, P.R.: Editorial Universitaria.

———. 1985 [1953]. La personalidad puertorriqueña en el Estado Libre Asociado. In *Del cañaveral a la fábrica: Cambio social en Puerto Rico*, ed. Eduardo Rivera Medina and Rafael L. Ramírez, 99–108. Río Piedras, P.R.: Huracán.

———. N.d. Puertorriqueños y cultura. Section V: Governor of Puerto Rico, 1949–1964; Series 17: Miscellaneous documents; Subseries 8: Notes for writings; Folder 63. Fundación Luis Muñoz Marín, Trujillo Alto, P.R.

Muschkin, Clara G. 1993. Consequences of Return Migrant Status for Employment in Puerto Rico. *International Migration Review* 27 (1): 70–102.

Myrdall, Gunnar. 1944. *An American Dilemma: The Negro Problem and Modern Democracy*. New York: Harper.

National Geographic Magazine. 1900. The First American Census of Porto Rico. 11 (8): 328.

———. 1901. Cuba and Porto Rico. 12 (2): 80.

Navarro, Mireya. 2000. Puerto Rican Presence Wanes in New York. Electronic document. ⟨http://www.nytimes.com/library/national/regional/022800ny-pr-immig.html⟩.

Negrón-Muntaner, Frances, and Ramón Grosfoguel, eds. 1997. *Puerto Rican Jam: Essays on Culture and Politics*. Minneapolis: University of Minnesota Press.

New York Academy of Sciences, Porto Rico Committee. 1915. Minutes of the Meeting of January 26. Franz Boas Papers, American Philosophical Society, Philadelphia.

———. N.d. Expenses of Franz Boas in Account with the Appropriation for the Survey of Porto Rico. Franz Boas Papers, American Philosophical Society, Philadelphia.

Nieto-Phillips, John. 1999. Citizenship and Empire: Race, Language, and Self-Government in New Mexico and Puerto Rico, 1898–1917. *Centro* 11 (1): 51–74.

NMAA Press Release. 1997. Colonial Art from Puerto Rico. Electronic document. ⟨http://nmaa-ryder.si.edu/nmaainfo/pr-vidal.html⟩.

Ober, Frederick A. 1893. *In the Wake of Columbus: Adventures of the Special Commissioner Sent by the World's Columbian Exposition to the West Indies.* Boston: D. Lothrop.

———. 1899. *Puerto Rico and Its Resources.* New York: D. Appleton.

Oboler, Suzanne. 1995. *Ethnic Labels, Latino Lives: Identity and the Politics of (Re)Presentation in the United States.* Minneapolis: University of Minnesota Press.

O'Connor, Donald. 1947. Letter to Teodoro Moscoso, July 22. Section IV: President of the Senate, 1941–1948; Series 2: Insular Government; Subseries 1: Fortaleza; 1C: Office of Puerto Rico in Washington; Folder 22. Fundación Luis Muñoz Marín, Trujillo Alto, P.R.

———. 1948. Mainland Labor Force Needs in 1948–49 and Puerto Rico's Opportunities to Exploit Them. Memorandum to Jesús T. Piñero and others, August 10. Section IV: President of the Senate, 1941–1948; Series 2: Insular Government; Subseries 1: Fortaleza; 1C: Office of Puerto Rico in Washington; Folder 18. Fundación Luis Muñoz Marín, Trujillo Alto, P.R.

Office of Management and Budget. 1997. Revisions to the Standards for the Classification of Federal Data on Race and Ethnicity; Notices. *Federal Register* 62 (210) (October 30): 58782–90.

Ojeda Reyes, Félix, ed. 1998. 1898: *Los días de la guerra.* San Juan: Universidad Interamericana, Recinto Metropolitano; Instituto de Estudios del Caribe, Universidad de Puerto Rico; Centro de Estudios Avanzados de Puerto Rico y el Caribe; Archivo General de Puerto Rico.

Olmeda, Luz H. 1997. Aspectos socioeconómicos de la migración en el 1994–95. In Junta de Planificación, *Informe económico al Gobernador,* 6–12. San Juan: Junta de Planificación de Puerto Rico.

Olwig, Karen Fog, and Kirsten Hastrup, eds. 1997. *Siting Culture: The Shifting Anthropological Object.* London: Routledge.

Olwig, Karen Fog, and Ninna Nyberg Sørensen. 1999. Mobile Livelihoods: Life and Work in a Globalizing World. Unpublished manuscript, Centre for Development Research, Copenhagen, Denmark.

Omi, Michael, and Howard Winant. 1994. *Racial Formation in the United States: From the 1960s to the 1990s.* 2d ed. London: Routledge.

Ortiz, Vilma. 1994. Circular Migration and Employment among Puerto Rican Women. *Latino Studies Journal* 4 (2): 56–70.

Pabón, Carlos. 1995a. Albizu y Madonna o la política de la representación. *Bordes* 2:129–30.

———. 1995b. De Albizu a Madonna: Para armar y desarmar la nacionalidad. *Bordes* 1:22–40.

Padilla, Elena. 1958. *Up from Puerto Rico.* New York: Columbia University Press.

Pantoja, Antonia. 1989. Puerto Ricans in New York City: A Historical and Community Development Perspective. *Centro* 2 (5): 20–31.

Pantojas-García, Emilio. 1990. *Development Strategies as Ideologies: Puerto Rico's Export-Led Industrialization Experience.* Boulder, Colo.: Lynne Rienner.

Pearce, Susan M. 1992. *Museums, Objects, and Collections: A Cultural Study.* Washington, D.C.: Smithsonian Institution Press.

Pedraza, Silvia, and Rubén G. Rumbaut, eds. 1996. *Origins and Destinies: Immigration, Race, and Ethnicity in America*. Belmont, Calif.: Wadsworth.

Pedreira, Antonio S. 1992 [1934]. *Insularismo*. Río Piedras, P.R.: Edil.

Pérez, Gina. 2000. *Los de afuera*: Migration, Community, and the Politics of Identity. Paper presented at the XXII International Congress of the Latin American Studies Association, Miami, Fla., March 16–18.

Pérez, Marvette. 1996. La "guagua aérea": Política, estatus, nacionalismo y ciudadanía en Puerto Rico. In *América Latina en tiempos de globalización: Procesos culturales y transformaciones sociopolíticas*, ed. Daniel Mato, Maritza Montero, and Emanuele Amodio, 187–200. Caracas: CRESALC.

Pérez, Moira. 1998. From Mask Makers to Bell Boys: Tourism and the Politics of Community Organization in Puerto Rico. Ph.D. diss. proposal, University of California, Berkeley.

Pessar, Patricia R., ed. 1997. *Caribbean Circuits: New Directions in the Study of Caribbean Migration*. New York: Center for Migration Studies.

Picó de Hernández, Isabel, Marcia Rivera, Carmen Parrilla, Jeannette Ramos de Sánchez de Vilella, and Isabelo Zenón. 1985. *Discrimen por color, sexo y origen nacional en Puerto Rico*. Río Piedras, P.R.: Centro de Investigaciones Sociales, Universidad de Puerto Rico.

Portes, Alejandro. 1998. Latin Americans in the U.S. and the Rise of Transnational Communities. Paper presented at the XXI International Congress of the Latin American Studies Association, Chicago, September 24–26.

Portes, Alejandro, and Rubén G. Rumbaut. 1996. *Immigrant America: A Portrait*. 2d ed. Berkeley: University of California Press.

Powell, J. W. 1903. *Twenty-first Annual Report of the Bureau of American Ethnology to the Secretary of the Smithsonian Institution, 1899–1900*. Washington, D.C.: Government Printing Office.

Price, David. 2000. Anthropologists as Spies. *The Nation*, November 20. Electronic document. ⟨http:/www.thenation.com⟩.

Price, Sally. 1989. *Primitive Art in Civilized Places*. Chicago: University of Chicago Press.

Provincia de Puerto Rico. 1882. *Feria de Ponce: Programa de los festejos. Año 1882*. Ponce, P.R.: El Vapor.

Puerto Rican Forum. 1975. *The Puerto Rican Community Development Project*. New York: Arno.

Puerto Rico Community Development Project. 1964. Training Institute. Section V: Governor of Puerto Rico, 1949–1964; Series I: General Correspondence; Subseries: Proposals; Folder 326. Fundación Luis Muñoz Marín, Trujillo Alto, P.R.

Puerto Rico y Nueva York: Magazine Mensual Ilustrado. 1955. 2 (8).

Pura Belpré Papers. 1897–1985. Series IV: Subject File; Series V: Photographs; Series VI: Clippings. Centro de Estudios Puertorriqueños, Hunter College, New York.

Quintero, Bobby. 1963. Nacimiento . . . vida . . . pasión . . . y . . . futuro de El Barrio. *Semana de la Prensa*, September 15, 11–13.

Quintero Rivera, Angel G., ed. 1998. *Vírgenes, magos y escapularios: Imaginería, etnicidad y religiosidad popular en Puerto Rico*. Río Piedras, P.R.: Centro de Investigaciones Sociales, Universidad de Puerto Rico.

Quintero Rivera, Angel G., José Luis González, Ricardo Campos, and Juan Flores. 1979.

> *Puerto Rico: Identidad nacional y clases sociales (coloquio de Princeton).* Río Piedras, P.R.: Huracán.

Radcliffe, Sarah, and Sallie Westwood. 1996. *Remaking the Nation: Place, Identity, and Politics in Latin America.* London: Routledge.

Rainey, Froilich G. 1940. Porto Rican Archaeology. *Scientific Survey of Porto Rico and the Virgin Islands* 18 (1): 1–208.

Ramírez, Rafael L. 1976. National Culture in Puerto Rico. *Latin American Perspectives* 3 (3): 109–16.

———. 1985. El cambio, la modernización y la cuestión cultural. In *Del cañaveral a la caña: Cambio social en Puerto Rico,* ed. Eduardo Rivera Medina and Rafael L. Ramírez, 9–64. Río Piedras, P.R.: Huracán.

Ramírez de Arellano, Rafael. 1926. *Folklore puertorriqueño: Cuentos y adivinanzas recogidos de la tradición oral.* Madrid: Centro de Estudios Históricos.

Renan, Ernest. 1990 [1882]. What Is a Nation? In *Nation and Narration,* ed. Homi Bhabha, 8–22. London: Routledge.

Revista Record. 1957a. 1 (1).

———. 1957b. 1 (2).

Ribes Tovar, Federico, ed. 1968. *El libro puertorriqueño de Nueva York: Un siglo de vida en la ciudad de Nueva York.* 2 vols. New York: Plus Ultra.

The Rican. 1973. An Interview with Joseph Monserrat. 3:38–47.

Rice, Edward R. 1899. Letter to the Board of Management, October 9. RU 70, Series 14, Box 52, Folder 26, Smithsonian Institution Archives, Washington, D.C.

Richardson, Bonham C. 1992. *The Caribbean in the Wider World, 1492–1992: A Regional Geography.* Cambridge: Cambridge University Press.

Rivera, Angel Israel. 1996. *Puerto Rico: Ficción y mitología en sus alternativas de status.* San Juan: Nueva Aurora.

Rivera-Batiz, Francisco, and Carlos E. Santiago. 1994. *Puerto Ricans in the United States: A Changing Reality.* Washington, D.C.: National Puerto Rican Coalition.

———. 1996. *Island Paradox: Puerto Rico in the 1990s.* New York: Russell Sage Foundation.

Rivera Ramos, Efrén. 2001. *The Legal Construction of Identity: The Judicial and Social Legacy of American Colonialism in Puerto Rico.* Washington, D.C.: American Psychological Association.

Rivero, Angel. 1973. *Crónica de la Guerra Hispanoamericana en Puerto Rico.* 2d ed. New York: Plus Ultra.

Roberts, Peter. 1997. The (Re)Construction of the Concept of "Indio" in the National Identities of Cuba, the Dominican Republic, and Puerto Rico. In *Caribe 2000: Definiciones, identidades y culturas regionales y/o nacionales,* ed. Lowell Fiet and Janette Becerra, 99–120. Río Piedras, P.R.: Facultad de Humanidades, Universidad de Puerto Rico.

———. 1999. What's in a Name, an Indian Name? In *Taíno Revival: Critical Perspectives on Puerto Rican Identity and Cultural Politics,* ed. Gabriel Haslip-Viera, 57–73. New York: Centro de Estudios Puertorriqueños, Hunter College.

Roche, Mario Edgardo. 1997. Hasta luego a la colección Vidal. *Diálogo,* August, 8–9.

Rodríguez, Clara. 1974. *The Ethnic Queue in the United States: The Case of Puerto Ricans.* San Francisco: R & E Research Associates.

———. 1988. Puerto Ricans and the Circular Migration Thesis. *Journal of Hispanic Policy* 3:5–9.

——. 1989. *Puerto Ricans: Born in the U.S.A.* Boston: Unwin Hyman.

——. 1990. Racial Identification among Puerto Rican Men and Women in New York. *Hispanic Journal of Behavioral Sciences* 12 (4): 366–79.

——. 1992. Race, Culture, and Latino "Otherness" in the 1980 Census. *Social Science Quarterly* 73 (4): 930–37.

——. 1994a. Challenging Racial Hegemony: Puerto Ricans in the United States. In *Race*, ed. Steven Gregory and Roger Sanjek, 131–45. New Brunswick, N.J.: Rutgers University Press.

——. 1994b. Puerto Rican Circular Migration Revisited. *Latino Studies Journal* 4 (2): 93–113.

——. 1996. Puerto Ricans: Between Black and White. In *Historical Perspectives on Puerto Rican Survival in the United States*, ed. Clara E. Rodríguez and Virginia Sánchez Korrol, 23–36. Princeton: Markus Wiener.

——. 1997. Rejoinder to Roberto Rodríguez-Morazzani's "Beyond the Rainbow: Mapping the Discourse on Puerto Ricans and 'Race.'" *Centro* 9 (1): 115–17.

——. 2000. *Changing Race: Latinos, the Census, and the History of Ethnicity in the United States.* New York: New York University Press.

Rodríguez, Clara E., and Héctor Cordero-Guzmán. 1992. Placing Race in Context. *Ethnic and Racial Studies* 25 (4): 523–42.

Rodríguez, Luisantonio. 1998. Tibes: Lugar enigmático. *Notisur*, January 15–21, 17.

Rodríguez, Magdalys. 1997. Pedido de libre tránsito. *El Nuevo Día*, March 14, 12.

Rodríguez, Miguel. 1984. *Estudio arqueológico del Valle del Río Cagüitas, Caguas, Puerto Rico.* Caguas, P.R.: Museo de la Universidad del Turabo.

Rodríguez, Víctor M. 1997. The Racialization of Puerto Rican Ethnicity in the United States. In *Ethnicity, Race, and Nationality in the Caribbean*, ed. Juan Manuel Carrión, 233–73. San Juan: Institute of Caribbean Studies, University of Puerto Rico.

Rodríguez-Cortés, Carmen. 1990. Social Practices of Ethnic Identity: A Puerto Rican Psycho-Cultural Event. *Hispanic Journal of Behavioral Sciences* 12 (4): 380–96.

Rodríguez Cruz, Juan. 1965. Las relaciones raciales en Puerto Rico. *Revista de Ciencias Sociales* 9 (4): 373–86.

Rodríguez-Fraticelli, Carlos, and Amílcar Tirado. 1989. Notes Towards a History of Puerto Rican Community Organizations in New York City. *Centro* 2 (6): 35–47.

Rodríguez-Morazzani, Roberto P. 1996. Beyond the Rainbow: Mapping the Discourse of Puerto Ricans and "Race." *Centro* 8 (1–2): 150–69.

Rodríguez Olleros, Angel. 1974. *Canto a la raza: Composición sanguínea de estudiantes de la Universidad de Puerto Rico.* Río Piedras, P.R.: Colegio de Farmacia, Universidad de Puerto Rico.

Rodríguez Vecchini, Hugo. 1994. Foreword: Backward and Forward. In *The Commuter Nation: Perspectives on Puerto Rican Migration*, ed. Carlos Antonio Torre, Hugo Rodríguez Vecchini, and William Burgos, 29–102. Río Piedras, P.R.: Editorial de la Universidad de Puerto Rico.

Rogler, Charles C. 1940. *Comerío: A Study of a Puerto Rican Town.* Kansas: University of Kansas.

——. 1972a [1946]. The Morality of Race Mixing in Puerto Rico. In *Portrait of a Society: Readings on Puerto Rican Sociology*, ed. Eugenio Fernández Méndez, 57–64. Río Piedras, P.R.: University of Puerto Rico Press.

——. 1972b [1944]. The Role of Semantics in the Study of Race Distance in Puerto Rico. In *Portrait of a Society: Readings on Puerto Rican Sociology*, ed. Eugenio Fernández Méndez, 49–56. Río Piedras, P.R.: University of Puerto Rico Press.

Rosario, José Colombán, and Justina Carrión. 1951. *El negro: Haití—Estados Unidos— Puerto Rico*. 2d ed. Río Piedras, P.R.: División de Impresos, Universidad de Puerto Rico.

Rosenblum, Gerald. 1973. *Immigrant Workers: Their Impact on American Labor Radicalism*. New York: Basic Books.

Rosenblum, Naomi. 1984. *A World History of Photography*. New York: Abbeville.

Rouse, Irving B. 1992. *The Taínos: The Rise and Decline of the People Who Greeted Columbus*. New Haven: Yale University Press.

Rouse, Roger. 1991. Mexican Migration and the Social Space of Postmodernism. *Diaspora* 1 (1): 8–23.

——. 1995. Questions of Identity: Personhood and Collectivity in Transnational Migration to the United States. *Critique of Anthropology* 15 (4): 351–79.

Routté-Gómez, Eneid. 1995. A Conspiracy of Silence: Racism in Puerto Rico. *San Juan City Magazine* 4 (8): 54–58.

Roy-Fequiere, Magaly. 1997. The Nation as Male Fantasy: Discourses of Race and Gender in Emilio Belaval's *Los cuentos de la Universidad*. In *Ethnicity, Race, and Nationality in the Caribbean*, ed. Juan Manuel Carrión, 122–58. San Juan: Institute of Caribbean Studies, University of Puerto Rico.

Ruby, Jay. 1996. Visual Anthropology. In *Encyclopedia of Cultural Anthropology*, ed. David Levinson and Melvin Ember, 4:1345–51. New York: Henry Holt.

Ruggles, Steven, et al. 1997. Integrated Public Use Microdata Series: Version 2.0. Enumerator Instructions. Electronic document. ⟨http://www.ipums.umn.edu⟩.

Rydell, Robert W. 1993. *World of Fairs: The Century-of-Progress Expositions*. Chicago: University of Chicago Press.

——. 1994. *All the World's a Fair: Visions of Empire at American International Expositions, 1876–1916*. Chicago: University of Chicago Press.

——. 1998. Souvenirs of Imperialism: World's Fairs Postcards. In *Delivering Views: Distant Cultures in Early Postcards*, ed. Christraud M. Geary and Virginia Lee-Webb, 47–64. Washington, D.C.: Smithsonian Institution Press.

Rydell, Robert W., John E. Findling, and Kimberly D. Pelle. 2000. *Fair America: World's Fairs in the United States*. Washington, D.C.: Smithsonian Institution Press.

Said, Edward W. 1978. *Orientalism*. New York: Pantheon.

——. 1994. *Culture and Imperialism*. New York: Vintage.

——. 2000 [1989]. Representing the Colonized: Anthropology's Interlocutors. In *Reflections on Exile and Other Essays*, 293–316. Cambridge: Harvard University Press.

Sánchez, Luis Rafael. 1987. The Flying Bus. In *Images and Identities: The Puerto Rican in Two World Contexts*, ed. Asela Rodríguez de Laguna, 17–25. Translated by Elpidio Laguna-Díaz. New Brunswick, N.J.: Transaction.

Sánchez Korrol, Virginia. 1994. *From Colonia to Community: The History of Puerto Ricans in New York City*. 2d ed. Berkeley: University of California Press.

San Juan News. 1900. A "Little Puerto Rico." March 4, 1.

Santiago, Carlos E. 1993. The Migratory Impact of Minimum Wage Legislation: Puerto Rico, 1970–1987. *International Migration Review* 27 (4): 772–95.

Santiago, Esmeralda. 1994. *When I Was Puerto Rican*. New York: Vintage.

Santiago-Rivera, Azara L., and Carlos E. Santiago. 1999. Puerto Rican Transnational Migration and Identity: Impact of English Language Acquisition on Length of Stay in the United States. In *Identities on the Move: Transnational Processes in North America and the Caribbean*, ed. Liliana Goldin, 229–44. Austin: University of Texas Press.

Scarano, Francisco. 1984. *Sugar and Slavery in Puerto Rico: The Plantation Economy of Ponce, 1800–1850*. Madison: University of Wisconsin Press.

——. 1996. The Jíbaro Masquerade and the Subaltern Politics of Creole Identity Formation in Puerto Rico, 1745–1823. *American Historical Review* 101 (5): 1398–1431.

Schemo, Diana Jean. 2000. Despite Options on Census, Many to Check "Black" Only. *New York Times*, February 12. Electronic document. ⟨http://archives.nytimes.com⟩.

Scherer, Joanna Cohan. 1990. Historical Photographs as Anthropological Documents: A Retrospect. *Visual Anthropology* 3:131–55.

——. 1992. The Photographic Document: Photographs as Primary Data in Anthropological Enquiry. In *Anthropology and Photography, 1860–1920*, ed. Elizabeth Edwards, 32–41. New Haven: Yale University Press.

Schiller, Nina Glick, Linda Basch, and Cristina Blanc-Szanton, eds. 1992. *Towards a Transnational Perspective on Migration: Race, Class, Ethnicity, and Nationalism Reconsidered*. New York: New York Academy of Sciences.

Schiller, Nina Glick, Linda Basch, and Cristina Szanton Blanc. 1995. From Immigrant to Transmigrant: Theorizing Transnational Migration. *Anthropological Quarterly* 68 (1): 48–63.

Seda Bonilla, Eduardo. 1968. Dos modelos de relaciones raciales: Estados Unidos y América Latina. *Revista de Ciencias Sociales* 12 (4): 569–97.

——. 1972. El problema de identidad de los niuyoricans. *Revista de Ciencias Sociales* 16 (4): 453–62.

——. 1973. *Los derechos civiles en la cultura puertorriqueña*. 2d ed. Río Piedras, P.R.: Bayoán.

——. 1980. *Réquiem para una cultura*. 4th ed. Río Piedras, P.R.: Bayoán.

Segal, Aaron. 1996. Locating the Swallows: Caribbean Recycling Migration. Paper presented at the XXII Annual Conference of the Caribbean Studies Association, San Juan, May 27–31.

Senior, Clarence. 1947a. Letter to Donald J. O'Connor, March 20. Section IV: President of the Senate, 1941–1948; Series 2: Insular Government; Subseries 1: Fortaleza; IC: Office of Puerto Rico in Washington; Folder 22. Fundación Luis Muñoz Marín, Trujillo Alto, P.R.

——. 1947b. *Puerto Rican Emigration*. Río Piedras, P.R.: Social Science Research Center, University of Puerto Rico.

——. 1965. *The Puerto Ricans: Strangers—Then Neighbors*. Chicago: Quadrangle.

Senior, Clarence, and Don O. Watkins. 1966. Toward a Balance Sheet of Puerto Rican Migration. Study done for the United States–Puerto Rico Commission on the Status of Puerto Rico, 1966. Mimeographed copy. Río Piedras, P.R.: Social Science Research Center, University of Puerto Rico.

Senior, Clarence, with Carmen Isales. 1948. *The Puerto Ricans of New York City*. New York: Employment and Migration Bureau, Puerto Rico Department of Labor.

Sereno, Renzo. 1947. Cryptomelanism: A Study of Color Relations and Personal Insecurity in Puerto Rico. *Psychiatry* 10 (3): 253–69.

Siegel, Morris. 1948. A Puerto Rican Town. Unpublished manuscript. Río Piedras, P.R.: Social Science Research Center, University of Puerto Rico.

Sierra Berdecia, Fernando. 1956. *La emigración puertorriqueña: Realidad y política pública*. San Juan: Editorial del Departamento de Instrucción Pública.

Silva Gotay, Samuel. 1997. *Protestantismo y política en Puerto Rico, 1898–1930*. Río Piedras, P.R.: Editorial de la Universidad de Puerto Rico.

Skinner, Charles M. 1900. *Myths and Legends of Our New Possessions and Protectorate*. Philadelphia: J. B. Lippincott.

Smith, Anthony D. 1986. *The Ethnic Origins of Nations*. Oxford: Blackwell.

——. 1991. *National Identity*. Reno: University of Nevada Press.

——. 1995. *Nations and Nationalism in a Global Era*. London: Polity Press.

——. 1998. *Nationalism and Modernism*. London: Routledge.

Smith, Michael Peter, and Luis E. Guarnizo, eds. 1998. *Transnationalism from Below*. New Brunswick, N.J.: Transaction.

Smithsonian Institution, National Museum of American History. 1998. A Collector's Vision of Puerto Rico. Electronic document. ⟨http://www.si.edu.nmah/ve.vidal/index.htm⟩.

Smithsonian Institution Research Reports. 1998. Vidal Collection Sheds Light on Puerto Rican History and Culture. No. 93, summer. Electronic document. ⟨http://www.si.edu/researchreports/9893/vidal.htm⟩.

Smithsonian Institution Task Force on Latino Issues. 1994. *Willful Neglect: The Smithsonian Institution and U.S. Latinos*. Washington, D.C.: Smithsonian Institution.

Special Committee on Exhibits from Outlying Possessions. 1899. Memorandum of Action, December 9. RU 70, Box 52, Folder 26, Smithsonian Institution Archives, Washington, D.C.

——. 1900. Minutes of the Meeting of the Special Committee on Exhibits from Outlying Possessions, October 31. RU 70, Series 14, Box 52, Folder 26, Smithsonian Institution Archives, Washington, D.C.

——. 1901. Memorandum of Action Taken by the Board of Management, US Government Exhibit, Pan-American Exposition, 1901. RU 70, Series 14, Box 52, Folder 13, Smithsonian Institution Archives, Washington, D.C.

Spier, Leslie. 1918. The Growth of Boys: Dentition and Stature. *American Anthropologist* 20:37–48.

——. 1919. The Growth of Boys, with Special Reference to the Relation between Stature and Dentition. *Journal of Dental Research* 1:145–57.

Spurr, David. 1993. *The Rhetoric of Empire: Colonial Discourse in Journalism, Travel Writing, and Imperial Administration*. Durham: Duke University Press.

Stahl, Agustín. 1889. *Los indios borinqueños: Estudios etnográficos*. San Juan: Imprenta Librería de Acosta.

Stalin, Joseph. 1994. The Nation. In *Nationalism*, ed. John Hutchinson and Anthony D. Smith, 18–21. Oxford: Oxford University Press.

Stejneger, Leonhard. 1904. *Herpetology of Porto Rico: A Report of the Smithsonian Institution and the U.S. National Museum*. Washington, D.C.: Government Printing Office.

Steward, Julian H., Robert A. Manners, Eric R. Wolf, Elena Padilla Seda, Sidney W. Mintz, and Raymond L. Scheele. 1956. *The People of Puerto Rico: A Social Anthropological Study*. Urbana: University of Illinois Press.

Stocking, George W., Jr. 1992. *The Ethnographer's Magic and Other Essays on the History of Anthropology*. Madison: University of Wisconsin Press.

——, ed. 1985. *Objects and Others: Essays on Museums and Material Culture*. Madison: University of Wisconsin Press.

——. 1991. *Colonial Situations: Essays on the Contextualization of Ethnographic Knowledge*. Madison: University of Wisconsin Press.

Sued Badillo, Jalil. 1978. *Los caribes: ¿Realidad o fábula?* Río Piedras, P.R.: Antillana.

——. 1995a. The Island Caribs: New Approaches to the Question of Ethnicity in the Early Colonial Caribbean. In *Wolves from the Sea: Readings in the Anthropology of the Native Caribbean*, ed. Neil L. Whitehead, 61–89. Leiden: KITLV Press.

——. 1995b. The Theme of the Indigenous in the National Projects of the Hispanic Caribbean. In *Making Alternative Histories: The Practice of Archaeology and History in Non-Western Settings*, ed. Peter R. Schmidt and Thomas C. Patterson, 25–46. Santa Fe, N.Mex.: School of American Research Press.

Taft, William H. 1907. Some Recent Instances of National Altruism: The Efforts of the United States to Aid the Peoples of Cuba, Porto Rico, and the Philippines. *National Geographic Magazine* 18 (7): 429–38.

Thomas, Nicholas. 1994. *Colonialism's Culture: Anthropology, Travel, and Government*. Princeton: Princeton University Press.

Thomas-Hope, Elizabeth. 1986. Transients and Settlers: Varieties of Caribbean Migrants and the Socio-Economic Implications of Their Return. *International Migration* 24 (3): 559–71.

——. 1992. *Explanation in Caribbean Migration: Perception and the Image—Jamaica, Barbados, St. Vincent*. London: Macmillan Caribbean.

Thompson, Lanny. 1995. *Nuestra isla y su gente: La construcción del "otro" puertorriqueño en "Our Islands and Their People."* Río Piedras, P.R.: Centro de Investigaciones Sociales y Departamento de Historia, Universidad de Puerto Rico.

——. 1998. "Estudiarlos, juzgarlos y gobernarlos": Conocimiento y poder en el archipiélago imperial estadounidense. In *La nación soñada: Cuba, Puerto Rico y Filipinas ante el 98*, ed. Consuelo Naranjo, Miguel A. Puig-Samper, and Luis Miguel García Mora, 685–94. Madrid: Doce Calles.

Tienda, Marta. 1989. Puerto Ricans and the Underclass Debate. *Annals of the American Academy of Political and Social Science* 501 (January): 105–19.

Tienda, Marta, and William Díaz. 1987. Puerto Ricans' Special Problems. *New York Times*, August 28, A31.

Tió, Teresa. 1993. *Esencia y presencia: Artes de nuestra tradición*. San Juan: Banco Popular de Puerto Rico.

Tió Nazario, Juan Angel. 1979 [1921]. *Esencia del folklore puertorriqueño*. San Juan: Hipatia.

Torre, Carlos, Hugo Rodríguez Vecchini, and William Burgos, eds. 1994. *The Commuter Nation: Perspectives on Puerto Rican Migration*. Río Piedras, P.R.: Editorial de la Universidad de Puerto Rico.

Torres, Andrés, and José E. Velásquez, eds. 1998. *The Puerto Rican Movement: Voices from the Diaspora*. Philadelphia: Temple University Press.

Torres, Arlene. 1998. La Gran Familia Puertorriqueña "Ej Prieta de Beldá." In *Blackness in Latin America and the Caribbean*, ed. Arlene Torres and Norman E. Whitten Jr., 2:285–306. Bloomington: Indiana University Press.

Torres Martinó, J. A. 1991. Fondos sólo para proyectos con encantos electorales. *El Nuevo Día*, September 4, 60.

Trelles, Carmen Dolores. 1993. Teodoro Vidal: El coleccionista y su mundo. *Revista Domingo, El Nuevo Día*, April 4, 18.

True, Frederick W., William H. Holmes, and George P. Merrick. 1903. *Report on the Exhibit of the United States National Museum at the Pan-American Exposition, Buffalo, New York, 1901*. Washington, D.C.: Government Printing Office.

Tsang, Jia-sun. 1998. A Closer Look: Santos from Puerto Rico. Electronic document. ⟨http://www.si.edu/scmre/santos_e.hmtl⟩.

Tucker, Clyde, Ruth McKay, Brian Kojetin, Roderick Harrison, Manuel de la Puente, Linda Stinson, and Ed Robinson. 1996. *Testing Methods of Collecting Racial and Ethnic Information: Results of the Current Population Survey Supplement on Race and Ethnicity*. Bureau of Labor Statistical Notes no. 40.

Underwood & Underwood. 1905. *Original Stereographs Catalogue no. 25*. New York: Underwood & Underwood.

———. N.d. *Catalogue 28: The Underwood Travel System*. New York: Underwood & Underwood.

Underwood & Underwood Glass Stereograph Collection. 1895–1921. Photo lot 143, Archives Center, National Museum of American History, Smithsonian Institution.

United Confederation of Taíno People. 1998. La Voz del Pueblo Taíno: The Official Newsletter of the UCTP. Electronic document. ⟨http://www.members.tripod.com/~Taino_3⟩.

United States–Puerto Rico Commission on the Status of Puerto Rico. 1966. *Report of the United States–Puerto Rico Commission on the Status of Puerto Rico*. Washington, D.C.: Government Printing Office.

Urciuoli, Bonnie. 1996. *Exposing Prejudice: Puerto Rican Experiences of Language, Race, and Class*. Boulder, Colo.: Westview.

U.S. Bureau of the Census. 1921. *Fourteenth Census of the United States: 1920. Bulletin. Population: Porto Rico. Composition and Characteristics of the Population*. Washington, D.C.: Government Printing Office.

———. 1932. *Fifteenth Census of the United States: 1930. Agriculture and Population: Porto Rico*. Washington, D.C.: Government Printing Office.

———. 1943a. *Sixteenth Census of the United States: 1940. Puerto Rico: Population. Bulletin no. 2: Characteristics of the Population*. Washington, D.C.: Government Printing Office.

———. 1943b. *Sixteenth Census of the United States: 1940. Puerto Rico: Population. Bulletin no. 3: Occupations and Other Characteristics by Age*. Washington, D.C.: Government Printing Office.

———. 1946. *Sixteenth Census of the United States: 1940. Puerto Rico: Population. Bulletin no. 4: Migration between Municipalities*. Washington, D.C.: Government Printing Office.

———. 1952. *United States Census of Population: 1950. General Characteristics: Puerto Rico*. Washington, D.C.: Government Printing Office.

———. 1953a. *Census of Population: 1950. Vol. 2, Characteristics of the Population. Parts 51–54: Territories and Possessions*. Washington, D.C.: Government Printing Office.

——. 1953b. *U.S. Census of Population: 1950. Special Reports: Puerto Ricans in Continental United States*. Washington, D.C.: Government Printing Office.

——. 1963. *U.S. Census of Population: 1960. Subject Reports: Puerto Ricans in the United States*. Washington, D.C.: Government Printing Office.

——. 1973. *1970 Census of Population. Subject Reports: Puerto Ricans in the United States*. Washington, D.C.: Government Printing Office.

——. 1993a. *1990 Census of Population: Social and Economic Characteristics*. Washington, D.C.: Government Printing Office.

——. 1993b. *1990 Census of Population: Social and Economic Characteristics. Puerto Rico*. Washington, D.C.: Government Printing Office.

——. 2001. American Factfinder: Census 2000 Data. Electronic document. ⟨http:www. census.gov/main/www/cen2000.html⟩.

U.S. National Museum. 1901. *Annual Report, 1899*. Washington, D.C.: Government Printing Office.

Vázquez Calzada, José Luis. 1963. La emigración puertorriqueña: ¿Solución o problema? *Revista de Ciencias Sociales* 7 (4): 323–32.

Vega, Ana Lydia. 1981a. Pollito Chicken. In *Vírgenes y mártires*, by Carmen Lugo Filippi and Ana Lydia Vega, 73–80. Río Piedras, P.R.: Antillana.

——. 1981b. Trabajando pal inglés. In *Vírgenes y mártires*, by Carmen Lugo Filippi and Ana Lydia Vega, 99–108. Río Piedras, P.R.: Antillana.

Vega, Bernardo. 1994 [1977]. *Memorias de Bernardo Vega: Contribución a la historia de la comunidad puertorriqueña en Nueva York*. Edited by César Andreu Iglesias. 5th ed. Río Piedras, P.R.: Huracán.

Velásquez, Steve, comp. 1999. Records Catalogue of the Vidal Collection. Smithsonian Institution, National Museum of American History, Division of Cultural History, Accession no. 1997.0097. Unpublished manuscript.

Velázquez, Nydia. 1992. Informe sobre labor realizada, 1986–1992. Archivos Históricos de la Migración Puertorriqueña, Centro de Estudios Puertorriqueños, Hunter College, New York.

Vidal, Jaime R. 1994. Citizens yet Strangers: The Puerto Rican Experience. In *Puerto Rican and Cuban Catholics in the U.S., 1900–1965*, ed. Jay P. Dolan and Jaime R. Vidal, 11–143. Notre Dame: University of Notre Dame Press.

Vidal, Teodoro 195?. *Manual de protocolo, Mansión Ejecutiva, Estado Libre Asociado de Puerto Rico*. N.p.: n.p.

——. 1957. Memorandum to doña Inés [Mendoza] for a TV program on historic monuments, September 18. Section V: Governor of Puerto Rico, 1949–1964; Series I: General Correspondence; Folder 99: "Asistentes, Teodoro Vidal." Fundación Luis Muñoz Marín, Trujillo Alto, P.R.

——. 1964. *La Fortaleza o Palacio de Santa Catalina*. San Juan: Talleres de Artes Gráficas del Departamento de Instrucción Pública.

——. 1974. *Los milagros en metal y en cera de Puerto Rico*. San Juan: Alba.

——. 1979. *Santeros puertorriqueños*. San Juan: Alba.

——. 1983. *Las caretas de cartón del Carnaval de Ponce*. San Juan: Alba.

——. 1986. *San Blas en la tradición puertorriqueña*. San Juan: Alba.

——. 1987. *Una dama del siglo XVIII, pintada por Campeche*. N.p.: n.p.

——. 1988a. *Las caretas de los vejigantes ponceños: Modo de hacerlas*. San Juan: Pronto Printing.

——. 1988b. *Tres retratos pintados por Campeche*. San Juan: Alba.

——. 1989. *Tradiciones en la brujería puertorriqueña*. San Juan: Alba.

——. 1994. *Los Espada: Escultores sangermeños*. San Juan: Alba.

——. 1997. Letter to José Roberto Martínez, June 10. Fundación Luis Muñoz Marín, Trujillo Alto, P.R.

——. 1998a. La imaginería popular: Arte y tradición puertorriqueña. In *Puerto Rico: Arte e identidad*, ed. Hermandad de Artistas Gráficos de Puerto Rico, 91–108. Río Piedras, P.R.: Editorial de la Universidad de Puerto Rico.

——. 1998b. Letter to José Roberto Martínez, July 26. Fundación Luis Muñoz Marín, Trujillo Alto, P.R.

——. 2000. *Cuatro puertorriqueñas por Campeche*. San Juan: Alba.

——. N.d. *La bandera de Puerto Rico*. San Juan: Estado Libre Asociado de Puerto Rico.

Viglucci, Andrew. 1997. Question: Who Sprang Up for the Luncheon Bill. *San Juan Star*, September 28, 123.

Viña, Andrés. 1854. *Memoria descriptiva de la primera esposición pública de la industria, agricultura y bellas artes, de la isla de Puerto-Rico, en junio de 1854*. Puerto Rico: Est. Tipográfico de D. I. Guasp.

El Visitante. 1992. Museo de Artes y Tradiciones. January 25, 5.

Vivoni Farage, Enrique, and Silvia Alvarez Curbelo, eds. 1998. *Hispanofilia: Arquitectura y vida en Puerto Rico, 1900–1950*. Río Piedras, P.R.: Editorial de la Universidad de Puerto Rico.

Vizcarrondo, Alicia. 1994. *Puerto Rico mi gran comunidad*. Río Piedras, P.R.: Cultural Panamericana.

Wade, Peter. 1997. *Race and Ethnicity in Latin America*. London: Pluto.

Warshaw Collection of Business Americana. 1901. 1901 Buffalo Pan-American Exposition. World Expositions, Box 10, Archives Center, National Museum of American History, Washington, D.C.

——. 1904. 1904 St. Louis Louisiana Purchase Exposition. World Expositions, Box 11, Archives Center, National Museum of American History, Washington, D.C.

——. 1939. New York's World Fair, 1939. World Expositions, Box 16, Archives Center, National Museum of American History, Washington, D.C.

Washington Post. 1902. Helen H. Gardener to Wed. March 20, 2.

Wheeler, Algar M. 1899. Letter to William V. Cox, August 17. RU 70, Box 53, Folder 5, Smithsonian Institution Archives, Washington, D.C.

White, Trumbull. 1898. *Our New Possessions*. Boston: Adams.

Willets, Gilson, Margherita Arlina Hamm, and Peter McIntosh. N.d. *Photographic Views of Our New Possessions*. Chicago: Waberly.

Williams, Patrick, and Laura Chrisman, eds. 1994. *Colonial Discourse and Post-Colonial Theory: A Reader*. New York: Columbia University Press.

Willoughby, William F. 1902. Some of the Administrative and Industrial Problems of Porto Rico. *National Geographic Magazine* 13 (12): 466–70.

——. 1905. *Territories and Dependencies of the United States: Their Government and Administration*. New York: Century.

Winant, Howard. 1994. *Racial Conditions: Politics, Theory, Comparisons*. Minneapolis: University of Minnesota Press.

Wolfson, Alan R. 1972. Raza, conocimiento del inglés y aprovechamiento social entre los inmigrantes puertorriqueños de Nueva York: Una aplicación de la teoría de grupos de referencia. Master's thesis project, School of Social Work, University of Puerto Rico.

Zenón Cruz, Isabelo. 1975. *Narciso descubre su trasero: El negro en la cultura puertorriqueña.* 2d ed. 2 vols. Humacao, P.R.: Furidi.

Zentella, Ana Celia. 1997. *Growing Up Bilingual: Puerto Rican Children in New York.* Malden, Mass.: Blackwell.

Zwick, Jim. 2000. Stereoscopic Visions of War and Empire. Electronic document. ⟨http://www.boondocksnet.com/stereo⟩.

Index

Aborigines of Porto Rico and Neighboring Islands, The (Fewkes), 65–66

Acosta, José Julián, 263

African Americans, 25, 31, 34, 149, 164, 217, 238, 244, 246, 254

African contributions to Puerto Rican culture: neglected by nationalist intellectuals, 19, 25, 78, 278; neglected by American anthropologists, 62, 76, 86; in folklore, 76, 78, 290 (n. 11); as opposed to Taíno heritage, 84, 86, 262, 271, 278, 280; downplayed in photographs, 89; in music, 159; and Vidal Collection, 161, 163; in seal of Institute of Puerto Rican Culture, 271

Afro–Puerto Ricans, 25, 27, 243, 244

Agapito's Bar speech (Muñoz Marín), 125, 126

Aitken, Robert T., 81, 274

Alaska: at world's fairs, 39–51 passim, 289 (n. 5); U.S. colonial discourse on, 52, 85; statehood in, 121, 292 (n. 16); as racial category in census, 238, 253, 296 (n. 2)

Albizu Campos, Pedro, 17, 124, 287–88 (n. 7), 293 (n. 2)

Alegría, Ricardo, 128–31; as cultural nationalist, 124, 125, 292 (n. 2), 293 (n. 6); biographical sketch, 128–29; as director of Institute of Puerto Rican Culture, 129–31, 272, 279; as archaeologist, 264; depiction of Taínos, 264–65, 268, 270

Alianza Obrera Puertorriqueña, 187–88

Alicea, Marixsa, 215, 288 (n. 13)

Alindato, Juan, 159

Alonso, Manuel, 290 (n. 12)

Alvarez Nazario, Manuel, 271

American Anthropological Association, 64, 65, 74

American anthropologists in Puerto Rico, 58, 59–86 passim, 239

Americanization of Puerto Rico, 1, 22, 124, 128, 162, 163

American Museum of Natural History, 67, 292 (n. 3)

American Philosophical Society, 76

Anderson, Benedict, 8, 15, 37

Anthropological Society of Washington, 64

Anthropology: and world's fairs, 41, 47–48, 87, 281; and colonialism, 59–65, 83–86

Aparicio, Frances, 34, 288 (n. 13)

Appadurai, Arjun, 29

Art and Mythology of the Taíno Indians of the Greater West Indies (Fernández Méndez), 165

Arts Museum of Puerto Rico, 147

Ashford, Bailey K., 119, 292 (n. 15)

ASPIRA, 202

Assimilation, cultural, 18, 34, 36, 119, 134, 166, 175, 179, 184, 202, 207, 213. *See also* Americanization of Puerto Rico

Ateneo Puertorriqueño, 279

Atrévete, 181, 182

Ausentes, 173–74

Autonomism, 17, 21, 126, 131–32, 162, 281

Ayala, César, 282

Babín, María Teresa, 269, 271

Bailey, Benjamin, 295 (n. 8)

Bainter, E. M., 77

Balibar, Etienne, 8

Banco Popular, 146, 160

Barradas, Efraín, 31

Barrio, El. *See* Spanish Harlem

Barrio Gandul, 236, 237, 246

Baseball: and Puerto Rican migrants, 189–90, 192–93, 197

Bateson, George, 87

Beckwith, Paul, 42–43, 108, 109

Benedict, Burton, 40

Benedict, Ruth, 75, 132

Benítez, Jaime, 170

Berríos, Rubén, 16, 195

Betances, Samuel, 243

Betanzos, Amalia V., 193

Bhabha, Homi K., 71

Bilingualism, 20, 32, 202, 213–14, 218, 231, 282. *See also* English language use in Puerto Rico; Linguistic nationalism; Nuyoricans; Spanish language

Blackness. *See* African contributions to Puerto Rican culture; Afro–Puerto Ricans; Racial prejudice

Blanco, Tomás, 21, 25, 240, 242

Boas, Franz: at World's Columbian Exposition, 41; on salvage ethnology, 59; on Puerto Rico, 61, 74–75, 81–82, 84, 86, 274, 290 (n. 14); and historical particularism, 63; on scientists as spies, 63–64; correspondence with John Alden Mason, 74, 75–82, 269

Bodegas, 191–92, 198, 200

Bomba, 157, 198, 203

Bonet, Desmonique, 34

Boricua, 28, 30, 188, 193, 205, 206, 245, 255, 280

Borinquen, 192–93, 275, 280

Botello, Angel, 292 (n. 3)

Bourgeoisie. *See* Creole elite in Puerto Rico

Brau, Salvador, 67, 68, 83, 263, 269

Braun, Elizabeth, 151

Brazil, 239, 241, 258

Brigham, J. H., 44

Britton, Nathaniel Lord, 74

Bryant, Henry, 288 (n. 1)

Buchanan, William I., 44–45, 47

Bureau of American Ethnology, 42, 43, 65, 73

Burgos, Julia de, 182

Cabán group, 151

Caborrojeños Ausentes, 173–74

Cabranes, José, 55

Caguana, Centro Ceremonial Indígena, 66, 81, 83, 130, 272, 273, 274

Calderón, Sila María, 183

Campeche, José, 48, 138, 144, 150, 163, 204

Capetillo, Luisa, 158

Carib Indians, 66, 69, 265, 267, 269, 276. *See also* Taínos

Carreta, La (Marqués), 166

Carrión, Juan Manuel, 14, 16, 287 (n. 4)

Carrión, Justina, 242

Carroll, Henry K., 291 (n. 4)

Casa Blanca Fortress, 47

Casitas, 7, 34

Castro, Román Baldorioty de, 204

Castro Pereda, Rafael, 146

Catalonia, 9, 282, 287 (n. 4)

Catholicism in Puerto Rico, 19, 23, 71–72, 100, 140, 154, 158, 162, 165, 193

Cemíes, 155, 265, 272, 275, 277

Census. *See* U.S. Bureau of the Census

Center for Archaeological Research, University of Puerto Rico, 128–29, 264, 273

Centro de Estudios Puertorriqueños, Hunter College, 167, 186

Cepeda, Rafael, 157

Chapman, Murray, 210, 294 (n. 1)

Chatterjee, Partha, 261

Chenoweth, Mary Alice. *See* Gardener, Helen Hamilton

Circular migration, 2–3, 208–35 passim, 288 (n. 13), 294 (n. 9); defined, 32–33, 294 (n. 1); implications for cultural identity, 37, 211, 213–15; relationship to return migration, 208; in the Caribbean, 209–10, 223, 233, 235; estimates of, 216, 223

Civil rights movement, 164, 176, 202, 206

Cockfights, 97, 100–101

Code-switching, 32, 203, 213–14. *See also* Bilingualism; Spanglish

Cofresí, the pirate, 157

Collins, Jane, 87

Coll y Toste, Cayetano, 67, 81, 84, 263, 269

Colón, Jesús, 187

Colón, Willie, 32

Colonial discourse, U.S., 44–45, 51–52, 60, 65, 71, 87; on Puerto Rico, 39–40, 49, 53–58, 62, 84–85, 88–90, 116–19, 281, 283; on the Philippines, 53–58, 85, 116–19, 283

Colonial exhibits. *See* World's fairs

Colonial immigrants, 217

Colonialism, 1, 15, 16, 23, 54, 59–60, 112, 124, 161, 272

Commonwealth government of Puerto Rico, 1, 2, 15–16, 122–34 passim, 141, 146, 162–85 passim, 195, 206, 252, 257–58, 260

Community organization of Puerto Ricans in the United States, 172, 183, 184, 185–87. *See also* Voluntary associations of Puerto Ricans in the United States

Commuting, 34, 209, 217, 231

Congo, Melitón, 78

Connors, Andrew, 151

Conway, Dennis, 209, 210, 223

Corretjer, Juan Antonio, 22, 267

Costumbrismo, 263

Crampton, Henry Edward, 77

Creative writers: and Puerto Rican nationalism, 14, 20–21, 26–34, 167, 263, 267, 279

Creole elite in Puerto Rico: views of the nation, 19–21; and world's fairs, 47–48; and women, 54–55; excluded from photographs, 89; in Helen Hamilton Gardener Collection, 108, 115, 119; and cultural nationalism, 124, 132, 134; and aboriginal culture, 262
Creolization, 22, 161, 163
Crew, Spencer, 151, 293 (n. 5)
Criollo, 159, 162–63, 263
Crystal Palace Great Exhibition, London, 40
Cuatro, 135, 148, 159, 198
Cuba, 1, 25, 26, 42–52 passim, 85, 91, 120, 149, 247, 283, 291 (n. 5)
Cubans in Puerto Rico, 13, 14, 20, 25–27, 35, 284
Culberson, George William, 238–40
Cultura de Puerto Rico, La (Babín), 271
Cultural nationalism: as opposed to political nationalism, 2, 124, 262, 284; defined, 5, 17, 33–34, 123; popularity of, 15, 29, 35; significance of, 18, 135–36, 279–80; and Generation of 1930, 21–22, 125, 292 (n. 1); as anticolonial movement, 86, 261, 280; as official state ideology, 123–24, 134, 277; anthropological influence on, 124, 125; exclusion of the diaspora, 133, 139, 166, 168; and Vidal Collection, 160; and archaeology, 265. See also Political nationalism
Cultural studies, 137, 138
Current Population Survey, 256–57
Curtis, Edward S., 157

Danza, 48, 194
Dávila, Arlene, 17–18, 271, 280
Dávila, Jorge L., 147
Day, Selden Allen, 106–7, 108, 291 (n. 8)
Decolonization, 14, 59, 122, 165, 261, 281
Delano, Jack, 145, 158, 159, 291 (n. 10)
Democracia, La, 125
Democratic Party (U.S.), 187, 189
Department of Puerto Rican Community Affairs in the United States, 168–85 passim, 207
Deterritorialization, 36, 168, 216, 235, 283, 284. See also Translocal nation; Transnationalism
Diario–La Prensa, El, 193
Diaspora, 20, 26, 29, 36, 135
Díaz, Luis R., 197

Díaz Quiñones, Arcadio, 31, 162, 288 (n. 10)
Díaz Schuler, Odette, 160, 161
Domínguez, Virginia, 295 (n. 6)
Dominicans in Puerto Rico, 13, 15, 20, 25–28, 35, 209, 284, 294 (n. 4)
Doty, Charles Edward, 291 (n. 5)
Duchesne Winter, Juan, 288 (n. 12)
Duncan, Ronald, 271
Durand, Jorge, 294 (n. 6)

Economic Development Administration (Puerto Rico), 142, 147
Ellis, Mark, 209
English language use in Puerto Rico, 19, 21, 29–30, 126, 158, 162, 219, 232
Erasmo Vando Papers, 186
Espada, Felipe de la, 143, 150–51, 156, 158
Espada, Tiburcio de la, 143, 150–51, 156, 158
Espinosa, Aurelio M., 75, 76, 79–80
Espiritismo, 154
Estado Libre Asociado. See Commonwealth government of Puerto Rico
Ethnic Origins of Nations, The (Smith), 9
Evangelical cults, 195–97, 207. See also Protestantism in Puerto Rico
Evolutionism, 57, 62–63, 64, 66, 103, 264, 269, 276
Exvotos. See Milagros

Farrow, Jeffrey, 4
Feast of Saint John the Baptist, 180, 193, 204–5, 206
Fernández Juncos, Manuel, 67
Fernández Méndez, Eugenio, 131–33; as cultural nationalist, 124, 125, 132, 264, 276–77; biographical sketch, 131; president of Board of Directors of Institute of Puerto Rican Culture, 131; concept of culture, 132–33; view of the diaspora, 166; on Taíno art, 265, 268
Fernós-Isern, Antonio, 171
Ferré, Luis A., 178, 195
Ferré, Rosario, 31, 288 (nn. 10, 12)
Fewkes, Jesse Walter, 62–86 passim; on annexation of Puerto Rico, 42, 61; travels to Puerto Rico, 43, 63, 264; as evolutionist, 62; diaries and notebooks on Puerto Rico, 62, 71; as colonialist, 125
Field Museum of Natural History, 64, 74
Fiestas patronales, 174–75
Filipinos: compared to Puerto Ricans, 39–

40, 49, 51–56, 65, 71, 84, 217; in native villages, 41, 46, 50, 56; as conquered people, 217–18. *See also* Philippines, the
Flores, Juan, 31, 32, 122, 288 (n. 10)
Folklore, Puerto Rican, 25, 75–81, 138, 139, 142, 143, 180, 204, 278
Food: as symbol of Puerto Rican identity, 32, 186, 188–89, 198–201, 206, 271
Ford Foundation, 181
Fortaleza, La, 130, 141, 142, 158
Fulbright, J. W., 239

Gamio, Manuel, 63, 264
García, Osvaldo, 291 (n. 6)
García Canclini, Néstor, 5
García Passalacqua, Juan Manuel, 287 (n. 6)
García Ramis, Magali, 27
Gardener, Helen Hamilton, 90, 106–20 passim, 291 (nn. 8–11)
Géigel Polanco, Vicente, 21
Gellner, Ernest, 8, 9
Generation of 1930. *See* Cultural nationalism
Genoveva de Arteaga Papers, 186
Gíbaro, El (Alonso), 290 (n. 12)
Ginorio, Angela, 295 (n. 9)
Glasser, Ruth, 197
Globalization. *See* Transnationalism
Godreau, Isar, 295 (nn. 2, 5)
Goldsen, Rose Kohn, 244
González, Libia, 48
González, Velda, 145
Gordon, Maxine, 242–43
Graham-Brown, Sarah, 119
Great Puerto Rican Family, the: as metaphor for national identity, 20, 24–25; and Vidal Collection, 139, 159, 160, 161, 163, 165
Grosvenor, Gilbert Hovey, 88
"Guagua aérea, La" (Sánchez), 33–34
Guam, 44, 85, 149, 283
Guesde Collection, 42
Gutiérrez, Luis, 3
Gutiérrez Igaravidez, Pedro, 292 (n. 15)

H. C. White Company, 91
Halstead, William Freeman, 290 (n. 6)
Hammond, William, 107
Handler, Richard, 140
Hawaii: at world's fairs, 39–52 passim, 289 (n. 5); U.S. colonial discourse on, 53, 85;

in photographs, 108; statehood in, 121, 292 (n. 16); Japanese Americans in, 164; Hawaiians as conquered people, 217–18; Hawaiians as racial category in census, 253; census of, 295 (n. 6)
Helen Hamilton Gardener Photographic Collection, 90, 106–21 passim
Herbstein, Judith, 176
Hernández, Carmen Dolores, 31
Hernández, David, 288 (n. 13)
Hernández, Rafael, 109, 197
Hernández Colón, Rafael, 25, 145, 178, 180, 181
Hernández Cruz, Juan, 288 (n. 13)
Hernández Vázquez, Olga, 293 (n. 10)
Heyman, I. Michael, 151
Hill, Robert T., 42, 54–55, 247
Hispanic heritage: significance for Puerto Rican nationalism, 19, 22, 24, 120, 128, 138, 162; in architecture, 47, 120, 278, 289 (n. 3); in Puerto Rican folklore, 75–76, 80; and Vidal Collection, 140
Hispanics, 238, 249, 253–56, 259, 282, 295 (n. 8)
Hispanophilia. *See* Hispanic heritage
Historia de nuestros indios (versión elemental) (Alegría), 264–65
Historical Archives of the Puerto Rican Migration, 195
Historical particularism, 63, 79–80, 264. *See also* Boas, Franz
Historical patrimony, 19, 133, 140, 144, 147, 148, 163, 184, 265, 266, 272, 279
Historic preservation, 141–42, 144, 277–78
Hobsbawm, Eric, 8
Holmes, William H., 43
Hometown clubs, 172–75, 176, 177–78, 202, 207
Hostos, Adolfo de, 264, 273
Hostos, Eugenio María de, 267
Hulme, Peter, 269
Hunt, William, 67
Hutchinson, John, 16, 134
Hybridity, 2–3, 5, 23, 29, 32, 36, 254, 280
Hyphenation. *See* Puerto Rican–Americans

Identities. *See* Colonial discourse, U.S.; Cultural nationalism; Racial identity of Puerto Ricans; Representation of cultural identities; Transnationalism
Iglesias Pantín, Santiago, 187

Imagined Communities (Anderson), 8, 15
Immigration to Puerto Rico, 13, 211–12, 248, 284. *See also* Circular migration; Cubans in Puerto Rico; Dominicans in Puerto Rico
Indiera, La, 68, 69, 80, 81, 270
Indigenismo, 263, 264, 267, 274
Indio, 244, 252, 259, 269, 270–71
Institute of Puerto Rican Culture: and cultural nationalism, 23, 123, 129, 135, 272; activities, 83, 277–78, 281, 292 (n. 2); Teodoro Vidal's participation in, 139, 141, 144; as model for the Puerto Rican diaspora, 182, 204; controlled by New Progressive Party, 266; official seal of, 277
Insularismo (Pedreira), 21–22
International Colonial Exposition, Paris, 289 (n. 5)
International expositions. *See* World's fairs
International Folk Art Museum of New Mexico, 146
International School of American Archaeology and Ethnology, 74
Ireland, 284

Jenks, Albert E., 50
Jesús Colón Papers, 186
Jíbaro: as symbol of Puerto Rican identity, 7, 19–29 passim, 83, 135, 137, 203, 204, 281; racial characterization of, 19–20, 77, 81, 83, 95; as object of anthropological study, 77; visual images of, 109, 205; and Vidal Collection, 151, 163
Jíbaros, Los (club), 188–89
Jiménez, Manuel "Canario," 197
Juan Bobo stories, 75, 204
Junghanns, Robert L., 77, 80, 263, 290 (n. 10)
Justo A. Martí Photographic Collection, 186, 196–97

Kearney, Michael, 218, 235
Kedourie, Elie, 8, 9
Keystone View Company, 51, 54, 93, 289 (n. 6), 296 (n. 3)
King, Walter W., 119, 292 (n. 15)
Klumb, Henry, 273
Kroeber, Alfred, 74

Labor movement, 158–59, 185, 191, 206, 288 (n. 14)
La Gorce, John Oliver, 88

Laguerre, Enrique, 267
"Lamento borincano" (Hernández), 109, 197
Lapp, Michael, 169, 176
Latimer, George, 263
Latimer, William Henry, 67–68
Latimer Collection, 42, 67, 292 (n. 3)
Latin American Migration Project, 294 (n. 6)
Latinos in the United States, 31, 138–64 passim, 238, 283, 295–96 (n. 9). *See also* Hispanics; Mexicans in the United States
Laviera, Tato, 32, 288 (n. 10)
Ledesma, Gregorio, 157
Liga Puertorriqueña e Hispana, 176, 188–89
Lindsay, John V., 201
Linguistic nationalism, 10, 19, 29, 31, 134, 279–80, 282. *See also* Cultural nationalism
Lite colonialism, 122, 287 (n. 2). *See also* Postcolonial colony
Lite nationalism, 14, 17, 284, 287 (n. 2). *See also* Cultural nationalism
Lloréns Torres, Luis, 194, 263, 268–69
Loíza, Puerto Rico, 76–80, 129, 155, 158, 221, 224–27, 290 (n. 11), 294 (nn. 7, 8)
Long-distance nationalism, 15, 187
López, Diana, 265
López, Mayra, 293 (n. 1)
López Bauzá, Juan, 288 (n. 12)
Lothrop, Samuel, 63
Louisiana Purchase Exposition, St. Louis, 39–58 passim
Luis Muñoz Marín Foundation, 148
Lutz, Catherine, 87

McCornick, J., 50
McGee, William J., 41, 61, 62
McKinley, William J., 91, 289 (n. 2), 291 (n. 4)
Madero, Francisco, 289 (n. 4)
Malaret, Marisol, 201
Maldonado-Denis, Manuel, 166–67
Malinowski, Bronislaw, 132
Manifest Destiny, 41, 53, 89
Mari Bras, Juan, 13
Marqués, René, 22, 26, 166, 171, 267
Marqueta, La, 200–201
Martí, Justo A., 197
Martín, Angel, 145

Martínez-Fernández, Luis, 288 (n. 1)

Marxism, 23

Más Ferrer, José, 157

Mason, John Alden, 62–86 passim, 269, 274, 289 (n. 3), 290 (nn. 9, 13)

Mason, Otis T., 41, 42, 43–44, 61, 62, 65, 66, 73, 263

Massey, Douglas S., 208, 221, 224, 294 (n. 6)

Matienzo Cintrón, Rosendo, 288 (n. 14)

Maxwell, Anne, 51, 119

Mead, Margaret, 87

Meléndez, Edwin, 288 (n. 13)

Men, Women, and Gods, and Other Lectures (Gardener), 107

Mendoza, Inés, 142, 148

Mestizaje, 25, 263, 264, 280

Metropolitan Museum of Art, 147

Mexican Migration Project, 221, 222, 224

Mexicans in the United States, 208, 209, 218, 222, 224, 233, 234–35, 253, 283

Middle class, 16, 20, 23, 88, 91, 159

Migration. *See* Circular migration; Diaspora; Puerto Rican diaspora; Puerto Rican migration; Return migration

Migration Division, Labor Department, 7, 168–85 passim

Migration policy: of Puerto Rican government, 170–71, 182–84, 207, 217, 282

Milagros, 143, 144, 148, 154, 158, 164

Mills, C. Wright, 244

Mintz, Sidney W., 23

Miss Universe Beauty Pageant, 123, 201, 205

Mobile livelihoods, 4, 11, 210–35 passim

Mohr, Nicholasa, 30–31, 203

Monserrat, Joseph, 175, 176–77, 178

Montalvo Guenard, José Leandro, 273

Morales, Iris, 288 (n. 10)

Morales Cabrera, Pablo, 264

Morales Carrión, Arturo, 124

Morel Campos, Juan, 48

Moreno, 236, 237, 252, 269

Morgan, Jaime, 147

Morgan, Lewis Henry, 66

Morley, Sylvanus, 63

Morro Castle, El, 47, 67, 291 (n. 8)

Moscioni, Attilio, 108, 114, 291–92 (nn. 12, 14)

Moscoso, Francisco, 265

Moscoso, Teodoro, 171

Moss, Alan, 292 (n. 3)

Multiculturalism, 140, 164

Muñoz Marín, Luis, 125–28; and cultural nationalism, 17, 125–28, 287 (n. 4); and commonwealth status, 122–23; definition of cultural personality, 124, 126–27, 136, 272; biographical sketch, 125–26; concept of culture, 127; relationship to Teodoro Vidal, 139, 144, 160; friendship with Clarence Senior, 170; on Puerto Rican migration, 172, 174, 195, 240, 293 (n. 1); appointment of Joseph Monserrat, 176; in New York, 187

Muñoz Rivera, Luis, 204

Museo del Barrio, 148, 180, 181

Museo del Indio, 270, 273

Museum of Aboriginal Cultures, 273

Museum of America (Madrid), 146

Museum of History, Anthropology, and Art, University of Puerto Rico, 129, 264, 273, 278

Museum of Our African Root, 276

Museum of the Americas, 129, 276

Museum on the African Man and Woman, 278

Museum on the Legacy of African Cultures, 276

Museums and national identity, 8, 137, 139–40, 159, 165, 218

Music: as symbol of Puerto Rican identity, 186, 197–98, 206

Nation: definitions of, 3, 7–10, 12, 15, 37

Nation, The (journal), 63

National American Woman Suffrage Association, 107

National anthem of Puerto Rico, 35, 69, 123, 135, 201, 272, 282

National Anthropological Archives, 42, 65, 107, 291 (n. 5)

National flag of Puerto Rico, 17, 18, 35, 123, 135, 172, 195, 201, 204, 205, 272, 282

National Geographic Magazine, 42, 87–88, 94, 106, 118, 119, 250, 289 (n. 4)

National identity. *See* Nation

Nationalism. *See* Cultural nationalism; Political nationalism

Nationalist discourse, 9–10, 16, 24–25, 29, 34, 90, 139, 169, 183

Nationalist intellectuals: and Hispanic heritage of Puerto Rico, 13–14, 138–39; concern with moral regeneration, 16; attitude toward Cubans in Puerto Rico, 26; relations with Luis Muñoz Marín, 127; and historical patrimony, 134, 279;

and Vidal Collection, 148; and Taínos, 262, 268
Nationalist Party, 16, 128, 287–88 (n. 7)
National Museum of American Art, 150–51, 158
National Museum of American History, 50, 93, 138, 140, 141, 149, 150, 151, 157, 161, 165, 293 (n. 5)
National Museum of Natural History, 42, 65, 90
National Museum of Popular Arts and Traditions, 145, 147, 149
Native Americans: at world's fairs, 40, 41, 46, 56; as objects of anthropological study, 59, 65, 73; in photographs, 89, 106; at National Museum of American History, 149; as conquered peoples, 217–18; as racial category in census, 238, 253, 256, 295 (n. 9)
Native villages, 40–41, 45–46, 50–51, 56
Navarro Tomás, Tomás, 76
Nazario, José María, 263
Negrón-Muntaner, Frances, 32
Neonationalism. See Lite nationalism
Neumann Collection, 292 (n. 3)
New Progressive Party, 146, 178, 182, 266
New York Academy of Sciences, 7, 61, 74, 82, 83
New York Herald, 67, 290 (n. 6)
New York Times, 288 (n. 120)
New York world's fair, 47
Nuevo Día, El, 160
Nuyoricans: as ethnic minority, 13, 186, 214; and assimilation to the United States, 23, 29, 31–32; defined, 23–24; and nationalist discourse in Puerto Rico, 28–29, 30, 167; in literature, 30–31, 34, 203; and language, 36–37, 166–67; as social networks of circular migrants, 230, 234

Ober, Frederick, 54, 288 (n. 1), 289 (n. 5)
O'Connor, Bill, 145
O'Connor, Donald J., 170–71
O'Daly, Isabel, 157
Old San Juan: as historical patrimony, 47, 130–31, 273, 278
Oller, Francisco, 48, 273
Olympic sports, 5, 17, 123, 282
Operation Access to the East, 3
Operation Bootstrap, 128, 136, 162, 163, 217
Operation Serenity, 123, 126, 128, 136, 141, 148, 165, 272

Ortiz, Vilma, 288 (n. 13)
Ortiz Cofer, Judith, 32
Our Islands and Their People, 88–90, 290 (n. 8)
Outlying possessions of the United States. See Alaska; Cuba; Guam; Hawaii; Philippines, the; Samoa; U.S. Virgin Islands

Pabón, Carlos, 14
Padilla, Elena, 185
Pagán, Leonardo, 159
Palace of Santa Catalina. See Fortaleza, La
Panama Canal, 107, 119
Pan-American Exposition, Buffalo, 39, 43, 44–58
Paris Universal Exposition, 40
Pava, 7, 51, 155, 158, 198, 204
Peabody Museum of Archaeology and Ethnology, Harvard University, 65
Pedreira, Antonio, 21–22
Pentecostalism. See Evangelical cults; Protestantism in Puerto Rico
Pérez, Marvette, 29, 150, 151, 160, 161, 293 (n. 11)
Pérez, Moira, 294 (n. 7)
Petty bourgeoisie. See Middle class
Philippines, the: at world's fairs, 39, 44, 47, 50, 289 (n. 5); in museums, 49; independence of, 55, 122; stereo views, 91; public education in, 114; photographs of, 120. See also Filipinos
Photographic realism, 88, 89, 103
Photographs: as historical and ethnographic documents, 87, 89, 90, 103, 106, 119–20, 186, 195, 196, 197
Picó, Rafael, 171
Pike, Dorothy, 292 (n. 3)
Plebiscite on Puerto Rico's political status, 13, 17, 31, 167, 260
Plena, 159, 194, 197, 198, 203
Political nationalism, 2, 5, 123, 124, 283
Political status of Puerto Rico. See Commonwealth government of Puerto Rico; Pro-independence movement in Puerto Rico; Pro-statehood movement in Puerto Rico
"Pollito Chicken" (Vega), 30
Ponce Art Museum, 181
Ponce fair, 47, 48
Pons de Alegría, Carmen, 265
Popular Democratic Party: and Estado Libre Asociado, 122; and dependence on

the United States, 124; and cultural nationalism, 128; and Ricardo Alegría, 129; autonomist ideology of, 132; and Teodoro Vidal, 146; control of Migration Division, 169; and Clarence Senior, 170; and migration policy, 171; and Joseph Monserrat, 176; electoral hegemony of, 178; and Institute of Puerto Rican Culture, 266

Portes, Alejandro, 294 (n. 2)

Porto Rican Brotherhood, 189, 191, 198

Porto Rican League, 187–88

Post, Regis H., 292 (n. 13)

Postcolonial colony, 4, 122, 123, 136

Postcolonial studies, 6, 61, 85, 138, 139, 261

Postmodernism, 13–14, 23, 60, 138, 284

Poststructuralism, 14, 138

Powell, John Wesley, 43, 62

Pratt, Mary Louise, 49

Pro-independence movement in Puerto Rico, 2, 14, 15, 16, 17, 18, 24, 25, 176, 296 (n. 10)

Proletariat. See Working class

Pro-statehood movement in Puerto Rico, 2, 17, 134, 182, 296 (n. 10)

Protestantism in Puerto Rico, 19, 22, 32, 54, 68, 100, 161, 162

Prothero, R. Mansell, 210

Public education in Puerto Rico, 49, 113–14, 158, 296 (n. 3)

Puck (magazine), 52

Puerto Rican–Americans, 28, 34, 154, 187, 283

Puerto Rican Community Development Project, 202–3

Puerto Rican Day Parade, 180, 182, 195–96, 204–5, 293 (n. 2)

Puerto Rican diaspora, 5, 28, 135, 139, 164–81 passim, 206, 215, 282, 283. See also Puerto Rican migration

Puerto Rican Folk Festival, 180, 194–95

Puerto Rican House of Representatives, 250–51

Puerto Rican Independence Party, 16, 195

Puerto Rican migration: to the United States, 13, 20, 23, 159, 167, 211–12; to New York City, 20, 128, 167, 172, 211, 226–27, 244, 293 (n. 1)

Puerto Rican Planning Board, 252–53

Puerto Rican Senate, 170

Puerto Ricans in Florida, 226–27

Puerto Rican Socialist Party, 187

Puerto Rican Studies Association, 28, 288 (n. 10)

Puerto Rican Telephone Company, 19

Puerto Rican Tourism Company, 147, 160

Puerto Rico and Its Resources, 48–49

Puerto Rico Federal Affairs Administration, 183

"Puertorriqueño dócil, El" (Marqués), 22

Pura Belpré Papers, 186

Putnam, Frederick W., 41

Quebec, 9, 282, 287 (n. 4)

Quintero Rivera, Angel, 288 (n. 10)

Racial classification systems, 237, 241, 296 (n. 9)

Racial identity of Puerto Ricans, 54–56, 67, 71, 84, 85–86, 103, 221, 236–60 passim, 293–94 (n. 3), 295 (n. 3), 296 (n. 3)

Racialization, 27, 55–56, 71, 84, 245, 257, 258

Racial mixture, 25, 62, 67, 81, 84, 237, 239, 245, 253, 258, 260. See also Mestizaje

Racial prejudice: in Puerto Rico, 22, 24–25, 27, 81, 240, 245–46, 249; in the United States, 54, 89, 240, 242, 258, 263, 278

Radical democracy, 14

Rainey, Froilich, 82, 264

Regional differences in Puerto Rico, 18, 155, 174–75, 185, 206, 207. See also Hometown clubs

Renan, Ernest, 12, 37

Representation of cultural identities, 6, 10, 37, 39, 140

"Representing the Colonized: Anthropology and Its Interlocutors" (Said), 59

Research methodology, 6–7, 20–21, 78, 219–23, 235

"Retrato del dominicano que pasó por puertorriqueño y pudo emigrar a mejor vida a Estados Unidos" (García Ramis), 27–28

Return migration, 208, 211–13, 221, 293 (n. 1), 294 (n. 4), 295 (n. 10). See also Circular migration

Revolving-door migration. See Circular migration

Richmond, Charles, 43

Rincón de Gautier, Felisa, 195

Rockefeller, Nelson A., 201

Rodríguez, Clara, 244, 245, 254, 257, 288 (n. 13)

Rodríguez, Miguel, 265
Rodríguez, Víctor, 245
Rodríguez Cruz, Juan, 243
Rodríguez-Morazzani, Roberto, 245
Rodríguez Vecchini, Hugo, 34, 216
Rogler, Charles, 241, 242, 249
Romanticism: in treatment of transna-
    tionalism, 12; and the *jíbaro*, 19, 22, 86,
    290 (n. 12); in treatment of Taínos, 35,
    115–16, 263, 265, 267; and cultural
    nationalism, 124, 134; and noble peasant,
    137
Romero Barceló, Carlos, 180
Romero Rosa, Ramón, 288 (n. 14)
Rosario, José Colombán, 242
Rosselló, Pedro, 4, 146, 147, 182, 253
Rouse, Irving, 264
Ruffins, Fath Davis, 160, 161
Rydell, Robert, 40

Said, Edward, 59
Salsa music, 19, 32, 34–35, 198
Samoa, 39, 40, 51, 106, 283, 289 (nn. 5, 6)
Sánchez, Juan, 32, 288 (n. 10)
Sánchez, Luis Rafael, 33–34
Sánchez Korrol, Virginia, 182
San Cristóbal Fort, 109
Sanes Rodríguez, David, 3
San Jerónimo Fort, 109, 291 (n. 8)
San Juan Star, 145, 151
Santería (religion), 154
Santería (sculpture), 135
Santiago, Esmeralda, 288 (n. 11)
Santiago de Curet, Annie, 145
Santos, 138–58 passim, 281, 293 (n. 5)
Sapir, Edward, 74
Scarano, Francisco, 288 (n. 2)
Scherer, Joanna C., 89, 90
Schmidt-Nowara, Christopher, 61
*Scientific Survey of Porto Rico and the Vir-
    gin Islands*, 74, 82–83
Scotland, 9, 282, 287 (n. 4)
Section 936, Internal Revenue Service
    Code, 226
Seda Bonilla, Eduardo, 23–24, 167, 241–42,
    243, 245, 246
Segal, Aaron, 209–10
Seis chorreaos, 204
Senior, Clarence, 169–70, 171–72, 175, 176,
    193, 244
Serrano, José, 3, 147
"Sex in Brain" (Gardener), 107

Shiwdhan, Naragandat, 209
Siegel, Morris, 242
Smith, Anthony D., 9–10, 35
Smithsonian Institution: general charac-
    teristics of, 7, 149; interest in Puerto
    Rico, 39–56 passim, 61, 83, 288 (n. 1);
    acquisition of Vidal Collection, 138,
    146–51; Latinos at, 149–50
Smithsonian Institution Center for Latino
    Initiatives, 150
Smithsonian Institution Task Force on La-
    tinos, 150
Social Science Research Center, Univer-
    sity of Puerto Rico, 169–70
Sociedad Guaynía, 274
Spanglish, 30, 31, 203. *See also* Bilingual-
    ism; Code-switching
Spanish-American War. *See* Spanish-
    Cuban-American War
Spanish-Cuban-American War: impact on
    Puerto Rico, 1, 6, 42, 58, 60, 72, 106, 112–
    13, 121; Puerto Rican reactions to, 55, 158;
    stereo views, 91; nomenclature, 287 (n. 1)
Spanish Harlem, 185, 187, 188, 193, 197,
    200–201, 213
Spanish language: as symbol of Puerto
    Rican identity, 14, 19, 21, 29, 31, 49, 126,
    127, 130, 135, 182, 184, 186, 201–2, 205; as
    spoken in Puerto Rico, 49, 76–77, 79,
    80, 271
Special Committee on Exhibits from Out-
    lying Possessions, 44, 46, 56
Spinder, Herbert, 63
Sports. *See* Baseball; Olympic sports
Spurr, David, 73
Stahl, Agustín, 48, 263, 267–69, 288 (n. 1)
Stahl Collection, 67, 292 (n. 3)
Stalin, Joseph, 28
Starin, John H., 50
Starin, Myndert, 50
Stejneger, Leonhard, 43
Stereographs, 51, 90–91
Steward, Julian, 18, 132
Strohmeyer, H. A., 94
Suárez, Jaime, 145
Subaltern studies, 138
Sued Badillo, Jalil, 265, 269
Suthar, Basil N., 81
Swallow migration. *See* Circular migration

Taft, William H., 88, 91, 119, 291 (n. 3)
Taíno Inter-Tribal Council, 296 (n. 4)

Taíno nation movement, 262, 276
Taíno revival, 19, 261–80 passim, 296 (n. 4)
Taínos, 25, 35, 62, 66, 129, 131, 161, 162, 269–70, 281
Taller Boricua, 180
Tapia y Rivera, Alejandro, 67
Teachers Association of Puerto Rico, 126
Thompson, Lanny, 41–42, 88–89
Three Wise Men, the, 32, 156, 171, 293 (n. 8)
Tibes Ceremonial Center, 274–75
Tió, Lola Rodríguez de, 204
Tió, Salvador, 170
Tió, Teresa, 145
Tischer, Walter, 145
Torres Aguirre, Lillian, 252
Torres Martinó, José A., 146
"Trabajando pal inglés" (Vega), 26–27
Translocal nation, 4, 5, 168, 184, 282–83
Transnationalism, 2, 6, 19, 34, 36–38, 213, 216, 218, 230–31, 234, 284
Trigueño, 236, 237, 238, 240, 252, 255, 258–59, 295 (n. 5)
True, Frederick W., 44

Uncle Sam's burden, 51, 106
Underwood, Bert, 91
Underwood, Elmer, 91
Underwood & Underwood Glass Stereograph Collection, 90–106 passim
United Confederation of Taíno People, 296 (n. 4)
United Nations, 122, 129
United States–Puerto Rico Status Commission, 129
University of Pennsylvania Museum of Anthropology and Archaeology, 74, 76
University of Puerto Rico, 23, 128, 129, 181, 243, 264, 270, 273, 279, 292 (n. 12), 295 (n. 5)
Upper class. *See* Creole elite in Puerto Rico
U.S. Army, 123, 141, 160, 217, 292 (n. 12)
U.S. Bureau of the Census, 7, 238, 244, 249–52, 257, 258, 295 (nn. 2, 7)
U.S. citizenship of Puerto Ricans, 1, 2, 13, 15, 16, 37, 54, 57, 89, 210, 282
U.S. Civil Service Commission, 107
U.S. Congress, 1, 55, 57, 122, 289 (n. 2), 291 (n. 4)
U.S. Constitution, 287 (n. 2)

U.S. Department of Agriculture, 43, 47, 49, 294 (n. 5)
U.S. Geological Survey, 42
U.S. House of Representatives, 56, 147, 182
U.S. Immigration and Naturalization Service, 294 (n. 5)
U.S. National Museum, 42, 43, 44, 46, 73, 149
U.S. Navy, 3–4
U.S. Supreme Court, 1
U.S. Virgin Islands, 40, 74, 289 (n. 5)
Utuado, Puerto Rico, 64, 67, 68, 76–78, 81, 155, 276, 290 (n. 11). *See also* Caguana, Centro Ceremonial Indígena

Vaivén, el, 2–3, 32. *See also* Circular migration
Vall y Spinosa, Federico, 68, 290 (n. 7)
Vando, Erasmo, 188
Vasconcelos, José, 264
Vega, Ana Lydia, 26, 30–31
Vega, Bernardo, 188, 197, 202, 293 (n. 1), 295 (n. 4)
Vejigantes, 148, 158, 159, 160, 203, 204
Velázquez, Nydia, 3, 181, 182
Velorio, El (Oller), 273
Vidal, Teodoro, Jr., 124, 138–45, 162, 292 (n. 3)
Vidal, Teodoro, Sr., 141
Vidal Collection, 138–65, 166
Vieques, Puerto Rico, 3–4, 19, 108, 109
Virgin of Montserrat, 156, 157, 158, 293 (n. 8)
Visual anthropology, 87
Visual representations, 7, 43, 86–90; of Puerto Rico, 51–53, 94–120 passim, 277, 281
Vogel, Dr., 119
Voluntary associations of Puerto Ricans in the United States, 175–77, 185–97 passim, 206, 293 (n. 1)

War Department, 46, 246
War of 1898. *See* Spanish-Cuban-American War
War on Poverty, 179, 206
Warshaw Collection, 50
Washington Post, 155, 161
When I Was Puerto Rican (Santiago), 288 (n. 11)
Whitening of Puerto Rican population, 25, 62, 86, 237, 242, 243, 247–48, 258

Willoughby, William F., 88, 119, 290–91 (n. 2)

Women: in literature, 24; as objects of desire, 54–55, 103; photographic images of, 101, 103–5, 106, 107, 111, 115, 120; segregated from men, 101, 158; suffrage movement of, 106, 107; prejudice against, 107; as photographers, 119; as folk artists, 156; as migrants, 230–31

Working class, 16, 20, 23, 24, 27, 94–95, 103, 185, 187, 211, 284

World's Columbian Exposition, Chicago, 40, 48, 288 (n. 1)

World's fairs, 39–58 passim. *See also* Crystal Palace Great Exhibition, London; International Colonial Exposition, Paris; Louisiana Purchase Exposition, St. Louis; New York world's fair; Pan-American Exposition, Buffalo; Paris Universal Exposition; World's Columbian Exposition, Chicago

Wyman, H. W., 94

Young, R. Y., 94

Young Lords Party, 203

Zapata, Rafael, 294 (n. 7)

Zenón Cruz, Isabelo, 243, 263

Zentella, Ana Celia, 36, 213

Zim Collection, 50